CHANEL

Her Life, Her World,
the Woman Behind the Legend

Edmonde Charles-Roux

Translated from the French by Nancy Amphoux

MACLEHOSE PRESS
QUERCUS · LONDON

First published in Great Britain in 1976 by Jonathan Cape Ltd
This edition published in 2009 by

MacLehose Press
an imprint of Quercus
21 Bloomsbury Square
London WC1A 2NS

Originally published in France as
L'IRREGULIERE OU MON ITINERAIRE CHANEL

A CIP catalogue reference for this book is available
from the British Library

ISBN 978 1 906694 24 1

10 9 8 7 6 5 4 3 2 1

Printed and bound in Great Britain by Clays Ltd, St Ives plc

To G.D.

"... and besides, there are no men without tragedies, there is only
   what you believe.
Everything is costume.
Everything seems the way you see it on the street, unconcerned,
   ambling along the pedestrian crossing of appearance.
Everything smells of rules, and keeps its secret."

— LOUIS ARAGON, *Henri Matisse*

CONTENTS

PICTURE CREDITS

ACKNOWLEDGMENTS

The author wishes to take this opportunity to thank, for the help that she has received in putting together this work, Baron Ferreol de Nexon, Mme Gaudin-Leclerc, and M. Hervé Mille, as well as the following people in various countries:

In England – Lady Diana Duff Cooper; Lady Harlech; Mrs Jeremy Hutchinson; Sir Michael Creswell; Beatrix Miller; and The Reverend Jean Charles-Roux.

In Italy – General Lombardi.

In Germany–M. Theodor Momm; Dr Carlo Schmid; and Professor Eberhard Jäckel.

In Canada – Mme Wright, née Fleming.

In France – Mme Etienne Balsan; Paul Morand; Mme René de Chambrun; Maurice Goudeket; Marcel Jouhandeau; Georges Wormser; Baron Edouard de Nervo; M. et Mme de Beyser; Mme Marcelle Campana, French ambassadress; Mme Stanislas Fumet; M. le curé of Ponteils; Pierre Chanel; Marcel Genermont; Abbé Chaudagne, curé of Souvigny; Baroness Foy, née Orlandi; Sheila de Rochambeau; Countess Dessoffy; Marguerite Vincent; Paule Gaspart, of Caroline Reboux, Inc.; Gabrielle Dorziat; Boris Kochno; Dominique Paulvé; Mme Denis; Mmes Antoinette Laget and Gabrielle Maurin, nées Chanel; Mme Lucien Chanel; Mme Valet; Mme J. B. Reday; M. Jean Poggioli; Mlle Orsoni; Paule d'Alayer; M. Marcel Benabou; and M. Gernet, archivist of the Bibliothèque municipale in Marseilles.

FOREWORD

In the south of France there lies a never-conquered land. Only surface-scratched.

Hannibal, at the head of his elephants and Carthaginians, chose the long way around rather than hazarding a frontal attack on the Cévennes, that granite barrier that forms the southeastern edge of the Massif Central range.

Came the time of the Caesars. The natives let themselves be Romanized, but from afar.

When the Empire disintegrated the barbarians sacked Rome, but those same barbarian waves surged up to and fell back at the foot of the Cévennes. And two centuries later the Gévaudan mountaineers and the shepherds of Villefort stood fast at their posts high, very high above the narrow valleys along which glided the cruel shadows of the horsemen of Islam. The Arabs: they too gave up.

Thus nothing – neither the Saracens nor the English of the Black Prince nor even the plague – nothing over the course of the centuries seriously interfered with this isolation, apart from a few robbers and some wolves.

It was not until Protestantism reached France, and the outbreak of the Holy Wars, that these lost lands were shaken. Their notion of Christianity was never that of the pope. They aspired to purity, to the perfection of the early Christians. *Purity*, nothing less is worth dying for, is it? Perfection at any price. In those years, the Cévennes soul revealed its hidden resources of sternness, and of violence too.

The intransigent breed endured. The people of the Cévennes lived on unaltered. And thus the theater of their exploits must be seen as something more than an accident of terrain.

A heart of granite whose schists glitter like so many jet suns. A wind of madness, the Mistral, is born here. That fierce, cold dry wind that blows down the Rhône valley and carries the snow-chill into the very streets of Arles, rips tiles from roofs and lines the sky with cobalt, flattens ripe wheat and turns the regal cypresses of the Crau into the frenzied torches van Gogh liked to paint.

Here, in the astonishing glare of this mineral landscape, a family was also born, tough and untaught, a family ruled imperiously by the will to procreate: the Chanels.

One descendant of the prolific tribe can be described in terms which might fit any of them: the physical type – the Gabalitan beauty, the same vigor, the same will to perfection, the same compulsion to produce (that is, to outlive oneself), the same harshness, the same authoritarian way of speaking, the same inability to compromise, the same violence, and the same passion. Subject, like them, by profession, to the inflexible round of the seasons and, like them, subordinating all other things to her work, this one, Gabrielle Chanel, was raised to celebrity by thousands of women who detected in her an exceptional gift: the gift for embellishment. It was these women, the exacting mistresses, anxious lovers, millionaires, or simple bourgeoises in search of costume harmony, who compelled this penniless girl to make elegance and luxury her only objects. It is they who forced her into the world of fashion.

Gabrielle Chanel took longer than people suppose to make up her mind. It was only at the end of a long process, and when she saw that there was *no other way out*, that she let herself be convinced.

Her work? A means of escape. She seized it in both hands and plunged into her new life head down, like a whirlwind, like a Cévennes mountain torrent.

No intrusion of culture or erudition in the style she created, no historical reminiscences. She was an inventor.

The forms we owe to her are what they are, no more and no less, with no sidelong glances or allusions. This came from her refusal to bow to anything outside the demands of everyday life, to follow any current that did not come out of her old peasant heritage. That refusal had a name: common sense.

Whenever, feeling the need for something that already existed, she turned to a detail of a former fashion, she instinctively discarded the aristocratic and searched only her own peasant past. She took over for her purposes articles previously considered too humble for use: the garments of rest, work, movement. Her creative act was a subversive act. She refused the oppression of ceremony.

The quality of her style came from this breath of naturalness running through it; and its alliance of the explicitly functional with the ultra-refined is not the least of the paradoxes of a style that can no more be dissociated from the stage of our time than from the drama being played out upon it.

*

Chanel's life abounds in inconsistencies.

She was a couturière who would have nothing to do with frivolity; an executive who broke every rule and overstepped her rights without compunction; a creator of original designs who was only happy when being plagiarized by others.

She amassed an immense fortune far from all traffic with what ought logically to have been her world: big business and everything connected with it, banks, stockmarkets, politicians, financiers – with power, in a word. Never was she heard to glorify riches or sing hymns to money. Possessing certainly gave her pleasure, but the essence of that pleasure lay in measuring the distance between it and the days when she had possessed nothing.

Although living in an age when travel had become a professional obligation on which the impact of any large firm depended to a considerable degree, she felt nothing but contempt for all who gave obeisance to the business trip, and traveled only for pleasure.

She could recognize the talents of the most prominent artists, and among them made the only friends on which she prided herself. And yet she could not bear to hear people associate her work with theirs, and hated to hear the word "genius" applied to herself. She wanted to be a craftsman.

She seemed invincible; and the magic of her personal attractiveness, her extraordinary charm, contributed to the success of her enterprise. But in the center of that success she lived as an exile, having failed in what mattered most to her: her life as a woman. In her professional life she was the equal of men, often their superior, but Gabrielle Chanel confronted the yearnings of the private heart unarmed. The worst of it was that although clothes might be the focus of her life, its only real concern was romance. And there she met nothing but disillusionment.

Formed, discovered, and invented by men, she worked for women all her life without liking them enough to forget herself in beautifying them. Every member of her own sex was regarded by this creature of passions as a potential rival, to such an extent that until her dying breath, still seeing herself not as she was then but as she had been in her years of glory, Chanel secretly dedicated her most provocative artifices to herself.

Every one of her collections was like a lonely look back, a long, unconfessed voyage into her past . . . that past she never spoke of.

For the most arresting feature of her life is not its spectacular success, not her popularity or the vast audience over which she held sway: it is the enigma she contrived to present to everyone who came near her, the exhausting feats she undertook and accomplished in her attempts to mask her origins.

The most arresting feature of this remarkable life (or such, at least, is the premise of this book) is the art she lavished upon rendering herself *unintelligible*, and, having done that, the persistence with which she perpetuated her disguise, remaining confined within it as in the most hermetically sealed prison.

She lived *possessed* by her legend.

What follows is what I discovered to have been her life.

I

Origins 1792–1883

"It is accepted that a man's first truth is what he hides."

— ANDRÉ MALRAUX, *Antimemoirs*

THE LAIR

Ponteils, the hamlet where Chanel's paternal ancestors came from, is in the Cévennes north of Nîmes. It has only three dwellings, so perfectly in keeping with their surroundings that they seem to have sprouted up out of the depths of the earth. These roofs of overlapping slabs – steep, half caved-in, blackened by the moss encrusting them – and these massive rustic walls (all, roofs and walls alike, made of the same wicked metallic schist that cuts into slender splinters sharp as razors): what were they originally designed to shelter, man or beast? One can't be sure. At the bottom of the valley, minute rivulets swell with the lightest shower and parch in the first ray of sunlight. Where do they come from? Where are they going? But why ask? Nothing here goes anywhere, nothing passes through this hamlet. The road ends here, blocked by a tall church steeple that rises like a lighthouse above the howling hills. Why that church? For what congregation? The entire population of a market town could not fill it. So what is it doing here, all alone?

Look through the open doorways: inside the buildings, see the signs of a former life – long, shadowy barns where halters hang and ancient harrows rust, and overturned carts gray with dust poke their naked shafts, massive as battering rams, at the breaches in the roof. The puzzle remains. A strenuous past stares back at us. The mystery of peasant life. What can have happened to bring about this desolation?

Apulian trulli, with their conical roofs, Sardinian nuraghes with their fortified chambers and secret passages, are slumbering edifices that bring to mind man's most mysterious imaginings. But these are only austere Cévennes farmhouses holding out against decay, the obstinate souvenirs of a time when this land was alive and men made their living from it.

That time is long gone now. The exodus began nearly a century ago, when the dense wall of forest that ringed the hamlet over thousands of acres, the chestnut trees precious as bread, began to thin until nothing was left but a shattered stockade.

Chestnuts: they were the source of Ponteils's prosperity. People earned their living from them, sold them, ate them, morning, noon, and night. They were sustenance and coin. On the hearth an earthenware pot – the *toupie* – heated, and in it simmered the family ration. The nuts that would feed the livestock in the winter dried on latticed trays. And when leases and rents fell due and the leaseowners came up from the county seat to claim their tithes, they were paid in kilograms of chestnuts.

Early in October everything that bore wheels in Ponteils began to roll, barrows, carts, and wagons loaded to bursting point with bags marked with their owners' initials – F for Fraisse, C for Causse, V for Vidal. Stenciled hastily, for there was no time to lose. The entire crop had to be sold before sales began to slacken and prices fell below cost. A deep rumble rose from the forest, an incessant hum of voices. The forest, the hive: everything came from it, everything depended on it.

In good years, when the chestnut trees seemed in danger of collapsing under the weight of their fruit, farmers hired as many as thirty horses to ensure more rapid transport to the markets in the valley, because up here there wasn't a single horse – at most, one mule per farm, and not always that. Nevertheless, those were good times in Ponteils; that was its golden age.

In that season one little room with its scrap of arbor, sole gathering place of the local peasantry, was continually full. The wine shop . . . long tables, narrow benches. The whole life of the hamlet was concentrated here, between the four walls of one house distinguished from the rest by its cyclopean foundations. Over the door, carved in the white keystone, two initials: A. B. – those of its first occupants, the Boschets; and a date – 1749, that of its construction, and also the beginning of the hamlet's prosperity. But it was not until the first years of the nineteenth century and the apogee of the chestnut era that the honest peasant dwelling was transformed into a tavern.

There, dry-throated farmers, hired men come to help get in the crop, weavers looking for work, peddlers up from town to sell their goods, all drew up to the tables alongside those who, winter and summer alike, were kept in Ponteils by the land and its needs: the large work force of the families, boys and men of every age, woodcutters, shepherds, silkworm breeders; and, too, crowding near the hearth, trembling a little, their legs slightly spread, the eternal aged with their knotted hands.

The tavern stood far up, overlooking the valley. The people went there to find life, noise, an echo of events happening elsewhere. Also, to marry. For the men of the house . . .

"You know my boy . . ."

Really, they had to go to the tavern for that. Where else could they more comfortably discuss their children's futures? There, in front of Noé Roure, the curate, they exchanged those "shakes" that were better than a bond for more than one contract. And afterward, you sealed it with a drink. And why look elsewhere for a witness? It was always the same one, always the tavern-keeper who did duty for baptisms, weddings, and burials. Did it gladly, too, experience having taught him that once the ceremony was over, the families . . . thirsty, you know. So, leaving his wife to fill the jugs, he stepped across to the church to scrawl the six letters of his name at the foot of divers documents: Chanel, Joseph, tavernkeeper, born at Ponteils in 1792.

No name crops up in the records more often than his. Chanel, Joseph, tavernkeeper – Gabrielle's great-grandfather. After his marriage, he appears to have spent as much time in the church as behind his bar.

Before marrying, like so many peasants of the region, he had been both journeyman and craftsman, now donning heavy saw-toothed clogs to husk a neighbor's chestnuts on the ground, now working through the long winter nights for some young couple, cutting wood from the forest to make their bed, their cupboard, or a few household utensils.

"Love only what is thine" went the centuries-old Cévennes saying. To express this attachment to acquisitions gained by the sweat of one's brow, everything must be decorated, carved, down to the least little spoon or flour scoop. Put your mark on it: a custom akin to the animal's instinct for his lair, his nest, the very meaning of the peasant's past.

Embellishing: no one had a greater liking for the task than Joseph Chanel, even though he always worked for others, for those who possessed land, timber, a roof over their heads and a bed to lie down in and a plot already marked with a cross in the churchyard. Never for himself. Besides, on what could he have carved his initials? No Chanel ever owned an inch of land in Ponteils, or even so much as a tomb.

Things began looking up for Joseph on the day, not far from his fortieth birthday, when his "understanding" with a Thomas girl was celebrated; her family, also from Ponteils, owned a bit of property. A modest dowry enabled the newlyweds to rent – by no means the whole of that stout Boschet house, whose owners had already grown rich and moved away to start a business in the valley, but its main room – the country kitchen: one big rectangle with the central hearth and a baking-oven giving onto it, as well as a little nook to set up a bed in. Attic over, cellar under, and from dawn till dark they had to make the best of that, because the rest – the woodshed, store-rooms, cow barn, sheepfold, the granary and farmyard black as a well – all of that still belonged to the Boschets. What could the Chanels have done with it, anyway? They owned nothing, neither cow nor flock.

The room had to be furnished. Joseph built tables and rudimentary benches on which, at last, he could carve a name that was his own. He contented himself with a double initial, two large C's forming a circle around a labarum* – the sign of his faith, as opposed to the dove of the Protestants – an essential mark in this country of warring congregations. Two large C's: less than a century later, braced against each other, they were to become the distinctive mark of Gabrielle's creations and the symbol of the biggest empire ever built by any woman with her own hands. Two large C's on chiffon squares, handbags, powder compacts, little nothings . . . that mania she had for putting her mark on everything. What is a human being, after all, but the sum of the alphabet of his race?

Once the furniture was in place Joseph Chanel laid in a stock of a full-bodied local wine, much appreciated by his neighbors. The first step was taken. The bride turned to her oven and offered the bread of hospitality. Soon a sign hung over the Boschets' door, promising all who entered "Good bread. Good wine. Lotto. Spirits. Sweets." That was The Chanel, a country tavern.

That was what the local people called it and still do.

Today the arbor supports the dying limbs of one consumptive plant and the few tall chestnuts still standing around the house carry as much dead wood as foliage among their branches. The sign has faded. The tavern room itself is almost unchanged. Still the bread oven, the long tables and narrow benches.

A century and a half has passed since the days when Gabrielle Chanel's great-grandfather poured out wine in the bar. And his son after him . . . and after that, nothing. The doors are gone from the sheepfold. No more movement around this house. And the schist-coiffed roof, so often, so long lashed by the winds, sags dangerously. And the shutters gape in the breeze.

Open to the snows in the churchyard that gives straight onto the mountainside, those who lived their hard-working days in Ponteils repose under mossy slabs, united by pride in their work and love of the soil. Here are the Daudes, the Nègres and the Rouxs, the Castaniers and the Sylvain Chambons, here are the "died for France," and a curate at Arles, a sailor in Africa, a carpenter at Brest: all come home to the village, all ultimately handed back to the earth, like its stones . . .

But no trace of a single Chanel.

The name alone has remained, linked forever with that of a little tavern. And somehow or other there are still one or two old folk who remember. They say:

---

* The military standard of the Christian Roman emperors, incorporating the Chi-Rho (X + ρ =$\rlap{/}\rho$), the sacred monogram of Christ.

"I've heard there used to be a tavern over there . . . The Chanel."
Wistfully.

A TAVERNKEEPER AND HIS SONS

Always too many children at the Chanels', and always more boys than girls, more offspring than money, and low-ceilinged houses filled with wailing.

In the year 1830 a firstborn arrived at the tavern of Ponteils and was christened Joseph like his tavernkeeper father. In the spring of 1832, early in April, another birth, a second son. In the presence of the mayor and two witnesses, both landowners and good customers at the tavern, the parents stated that they wanted this son to be named Paulin-Henri-Adrien. Fine. No objections. Written down, dated, initialed. Now that's out of the way . . .

Chanel's grandfather had just been born.

In 1835 the tavernkeeper toasted a third birth, that of Jean-Benjamin, and in 1837 a fourth, with the arrival of little Ernest; at last, in 1841, the first daughter came along, Josephine. Those are the names recorded at the beginning of a long dynasty.

A steady stream of new Chanels was brought to the curate of Ponteils to be baptized; and in those same years, and with a wholly Latin single-mindedness, other villagers of the same name, brothers or cousins, were procreating at a similar rate.

Between 1830 and 1860 no fewer than a score of Chanels first saw the day at Ponteils, and in them may already be detected a predilection (that was to endure) for masculine names with historic overtones; while set against these males more gifted at dalliance than duty, their only true occupation lovemaking, set against these Chanel Marius, Chanel Auguste, Chanel Alexandre, Urbain, or Jules-César, stood the fiancées of Ponteils, the dark-haired girls with the amber skin, all those Maries, Virginies, Apollonies who fell into their arms and were, for two generations, what every Chanel spouse without exception has been: zealous victims, industrious bees who did all the work of the hive at once; females and feeders and fosterers until death . . .

We are in 1850. In their work, the Chanels were still dependent on demand or lack of it. Apart from the eldest son, who followed his father behind the tavern counter, the others – penniless journeymen – were not even under the orders of men. They were ruled by the land.

And the land was in a bad way.

Two dread enemies were beleaguering the chestnut forest, two diseases: black canker and endothia, or chestnut blight.

The puzzled elders counted up the dead trees.

In all their lives they'd never seen the likes of it. You'd think the chestnut trees had a fever. The leaves swelled and dropped off. A calamity. The ministry of agriculture was mute. Ponteils is still waiting for the specialist from Paris who never came. Who remembers Ponteils, who thinks of this forsaken hamlet?

Tavern customers grew scarce and conversation gloomy. An evil spell was feared, the maleficent action of some Satan or other. The part of the peasant soul that had remained pagan suddenly revived. In their panic, the most Christian proved to be only half-Christian. The old fetishes were brought out, the old wives' remedies. Furtively the women traded talismans. Was it better to nail the body of an owl to an infected trunk, would that work better than the four paws of a mole? Or would a toad . . . ? They say a cross made of thistles, too . . . The curate turned a deaf ear to what he chastely termed "old customs."

The only people who profited from the general woe were the peddlers. The residents of Ponteils argued over every little pamphlet on prophecy or the counterconjuration of spells. *The Authentic Red Dragon, or the Art of Commanding Evil Spirits*, and *Little Alfred's Wonderful Secrets, or Natural and Cabalistic Magic* sold like hot cakes. In the evenings around the single candle flame no one read anything else. But it was all wasted effort. Nothing did any good.

A few years of waiting and hoping went by. But all things come to an end, even hope. How quickly change came then. And how easy to explain the depopulation of Ponteils.

The forest burgeoning with wealth and with the people's trust in it fell to ruins. The trees were wilting. The chestnuts: most powerful, most mysterious fruit of the earth. Why struggle?

It was time to go.

The poorest went first.

The earliest emigrants were the tavernkeeper's younger sons: Henri-Adrien, his brother Benjamin, and little Ernest. The nephews and cousins followed.

They all went.

For the Chanels it was the beginning of a period of migration, and of the loneliness of cities.

AN ITINERANT GRANDFATHER

Henri-Adrien Chanel was twenty-two years old when he left Ponteils. He was unmarried and had no skill or knowledge other than what he drew from the land and the forest. He was to lose both land and forest, and find himself seeking work thirty miles from home. First drop, first step down.

Jobless and a stranger, whereas at Ponteils everybody knew him, Henri-Adrien felt his first humiliation. Would he manage to find work? He spent eight months at Travers de Castillon, a little village at the foot of the Cévennes, neither forest nor mountain, nor yet plains or town. Jobs were scarce. People said that in Alès . . . That was true, Alès, mines, coal, jobs . . . But he hesitated. It meant going even farther away. Weren't they already saying he "came from afar"? What would it be like elsewhere? He hunted, groped. Something rustic in him still resisted the allure of the town, the dreams of high life.

At last some local farmers, the Fourniers, offered him a job. What luck, a haven in sight: the Fourniers' silkworm farm at Saint-Jean-de-Valeriscle. Thither he went. Henri-Adrien liked everything about peasant life, so why not mulberries and cocoons? Alas, the Fourniers also had a daughter, Virginie-Angelina, sixteen years old and no sooner seen than seduced. Making love to an underage child! The whole village was aghast. It was indecent, immoral. A no-good, that Chanel boy. The Fourniers threatened, demanded reparation. Otherwise Henri-Adrien, Gabrielle Chanel's grandfather, would be thrown in jail.

But he took it like a man. He married, in the presence of his father and mother, who had raced down from their mountain in a terror. A hasty wedding, celebrated at Gagnières at seven o'clock one morning in 1854. The mayor was also lord of the manor, a nobleman, Alphonse de Lanouvelle, and the bride's witnesses most respectable people: the schoolmaster and a local landowner, Casimir Thomas. All three penned faultless signatures at the bottom of the page. The schoolmaster weighed in with his fairest flourish, and the capital A of the mayor's chilly and elegant hand towered like a feudal dungeon over the pitiful scrawl representing the tavern keeper's best effort. As for the women, book learning was not their strong point. Angelina was no better at penmanship than her new mother-in-law. As duly noted by Monsieur de Lanouvelle: ". . . having read which, declared themselves unable to sign."

As soon as the wedding was over, Henri-Adrien went off with his child bride as far as he could go. He never saw his parents-in-law's farm again. Driven out . . . Second drop, second step down.

Because one of his brothers lived there (Ernest had become a fish-monger), it was to Nîmes that Henri-Adrien and Angelina proceeded, and it was there also, no doubt from his memories of the peddlers who emerged unscathed from catastrophes and to whom the villagers gave the fine name of "wayfarers," that Henri-Adrien invented his new job. It was more than a change of life for him, almost a change of skin: he became an itinerant market trader.

"Henri-Adrien Chanel, one-time farmer . . ."

This is the mournful appellation found at the top of some of the official papers dating from this period and bearing his signature. From this time onward the one-time farmer became, depending upon the season, a small-wares salesman offering bootlaces and caps to the boys, a purveyor of baubles for babies and frills for young females. That was Gabrielle Chanel's grand-father, then: a wayfarer.

If his matrimonial saga deserves to be told, it is only as a preview of the lives of his sons and grandsons.

With this footnote: the further they drifted from their ancestral forest, the more thoroughly the males of the Chanel tribe abandoned their ances-tral virtues. Very soon, insincerity and boastfulness overcame their peasant probity. Very soon, they learned all the lures and snares of the fairground fascinator, and they used them. A goodly number of them, like Granddad, led maidens astray . . . got them pregnant. Sometimes with no thought of reparation or recognition.

The Chanel sons had to have women, every woman, every day. They took them without affection or scruple. Father and son, all of them were lady killers as well as wayfarers.

For the first time, a city. Everywhere, crowds and unfamiliar noises.

Nevertheless, in some almost inexpressible way Nîmes was still reminis-cent of the lost countryside. Not only because of the sylvan street names: Spanish Mulberry Street, Orange Tree Street, Violet Street; and not only because so many families from Ponteils had reassembled there; no, not only because of that. It was a world of perfumes from the past, when the wind blew down from the Causses on the *garrigue*, carrying the smell of ever-green oak and balm all the way to the square in front of St Castor. The Chanels of Ponteils never went home again, except along these imaginary paths.

They lived with their noses to the wind.

Henri-Adrien and Angelina found lodgings at number 4, rue du Bat d'Argent, just off the central market. Their house, with a stable and two stone troughs flanking the low door, seemed to be awaiting the arrival of invisible flocks, for the narrow little street had long served as a gathering place for livestock dealers. Most curious of houses: the cellars, a labyrinth of vaultings and gigantic walls, must have been used as an abattoir, for there were traces of blood and the floor slabs resembled sacrificial altars.

It was there, on the rue du Bat d'Argent, that Albert, father of Gabrielle Chanel, was conceived in 1856.

When her time drew near, Angelina, aged nineteen, was admitted to the Hospice d'Humanité of Nîmes – the poorhouse hospital. Her husband? Absent, detained at a village fair. She was delivered of her firstborn alone. Even though many a Chanel had settled in Nîmes, no cousin or relative came to her bedside. Very peculiar. What should she do, where register her son? Three hospital employees, one aged seventy, volunteered to declare Albert's birth for her. The youngest made the declaration and the other two bore witness, but the declarer made a mistake and had the baby written down as "Charnet," which gave rise to no end of complications later in his life. And the document bears no witnesses' signatures. "Unable to sign," wrote the registry office employee, according to custom. The witnesses were illiterate.

Apart from an occasional variation in detail, and in whatever town they might happen to find themselves, similar circumstances surrounded the births of subsequent generations of Chanels. The lodging? Always within a stone's throw of the central marketplace, and always run-down and shabby. The mother? Always at the public hospital and always alone. The father? Always "traveling." And the witnesses always signed with an X.

THE RURAL EXODUS

Nîmes looked promising. It was possible to find shade in the narrow streets, and to live "among our kind," that is, among people of the Cévennes. The Ponteils clans had been more or less reconstituted; there were the Castaniers, whose daughters Olympe and Julienne always went everywhere together, while their brother Bonaparte had found a job at the firing range. There were the Magnes, whose boy Charles clerked in a clothing shop. There were the unattached of Ponteils who remained unattached at Nîmes: Bonaventure Cucurul, the cowherd, now a bartender; and Zélie Dessous, the unmarried mother, now an unmarried prostitute. There were more solid citizens, who had also been driven down by natural disaster: livestock carried off by flood, crops burned – such as the fair Arthémise of the Bouzigue clan, forever in her ruched beribboned bonnet, whose husband Ulysse had been transformed from the farmer he once was into an office clerk in a licorice factory.

But mostly, there were the Chanels, all living within a few streets of one another, all close to the Place aux Herbes, and each endowed with a child bride in permanently swollen condition. For Angelina was not the only one breeding: her sisters-in-law, large-bellied little girls, also advanced from pregnancy to pregnancy.

Thus it was that a fresh dozen Chanels, all cousins, saw the light of day not, this time, at Ponteils, but at Nîmes. Among them all, the will to beget was as powerful as a religious faith. As in the days when their fortunes had hung once a year on the branches of the chestnut tree, the Chanels, urban though they had become, were still ruled by that immemorial terror of impermanence shared by peasants the world over. There they were at Nîmes, reproducing themselves at the rate of one baby a year – and even more: sometimes two Chanels were born of the same mother and father, in January and December of the same year. And the eldest in each family was always called Joseph, an exile's homage to the chieftain of the tribe, the patriarch, the tavernkeeper of Ponteils, who was aging slowly among his memories of lost laughter and singing noondays under the arbor.

Now appeared the first breach in the ranks of the clan. Its sedentary members grew further and further away from the itinerants, and were ultimately lost sight of. Some indeed managed to change themselves into craftsmen or sneak into business through the smallest back door – and a few among those, by dint of tenacity, fulfilled their dream (a small minority): they were always to be found in the vicinity of a railway station, and they succeeded, after two generations, in becoming railway employees, the most highly remunerative occupation to which any Chanel ever pretended. But the rest, endlessly on the move from one market to another, remained what they were when they began: migrants.

Gabrielle Chanel's grandfather, Henri-Adrien, was one of those. He left Nîmes with his wife and infant scarcely a year after arriving there. Soon, in the nature of his type of work, he was changing house and town every year, every season.

How can one forget that it was this, the "wayfaring" branch of the clan, that produced Gabrielle? One might have expected to find her antecedents among those who had scraped their way into small businesses and owned their own homes. To our endless surprise, however, this was not the case.

*

Where were the days when generations were born, lived, and died one after the other in the same village? Henri-Adrien Chanel, his wife and children spent their lives "on the road" but never completely lost touch with the earth, presumably because they hardly ventured outside the Midi, that southern region of France where the markets, their smells and noises, still retained a quality of the village fête.

Henri-Adrien never dared to cross the imaginary frontier that forbade a southerner like him to display his wares where food was cooked without oil and roofs made without tiles, and where you could stand up in the wind. His children were born wherever he happened to be stopping, most often in the Gard section of the south of France: Louise, who was later to take care of Gabrielle, was born in 1863 in the heart of the Cévennes, Hippolyte in 1872 in Montpellier, Marius in 1877 at Alès.

Gabrielle's grandfather, thus, never roamed very far. He traveled as he had worked the fields before, with his nose glued to a calendar and his routes dictated by his old peasant sense, although it was no longer the sun's last rays or the first frosts that guided his steps. Now he was subject only to the festivals of the earth, and to everything a rural faith – that vast need to believe and hope – had added to them.

Back in the 1860s, a Chanel from Ponteils was standing upstream of the dawn listening for the milling and mutter that herald all peasant gatherings. That noise? Beasts and humans taking to the road, moving slowly, the cattle in front. Those marks in the almanac? Reminders of dates when some town was holding its harvest festival or some guild feasting its patron saint, when wreaths would be festooned across the streets and a venerated statue would emerge from the church and be paraded, bejeweled like an idol and robed in velvet. Then he moved too. He had to follow the same route and he had to move fast, for there was not one of these very Christian celebrations that did not have its fair.

This way, ladies and gents, this way, step right up, step right up! Psalms and drinking songs, rosaries and sugar candy pipes, processions and wooden horses, relics displayed next to nougat stands, incense and the smell of waffles, genuflexions and face-making contests: they all went together. These hawkers' stalls adorned like wayside altars, this tangle of sermon and brass band, these chaotic, dusty markets and carnivals provided the daily bread of Chanel's grandparents. And continued until Henri-Adrien's death at eighty-odd.

His older children, Louise and Albert, were taught in this school. The other kind, the "real" school, they seldom saw the inside of – a few months each year, during the off-season in January and February, when there was so little work in the markets that the head of the family could manage alone. The amazing thing is that in spite of such summary schooling, both children learned to read and write.

A FAMILY TO DISOWN

Gabrielle Chanel's father and her Aunt Louise had little enough in common. Louise was more refined than her brother, and quieter too. Cheerful, clever, and vivacious, with a profound sense of duty, she took after her mother: she was a Fournier to her fingertips. Albert Chanel resembled his father: the same sturdy neck, the same short nose, the same stubborn brow and the same straight black hair. And as for his character: hot-tempered as his father and a braggart and woman chaser, too.

As working partners throughout their childhood and teens, Albert and Louise were never separated. Their work was harder than one might suppose. They had to do more than carry the family baskets of wares and hawk during the season: at other times of the year, for the haying, the harvesting, the grape picking, the two elder children hired themselves out to farmers. Louise assisted the wife at her stove, Albert went to the fields with the men. A supplement to the family income. Perhaps it was the hardworking adolescence they shared that accounted for the lifelong loyalty between them.

Their branch of the Chanels remained united for many years.

Albert, Gabrielle's father, was not finally separated from them until his marriage, at the age of twenty-eight and in circumstances strangely reminiscent of those surrounding the marriage of his own father . . . albeit slightly aggravated.

Albert lived only to seduce, procreate, run away, and begin again.

His sister Louise, his good angel, did not marry until she was twenty-three. Her fiancé came from Ponteils, and worked for the railroad, in an office. What a step up! To the Chanels, eternal wayfarers, their future son-in-law seemed like a sort of government official, a man who could count on a regular monthly salary – what bliss – and, who knows, on promotion, too. Wasn't he from the Cévennes, as well? Louise was making a good marriage.

Her betrothed worked in Clermont-Ferrand, the big city, and so that was where they all had to go for the wedding, which was attended by the entire family and the "Tout-Ponteils." In order not to cut too sorry a figure in front of this new addition to the family, the bride's father declared on the marriage certificate that he was a "merchant." That sounded a bit better than "itinerant," after all. Albert Chanel, the bride's brother, rejoined the family for the occasion and acted as witness for his sister. He described himself the same way. All merchants here . . . only Angelina, the bride's mother, refused to pass herself off as something she wasn't. During all the long years since her own marriage she still hadn't learned to write. Why deny it? So she refused to sign.

"Declared unable," noted the registry official once again.

Here we are, a few years from the birth of Gabrielle Chanel.

How many inaccuracies in the stories she told! It is impossible at this point not to mention her ability to ensnare her listeners. She watched them with the smug ferocity of a waiting spider. But she also knew how to feel contempt, and her contempt went deep. Too gullible, her prey, too easy . . .

For her, everything was more important than the truth.

It is interesting to observe that one can search all her confessions in vain for a single acknowledgment of her humble origins. A peasant, she? Never did the name of her ancestors' hamlet cross her lips. Oh, weakness! Obstinate weakness! Sometimes she pretended to come from Auvergne, like her forebears . . . who did not; sometimes from Provence, like her father . . . who did not; sometimes she said she was of Protestant stock, like a grandmother . . . who was not. She defended her legend with noble desperation and even when she was driven to the wall and beginning to go under, this woman about whom everything was known – her friends, her income, her love affairs, her opinions, her tastes, her successes, her sorrows, her failures – was still striving at the close of her life to disguise her origins and mislead her pursuers, if only by a few miles.

How is it possible that this garrulous woman, who adored talking about herself, was never once tempted to confess what the real lives of her grandparents and parents had been, their stubborn struggle, so deeply rooted in her country's past? Her ancestors: like boulders, like those steles found around Alès, those menhirs; and they stood as firmly, planted upright in the earth. What cause did Gabrielle have to reject them? And from that first rejection followed all the rest . . . She rejected the injustice, the neglect, the oppressive inequality of which the peasant population has always been victim. All of it, rejected . . . and rejected, too, their long march toward a better life.

Why, in preference to her true origins, should she choose such a web of mediocrity upon which to weave her biography? Did she honestly believe her legend was going to flourish on such platitudes? Think of the woman her mother was, and lean on that memory as on a shoulder . . . Think of the unyielding Jeanne, daughter of a seamstress and a carpenter, Jeanne the orphan . . . Was there never any place in Gabrielle for the memory of her mother? And her bawdy, skirt-chasing father? Wouldn't it have been better to present him as he was, rather than make up a father out of a seventh-rate novel, a cheap soap-opera character?

To tell lies – decidedly, that was Gabrielle Chanel's permanent preoccupation. To tell lies, to the newspaper reporters who came to interview her, to the writers whom she expected to prepare her memoirs for her, to her friends.

We shall see the nature of the wound that must be held responsible, the disappointment that caused her to be inescapably ashamed of her origins. Love, ambition, hope: so many areas in which a series of misfortunes transformed her into a virtual parricide for the greater part of her life.

A ROVING FATHER

Albert Chanel exploited his "business bump" very thoroughly, far more thoroughly than his father had.

The itinerant life and its hazards suited him down to the ground.

First of all, he had to get out of the Gard. Why rot in Alès? France had better things to offer elsewhere. A glutton for fairs, wine, and women, Albert sensed what wealthier and more populous provinces might hold for him.

He went north.

He felt his way cautiously at first, and paused for a time in Ardèche, the next département. At Aubenas they made a nice little wine that went down easily. It was a rare item: vines that had escaped phylloxera were scarce as hen's teeth around 1880. Now, why not take this little wine on the road, carry it for the local wineshops? Become a sort of traveling salesman, add another string to his bow: wine. Wine, bonnets and buttons, overalls, kitchen aprons – they would all mix together perfectly well at the fair. Such were the visions of the future slowly germinating in Albert's mind. No doubt about it: Aubenas was not a bad place. But it wasn't the end of the rainbow, either. Come on, look farther afield. Farther . . .

Throughout his childhood Albert had heard tell of the fairs held at Puy-en-Velay on the feast of the local Our Lady, a colossal statue cast from the bronze of 213 cannon captured at Sevastopol by the soldiers of Napoleon III. In 1860, four years after Albert was born, the effigy of the Good Lady of September had been erected on a hilltop. His parents had always dreamed of that fair. To go there . . .

At last Albert reached the holy town and its monument. He spread out his wares. What a crowd! It was summer. The whole département was there. Paradise . . . not one church in the vicinity, not one monastery without its own Black Virgin – carved of black stone, left from the Middle Ages – however minimally miraculous. There were so many of them that September didn't have enough Sundays to honor them all. Some place or other held a celebration every single day of the week.

And here was Albert Chanel on the threshold of that part of France where fairs were taken fully as seriously as prayers. Here he was wending his way through the holy province.

He mustn't leave a single stone unturned. He stopped everywhere.

One day, he turned up at Courpière. A fair day, of course, the last of the year. Suddenly it was all clear. The banks of the Dore, the village with its narrow passageways, the wood and stone houses looking down on the valley, neatly grouped around the church in that precise arrangement that seems designed solely to provide good picture postcards, the square where the hawkers had already set up their shooting range: it was all waiting for him. And the constable? In his dress uniform, shirt, two-cornered hat and shoulder strap, old "Father Law," terror of the striplings, yes, the constable was waiting for him too, and the year's army recruits with flowers in their buttonholes, and the bear trainer, and all the maidens who had been awarded rose wreaths for good conduct, sweetly aligned in front of the church.

The bad season was drawing near. Albert Chanel decided to take up winter quarters in Courpière. He found lodgings, in November 1881, in the house of Marin Devolle, carpenter and carpenter's son, who had space to spare.

When they first got to know each other, Marin was twenty-three and Albert twenty-five. The two young men became friends. Marin had inherited his father's carpentry shop at an early age: his mother had died when he was ten, his father when he was seventeen. At twenty-one he escaped the army because he counted as a head of family: his little sister Jeanne, although living with a maternal uncle, Augustin Chardon, was financially and morally in Marin's charge. The girl was planning to be a seamstress, like her mother before her. She spent some time every day at Marin's, where she did the housework.

Albert soon began behaving like the cock of the walk. Marin lacked his self-assurance, his aura. Albert had been a soldier, he had experience, he had regimental reminiscences, the gift of gab, an appealing accent, a fertile memory, he knew how to discourse with the older women and prattle to the village maids. He charmed them all – most of all Jeanne, who had never been outside Courpière. This man from nowhere gave new meaning to her life.

One night he asked her to wait for him in the shadow of the barn. She was the invisible, silent conquest he was seeking.

But the days began to lengthen, and Albert had plenty of reasons for moving on. The fairs were starting up again. Soon it would be the feast of St Vincent, for the winegrowers; then it would be Chandeleur, with its pancakes and the hundreds of tapers to chase away the wintry darkness at the feet of the Black Virgins; then the feast of St Blaise, patron of tillers, and the slow processions through the fields; and then . . . Then it would be Carnival and the towns filled with noise. Ah, the towns, the towns! And away from Jeanne's sighs, which were becoming embarrassing. Away . . .

In January 1882 Albert packed his bags and vanished, leaving no address. But he did leave a few broken hearts behind him in Courpière, and many regrets, and one pregnant girl: nineteen-year-old Jeanne Devolle.

When Jeanne's "fall" could no longer be kept secret, her uncle the winegrower, with due regard for convention, threw her out. She took refuge with Marin, in the house where she had been born.

The only problem then was to locate Albert Chanel. The mayor would have to take a hand. Victor Chamerlat, whose name still graces a street in Courpière, did his best to calm young Devolle's avenging fury. How could they forget that one Devolle was a notary's clerk? And that the whole family was respected? Action must be taken. That unscrupulous vagabond, that blackguard Chanel, must be forced into marriage or, at least, into recognizing the child: this the mayor undertook to accomplish.

Albert Chanel had left a few traces of his passage. In the mayor's office, for instance, the same old story, the alteration of his name on the records. This nuisance followed him everywhere. Even though a decree correcting the error had been officially recorded in the archives at Nîmes, every time the mistake was made there had to be letters, a check, a request for a certificate from his father. Monsieur Chamerlat had taken the necessary steps. And then, as Albert had said he wanted to become a resident of Courpière, his name had been entered on the electoral list. In other words, the name and address of Albert Chanel's father could be found in the mayor's office at Courpière. There were a few other particulars in the notary's files, for Albert Chanel had been serious enough in his intentions to acquire part of a butter merchant's business. The address of the father, the mother, their registrations . . . more than enough to begin the search.

A few months passed before the whereabouts of the culprit's parents were discovered. The peddler and his wife were still changing residences as often as in their younger days.

But there they were at last, at Clermont-Ferrand, where Henri-Adrien and Angelina were finally apprised of Courpière's search. Their son? It wasn't the first time the Chanels had been called to account. Now what scrape had he got himself into, that scamp of an Albert? But this time his parents turned a deaf ear. So many children had been born to them since Albert's appearance! Sons and more sons. If they had to keep an eye on them all . . . So the senior Chanels feigned ignorance.

And Jeanne was losing patience.

She was one month from her confinement.

Urged on by the mayor, Marin Devolle and two of his uncles set out for Clermont-Ferrand. The idea was to give Henri-Adrien and Angelina the straight facts: Albert had knocked up a girl.

The men of Courpière arrived mouthing menace. They would go all the way; if need be they would demand satisfaction from the courts. And they had the means to obtain it.

Angelina instantly imagined the worst: Albert, her boy Albert on Devil's Island, in some hard labor camp . . . The frightened Chanel parents finally confessed: the guilty party was at Aubenas.

The gates of hope opened for Jeanne. The moment she heard the name, off she scurried. And nobody was to interfere. Albert would never be intimidated by threats. She alone could overcome his hesitations.

Jeanne Devolle reached Aubenas in the last days of her pregnancy. Albert was at the local tavern. That was where he lived and transacted his business affairs. That was where, almost as soon as she arrived, Jeanne Devolle gave birth to a baby girl one evening at eight.

The father agreed to recognize the child but refused to marry her mother. He wouldn't mind a companion, but no wife. But was it necessary to officialize such goings-on? That old dread of authority. And besides, nobody could keep a secret in Aubenas.

So they decided to act as if . . .

Jeanne was declared the lawful wedded wife of Albert Chanel. Their innkeeper landlord was taken into their confidence and agreed to act as witness to register the birth. And so it was that Julia Chanel, Gabrielle's older sister, born on September 11, 1882, in the public tavern of Aubenas, was declared the child of wedded parents.

Not enough, but more than Jeanne had hoped for.

A GUILTY MOTHER

Go back home after this? How could she? Thereafter Courpière would be nothing but turned backs, icy stares from her family, a ponderous silence from cousin Etienne the notary's clerk, snide remarks from cousin Claudine the cook, and from the wine-growing uncle . . . Jeanne knew it. That, then, was out of the question.

Her bridges were burnt.

Albert Chanel, meanwhile, was trying to put as much distance as possible between himself and the province containing double perils of proximity: his parents' and Jeanne's. Besides, fortune was frowning: business was bad. Jeanne's presence drove away his good luck.

What did he have in mind, at the end of 1882, when he decided to travel right across France? What could he have hoped to find in Saumur? This was more than running away. It was an atavism, a throwback to his tavern-keeping grandfather and to his old and never-fulfilled dream of settling down in a wine-growing region and running a business there. It was also his desire to get rid of Jeanne. Would she embark upon such a journey, trailing after a man who wasn't even her husband and dragging a newborn baby with her? Could she dare?

Albert told himself that maybe . . .

Which showed how little he knew her.

Jeanne had no choice. Albert was leaving, and all she could do was follow him, because the moment his back was turned the tavernowner would throw her and her infant out into the street. All attempts to dissuade her were therefore futile. On the strength of his rights as a male, however, Albert Chanel had no intention of sparing her. So she was stubborn, was she? She wanted to come with him? And she wanted him all to herself? All right, she would have him . . . Before her daughter was three months old, Jeanne Devolle was pregnant again. And in January 1883 she arrived in Saumur more lost than ever, having to find both a job and a place to live.

Saumur. There lies the town in all its majesty and there flows the Loire, perhaps the best of nature's gifts to France.

What if the influence of even a temporary environment, even one resulting from sheer chance, could be proved? One would then try to define what a being owes to his birthplace by immersing oneself in that environment and its particular features. One would try to assemble enough certainties, if not to explain a personality, at least to shed light on its more obscure corners. Every iota of that environment would become swollen with previously unsuspected meaning.

Thus Saumur, where Gabrielle Chanel was born.

What did she owe to Saumur, to this town that was giddy as a boarding school on the night before holidays begin, strict as a convent, and committed heart and soul to the worship of horsemanship? She never denied that in her mad younger years horses were her one and only passion. She was born in 1883; is it so absurd to see something like a secret understanding between her and the town in those years? Was it pure chance that she, the woman who strove her whole life long to impose on fashion a form of freedom and an outdoor spirit that tolled the knell for frills and furbelows, was born at a time when the riding instruction there was founded as much on cross-country training as on work in the traditional ring? Also, 1883 happened to be a year of influence from across the Channel. That year, Saumur was importing large numbers of hunters, the school's saddlers were beginning to build English saddles, and the riding masters were adopting – oh, horror; oh, revolution! – the rising (posting) trot in preference to the sitting trot, a hitherto sacrosanct principle of the French school. In Paris drawing rooms words such as *bal, tir au pigeon, réception*, and *promenade* were banned because fashion dictated that one had to say "night party," "gun club," "rout," and "footing." And the ladies no longer spoke of that raspberry-hued *drap* that had made such a hit in London, because "lady-cloth" was its name this year. They had ceased to have *déjeuners* anymore, too; now they *lunch aient*.

This was the beginning of a fascination with things English, from which, thirty years later, Chanel's art was to be born.

It was also a time when the cavalry uniform was gaining in simplicity and style. No more full parade coats or dress sabers, but a short fitted jacket with frogs and loops; and the peaked cap had definitively ousted the shako. As for the infantry: epaulets were passé and were replaced by passementerie braid and gilt buttons.

The Second Empire styles, the light-opera cavaliers with their brash, swashbuckling poses, were disappearing from the streets of Saumur. But can anyone imagine today what this equestrian Mecca was like then? Wasn't Saumur alone responsible for that miracle, the renaissance of the French cavalry? Renaissance because no branch of the army had suffered more in the Franco-Prussian war, a war that was still fresh in every memory. How could it have been forgotten – the defeat, Paris occupied, the emperor deposed, the Tuileries burned? It was less than thirteen years in the past. And it was the traces of these memories people were endeavoring to efface when Gabrielle was born.

When the so-called M. and Mme Chanel arrived, Saumur was the only town in France in which the shops stayed open after dark. Masters and cadets reigned supreme in the stronghold of the horse, and it lived on them and for them. What bound them together? A contract in the form of a romance. The entire population marched in step with the rhythm of military life.

Thus, the "certified purveyors to the gentlemen officers" held themselves in readiness until all hours to satisfy the whims of the playboys and rich men's sons, their yearnings for a last-minute purchase or an elegant meal. And continued to do so even though those same young bloods were in a far greater hurry to be served than to settle their accounts. Everybody knew it . . . even the locals, the civilian scum who stood by watching the cost of their own purchases soar. Were they paying for the cavalry? No doubt about it. But never mind that! What wouldn't they have done to keep up the morale of the army!

Such was Saumur in 1883, a town that never slept until the lights in the *beuglants* – noisy combination café-bars, music halls, and singing and drinking places – went out and the last songs faded away. The time for sleep came after silence had fallen in the Café des Arts, that pinnacle of Saumurois high life, and after the Blanchisserie and Hôtel Molière had closed their doors. And even then only if there was no ruckus that night, no brawls or practical jokes, no screams from the midwife when her sign was taken down and the coat-of-arms of the general and commanding officer of the riding academy put up in its place. Ah, no; and this was no town for dawdling in bed in the morning either. The whole place woke at the first bugle call, when cadets and grooms went racing for the stables where the horses were whickering and snorting as feeding time approached . . . Saumur's best time of day, that pause when dawn was just breaking among the smells of leather, hay, and shaken straw and Jeanne Devolle left her dwelling with little Julia on her arm and hurried off with the rest to her place of work.

There was no want of jobs in Saumur, and Jeanne, whose honest look inspired confidence, had a fairly easy time finding ways to sell her skills. What else could she do? Her pregnancy, as well as the baby, made it impossible for her to stand for hours in the raw market air. So until Gabrielle's birth, she had to stifle her desire to be with Albert Chanel on the Place de la Bilange, where he was now hawking his wares, offering corset covers, winter vests, and long flannel underwear accompanied by a heavy barrage of patter, oglings, and gallantries addressed to the ladies.

Jeanne, meanwhile – in the still gloomy pallor of early morning – hatless, wearing a broad-pleated apron, her belly heavy with Gabrielle whom she was carrying and Julia heavy on her arm, was heading for houses in which the cavernous kitchens awaited her, or the white neatness, the faint smell of yellow soap and the steam of a laundry, or . . .

There are no standard woes. Every age has its own. Jeanne's misfortunes are stamped with the seal of the time she lived in. To fight for a place as kitchen maid, ironing girl, or waitress; to know nothing of the Hôtel du Commandement, where General Danloux presided, except the pantry; and of the residence of the Commandant de Bellegarde, Ecuyer-en-Chef, only the ovens; and when that wasn't enough, to put in a few extra hours here and there, as sewing maid at the Maison des Trois Anges, which housed a boarding school for young ladies, or dish washer at the Hôtel du Belvedère, which provided meals for passengers from the *inexplosibles*, as the Loire steamboats were called: these, among other such odd jobs, were the labors Jeanne had to perform in the early days of her stay in Saumur.

Who will ever tell how far her instinct for preservation and the pangs of hunger drove her? Did she, as some say, stoop to taking jobs in Saumur's dishonored streets? Room cleaning on the rue du Relai or in the quartier des Ponts . . . "houses" for officers, "houses" for the enlisted men . . . Jeanne washing and bleaching, Jeanne carrying piles of sheets, waxing staircases where the customer's step was heard only after a female voice had called up in authoritarian tones, "All clear?" Jeanne bending over dubious beds, Jeanne as much a stranger there as elsewhere, as bewildered in these houses of ill-fame as in the public bar of the Belvedère among the inebriated bargemen, as uncomfortable at the "Grand 3" on the rue de Relai as among the maidens in the Maison des Trois Anges whose mildness and grace put her in mind of her days at Courpière, her age of innocence when she used to run over to Marin's house in her light skirt, her black apron and tightly laced bodice. Jeanne listening, Jeanne hearing but not understanding a single word spoken around her . . . What had got into those officers to make them wrangle so? What was this battle nobody had heard of except at Saumur? A battle of spurs and crops . . . Jeanne a foreigner to the words, foreign to everything, jostled from phrase to phrase like a deaf-mute, lurching like a cork on the crests of the tall waves blown up by the inextinguishable quarrel between Auristes and Bauchéristes.* What sense could Jeanne have made of it all? Their voices started to rise the moment certain words were uttered: "mouth," "tickle." . . . Whose mouth and tickle what? Fists thundered down on the table. Glasses trembled. Jeanne came running, dish towel in hand. But what on earth made them work themselves into such a furor? Madmen, these horse people, fanatics. Why did the spur fans have to be called "butchers' boys" by the other lot, the crop fans? The latter affirmed, "The crop's quite enough!" Whereupon, roars. The partisans of the spur accused their adversaries of outrageous cruelty: "Whipping a horse, flogging it! Really, what next! As if a crop were meant to be used, I mean to say! Spurs are quite enough . . ."

The meals ended in a salvo of slammed doors and Jeanne walked home again wondering whether the roving ache in her body was weariness, or panic at being unable to escape from what she was seeing and hearing for the first time.

A FAKED FAMILY

Jeanne and her lover found a place to live in a two-story house, of which they occupied only a north-facing garret. From there it was only a few minutes' walk to the two marketplaces of Saumur: the Bilange where the local gentry did their shopping, and the more "working class" market in the medieval setting of the Place St Pierre; in this respect Albert Chanel's address was in keeping with family tradition. Located in a busy street in the heart of a ramshackle part of town, it was one of those houses that sag with age, grow gaunt and bowed but keep standing all the same – and stand it still does, unchanged, with its three or four yards of frontage and high narrow windows, up to which float the costermongers' cries, "Oh, escarole, my fine escarole! Buy my escarole fine!"

On August 19, 1883, Jeanne Devolle rushed to the old Maison-Dieu, alone. Over a tall gateway which had formerly guarded the access to a leper house belonging to the Knights of St John, the word HOSPICE was engraved in gold capitals. The chapel, stuck like a sentry box plumb in the center of a stern gray courtyard, was the first thing to strike the eye, emphasizing the

---

* Followers of the comte d'Aure (1799–1863) and M. Baucher (1796–1873), two cele-brated horsemen whose methods were based on opposing principles. The French cavalry split into two enemy factions, which disputed the qualities and teachings of the two masters for over half a century and with unimaginable ferocity.

religious character of an institution staffed by the Sisters of Providence. It is possible, but by no means certain, that Jeanne, her pains having begun very suddenly, did not have time to be properly admitted to the hospital and gave birth to Gabrielle in the outer office. We will never know, but there was an anecdote to that effect among the Chanel employees for years. But what is certain is that Albert Chanel's signature appears neither on the registry office records nor on the certificate of baptism. Was the father really absent, as the hospital chaplain was told? Or was his absence feigned, in order to facilitate a false declaration?

On August 20, the infant had to be taken to the town hall. But who was to perform the task? Once again, a woman had come to give birth in the Hospice, alone. For a few pennies, three respectable persons offered their services as witnesses: a spinster, Joséphine Pélerin, aged sixty-two; and two men, Jacques Sureau, seventy-two, and Ambroise Podestat, sixty-two – all three hospital employees. To perform this favor for unaccompanied mothers was a regular custom, and the hospital workers stood only to gain by it. Presenting little Gabrielle to the deputy mayor, they announced that she was the daughter of one Albert Chanel, market trader, and a female trader named Jeanne Devolle, residing at 29, rue St Jean with her husband. Not being in a position to supply the least official document – but there was nothing surprising about that; wasn't it natural for the husband, the father, the absentee, to carry the family papers with him? – witnesses and declarers were equally unable to vouch for the spelling of the name Chanel. After a moment's hesitation, the deputy mayor improvised. And thus Gabrielle was registered with an *s* in her name. After Charnet, Chasnel . . . It was all in the family tradition. When the time came to sign, a fresh revelation: nobody knew how to write. Three hospital employees, three illiterates. All that remained for the deputy was to certify the fact according to the ritual phrase, "did not sign the above, which was read out in our presence, having declared themselves unable," and to place his own name at the bottom of a document that would otherwise, bearing no other signature, have been a sort of anonymous act.

August 21 was a baptism day. For the occasion, the hospital chaplain left his base. His parish was nearby: he was curate of one of the oldest and loveliest churches in Saumur, Notre Dame de Nantilly. It was he who baptized, among other infants, Gabrielle Chanel. The ceremony was performed in the hospital chapel, across from a major work by Philippe de Champaigne, *Siméon recevant l'enfant Jésus à l'entrée du temple*. The fourteen figures in the painting dominated the ceremony – among them, a tall slender feminine shape, the Virgin, whose mysterious elegance is always pointed out to lovers of beauty.

An acting godmother and godfather, Moïse Lion and the widow Chastenet, held out Jeanne Devolle's baby, calling it by the name of *Chasnel*. The priest of Notre Dame had no reason to question that this infant was the product of a legal marriage, since the people present on its behalf claimed so.

The father was traveling, the mother in hospital, neither had been born in Saumur.

In complete good faith, the priest wrote out a certificate that deviated in no particular from the traditions of these generations of itinerants. The family was absent, the name false, as was the legal position, and the godfather alone able to sign, the widow Chastenet "having declared herself unable."

Sixty years later Gabrielle Chanel presumed upon the credulity of her listeners to credit an anecdote she told to the effect that the nun instructed to hold her over the baptismal font had called her Bonheur (Happiness) in the hope that the name would be reflected in the landscape of her life. Nothing could be further from the truth. Jeanne – the first name of her mother and godmother – and Gabrielle are the only names on the document. But this invention was in keeping with her usual style: in defending the secret of her past, she could contrive to alter the truth only by amalgamating false actions and true characters – so that it has often been possible to glean accurate information from her stories in spite of her intentions. Thus, the tale of the imaginary name bears witness to a custom prevailing at that time in hospital institutions run by religious orders, and to the presence of one real person, the Sister of Providence who always attended the baptism of children born in the Hospice.

And there is no reason why it should not have been a nun, having complete freedom of choice, who was responsible for Mlle Chanel's first name of Gabrielle, which in Hebrew means strength and potency and, if onomancy is to be trusted, *guarantees enduring renown to those who bear it.*

LIFE IN SAUMUR

The ensuing year was unique for Jeanne and her two little girls – the only year they spent together not "on the road," the only one during which every town of Berry, Limousin, and Velay did not file past in succession, a year in which their continuous presence in Saumur is firmly established.

Although he was living in wine country, and despite his aspirations, Albert Chanel had still not become a wine merchant. He remained an itinerant, traveling by horse cart from fair to fair and market to market, living on his unrealistic expectations of financial triumphs to come. He owed to Jeanne alone the fact that he had a home and a roof, and also to her alone the help he had whenever he came to see her – for with the return of spring Jeanne, for whom love and sacrifice were the same, signed on to work under him, and the lovers of Saumur were increasingly often seen, by sellers and buyers alike, standing together behind their stall.

This outdoor life was good for the two little girls. Julia was beginning to walk, Gabrielle had just been weaned, and Jeanne, not yet exhausted by child-bearing and work, was a good nurse, a good mother, and a wise companion.

In the photographs that Eugène Atget, a roving artist, took some years later of other itinerants, Jeanne's brother tradesmen of the streets, there is a Jeanne – or a facsimile of her – and also, down to the last detail, there is the atmosphere of those markets, those windswept general stores in which Gabrielle spent the first months of her life. Those women, that gaunt figure of the young vendor behind her baskets, her weathered face raised to the passersby, her little girl, a few months old, nodding in the crook of her arm: she could be Jeanne holding the sleeping Gabrielle. That is her neatly skinned-back hair which the wind has loosened, the unpinned strands forming a sort of halo around her face, the little southerner's knot, round as a button, stuck down on the back of the skull; that is her twill skirt, her limp cotton blouse, her turned-down collar tightly secured around her neck by a string, and the full sleeve encircled at the elbow by a timid ruffle.

Reflect upon it: this image tells us far more about Gabrielle's childhood than pages of description could do. That look, that bearing, belongs only to Jeanne and the people of her condition. With the possible exception of the mattress carders, dog trimmers, and Romanys (gypsies), no group had a harder life than she did, working in the streets of those days. Judge from Atget's pictures; look, see with the photographer's eye how dressy and smart by comparison the bread girl is in her starched apron, how cozily clothed the flower girl in her full jacket and bonnet, her shoulders warm under the double points of her shawl. Whereas Jeanne . . . All the misery of the dying nineteenth century is there in the figure of a woman sitting on the ground displaying her shabby wares. Nothing can alter it.

Jeanne's misery lies in something evasive and reproachful in the eyes, in the smile that is not a smile – twelve years later, at the entrances to English coal mines, child laborers offered the same forced smile to the Lumière brothers – in the unutterably weary gesture of the hand lying limp on the basket rim, the deep hollow pressed into the apron by the weight of an infant and nobody to leave it with, the child always having to be carried, the hunger of that child, its crying, its tiredness, its sleep and immediately the fresh weight of the secondborn – the same hunger, the same crying.

After Julia, Gabrielle. But what does remain to be imagined is, upon that child, upon the innocence of that small body, the beauty which the perfect light of Saumur sheds upon all things . . . that caress. That child's future, however inconceivable it may seem, is irredeemably marked by what was seen as a dishonor by its contemporaries: the poverty of its origins.

What will Gabrielle's life be? You may say it is too soon to speak of it here; you may say . . . but never mind, since the image of Saumur on the day of her birth contained all of the Gabrielle to come. Look at them, in their ignorance of one another, these people who were the town, the people who *were* Saumur in 1883, whom the little girl sleeping in her mother's lap never saw. Listen to the hum of the marketplace, the constant cries of the vendors, forming the daily din that was her lullaby, the restless snorting of the horse tied to the standing cart, and everywhere, at all hours and in every street, the merry jingle of spurs of the gentlemen officers contending with Balzac's pebbly pavement. See them so sure of themselves and their boots. See the foreign cadets, mostly Russian, young Croesuses who will one day be the horse guards of His Majesty the Tsar. See the fabulous remittances sent monthly from St Petersburg by anxious mothers, and the incredulous eyes of the postal clerks who receive them in Saumur, see the who-can-smash-the-most-bottles contest at the Café de la Renaissance, one not to be forgotten for many a day – champagne it was, Madame, and they didn't even bother to uncork it – and see, finally, the French. All they could think about were their horses and their mistresses. If the little sleeping girl had only raised her head from her bib! Perhaps she would have seen the barouche of one of those . . . Behold the courtesans of Saumur, look at them. Better to be killed in the wars than alive in the bed of one of *those women*. Families lived in terror of them. What if their young man fell for one? Please God he could bring himself to break off when his time at Saumur came to an end! He was encouraged, the task was made easier for him. Come, come, my boy, one doesn't marry *those women*. One passed one's mistress on to a companion who could promise the forsaken one an equivalent standard of living and an equally fine barouche: that is how romances in Saumur usually ended.

If she had opened her eyes as one of them passed by, what could Jeanne Devolle's daughter have made of this life? And Jeanne herself? Could anyone imagine that twenty years later, officers identical to these in every respect – for they never changed – handsome horsemen, frequenting the same cafés and singing the same songs, surviving on the same superficial notions of love, life, and death, would be the first lovers of her sleeping infant? What if Gabrielle should turn into one of *those women*? Well, what harm was there in that? Hadn't they always existed? To encourage her to play that part; to coerce her, by proving to her that her head was full of impossible aspirations and preposterous dreams; to make her at once unsure of herself and aware of the unfathomable chasm separating her from them and all attainable joys: that was the work of the merry rich men's sons.

We find them woven into the background of Gabrielle's youth as one finds the sound of the sea in the heart of a shell.

II

Gabrielle's Youth 1884–1903

"*She was changeable. From that adjective to the other one: stubborn, which is supreme anathema to country folk, there is but a step.*"

— STENDHAL, *The Red and the Black*

A CHILDHOOD BEYOND THE PALE

In July 1884 Jeanne was offered what she had given up hoping for: marriage.

Although settling down, or settling anywhere, was the last thing in his mind, Albert had resigned himself to legality. He almost had to. Jeanne was pregnant again.

The wedding took place at Courpière, on November 17, 1884, in the presence of both those who had acted on Jeanne's behalf at the beginning of their liaison and those who had persecuted her subsequently. The officiating civil servant was the good mayor in person, Victor Chamerlat. Marin, the devoted brother, and Augustin Chardon, the uncle who had driven Jeanne from his home two years earlier and called her a shameless hussy, were the bride's witnesses, while a café owner – Albert always had one somewhere up his sleeve – stood up for the groom.

The senior Chanels, although apprehensively remembering the avenging zeal of the men of Courpière, were also present. They had been threatened in their own home, hadn't they? And since that time had judged it prudent to keep some distance between themselves and this awkward son.

The vanishing act was one at which all Chanels excelled; and so father and son had virtually lost touch with each other.

But marriage made everything different, and nothing more was needed to revive country good fellowship. So here was that rogue of an Albert settling down at last, and as soon as the ceremony was over they announced the existence of two children whom he recognized as his daughters: Julia and Gabrielle.

All that remained was to enter them in the margin of their parents' marriage certificate. No sooner said than done – but to everyone's considerable surprise.

Then, as though not to be outdone, Henri-Adrien Chanel announced that he, too, had cause for rejoicing – he was celebrating his thirtieth wedding anniversary; and he, too, had a surprise for them: he had just been made a father again.

So Albert learned on his wedding day that he had a sister the same age as his own daughter.

She had been born at Saintes and her name was Adrienne.

Gabrielle had no better friend in all her life.

The life of the new couple went on as before, with the sole difference that in the records office of a provincial town hall lay a document certifying that Albert and Jeanne were husband and wife.

Cold comfort. For as far as the rest was concerned, what had changed?

Albert's character was highly erratic. His affection was demonstrated only during the instant in which he embraced his wife before disappearing again. In order for him to take her with him he had to need her services so badly that he could not do otherwise; most of the time, however, Jeanne sat alone listening to him drive away. She heard the hoofs fading in the distance, and wondered whether Albert would come back.

She knew about his womanizing and his bragging. To enhance his image as a seducer, Albert embroidered upon his origins, failing to mention the irremediably itinerant nature of his family's occupations, claiming they owned land and vineyards and that his real trade was in wines. Meanwhile, Jeanne waited. She waited indefinitely.

The great problem was to select a town as a base, and then to find lodgings in it. The couple tried various biggish market centers whose predominantly agricultural activities seemed likely to afford them a decent living. In none of them was there a covered market. They worked exposed to every wind and weather, their goods displayed in the fiercest gales, the men wading through mud, the women soaked to the skin under umbrellas that protected precious little.

Nothing in France is more stable than the market site, a place of work that has witnessed the birth of many towns. Its internal organization obeys a tradition many centuries old: at the top of the square are the fruit and vegetable stands, with fresh meat, sausages, and cheese going along the sides; and in a double row down the middle, those vendors of gadgets, ready-to-wear, hats, and yard goods among whom stood Albert Chanel, and often his parents. More than once he chanced upon his father and mother and, alongside them, brothers and sisters he had never seen before, doing the same work on the same market square.

As important as the existence of the market itself, however, was the presence of the railway. At least in station towns one could be sure of finding activity, business, industry.

Issoire, where Jeanne and Albert spent some time shortly after their marriage, met all these requirements. Trains stopped there, and the marketplace was like a huge stadium surrounded by houses with eaves made of four tiered rows of tiles.

In this town, the base for their peregrinations for over two years, the Chanels lived in two places, both extremely modest and both located outside the nearly perfect oval of the old town, limited by the site of its medieval wall.

This eccentric (in the literal sense) quality of Gabrielle Chanel's childhood must not be forgotten: as a little girl, she grew up beyond the pale of every town she lived in.

At Issoire, her father showed a preference for crossroads. He wanted to have his back to the old town gates in undeveloped districts that were still more than half open ground. His windows looked out onto a reassuring vista, of roads parting and multiplying, each bearing the name of the village it led to – as though an inventory of all the possible places in which adventure might be awaiting him were spread before his eyes.

He was not exactly the smothering type of husband: Albert Chanel was a creature of movement.

To render domestic intimacy tolerable – the little girls' screams, Jeanne's nausea and dizzy spells toward the end of her pregnancies, his money problems; everything, in short, that ceased the moment he closed the door behind him – he needed the landscape of the open road.

Albert's sojourns at home were only badly dissimulated pauses between escapes.

First, we find Albert Chanel and his family living on the rue du Perrier and facing the route de l'Ouest, the road leading to towns whose names all end in *ac*, to little country markets smelling of truffles and fruit, to the Limousin.

There, on the rue du Perrier, on March 15, 1885, a first son was born. What sort of man was this child going to be? A more widely roaming wastrel than even his father was, a drinker and gambler, but also the only one of her brothers for whom Gabrielle showed any affection: Alphonse, her favorite, the one who always knew how to make her laugh and how to move her, the one for whom she kept a soft spot in her heart, until 1940, when she rejected him and cut off his pension.

Soon after his birth Jeanne, Albert, and the three children moved to another crossroads, this time on the rue du Moulin Charrier, facing the south and the hills of Auvergne.

Much has happened since the days when Gabrielle was growing up there, under a roof even then so ancient it seemed about to fall into the river millrace. Yet the house is still standing and engraves upon the mind a picture of an untender setting for tender years.

It was on a damp, narrow street, a dwelling not far from the towpath along the Couze de Pavin. A poor district . . . only craftsmen lived there, and everything manufactured up and down the street was for sale in the market on Saturday. A few wheels moved by the river, still turning the last mills. People were busy at break of day, some cutting stakes, others – candle-makers – pouring tallow.

The Chanels' neighbors wove the hemp the peasants brought in. The last job weavers, the last hemp retted and scutched on the farm. There were wax chandlers who said they were the only people in France who knew how to manufacture "genuine Roman tapers." There were hat-makers, from whom Albert Chanel bought his stock. And there were rope-makers, potters, and a nailsmith whose bellows was worked by a dog endlessly circling inside a wheel. The last hand-forged nails, the last forge dog . . .

Gabrielle's early childhood was spent in contact with these humble realities, and her first playmates were the children of these craftsmen.

By the time a third daughter, Antoinette, came along in 1887, the Chanels' financial circumstances had not noticeably improved. Jeanne had more work than ever looking after the children, and her health was deteriorating. She could hardly breathe. They decided to leave.

SUFFERING AND DEATH OF JEANNE

A prolific family suffocating within the walls of a furnished room suddenly breathed fresh air again: the return to Courpière.

For Jeanne it meant the end of being a stranger everywhere, it meant finding the little world of her own province again, and for Gabrielle and Julia it meant learning about the country, and a few years of happiness.

What attracted Albert to Courpière?

Nothing but the hope that Jeanne might take root there and thereby enable him to regain his lost freedom at last.

Uncle Augustin, described in contemporary documents now as proprietor, now as gardener – his property presumably being a garden – had a house. He took in his niece. Who could do less? This Mother Courage, burdened with four toddlers and a husband uncongenial to domestic bliss, aroused anxious compassion. She had never been sturdy, and now she was coming home thin and sunken-eyed. She was short of breath, her attacks of suffocation reminded Augustin Chardon of the malady that had carried off his sister Gilberte, Jeanne's mother. Had she contracted the same disease? He feared she was going to live in permanent danger of asphyxiation.

Augustin Chardon was not mistaken.

Jeanne Devolle suffered, like her mother, from a form of asthma that had grown steadily worse with the years. But one may reasonably express surprise upon learning that her daughter Gabrielle labored to portray her as a consumptive with blood-stained handkerchiefs. There is no doubt that in attributing to Jeanne Devolle the death of La Dame aux Camélias, in preference to that of Marcel Proust, she thought she was giving a better tone to her mother's demise. In Gabrielle's mind, being a tubercular incontestably added class to Jeanne Devolle: it was effective, therefore good. "Making Margot weep"* was a mainspring of the Chanelian narrative technique.

To get well again, Jeanne would have had to give up "touring" with Albert and remain in the pure air of Courpière, among the divine smells of the countryside and the twittering birds. But her husband's absence caused Jeanne such agonies of anxiety and irritation that she could not bring herself to do it. Why stay? Weren't the children in safe hands now? They ran no risks in Courpière, where she was leaving them in the care of an abundant family entourage.

Off she went, then, despite suspicions and quarrels, wearing herself out in Albert's wake. Never mind that she was ill. Getting well was less important to her than staying with him, every step of the way.

So great was her fear of being parted from him that she would no longer even risk having her babies anywhere except where she was living with Albert. In 1889, she gave birth to a son during the fair at Guéret, and once again she was living in furnished rooms, and once again in a country inn. It was there, in the public tavern, that Lucien was born, like Julia before him.

During this time, Gabrielle was in Courpière, spending the best years of a largely joyless childhood.

She was six when her mother came back from Guéret, with a little brother as a bonus. But who could care about him? Antoinette didn't count either,

---

*   An allusion to a famous couplet:

"Vive le mélodrame où Margot a pleuré
Et que tous les pédants frappent leur tête creuse."
(*Après une lecture*, by Alfred de Musset)

(Long live the melodrama Margot wept to watch / And let all pedants beat their hollow heads.)

she could hardly walk. Whereas Julia, one year her senior, and Alphonse, a year and a half her junior . . . (In all her stories Gabrielle Chanel, who often faked her own date of birth, claimed to be six years younger than Julia. It was all part of the game.) The three of them formed a group that was more than enough to transform their days at Courpière into one long holiday.

Now, from living with a family intimately tied to the soil, from racing wildly through the countryside and performing little household jobs for her good Uncle Augustin – the children helped him to push the wheelbarrow, to water and hoe – from the discovery of learning, on the benches of the friendly school where the three older children sat together, an entirely new notion of happiness was born in the mind of a gay and mischievous child. At Courpière, freed from maternal lamentations and the atmosphere of nagging suspicion that had hitherto comprised the essence of her family environment, Gabrielle learned to lead the life of a country child.

Poor Jeanne . . . At last a day came when she had to abandon forever her shuttles between the children at Courpière and her debt-ridden, fickle, and brutal husband who, although he greeted her with blows, felt compelled on each occasion to make her pregnant again, in order to be rid of her for a while. Perhaps, in her innocence, Jeanne imagined that he loved her! Perhaps she told herself that it ran in his family; but Albert was not like his father. He mounted her not as a proud stallion, but as a man taking revenge.

In March 1891, Jeanne returned to the family in Courpière. She was terribly changed. In May, Uncle Chardon, accompanied by a cousin – the respectable notary's clerk, Etienne Devolle – and his neighbor the flax carder, went to declare the birth of a child in his home: another boy, another of Jeanne's sons, called Augustin in his uncle's honor.

The child seemed unwell and cried constantly.

The father, as usual, was "traveling."

Soon afterward, little Augustin fell ill, and the poor creature died without anybody's really knowing why. He was carried to the churchyard, and almost the next day Jeanne began talking of leaving again. But where she said "duty," her family, more perceptive, read "obsession," "sickness." What sickness? Jeanne demanded to know. For her there was only one pain: being where Albert was not.

She wavered at length between various extremes of tenderness, hatred, and mad jealousy, sometimes speaking of divorce and sometimes of staying with Albert forever; at other times, realizing that he was the cause of her permanently ruined health, she would sink into a despairing silence.

Gabrielle was in her early thirties when she made the following remark to an *irrégulière** of her acquaintance: "My parents were ordinary people moved by ordinary passions." At over eighty years of age, that friend from the years of insecurity still remembered the tone in which those few words had been uttered – completely sincere and truthful. But can we assume that Gabrielle was referring to her mother? For, after all, *was* Jeanne's devouring passion so ordinary?

Until her last breath Jeanne Devolle, pregnant, deceived, and love-crazed, endured the same torture: either she must let Albert live as he pleased and lose him, or inflict her presence upon him and die of exhaustion.

Which is what she did.

In 1893, overruling her family's objections, Jeanne took to the road again, and the oldest girls, Julia and Gabrielle, went with her.

This departure had been precipitated by a letter from Albert. He had unearthed a young brother, Hippolyte, and gone into partnership with him. He also announced that he had set up in business as an innkeeper at Brive-la-Gaillarde and had found lodgings on the avenue d'Alsace-Lorraine.

It sounded good, and had the best possible effect upon Jeanne. Her hopes soared in every direction. She imagined herself happy at last by the side of a calm, quiet man who had achieved his heart's desire.

Albert was an innkeeper: that was enough to alter their whole relationship.

How could she have guessed what the letter didn't say?

At the inn, Albert was really only a waiter. Far from yearning for a reconciliation with a woman of whom he had had only occasional glimpses for the previous three years, what he wanted was to secure the services, at minimum cost, of the most devoted of domestics: his wife.

With her customary ardor, Jeanne labored to satisfy him, and in doing so lost what little strength she had left.

At the end of a few months she took to her bed. It was winter. She seemed to be suffering from something like a bad cold. She fainted from shortness of breath. But she would ask for neither help nor medical treatment: above all, she must not cost anything, she must avoid provoking both expenditure and ill-temper. Her condition – aggravated, no doubt, by bronchitis – worried her only in so far as it endangered her marriage.

On February 16, 1895, after several days of high fever and asthma attacks,

---

* The word was applied to a certain category of mistresses or kept women, by no means simple prostitutes, and implied a contrast to regular and regulation, as in regular army or lawful wife.

she was found dead. Dead of overwork. Worn to death. She was thirty-three.

Her husband was traveling.

Had the little girls seen her die? Gabrielle having said nothing on this point, no one will ever know.

It was Hippolyte, Jeanne's young unmarried brother-in-law, who made the arrangements for the last rites.

Such were the circumstances in which Gabrielle Chanel's mother died, and anything one might add to these few facts would be groundless speculation.

THE TRIBULATIONS OF
SCHOOLGIRL CHANEL

Although there is no shortage of witnesses – on the contrary – we must resign ourselves to having very few particulars of the ten years that passed between the winter of Jeanne's death at Brive and the period of her daughter Gabrielle's début at Moulins.

Those who knew Gabrielle between 1895 and 1906 have always met even the most inoffensive requests for information with stony silence.

What were they trying to hide, these intimate observers who knew everything of the calvary of a child? To what should the silence of Gabrielle's cousins be attributed?

Their reticence was probably the vestige of an old peasant grudge. Something along the lines of "She never did anything to give us a better life . . . we won't do anything to help her be better known." Because after she became rich, Gabrielle hardly had a thought for them, and they made no secret of their dislike for her.

It is also possible that Gabrielle's family thought her childhood too grim to relate. After all, Stendhal preferred to pass over some moments in the life of Julien Sorel in silence. Those years in the theological seminary: "Contemporaries who suffer certain things cannot think back upon them without being paralyzed with horror." There is no remedy for that horror. All decent people feel it when confronted by children who have been robbed of their childhood on the pretext that they were being saved, uplifted, instructed, cured, or kept out of trouble. Jean Genêt, in *L'Enfant criminel*, defines the origin of that feeling when he writes, referring to his own case: "We shall remain your remorse."

For her family, thus, Gabrielle Chanel was a source partly of resentment and partly of remorse, and for either or both of those reasons we shall never know with any exactitude how she was brought up.

If we wish to understand the kind of adolescence Gabrielle Chanel had, the only way is to make a careful comparison of the astonishingly contradictory versions she herself endorsed. It then becomes possible to isolate and analyze a few constants around which the truth must somehow certainly hover. As we know, Gabrielle Chanel occasionally resigned herself, in her efforts to invent her own past, to making use of real memories (so her tale would "sound true").

First of all, the horse-drawn buggy.

There can be no doubt that it was in such a vehicle, and driven by her father, that Gabrielle Chanel, then twelve years old, left the town in which her mother had died. She never contradicted herself on that point, and spoke of the incident in a wholly convincing tone.

Listening to her, one sensed that she was touching upon a major event of her life and that she had been permanently marked by the memory of that day of mourning, of a particular road leading out of Brive toward the mountains, and of the sound of the horse's hoofs trotting along it.

There, however, her truthfulness ended and we are plunged promptly back into soap opera.

"My parents couldn't bear mess and untidiness. They had a natural penchant for everything clean, fresh, of good quality; that is why people commented upon the note of elegance about our horse and buggy that was so uncommon in the countryside," she told Louise de Vilmorin, who did not mind talking about the days when Gabrielle Chanel was trying to persuade her to ghostwrite her memoirs.

And Louise de Vilmorin, unable to wring a word of truth from her, was driven to despair and soon abandoned an experiment whose pointlessness Gabrielle's own contemporaries made painfully clear: their testimony enabled her to measure the puerility of the myth she was being asked to transcribe.

No slightest degree of trust could be placed in Gabrielle Chanel's perpetually revised recital. Even the vehicle varied with her mood. It was called a cabriolet when she was investing her father with the authoritarian bearing of a powerful horse dealer, and it became a tilbury on days when he was cast in the role of a prosperous wine merchant. In this second version, she was giving a reality to the paternal aspirations that life was forever to deny. She even went so far as to assign Albert Chanel the part of a seductive, refined, free-spending fellow who owned extensive vineyards and – why skimp? – was fluent in English.

All of this, which brings both a smile and a sigh of pity to the lips, would not be worth a pause, and no one would care in the slightest whether the vehicle was a governess cart or a hay wagon, were it not that in these slivers of truth we have Albert Chanel's final appearance in the role of father – free at last, widower at last, driving his shabby little cart with two of his daughters in it to the orphanage.

Nothing could be stranger than the metamorphosis France's monasteries underwent after the Revolution had despoiled and robbed them of their statues, monks, abbesses and pasts. There is something fascinating in the mysterious similarity of their subsequent destinies. Think of Fontevrault, dear to the hearts of the Plantagenets, which became a national prison; or the Abbey of Poissy, haunted by the memory of St Louis, which became a home for delinquents: even Bec-Hellouin, occupied by soldiers until 1948. Barracks, solitary confinement, compulsory residence . . . it seemed written that these places were to harbor only single-sex communities.

And Aubazine?

No less handsome than the others, no less venerable, no less rich in abbots, saints, and relics, this monastery was destined to house a wistful and chilly world, the eternal gray of an orphanage for girls.

If some family traditions are to be credited, it was the doors of this institution that closed irrevocably upon the daughters of Jeanne Devolle. Why doubt it?

Aubazine was the chief orphanage of the region. The sisters of the Congregation of the Sacred Heart of Mary, who had been running the deserted monastery for twenty years or so, had made it so, and therefore it is likely that it was to this institution, nine miles from Brive, that Albert Chanel repaired.

The fact that the records which have been lost or destroyed are exactly those corresponding to the period when Julia and Gabrielle might have been living in the convent gives positive rather than negative support to the hypothesis. Searches, falsifications, and pressure exerted over the years by "important persons" desirous that some document should be removed or this or that erased from the Chanel files . . . revelations of this kind are not likely to amaze us where she is concerned. But it is impossible not to be amazed at the ferocity with which she tackled the impossible task of removing every single trace of the path she had traveled.

If there is one word above all others that never crossed her lips, it was the word "orphanage," a dread word, a word she carried within her until death, its virulent powers unabated. To understand what it meant to her and her feeling that fatal moment when she found herself in an orphan's uniform behind convent walls, it is necessary to refer to remarks she made many years later, referring to other tragedies. For example, Carlo Colcombet, a friend from her Vichy days, who was trying to comfort her after the loss of a loved one, recalled provoking this retort: "Don't tell me what I'm feeling," she said. "I have known it since my earliest childhood: they've taken everything away from me and I am dead . . . I knew that when I was twelve. You can die more than once in your life, you know."

We cannot doubt that the first days at Aubazine were this kind of death.

Abruptly removed from the shabby lodgings in which she had grown up, from the presence, on all sides, of families who suffered as much as her own from lack of air, space, and money, but had plenty of human warmth to offer, how bewildering the vast edifices of Aubazine must have seemed to the little girl suddenly transplanted there.

Perched on a summit encircled on all sides by vast forested expanses, the abbey, with its steep-pitched roofs and high walls, stands like a fortress.

And it is in this extremely severe setting that Gabrielle Chanel was to be educated. Like those daughters of the noble families of old who were placed in convents in early childhood, she spent the best part of seven years at Aubazine.

FRIAR ETIENNE'S ABBEY

Not a single decoration on the walls, not one carved figure. The only beauty is in mass, in volume; the only riches are those of naked stone, the only genius that of proportion. An outburst of Romanesque purity in all its immaterial loveliness.

Attentive to everything, as all children are, how did schoolgirl Chanel respond to such a setting?

Was it the monastery of Aubazine that gave her the taste for unadorned essentials she subsequently displayed, and her instinctive horror of everything immoderate – the distance she always kept between herself and any form of excess?

The convent buildings erected on the flank of the abbey church, the courtyard they enclosed, the fountain hollowed out of a single boulder and transported at what cost in manpower, the fish pond calmly containing the leaping waters of the Coiroux, a mountain stream that tireless stonemasons had contrived to channel a few miles away for the love of God or His poor. This was all the work of a handful of men living without rule or statute, wanderers dressed in sackcloth, so unwashed, possessionless, and vermin-infested that everyone treated them as tramps. Their vows were of silence and solitude and they followed a twelfth-century monk, a sort of Poverello, or St Francis of the banks of the Dordogne; a coarser, cruder companion, though, than the saint of the Portiuncula near Assisi, more of a pioneer and less of a seraph, more of a hermit and less of a preacher – another madman, yes, mad for God, but frail, homely, bald, as wrinkled at thirty as an ancient Buddhist priest, and a son of the people: Etienne d'Aubazine.

Etienne of Limousin, sower of priories and monasteries; Etienne the Flagellant, bare-foot Etienne, Etienne the Penitent, so acutely aware of his unworthiness that he demanded to be given the most repellent tasks: clearing cesspools, carrying excrement; Etienne, who longed to be not a Christopher carrying the Infant Jesus, but manure carrying the manure of his brothers. How often did schoolgirl Chanel have the tale of this exemplary life recited to her? Passages from it were read during walks, in class, at mealtimes, and a certain *Life of Etienne d'Aubazine*, published in 1888 and approved by the Bishop of Tulle, was treated by the sisters with as much reverence as the Gospels.

Gabrielle Chanel never wholly shed the influence of those readings.

Even in the days when, to obliterate the existence of the monastery where her father abandoned her, she had made Aubazine a forbidden word, snatches of the good hermit's story kept creeping into her conversation. She detached little pieces from it and inserted them into her anecdotes, telling herself that, after all, nobody could check any of it.

For example, mendicant monks of indescribable filth paraded through reminiscences of her imaginary childhood. She described them as bearded and sweaty, begging from door to door in rags. One wondered where she had unearthed them. She was suspected of having simply lifted some gripping scene from an opera, but the medieval setting of her monks was not that of *Khovanshchina* but rather of Etienne's first companions, the untutored builders of Aubazine. She thought she had given away nothing. She was mistaken. Those monks betrayed her as surely as if she had named the place.

Or what about Valette?

She liked to tell of dreary holidays spent with Julia and Antoinette in a convent of that name, huge and splendid, but unoccupied during the summer.

She thought there was no danger in the name: there have never been any nuns in this place, which, moreover, is not shown on any map. But why Valette?

Only an Aubazine orphan could know about the place where, in 1144, Friar Etienne had founded an abbey; almost nothing remains of it and it is mentioned in no guidebook or other publication – except for one tattered tome from which the sisters of the Sacred Heart of Mary endlessly recited. In this way, imagining that she was covering her tracks, Gabrielle Chanel unwittingly revealed one, the very one she was trying to hide.

Of the enormous building in which she was compelled to live, the huge halls swarming with children of every description, of the hours of rosaries, hymns, prayers, and the hours of silence, of the workroom, the lessons in household management, of the punishments, the walks, the long exercises in devotion, Gabrielle never spoke.

Nor did she ever speak of Sundays, when the orphans went on walks to the summits of the Coiroux, where the little girls could admire a landscape of unending forest. As far as the eye could reach, the same green, the same trees, the same dips and swells and, as though floating in the midst of a placid ocean, *their* monastery. Once again, the sisters related its secrets: a bell tower like no other on earth and its contradictory faces . . . and on the floor of one corridor, some unexplained signs, part of a mysterious mosaic each of whose figures, embedded in the stone, was derived from a single numeral, always the same.

"Why?" asked schoolgirl Chanel, fascinated. Why that number? Is a number stronger than a word? Stronger than an image?

The mysteries of the language of numbers were among those that troubled her most deeply. In her hour of success she remembered. What more magical than a number? The number five, say. Wasn't it a fine name for a perfume?

On that number her fortune was built.

Before nightfall, the Aubazine orphans were home again.

Two by two, the little flock crossed the village where the old men and women sat in their doorways. The children knew their faces. Greetings were exchanged.

Then the doors of a black and white universe closed upon them again.

White the orphans' blouses, washed and washed again, always clean. Black their skirts, box-pleated to last, and to allow them to take long strides. Black the nuns' veils and wide-sleeve robes. Ah, those sleeves, turned up to the elbow with a cuff deep enough to hide a handkerchief. But white the starched band around their heads and the wide wimple in the form of a ruff. White, too, the long corridors, and the whitewashed walls, but black the tall dormitory doors, a black so deep, so noble that if ever you see it, that black stays in your memory forever.

Such was Aubazine.

But Gabrielle never referred, directly or indirectly, to the little community that lived a prison life behind high walls.

The curious thing is that although her verbal aggressiveness was limitless, she never spoke out against the convent orders either . . . not one word of criticism. What did she feel about them fifty years later? What weight was there in the name of Aubazine?

There can be no doubt that for her the convent held the kind of fascination from which one never recovers. And although the memory of Aubazine may long have been a subject of odium to Gabrielle, it is possible that the violence of the shock wore off in time and she found in her most secret heart something like a vague, undetectable affection for the place and the women who had given her sanctuary.

And whenever she began yearning for austerity, for the ultimate in cleanliness, for faces scrubbed with yellow soap; or waxed nostalgic for all things white, simple and clear, for linen piled in high cupboards, whitewashed walls, an enormous padded table above which starched wimples and ruff wings fluttered like weightless petals, one had to understand that she was speaking in a secret code, and that every word she uttered meant only one word. Aubazine.

Resentment, hatred, animosity: she saved those for the people *outside* the convent walls who, by rejecting her, had driven her into this exile; saved them for that power which others called "family" and to which she, never having known it, could not even give that name. Her family? It was confined to Julia, Alphonse, little Antoinette, and the baby, Lucien. They and they alone were her family. What was left of them now? Would she ever see them all again?

She bore no grudge against her father: she could expect nothing from a person who had always made her mother cry and was always disappearing. He kept doing it. He would keep doing it forever.

Later, a long, long time later, she would meet him again, she was sure of it, and he would be the same as ever, unalterable vagabond.

No, she did not bear a grudge against her father.

But against a collection of unnamed and unnameable forces, a community of aunts, uncles, cousins, and grandparents whom she treated until her dying day with sovereign contempt. Poor and semipoor, clutching their meager savings . . . good-for-nothings, incompetents, petty people, provincials . . . She made no distinctions among them: all alike.

And when her father's sister, that Louise Costier who had married the man who worked for the railroad, took it into her head to offer the orphans a taste of the comforts of home; when that good and generous woman invited the little Chanels to spend their vacations at Varennes and live with her own children, it was too late: Gabrielle had to take it out on someone, *she had to*.

She knew better, but she nevertheless held her aunt to blame for her status as an orphan, for the ruthless rejection she had suffered, and for the dispersal of her brothers and sisters. So she met the holiday kindness with a defiant frown.

What had been done could not be undone.

She despised the woman before she even knew anything about her.

Therefore, we come to see the imaginary relatives with whom and by whom she pretended to have been brought up as the personifications of her hatred. They were two old maids, strict, unfair, hypocrites, two sisters of her father who never existed. That is what she wanted people to believe. These women *had to be* of the accursed race of skinflints – the filthy-rich females who had their own maids but never shared anything. Their way of welcoming the child *had to be* a barely disguised rejection. Gabrielle *had to feel* unwanted and banished *a priori*, everywhere.

These fictitious women, abused for over forty years, abandoned to the journalists' sarcasm with the support of an arsenal of endlessly renewed anecdotes, ridiculed on every occasion and in a thousand different ways, were the cold revenge of the child Gabrielle.

TO BE A HOSPICE CHILD

Whatever one may think of the fate of Albert Chanel's daughters, that of his sons seems still more cruel.

Alphonse and Lucien were ten and six years old respectively when their mother died. Since absolutely no one in their family was either able or willing to take charge of them, they were "placed" with a peasant family.

In those days, this was the fate reserved to orphans or infants abandoned at the Hospice turnstile.

The business of hospital management was entrusted to a half-religious, half-civic body which appointed a foster family and decided upon the allowance to be paid until the homeless child reached the age of apprenticeship. Alphonse and Lucien became what were known as Hospice children, for although not wholly orphaned, they were most definitely abandoned; and few objections were voiced, no doubt, by the itinerant tribe.

The Chanels would not have dreamed of opposing a practice with which they had been familiar since birth, and by which the people of Ponteils – beginning with Joseph Chanel the tavernkeeper and his wife, Marie Thomas – had long benefited. The old man had taken in as many as three foundlings at a time. One particularly hard winter, he lost two in one month. Dead.

The poorer the province, the more numerous the Hospice children and the higher their mortality rate. This was the case in Ponteils. Each of these children represented at least as much potential income as a chestnut tree, and they also provided a free labor force – of which, with rare exceptions, the peasants took scandalous advantage.

The Hospice child slept in the stable. Chestnut leaves were his litter. For him the farmer's voice became harsher, his hand heavier. The tut-tutting of the priests – as the curate of Ponteils agrees even today – had no effect upon this barbarous state of affairs. They chastised their flocks in vain.

Sometimes the foster family mislaid the child's papers, which were usually of the sketchiest anyway: a contract on which the orphan's first and last names were recorded, and for the foundling not even that. Just a number – the number of a report filed in some obscure drawer, declaring him abandoned. Sometimes a laboriously phrased letter was attached, affirming that somebody would come to fetch him someday. Then, so he could be more easily identified, a few snippets of clothing would be fastened to the record – an absurdly inadequate precaution, all trace of which soon disappeared.

As the years went by the child became known by a nickname derived from some physical or personality trait. His first name was forgotten, if he had ever had one. And for the rest of his life he remained a reflection of the unfathomable wickedness of humans, a body with no destination and no place in the village. He was "John from outside" or "the brat" or "the foundling"; he was two legs to haul with, two arms to perform only the heaviest tasks. If he fell ill and died they buried him in a corner of the churchyard. The priest recorded him under "death." But what can you say about a corpse that had no official existence? The report was succinct: "Death of a Hospice child. Was buried," state the archives of Ponteils.

The Hospice child could be beaten bloody, but the priest was there to see that he was taught. Yet very few peasants failed to get around this difficulty too, in order to make a better profit on their boarder. And what could anyone do about it? In winter the excuse was that the snow was too deep on the roads. Then the rains came; how could you send a child to school in weather that wasn't fit for a dog? The child stayed behind to sweat in the stable.

With the first warm weather he was sent up to the mountain pastures with the shepherds. He slept under the stars, always listening for animal noises. It was that much gain for the foster family: he was doing something useful without needing to be housed or fed. The priest complained to the administration, sent notice of the child's absence from catechism class. But complaints of this nature were so frequent that the bureaucratic languor was no longer even ruffled by them. Once again, what could anyone do about it? Were they supposed to send out the members of the welfare department, middle-class gentlemen in wing collars, to hunt for shepherd boys at an altitude of three thousand feet?

The child stayed up in his meadows.

He went on cheerfully sharing the shepherds' privations, and the village saw no more of him until the sheep came down again. The bellwether's distant tinkle heralded his return. The child reappeared, tanned and thinner than before, in a great cloud of dust. But it was the condition of the flock that interested the villagers, and only the sheep that were carefully inspected. After that was done, the child moved back into his barn, with the flock.

Until the age of thirteen Gabrielle Chanel's brothers knew no other life, and nothing that happened to them subsequently could ever completely sever them from that past. The peasant language was for many years the only one they understood immediately.

Was it to their grandparents or to the intervention of their Aunt Costier that they owed their placement, upon reaching the age of apprenticeship, with some market traders whose home base was Moulins?

Thereafter, Alphonse and Lucien led lives which were virtually the same as the one they had known while their mother was alive.

Despite the dispersal of the family, and their sorrows and their ignorance, which was great, and despite their father's abdication and their own ambitions too, a sort of impatience to "get somewhere" which they inherited from their father, they, like all the Chanels, were to live the harsh life of the itinerant.

Hawker of small wares, street crier announcing the passage of the Moulins *saccaraudes* (or costermongers), basket carrier in the market, Alphonse was all of those.

We know from his children that he often said, "I was put on the road at thirteen . . . always on the road."

To be on the road was his destiny.

Lucien's was the same.

HOLIDAYS AT VARENNES

In 1900 Gabrielle was approaching her eighteenth birthday, and after that age the sisters of the Sacred Heart of Mary kept on only girls aspiring to the novitiate. The others, those who did not appear disposed to take the vows, left Aubazine. But that did not mean they were abandoned to their fate.

Nowadays it is hard to imagine the influence and power of the convents. The nuns did more than place their orphans in apprenticeships and continue to provide them with room and board and supervision. Those who might distinguish themselves elsewhere were sent to other provinces, moved from convent to convent, and although the sisters could not guarantee their charges a social position, at least they did manage to find work for them and bene-factresses, and sometimes marriages.

On whose decision was Gabrielle sent to Moulins? That of the sisters who had brought her up? Or that of her neglectful family? Varennes-sur-Allier, the little town where Louise Costier lived with her white-collar husband, was only twelve miles from Moulins. Wasn't it tempting for this relative to remove her young nieces from their isolation, if only to put them in the way of earning a living? There was no future for them at Aubazine.

In any event, mere chance can hardly be responsible, and it was not by magic that Gabrielle Chanel, aged seventeen, was admitted to the religious institution in Moulins in which Adrienne Chanel, her contemporary and the last-born of her prolific grandparents, had been living for several years.

Hard by the venerable heart of the town – on the edge of the part of Moulins containing its collegiate church and belfry, and the streets in which ancient dwellings, leaning together, seem to be struggling to save one another from collapse – stands a rather dreadful building whose only noteworthy feature is that it has none, and it encloses the Notre Dame boarding school. Everything indicates that this is where Julia, Gabrielle, and Antoinette lived. It was run by canonesses, and attended by the best that Moulins had to offer in the way of solid citizenry. But in addition to the fee-paying school it also contained, as was customary in those days, a school for needy young women. On one side, then, the young ladies distinguished by advantages of birth and fortune, and on the other the poor girls.

Although the enrollment in the free part of the school was less peasant-dominated than at the orphanage of Aubazine, one can imagine what kind of resentment was aroused by this system and the distinctions it created.

Gabrielle in particular could not be insensitive to what, once again, made her *different*. She felt herself a victim of another injustice, and as though cheated.

Without Adrienne's affectionate welcome and her enormous curiosity about the town, it is likely that she would have been even more miserable at Moulins than she had been at Aubazine.

Entrusted to the canonesses of St Augustine at the age of ten and a pupil of the free school ever since, Adrienne, who was strikingly beautiful, had escaped the absentee childhood which had been the lot of all the other members of her tribe, whatever their generation.

She had been admirably brought up, and was spared many of the setbacks Gabrielle had suffered: the feeling of isolation in a boarding-school prison, the neglect. She had solid family attachments.

In fact, Adrienne had three families and two mothers, rather than one. First of all, the nuns. They had completely adopted her and taken pains to teach her all kinds of domestic skills. Adrienne knew how to do everything; she excelled at all domestic arts. Then there was Louise Costier, who, for some unknown reason, was never called anything but "Aunt Julia." The nuns allowed Adrienne to visit this sister, nineteen years her senior, whenever she liked. And thirdly, there were her father and mother. Henri-Adrien and Angelina had grown more settled with age. Not that they had given up tramping from fair to fair, but they began to show a preference for towns with covered markets where, when all was said and done, the work was easier. And the market in Moulins, built at the end of the century, was a particular favorite with the old man and his wife, especially in winter. Little by little, the eternal wanderers were beginning to want a rest. They looked for a home base, and decided on Moulins, where their dwelling, an attic on the rue des Fausses-Braies, put them within close reach of everything dearest to their hearts: the Halles (closed markets), the fairground, and their daughter Adrienne.

The real center of the family, however, was the low house and garden at Varennes-sur-Allier where the good Aunt Costier was always glad to entertain, however modestly, her young sister, nieces, nephews, and her old crony of a brother, that Albert Chanel with whom she had spent so many years of intimate association.

After dwelling among strangers and being entitled to nothing but solitude in a remote Corrèze village, Gabrielle was discovering a grandfather, a grandmother, two aunts of different generations, cousins younger than herself . . . it was too much. She rejected them *en masse* and, unlike her sisters, refused to acknowledge any obligations to a family community in which she was being given a place so tardily.

With one exception, however: Adrienne.

By her own admission this new aunt, "dreadfully family-minded" as she was, nevertheless became her intimate friend. They were inseparable. The resemblance between them was at least as striking as their good looks, and they were within a year of the same age. They also had in common an inexplicable elegance. Anyone seeing them for the first time took them for sisters.

They were not displeased by the mistake. Neither Adrienne nor Gabrielle troubled to undeceive people.

There was an air of sedateness and self-possession about Adrienne, a sort of trust in life that was painfully lacking in Gabrielle. Adrienne became the sole confidante of the girl from Aubazine, who was dizzy with longing for all things exalting and frightening. In the dormitory of the boarding school at Moulins, in the attic bedroom they shared during holidays at Varennes, they talked until dawn. Adrienne hoped, Gabrielle imagined. One strove to see straight, the other invented. They were already enemies, without knowing it . . . But isn't it always the same, with those perilous alliances formed on the threshold of adulthood? The first secret conspiracies, composed of dangerous acts and unconfessable promises. But this alliance did not follow the usual pattern and disintegrate at the first collision with reality. Later . . . only later. Much later, when Adrienne, after an endless wait for a respectable life, was finally about to enter into a delayed matrimony. Whereas Gabrielle . . .

As for Gabrielle's sisters: both were by nature restricted to minor roles. One a little slow-witted, the other too frail. Julia, the elder, passive and good-natured, was afraid of everything. Antoinette, eternally frustrated, didn't like anything. Neither of them had the constitution to confront the future on an equal footing with Gabrielle and Adrienne. They found themselves cast as walk-ons. To listen, follow, and swim in the wake of those dazzling beauties now still imprisoned within convent walls: those were the duties of Julia and Antoinette during their years at Moulins. Duties they would undoubtedly have gone on performing indefinitely, had they not both died young.

Nothing more French than Varennes-sur-Allier. A village? No. A little town, encircled by a road that dispensed quantities of pale dust, with a church and presbytery, its door topped by a stout cross of solid stone and decidedly funereal character.

Other unique edifices were the railway station and the inn, the former installed for the sole purpose, it would seem, of bolstering the importance of Uncle Paul Costier, and the other in order that officers garrisoned at Moulins would have a place to go when they wanted to drink and sing during maneuvers.

Nothing in the inn of Varennes had changed since the days of the stagecoach, and the old walls were full of charm, with double timbered balconies over which spilled a cascade of roses bursting with vegetable vitality, a paradise for bees.

Little or no commercial activity in Varennes: the fields grew straight out of the main street.

In fact, that was all Varennes was: a stop on the railway line, a freight station, a street drawn across the fields, overlooking rolling meadows, sedate dips and swells, moderate, with never a hint of ruggedness, however discreet, to break the harmony of a maddeningly reasonable landscape. What one might properly term a restful setting.

There was nothing of the peasant about "Aunt Julia's" house. It was a stone structure, set back from the road and covered with red tiles. Nothing pretentious about it either, no flight of steps before the door, no glassed-in entryway, but a shy suggestion of bourgeois austerity and some indefinably suburban quality expressed in an arbor, two impeccably symmetrical flower beds, and a garden shed whose shutters were always closed.

What any lonely child brought up as an orphan might have looked upon as the promised land appeared to Gabrielle to offer at least as many drawbacks as a convent, and perils all the more redoubtable for being less obvious. In Varennes one spent the holidays imprisoned by a different set of prohibitions, held back by other threats always stemming from the same fear: that one mistake, one rash move, one ill-advised expense would plummet these Chanels back into the proletariat from which they had just barely emerged. Terror of the unforeseen was the rule. Was that life? What a swindle, Gabrielle told herself. Her difference of opinion soon became manifest. Her family saw it as a sign of a bad character. Is it my fault, she told herself, if I am not as terrified of taking chances as they are? And why is this house so utterly unmagical?

In the course of her long talks with Adrienne she managed to bring her to share some of her own hopes, and to convince her that life had to be *something* else. Her gift for sarcasm was already well developed. Slowly,

Adrienne was won over. She, too, began longing to meet a little of that unforeseen her family dreaded so deeply.

But Gabrielle was the first to recognize that underneath this fear, in which her Aunt Julia lived as in a newly made shell – for she had acquired her lower-middle-class prudence only with her marriage – lay other qualities, sound and flourishing, that were not to be disdained: those provincial qualities that owe nothing to any sense of class and can be found in prosperous farmers and their hired hands alike.

There was imagination in Aunt Julia's fingers. She knew that endless wonders could be wrought with a skillfully starched piece of linen. Suddenly Gabrielle, who sewed just as beautifully as Adrienne – it was not for nothing that she had been a pupil of the nuns – sensed in Aunt Julia's efforts a quality hitherto unknown to her: imagination. In the convent, neatness and durability had been the only criteria. But imagination? Ingenuity? Not in the curriculum for orphans. And yet . . . She sensed that this was an important discovery.

Aunt Julia knew how to make a shirtwaist blossom with a cleverly crumpled carnation-fringed handkerchief. She knew how to take a remnant of linen and turn it into as many pleated collars and cuffs as were needed to give a lift to the strict attire of her convent charges. And her hats?

Hats were her one luxury.

To choose her hats, she made a special journey every year to certain shops in Vichy, the nearby town which became in Gabrielle's mind a synonym for luxury and opulence.

Gabrielle had never heard a woman talk about her hats.

That was a refinement unknown to the people of Aubazine.

Upon her return from her shopping expeditions, Aunt Julia would summon Adrienne and Gabrielle and, armed with a pair of scissors, proceed to attack the form she had bought and embellish it with certain notions of her own. Rims braid-bound, rippled and rolled, streamers . . . Adrienne and Gabrielle helped her to fashion a new marvel. But the basic form was almost always the same. Aunt Julia's inventions were all variations on the *capote*, a small Victorian bonnet with tie strings, and its indispensable accessory was the hatpin. She was inspired, here, by the unconscious heritage of all those women for whom the bonnet, that fragile miracle, had been an emblem of femininity.

When Aunt Julia sewed and when she cooked no pains were spared, and at those times the silent conflict between her and her rebellious niece faded away. What criticism was already being leveled at Gabrielle? That she had big ideas . . . that she was *different*. But this hostility, full of unconscious fears, gave way to their shared interest in a piece of work well done. The sewing room and the kitchen were two places where a fierce sense of economy, and the dread of "going short" which inexorably ruled the Varennes Chanels, proved less potent than that love of comfort that pervaded the last years of the century.

It was the age of buxom beauties . . .

An age when thinness caused shudders of revulsion . . .

An age ruled by the genius of the dinner table, when even the most modest housewife knew that a good meal required at its beginning – like all shared things: love, rest, or dreams – the pacifying vision of a white expanse, offered in all its gratuitous and perishable beauty.

Tablecloths . . . sheets . . . Every woman in the house bending over that whiteness.

A certain manner of speech, too, that was to haunt Gabrielle throughout life. She was still using it unconsciously half a century later, when she berated her apprentices: "You've gone and curved the edges of *my* pleats *for me* again! They look like mountain roads! What kind of work do you call that? You're not gifted, my girl! At your age I would have got that shirt front right in two shakes. What kind of foolishness is that? All right! Go press that over again for me . . . and try to get rid of that frizz."

Aunt Julia's manner of speech.

And while Uncle Paul's trains whistled in the distance and the rival sounds of church bell and tower clock clashed at regular intervals in the sky, aunt and nieces engaged in lengthy technical deliberations on the right amount of pressure for the iron stroke, the exact degree of dampness for the towel in which a piece of washing should be rolled; how to master the most complicated sleeve through the judicious use of the sleeve board; how you start a pleat by breaking the cloth with your thumb; how, with a cautious hand, you gauge the heat of the iron by holding it to your cheek; and how . . . All in the glow of the little cubes of embers on which the irons rested.

Whether she admitted it or not, and despite her hatred of her past, it was at Varennes-sur-Allier, in the house of her railway uncle, that the orphan from Aubazine learned the meaning of a word her convent years had stripped of its sense: home.

The extraordinary part of it was that all the connotations attached to that word, all the sweetness and softness it suggests, converged in her mind with a desire for escape.

A TOWN, ITS CLERGY,
AND THE ARMY

And what was Moulins to her?

Gabrielle was just a young peasant girl brought up by charity. During the two-year extension of her boarding-school term, she saw very little of the true features of the town except on occasions such as group excursions, or when Aunt Julia stopped at the Notre Dame school to collect her batch of convent girls and take them off together, Julia, Gabrielle and Antoinette walking behind Adrienne, the eldest, to the railway station, and from there to Varennes.

Gabrielle didn't miss a thing on those days, and nothing put her in a better mood. The town . . . life at last, coming toward her . . . it must be! But it was still impossible for her to do what she most longed to: to stop and look for a long, long time. And it became increasingly forbidden as she grew increasingly pretty, and was aware of being increasingly admired. But just to look? To follow the movements of the schoolboys when class let out? Even with her eyes? Forbidden.

But there was only one street, and not a very wide one at that, between the girls' boarding school and the boys' grammar school, where the recreation period was announced by a loud roll of drums. An old bearded "thumper" (drummer, in schoolboy language) was stationed in the middle of the playground. And off the boys ran . . . oh, to listen. To look. To follow from afar the pupils dashing over to the nearby grocer's shop and returning with their mouths full of croquignats – or nougat cakes, in the Bourbonnais patois. Hurry, look! Look at the old veteran shambling off with his drum under his arm to buy two sous' worth of chewing tobacco. The big boys gave themselves airs, they smoked *crapulos*, miniature cigars sold in pairs, which they lighted with infinite precautions to avoid being seen by the teacher on duty. Then, drifting on the wind, the aroma of the invisible cigars would curl up to Gabrielle's windows. A wisp of life, life again, like a reassurance. A life to inhale, to look at . . .

A comical-looking lot they were, those schoolboys, each in a long-sleeved, tightly belted black overblouse, beneath which showed two fingers of shorts that stopped just below the knee; then came a patch of bare calf, incongruous enough, then a generous strip of sock, and finally the very high uppers of the short boot. What weirdoes! Were it not for the touch of white of the short collar worn outside the belted smock, and the splash of color of the loose tie, they would have made as pitiful a spectacle, enveloped in

all that black, as the little chimneysweeps whose poignant cry could sometimes be heard from the dormitory. "Ah here's the sweep . . . !" And Gabrielle
longed to look and look at those little gentlemen whose mothers had bought
fine boots for them and who wore white collars as they played in the yard
across the way. She was scolded for it. What rational answer could she give?
Gabrielle liked to look.

It is hard to say why but two details, insignificant at first sight, were to
stick in her memory forever: the collars of the rue du Lycée schoolboys
with their floppy bow ties, and the black of their smocks.

One day, many years later, a highly fashionable young woman was to
adopt the same collar and floating tie that the young scholars wore tight
beneath their chins.

People instantly began to copy her.

A short time later she became a designer, this young woman, and the
women she dressed found themselves adopting the same collar. Then she
added a crepe de chine tie to it. Then she decided to make them black,
because black, she said, never went out of fashion. And suits were born the
likes of which had never been seen. They were so young-looking. Some
people thought them brazen.

And so for half a century a certain suit, saucy but black, black as the
linenette smocks of the Moulins schoolboys, adorned with the same collar
and the same tie, went trotting through the streets of Europe and the two
Americas. It was a worldwide best seller; more than that, more than a
keynote, more than a fashion: a style.

A style whose name no one could fail to know: Chanel.

Opportunities for outings were few at the Notre Dame boarding school and
the motives were always religious.

What would Gabrielle have preferred? The Place d'Allier and its cafés,
where the manille* players assembled. The Sunday concerts where La Lyre
Moulinoise played. To sit. To wait. To watch for the moment when the
conductor, with unctuous hand, would call forth the opening measures of
La Jolie Parfumeuse, making the kiosk and its round roof ring. *Et badadi et
badada* . . . Moulins, the people, rich and poor together, they were all there,
blissful.

But it was no place for a free-school pupil.

On Sundays the boarding school attended high mass in a body. The girls

---

*   A card game using a 32-card pack.

from the fee-paying classes sat in the center pews, while orphans and the needy were relegated to the side aisles – an inequality Gabrielle found hard to accept. Not a single boy in sight. It was the custom for pupils of the male sex to be put behind the high altar, where they could hardly hear the service, let alone see it.

The army children, conducted by the bemedaled survivor of a thousand deaths, and the *cagots* – as the church-school pupils were called by those from nonaffiliated schools – flanked by priests armed with their "signals" (six-to-eight-inch-long boxwood batons used to indicate the movements of the mass), appeared in their Sunday best – short navy-blue jackets with gilt buttons – and, after marching past the entire congregation, disappeared into the taper-hearses bristling with lights, as into flames licking at so many stakes. Seen no more. Heard no more. You might think they were dead, if the dry taps ordering them to kneel or rise had not reminded you of their presence. *Tac–tac–tac* . . . beyond the high altar, the signals sounded like castanets.

Soon, followed only by choir boys, the priests appeared in a proliferation of lace.

Mass at Moulins was invested with greater pomp, and lasted longer, than anywhere else in France.

This was a consequence of the long reign of one bishop, Monsignor de Dreux-Brézé, an opulent prelate with a keen sense of costume. Throughout the forty years of his ministry, the height of his miters, the length of his train (which a subdeacon and two choirboys specially selected for their strength were scarcely able to carry), the never equaled slowness of his processional tread, and the unctuousness he imparted to his most trivial blessings, all remained engraved in the memories of the people of Moulins, and six years after the dignitary's death his taste for the ecclesiastically over-done lived on in the interminable ceremonies. As for the oddities of the deceased, such as the little infirmity that had been the subject of much jesting among liberals in his lifetime – there were days when an imperative need compelled Monsignor to interrupt himself in mid-service and scurry (Jesus, help me!) to the sacristy facilities at a rate made perilous by his endless train – everyone had forgotten about that. In the days when Gabrielle was becoming acquainted with the town, one could believe the Roman Catholics of Moulins would remain loyal forever to the memory of a bishop who had combined such magnificence with the merit of high birth.

For his father had been a valiant defender of the Throne. He had also been a genuine marquis. And this marquis, topic of conversation in the Notre Dame boarding school almost as often as the bishop himself, was none other than the hapless grandmaster of ceremonies of the late Capetian. (After divesting Louis XVI of his string of titles and his head, the revolutionaries derisively referred to him as just plain Citizen Louis Capet.) It was he who, ordered to dismiss the Third Estate, had inspired the famous apostrophe of the comte de Mirabeau.* According to the professionally devout, the retort was typical of the loathsome Riqueti; but it remained, to the last, one of the few historical quotations ever used by Gabrielle.

Strange but true. She couldn't have cared less about the Revolution, or the revolutionaries or their ideas, but she loved to surprise people, and would quote, out of the blue and in ringing tones, "Go tell your master . . ." For her, it was a line in a play, a tirade like any other, almost a joke. Later, the words heard long before and carried secretly in her mind came back to her. Words dating from a youth composed wholly of masses, vespers, and communions; words from Sundays spent in the din of the great organ, old words from her Moulins days.

No matter how many masses they attended, the existence of the girls of the free school, and the devotional education imparted to them, would still not have been fully justified without processions.

And the girls were their crowning glory.

They moved with cadenced steps past a crowd of vigorously moustachioed peasants, bourgeois dressed in their best, prostrate families, businessmen drunk with devotion, and soldiers with lowered arms.

A providential parade for Gabrielle.

At last, she could see what she never saw: other people. She could do what she was always longing to do: look. And then, she herself was on display . . . She marched past a silent, prayerful public. The streets were as highly perfumed and decorated as a drawing room. White bouquets and golden hangings on all sides. She sang. She thrilled to the sound of her own voice. How she loved to sing! She walked, light as air. People looked at her. Especially men. She paced on without lowering her eyes.

The feast of Corpus Domini, in Moulins, was the occasion for an unbelievable amount of fuss. There were as many processions as parishes, and

---

* The words were, "Go tell your master that we are here by the will of the people and will be removed only by the force of bayonets," a reply made by Honoré Gabriel Riqueti, comte de Mirabeau and the greatest orator of the French Revolution, to the marquis de Dreux-Brézé, who, acting on orders from King Louis XVI, was trying to expel the representatives from the chamber of the Estates-General (1789).

as many wayside altars as processions. Every crossroads, and the front page of every newspaper, was cluttered with it for weeks.

On that day, the free-school girls led the procession. They marched in front of the taper-bearing canons, the local tots dressed as angels, the Holy Sacrament beneath its canopy, and the bishop in his rigid gold cope.

Upon reaching a wayside altar, the procession came to a halt. The celebrant laid down his burden and caught his breath. The canons mopped their brows. The choirboys replenished their censers and a fresh stock of petals was distributed to the angels.

Occasional wails would rise from the children's ranks. Desperate voices cried out "Mommy!" The mothers came running. With nervous fingers they patted wilting ringlets back to sausage plumpness, straightened a halo, or hastily unfastened the knickers of one tormented by an agonizing need to pee. The gentlemen of the Welfare Committee took advantage of the pause to withdraw discreetly, just long enough to knock back a glass of cherry brandy at the Café Chinois.

The customers on the café terrace crossed themselves.

Then the orphans broke into a final psalm and the procession swung away again in a swirl of incense.

The most grandiose of all the wayside altars was that erected by the cavalry regiments stationed at Moulins. The clergy made their longest pause there, and blessed away as though they would never stop. It was the star attraction, the surprise annually anticipated by local journalists.

The year of Gabrielle's arrival in Moulins, the ingenious horsemen had outdone themselves. Every single taper was planted in the barrel of a rifle or revolver. Beheld through the fumes of the censers, this conglomeration of weaponry guarded by impassive horsemen . . . really, one doubted one's eyes.

The press, however, saw nothing in it but a pretext for delighted commentary.

Here is one description of the *pièce de résistance* of this holy day: "The crossed sabers and artistically assembled lances, the chandelier suspended above an altar decorated with an arrangement of revolvers; the whole, forming an ornamentation of the finest decorative effect, was a little miracle of taste."

On this occasion Gabrielle realized that Moulins, in the shade of its linden trees, held more than convents and churches.

When Adrienne and Gabrielle reached their twentieth birthdays, life took a new turning.

Julia had already left the convent, and was helping her grandparents in the markets. Antoinette, still too young, stayed on in the care of the canonesses, while Adrienne and Gabrielle found themselves placed together as shop assistants to a respectable couple who ran a well-stocked little establishment on the rue de l'Horloge. À Sainte Marie, "specialists in trousseaux and layettes," is where Adrienne and Gabrielle lodged with their employers, sharing an attic room, just as they had at Varennes and in the convent.

Relations with Notre Dame were not broken off by the move, however, or at least, not right away.

Adrienne remained on friendly terms with the nuns who had brought her up. And although now employed in the town, she continued to be seen in their workrooms as well. As for Gabrielle, she needed no prompting when asked to swell the ranks of the free-school choir. Singing was a field in which she had ambitions.

The shop on the rue d'Horloge also made clothes for ladies and little girls, and the nuns' pupils quickly found themselves transferred to this branch of the business. These pupils sewed divinely. The news got around.

The region was liberally sprinkled with châteaux, which became the rallying points for all manner of elegant types during the racing season, for the Moulins course was located near some important stables. It was at Champfeu, after all, in the stud of the duc de Castries, that Frontin and Little Duke, winners of the Paris Grand Prix, had been foaled. And Field Marshal MacMahon, during his term as president of the Republic, had come in person to watch the races at Moulins. Out of friendship for the duc de Castries, who was his brother-in-law, of course; but also because, as was commonly known, that particular president had sounder views about horses than about statecraft.

Gabrielle watched her employers grow literally intoxicated reciting the names of those whom they saw as the sources of their fortune. And quite rightly so! That was the essence of the business sense, after all, and Adrienne was not far from sharing their bedazzlement. While Gabrielle . . . she seemed impervious, walled up inside her skepticism, which helped to sustain a certain irritation in her associates. Their presentiment? That she would escape them. Would not let herself be intoxicated, or influenced by the attitudes of others. She was no ordinary shop assistant. After long days and long months spent behind a counter, scissors in hand, ceremoniously greeting the haughty persons who, she sensed, lived *outside* everything that affected her, the social resources afforded by the neighborhood held no more secrets for Gabrielle.

Her employers had taken pains to reveal every detail of them. It was essential, wasn't it, absolutely essential that the new assistant should be as impressed as they were by such amazing riches. She learned, for instance, that there was a country seat at Tortezais whose owners had a mule in their coat of arms, and one of their ancestors had been a steward of King Charles VIII. Wasn't that wonderful? And so many princes! No fewer than four châteaux in Besson alone. All Bourbon-Parmas. Two châteaux, alas, had been turned into stables. Deplorable . . . but most fortunately, the Bourbon-Bussets, excellent customers, lived just around the corner and had been there for nearly five centuries. Their château was at Busset, and the identity of name between château and château-owner was an added mark of distinction to the shopkeepers. With obvious pleasure they would repeat, "The Bussets at Busset, the La Palices at La Palice, the Nexons at Nexon . . ." None of this, regrettably, struck Gabrielle as sufficient ground for oohing and ahing. The noble visitors who came to the shop awakened few thrills in her: her notion of elegance differed widely from that of her milieu. And to her their stately homes were merely austere – always clinging to some pinnacle, always corseted with walls, and all too often looking as though they had been designed for military use alone.

She dreamed of something different . . .

But was very careful to keep it to herself.

Later, when she had reached the age at which most people feel they can tell all, she never went beyond veiled allusions, but she did hazard a jest about her horror of châteaux. "The affection I may have felt for certain of their owners was never enough to make a stay in them tolerable to me," she would say.

III

A False Start 1903–1905

"You understand, when one army is beaten by another army, you change cockades and invent a new uniform, but it's still a uniform and still a cockade."

— LOUIS ARAGON, *Holy Week*

THE SCARLET BREECHES

The year 1903 was a crucial one for Gabrielle. She was beginning to lose patience. So many wasted days, hours! She was about to be twenty-one.

She took a room, in the rue du Pont Guinguet, the cheapest part of town. Because with her salary . . . hard to find anything better. Far away, beyond the rooftops, she could see the broad, calm waters of the Allier.

Now the haughty persons wishing to make alterations to their wardrobes came to her little room and consulted Gabrielle directly, without the knowledge of the good people in the rue de l'Horloge. If some statements can be credited, she even spent days in some of those crenellated châteaux.

Adrienne, less venturesome, hesitated before following her.

Then, a little while later, she too made up her mind. As "family-minded" as ever, and wholly nourished on the sap of the Notre Dame school, it was she who made sure that all ties with Aunt Julia's world were not severed.

And after all, what objection could be raised to the girls' decision? They might not be living on the rue de l'Horloge anymore, but weren't they still living together? And their work was the same as before.

The nuns themselves saw nothing reprehensible in the step.

Aunt Julia concurred.

Now, as the turning point approaches that will launch Gabrielle, and Adrienne after her, into an encounter with another world, hints of the temptations to which they will succumb begin to appear. The girls were now discovering the other Moulins – no longer the drowsy, edifying town seated upon its dignity, with the massive doors that seemed to open as though against their will, the houses with their huge porticoes dating from the days of heavy coaches; no longer the streets around the cathedral, so silent that walking along them felt like walking among convents. Now they became acquainted with the main streets and their linden-shaded shops.

Any garrison town must have pastryshops and tailors.

Moulins had both. And into their precincts, on the main street, came the officers quartered in the town.

Moulins was not a dreary place; there were several regiments there. But one and one only – from 1889 to 1913 without interruption – overshadowed the rest: the 10th Light Horse. It would be hard to find any more select. The 10th Light Horse contained both the scions of the Faubourg St Germain and the fine flower of the landed gentry.

Its commanders were Colonels de Chabot, d'Estremont de Maucroix, du Garreau de la Mécherie, Renaudeau d'Arc. The captains: Verdé de l'Isle, Marin de Montmarin, Anisson du Péron, de Gaullin des Bordes, de Valence de la Minardière, de Barbon des Places. The lieutenants: Doublet de Persan, de Barjac de Rancoule, d'Adenis de la Rozerie, de Vincens de Cauzans, d'Albufera, d'Espeyran, des Courtils de Montchal. The standard-bearers: Merle des Isles, de Ponton d'Amécourt, de la Moussaye, de la Bourdonnaye, de Sainte-Péreuse . . .

Leafing through the directory of officers of the 10th Light Horse gives one the disconcerting sensation of traveling back through time to the days when King Louis was calling up his chevaliers for the Crusades.

Once again, then, we find horsemen entangled in Gabrielle's destiny, a recurrent theme throughout her life; and here we have Gabrielle, only just come of age, entangled in barracks life.

The Light Horse were billeted in the Quartier Villars on the far side of the Allier, facing the old town and its crooked streets – in short, a good distance from the center.

But the moment they laid down their arms and bolted the box doors on their steeds, the officers overran the promenade, wearing scarlet breeches cut wider than the regulations permitted and peaked caps raked over one ear – but not too obviously so; nonetheless *supersmart*, and easily stuffed into a pocket in spite of their extremely long visors.

Gabrielle let herself be dazzled.

This was an army one had supposed dead – reported lost at Reichshoffen.* But here it was, the same army, composed of gentlemen enamored of war, braided to the shoulders and arrogant withal, and chauvinistic too, no more than half-cured of their love of foolhardy feats and doomed charges, deaf to all tactical innovations – an army convinced that its mission was to stupefy. The cavalry, too, the old traditional cavalry, bold and fanatic, sneering at a Republic that wanted it to learn how to spell and show respect for instructions which, if applied, would have meant the end of the whole

---

* Site of a Prussian victory on August 6, 1870, Reichshoffen was identified with the memory of a suicidal French cavalry charge. A military song immediately appeared to glorify the massacre, and remained popular for over forty years, just long enough for another war to break out between France and Germany.

romantic military ideal. What a notion! Why, the authorities were trying to forbid the cavalry "to hurl itself upon the enemy according to its personal ardor and the speed of its horse." What did they want? A collective conscience; a little forethought. The horsemen considered themselves insulted and the text too distressing for words.

Such was the army garrisoned at Moulins.

There were many distractions: dancing at the Café Chinois every Saturday, and quadrilles at the Alcazar on Sundays.

And the pastryshops were never empty. They were the rendezvous for the mothers, sisters, fiancées, and cousins who came to Moulins to embrace their heroes.

And then the tailors . . . They showed a singular want of *pschtt*,* and although one or two provincials, even among the Light Horse, were "green" enough to order their uniforms from them, it was understood among the young bloods supplied with private incomes and understanding papas that the purchase of a képi-cravat or a short jacket with seven goats'-hair frogs and three rows of gilt buttons and artistically passementerie-trimmed sleeves – and even more, perhaps, the acquisition of one of those sky-blue overcoats worn only by the cavalry – required a trip to the best tailors in Paris, those in the Place du Théâtre Français or the rue de Richelieu. Otherwise, one ran the risk of looking a fright and being taken for a *plouc* (hick).

The local tailors, therefore, caught only rare glimpses of the cavalry officers, when they dashed in to have a stripe sewn on or a button replaced.

Nevertheless, it was in a Moulins tailor's shop that everything began for Gabrielle.

It was at the height of the racing season, and the big day of the races run by the gentlemen officers was drawing near.

Five or six young men, all with moustaches and all lieutenants concerned more with equestrian glory than sartorial snobbery, came into the Modern' Tailleur for some last-minute alterations. Oh, nothing much . . . the replacement of those knee linings that were forever wearing out in the heat of training, or the addition of the removable armature worn steeple-chasing, a kind of crash-helmet made of cane or whalebone and designed to stiffen the cap . . . Nothing much, but it had to be done.

There they were, rushing about seeing to everything themselves, one in shirt tails, another cap in hand, when they caught sight of two girls busy at

---

* From Parisian "smart set" slang around 1900, this was a new word intended to replace "chic," corresponding to something like "pep," "pzazz," or "zip" in English.

their sewing in the next room – like two enchanted princesses in the thrall of an invisible bad fairy. What more singular sight than a king's daughters patching a pair of riding breeches?

The young men's surprise only increased when they observed that the girls never lifted their eyes from their work and behaved as though the young bloods weren't even there.

The boys asked questions.

They were told that the girls were employed in a ladies' dress shop, A Sainte Marie, on the rue de l'Horloge, and did occasional jobs for the tailor only when the racing season brought in more work than he could handle.

The young men waited for the girls to come out after work, and at the end of five minutes of conversation invited them to watch the jumping events the next day.

They deigned to accept. But how haughtily! The manners of royalty . . . One taller and fair, the other dark, smaller, and more deadly.

The young men were electrified.

That was the beginning.

This escort was composed of boys of varying origins. One could identify them all. There was a younger son of a wealthy family of Montpellier, there was a boy from the Béarn who was regarded as a desirable match but was to end his career, after joining the Cadre Noir as one might take religious orders, as a riding master – and a bachelor – in Saumur. The Cadre is a group of military horsemen, all dressed in black, commanded by a master, or Ecuyer-en-chef. The *reprise de dressage* of the Cadre Noir is as famous in Europe as the equestrian ballet of the Spanish Riding School of Vienna. And who could forget the merry marquis, another horse fanatic, who succumbed to the evils of the times in the forties and went off to do a turn in the LVF: the Légion des Volontaires Français against bolshevism, a unit in which French volunteers fought in German uniform alongside Reich troops in the campaigns against the USSR. It would be easy to complete the list: Robert Sabatier d'Espeyran, Charles du Breuil, and masses more. They were the irrefutable witnesses to Gabrielle's beginnings.

The first rendezvous took place at À la Tentation, an innocuous shop where people went to eat sherbets. Then various schemes were hatched. They might go to the Grand Café, meeting place of the local smart set. A little jewel of a spot . . . newly built, with beveled mirrors like those at Maxim's, wood paneling with carved intertwined vines, and here and there a touch of tiling like the Art Nouveau at Lipp's – all the latest thing.

In fact, the Grand Café, which succeeded in resembling neither Maxim's nor Lipp's, was inalterably provincial; but to the two girls it seemed unimaginably luxurious. They couldn't recall ever seeing anything gayer or prettier.

But the novelties that shone with a magical gleam in Gabrielle's eyes only aroused Adrienne's anxiety. She saw obstacles everywhere.

The transition from the atmosphere of the shop specializing in trousseaux and layettes to the Moulins-by-night of the lieutenants of the 10th Light Horse did not take place without a qualm.

It required all Gabrielle's energy and determination to pull Adrienne out of the rut with her.

One of the most certain proofs of Gabrielle's and Adrienne's success among their new friends would seem to be the imperishable impression left by that first meeting.

Half a century later, some of them could still recall their initial fascination.

One might wonder at this, knowing to what extent these young men were, with one or two exceptions, blasé, unrefined, and superficial, bothered by nothing, subject to neither scruples nor regrets, and far too preoccupied with themselves to be dominated by the past.

And it was nevertheless they who, year after year, from mess hall to drawing room, with comments dropped while in their cups and pillow confessions, were to provide a scrupulous, accurate report of the amazing beginnings of Gabrielle Chanel.

We cannot deny that she was already marked with that quality of strangeness which alone makes women memorable. A singular beauty . . .

Both girls were speedily enlisted to add to the attractions of evenings in Moulins. They relieved the officers' distressing sense of being imprisoned in a world from which women, apart from good-hearted but often silly or excessively vulgar professionals, were excluded.

The circle of Gabrielle's new acquaintances soon spread far beyond her original group of admirers. She became indispensable. The two little seamstresses, whose popularity soared until they were something like a craze, became the mascots of a milieu accustomed to having its whims obeyed. Gabrielle and Adrienne *had* to be part of every outing.

Which does not necessarily imply that they immediately had lovers too. What is hard to ascertain is just when they did begin "sleeping." Nothing clearly discernible on this point.

But the impression left by their witnesses' accounts leads one to suppose that as long as they belonged to all, they belonged to no one in particular.

It was with unencumbered hearts, therefore, that Gabrielle and Adrienne first set foot in La Rotonde.

This was a round pavilion with trellised walls, built around 1860 as a café and, according to the municipal council decree, a reading room. Any reading done must have taken place upstairs, however, for La Rotonde itself was crowned *à la chinoise* with a sort of pointed pagoda roof overlooking a garden – oh, no grand park, just a nice little provincial square, containing a full sampling of the trees and assorted accessories traditionally found in the public gardens of temperate zones: a cedar, an elm, a cypress, a few chestnuts, a ring of benches around a plot of lawn, a statue of the local poet in his dressing gown presiding in his bronze armchair, and lastly, paddling rhythmically on the surface of a pool, two sour-tempered old swans.

The fashion of café-concerts spread quickly throughout France, so La Rotonde had only the briefest of cultural careers.

Hardly two years after it was built, it was being used for singing. Whereupon the local authorities installed a solid iron fence around the pavilion, designed to keep the curious at a respectful distance, and heavy curtains to veil the bays.

La Rotonde became a *beuglant*, or low-class music hall. High time it did, too.

Here the name applies to little café-concerts opened for the use of the army in garrison towns. There were *beuglants* for officers and *beuglants* for the men, and in all a predominantly patriotic repertoire was applauded, with calls to revenge and threats to Germany. The word itself comes from *beugler*, to bellow or bawl, as a bull.

The other place, Le Bodard, on the promenade, could no longer hold all its customers. One positively smothered there; and so it was abandoned to the gendarmes, quartermaster sergeants, baggage train troops – everybody, in short, who was not the Light Horse.

From garrison to garrison, the word about La Rotonde soon got around. The men came running from all sides. Because there were limits, after all, to devotion to one's country and, in any case, devotion did not preclude enjoying oneself. Smoking, joining in the choruses of an essentially patriotic repertoire, drinking within reason – for their equestrian ambitions could scarcely tolerate abuse – bombarding the singer with cherry stones just to keep everybody on his toes: the distractions of the military did not exceed those limits. It was all redolent of foolishness and relatively innocent. This was a far cry from the "caf'conc' " so dear to Henri de Toulouse-Lautrec, and a far cry from Montmartre. La Rotonde offered neither the attractions of the Moulin Rouge nor the distinguished perversity of the Divan Japonais.

But only let a few infantry officers in the door, and the devil of a row broke out. If the singer whose job it was to belt out the military couplets made her entrance in a cavalry cap, the foot soldiers began to shout the place down. Or if, wearing a tricolor costume, she broke into a verse glorifying the infantry:

> *Le cheval court, le canon flambe!*
> *Mais pour donner l'assaut – Viens-y!*
> *Toujours joyeux, toujours ingambe*
> *C'est le fantassin qu'on choisit . . .*

(The horse can run, the cannon flame! / But to make the charge – come on! / Ever jolly, ever nimble, / It's the infantryman they choose . . .)

The outraged horse guard would launch a virulent counterattack, miming a charge, pounding fiercely on the tables, bawling *Les Cuirassiers de Reichshoffen* in unison and imitating bugle calls with "ta-ra-ta-ta's" loud enough to knock the plaster off the walls, or galloping across the room with their chairs between their legs and whipping their boots until a haggard director appeared to try and pour oil on the troubled waters:

"Gentlemen, gentlemen, please!"

The announcement that the next number would be a ballad to vibrate the ever sensitive strings of the spirit of revenge never failed to produce the desired effect. In complete silence, the men listened to *La vengeance du pharmacien de Strasbourg* ("The revenge of the Strasbourg pharmacist") or *Voilà mon fils, ce qu'est un prussien* ("That, my boy, is a Prussian"). Then a comic "turn" would be put in, some piece of contemporary vulgarity, good and coarse and strongly *gaulois: Une tempête dans une culotte* ("A tempest in a pair of knickers") and *L'arrière-train d'une dévote* ("The hindquarters of a pious dame") were tried and true favorites.

And Gabrielle? What was Gabrielle doing in the midst of all these flushed faces? She was listening, looking, and seeming to like what she saw.

Beneath all the racket and the din, a vague promise was mounting to the surface, which she alone could hear. Nothing more than a formless sound, like an opening door. *A way out?* Where did it lead? Gabrielle was far from guessing. But she could not let it pass, and would have to try it, come what may. For her only thoughts were these: to get out, to make good, to succeed; and her only ambition, to put an end to a condition of manifest inferiority. She was alone, however, and already knew it was up to her and no one else.

THE BEUGLANT

The initiative that led to a year's contract at La Rotonde was apparently hers alone, and she also found a situation there for Adrienne.

One can readily conceive the reaction of a music hall director confronted with a recruit like Gabrielle. In her wake trailed the best-provided-for hearts of the garrison. Could he hesitate?

Moreover, this novice was an unusual physical type.

It is true that she was exceedingly brunette. But a certain Spinelly, a ravishing brunette whose moment of glory began in 1901, was beginning to be talked about in Paris; she writhed about and cried, "*Un coup de piston!*" and Gabrielle was exactly the same type. And then, that mouth . . . Gabrielle's voracious mouth gave the lie to her grave, almost melancholy expression. Her very long throat was like that of Yvette Guilbert – "La Grande Yvette," the biggest café-chantant star around the turn of the century, who appears in many of Toulouse-Lautrec's pictures. The creature was all contradictions, at one moment convent-girl shy and the next diabolically daring. She certainly was too thin, but she had an indefinable charm. Would her defect eliminate her? There was also a woman named Polaire – who with her eccentric songs, suggestive undergarments and seventeen-inch waist, was a music-hall sensation just then – quaking spasmodically and showing the whites of her eyes, subjugating the Parisian public with a vision of unpadded flesh that would have been judged unacceptable five years earlier. [Her name remains linked to the play *Claudine à l' école*, by Willy and Luvay, directed by Lugné-Poe and first produced in 1906; it was her first stage appearance. " 'Claudines' were all the rage," Polaire wrote in her memoirs. Every nightclub and house of ill repute had its "Claudine."] So? So Gabrielle was highly employable. She had no voice to speak of, but she had her followers, and even a claque, for she had already hopped about the stage now and then, shaking a fairly lively leg to the great joy of her admirers. She clearly liked doing it.

A repertoire and traditions that had disappeared from Parisian café-concerts were still in circulation in the provinces.

In Moulins in 1905, for example, what were known as *poseuses* were still seen on stage in the *beuglants*: ten or so girls sitting in a semicircle behind the top-billed performers. They were there to provide a background, to raise the "tone" of the establishment and keep the audience from growing restless between numbers. As soon as the stage was empty they would stand and offer a song, each in turn. No one really listened to them. They were unpaid. One was elected to pass the hat among the tables, a custom Parisians would have considered hardly worthy of even a rural cabaret.

It was as *poseuse* that the granddaughter of the tavernkeeper of Ponteils made her début at La Rotonde. The atmosphere was friendly. Her fans in the house were lavish with their encouragement. She was hailed as a triumph almost before she got up from her chair.

Gabrielle weighed her chances.

Sitting beside her, more dead than alive, girls as totally inexperienced as she watched and waited, suffering the agonies of a condemned man hoping for reprieve, hoping for the applause on which their future depended. It was a cruel competition. Success was the only criterion. At the slightest sign of hesitation, all hope of an engagement was lost.

Gabrielle was the favorite among them all. She was the gentlemen's star yearling and she led the field by lengths in an easy canter. Every evening, with a little smile for her devotees, she rose and launched into one of the songs of her repertoire.

About this same time, love had brought to Moulins a young woman who had acquired a small reputation at the Théâtre de la Monnaie in Brussels. Her affection for a rich man's son, the comte d'Espous, had permanently curtailed a career in the ballet. Her lover was serving his time in the 10th Light Horse. She loved him passionately and gave up her career for him. He accepted the sacrifice, and did not marry her. Just another *irrégulière* . . . Her name has left few traces in other memories, but her own testimony was invaluable. She remembered Gabrielle's first appearances on the stage of La Rotonde very clearly: "She was a prude," she said, "and locked the door to change her dress. She had terrible stage fright, but it didn't show. Basically, she was an insecure *arriviste*."

The new recruit knew only two songs. She would start with a verse from *Ko Ko Ri Ko*, a revue which Polaire had turned into a hit in 1898 in a chic Parisian caf'conc', La Scala.

At La Rotonde, Gabrielle's appearance was traditionally hailed by various onomatopoeic noises in which the cackling of barnyard fowl predominated, to encourage her when she broke into a timid "Ko Ko Ri Ko" in her rusty voice that bore scant resemblance to the war cry of the rooster. Then she called in her second string, which always brought down the house with roars of delight. The tune was a touch out of date, but it still went over in a big way, and it was called *Qui qu'a vu Coco dans l'Trocadéro?* ("Who's seen Coco in the Trocadéro?") It was just about as old as the Eiffel Tower. Her good-luck song . . .

She put her whole heart into it. Singing it, she saw herself queen of the music hall, mistress of the Seine, having *arrived* at last.

To call for an encore, her public simply chanted the two syllables of the word common to both her songs, "Coco! Coco!"[1]

It was like a catchword that kept coming back every evening, every time Gabrielle sang.

The nickname stuck.

She was "Coco" to all the officers, to all her friends in the garrison. That's how it was; she had no choice in the matter.

After finishing her song, the débutante named Coco – not by her father, as she tried her whole life long to make people believe, but by an audience of soldiers out on the town – curtsied gracefully and returned to her seat.

As beautiful, even more beautiful, but less talented than she, Adrienne was assigned the task of passing the hat.

The La Rotonde experiment – this risk Gabrielle deliberately chose to run – did not seem to be having quite the results she had hoped for.

Moulins was not Paris.

Everything at the *beuglant* was second-rate: no water in the dressing rooms, no stars' names on the bill, only performers who were on the way out and no longer had the stuff to face competition from the young wolves in the capital.

Anyone but Gabrielle might have been content with this state of affairs, mistakenly supposing she had set her foot on the path to the stars. But not she, for whom the admiration of a few officers could not offset the indignity of performing among a cast of has-beens. How could one fail to see it? The shabbiness and triviality of the show were self-evident to the least sophisticated eyes, and Gabrielle was now beginning to have doubts. What was she doing there? There was nothing for her to learn.

She already had an inflexible will, and she said she was convinced of her calling. To make a name for herself, to proceed, like Yvette Guilbert, from back-room sewing to the footlights out front, to become somebody, by singing . . . It is possible that even in her Moulins days, Gabrielle had more specific aspirations. She dreamed of using the music hall as a steppingstone to operetta.

And for that, she would have to move on.

She would have to settle in a town that had some real theatrical life, a genuine stage, and in that town she would have to find work. And although she must go, she must also try to lose as few of her faithful followers as possible. Lastly, she must avoid alarming Aunt Julia, who knew nothing of the gladsome goings-on at La Rotonde.

The reason she didn't was that an impenetrable wall stood between the fine-looking gentlemen of the 10th Light Horse and the citizens of Varennes. Two worlds, each living in the margins of the other. They passed one another in the street and never saw one another, they jostled one another without ever daring to become acquainted.

But even if the Chanels had known, is it so certain they would have disapproved? Gabrielle Chanel said so. She spoke of threatening messages – transmitted by Antoinette from the Notre Dame school – and claimed that the family had sworn to have Adrienne and Gabrielle put in a reform school if ever they let themselves be seduced by some barracks masher.

Don't believe a word of it: they were both twenty-one. What danger was there? Besides, the people of Varennes could hardly talk – they had few lessons to give. Julia, Jeanne Devolle's eldest daughter and the only one to remain within the family circle, had got herself pregnant by a fairground vendor. She had just had the child. The father had recognized it, but made no move to marry the mother. Nevertheless, they lived under the same roof. There were traditions in the Chanel family too, after all, handed down from generation to generation.

But there is reason to think that this misfortune, suffered by a sister of whom she was fond and with whom she had spent so many sad years, could not fail to touch Gabrielle. This may be the true significance of a decision which aroused the indignation of the habitués of La Rotonde: Coco was leaving them. Was it possible? The creature was escaping her creators.

When the outcry subsided, they chose to be understanding.

She was going to Vichy for one season. But the resort town, which had grown increasingly fashionable since the Second Empire and Napoleon III's visits to take the waters there, was only thirty miles away. The Light Horse lads trooped over on the slightest pretext. Races, concerts, touring actresses, unknown beauties to quarrel over, a steady stream of proper and not-so-proper women . . . Vichy was the Baden-Baden of Monsieur Loubet's France: adventure to fit every pocketbook, and the garrison's holiday home. So they had to console themselves and consent, for a few months, to life in Moulins without Gabrielle. Adrienne was going too. Never apart, those two.

Promises were exchanged. They mustn't lose touch.

But just to be on the safe side, the Light Horse followed close behind the fugitives, in serried ranks.

Colonel de Chabot never had so many applications for leave to go to Vichy as in that summer of 1905. An epidemic . . .

One reaction was most unexpected, however – that of a trainee officer. He was frankly pessimistic about Coco's artistic future.

"You won't get anywhere," he told her. "You don't have a voice and you sing like a trombone."

She decided to ignore him, although there was no one she trusted more. Odd, wasn't it? He was an infantryman. Courted by so many horsemen, she favored a foot soldier. Her official suitor? Not yet, but he was very taken with her and made no secret of it. One witness to the evenings at La Rotonde went so far as to claim that the officer in question was her first lover. This is less certain. But there can be no argument about the fact that in 1905 Gabrielle Chanel had no serious interest in him. Fun and friendship, of course. But nothing more. If she had been in love with him, would she have gone?

His name was Etienne Balsan. He was much more real and natural than the flashy toffs from the Faubourg St Germain, and Gabrielle understood him much better. Neither tall nor slender, with an unspectacular moustache and a round face, nothing military in his bearing, none of the audacities of dress so cherished by the horsemen, not much distinction about him and no pretentiousness at all, he was assuredly less alluring and less elegant than they. But wildly energetic, visibly openhanded, and a master at making and keeping friends.

The last-named feature alone would suffice to describe him. No one could have more friends than he did.

What was he fond of? Wherein lay his happiness? In horses, to make them run; in women, to give him pleasure; in the light wines of his province, to make him laugh; and in good humor, good food, good-looking flesh, and the good life . . . If the term *bon-vivant* hadn't existed it would have had to be invented to describe Etienne Balsan.

He lived only a short distance from Moulins.

His family were from Châteauroux, a manufacturing town in which his parents had amassed a solid fortune. Dignity, sobriety, solemnity, quantities of competence, the French upper-middle class and its language of cold moderation – that was the Balsan family: a social class hitherto unknown to Gabrielle.

The common people and the army were all she knew of France.

The 90th Infantry had had its garrison at Châteauroux for thirty years; when the time came for Balsan junior to do his term of service, he was naturally assigned to that unit. Infantry . . . strange condition for a conscript whose sole ambition was to breed racehorses. The news plunged him into despair. What could he do? How could he escape from drill, from Châteauroux, the barracks, his family? He contrived to get himself transferred to Moulins, to a service for the study of Oriental languages. A neat trick. The Light Horse cheered his arrival. Those gentlemen regarded him as one of themselves. They had great hopes of a human dynamo like him.

They were not mistaken.

Their enthusiasm redoubled when they learned their friend had succeeded in persuading his chiefs that he had to learn an Indian dialect, since the interests of the country might one day require the dispatch of spies out there. But the dialect was so obscure that there was no one around sufficiently qualified to teach it . . .

It was skillfully done. Young Balsan was going to be able to take it easy, ride all the best horses, have a ball.

Thereupon, he met Coco. At first, he had no idea of abducting her. What could he have done with her? The young person's life-style did not indicate any great social talent. But he, like the rest, and indeed more than the rest, was intrigued by the idea of launching her. As what? That was the whole question.

Although he had grave doubts about Coco's vocal abilities, Etienne Balsan undertook to promote the Vichy endeavor.

He offered to help Gabrielle and Adrienne with their purchases, but was careful not to let it get around. He didn't like people to feel obligated to him. In later days, when Gabrielle Chanel's talent was taken for granted and her fame had spread far beyond French frontiers, he need only have told his story . . . But he had little wish to do so. What had he done? Why talk about it? He merely said, in a modest voice:

"I gave her a leg up."

Thanks to him, Gabrielle and Adrienne now entered the shop of those good folk on the rue de l'Horloge as customers, no longer as employees. It was not everything to know how to cut and stitch – you still had to buy the wherewithal to do it. They selected a few pieces of that new cloth all the women were so crazy about: surah. And then, they followed the advice of *L'Illustration*. The Light Horse read nothing else. The girls had no other guide.

The tyranny of the social columns of that publication weighed heavily upon any provincial female with pretensions to fashion. Their editor, the baronne de Spare, had won the vote of the bourgeoisie. Gabrielle and Adrienne did not escape her dictates. They avoided combinations of colors that the baronne decried, and for the same reason steered clear of "radhames satin," which was "loud" and made it "impossible to distinguish between a woman of society and an *horizontale*." For tailormades, the baroness recommended a "ladies' riding-cloth," affirming that nothing could be "more distinguished or becoming to wear." They bought some.

It would be reasonable, to say the least, to thank Balsan. They undoubtedly felt no less gratitude than amazement. How could they show it?

Etienne Balsan was never able to make out to whom Coco was referring when she told him: "I've already had one protector named Etienne. He performed miracles, too."

How could he guess which Etienne she meant? She never told him about Aubazine.

There were heated discussions on the subject of hats.

Following Aunt Julia's example in this matter, Gabrielle and Adrienne resolved to transform "ready-made" hats, as in their Varennes days. But on whom should they rely for guidance? The baroness could recommend no better hatter than Mélanie Percheron in Paris, but the Light Horse guffawed at the name, insisting that the women in their families would wear nothing but the creations of Caroline Reboux, the great lady of the rue de la Paix. How hopelessly confusing. Could the baroness be wrong? They didn't know what to do.

Gabrielle settled the matter. Her decision was inflexible: she would design her own hats. Adrienne had no choice but to like it.

Thus they came to Vichy in hats and gowns of their own confection.

The earliest known photographs of Gabrielle Chanel date from this period. In them we see something of the horsewoman about her and something that, despite her obvious femininity, acquires its severity from a highly romantic paraphrasing of the uniform. Squared shoulders, high collar, neat shirtwaist, belt firmly buckled, no embellishments but an imperceptible embroidery on the sleeve, in the same color as the background – a tentative homage to the cavalry braid.

What is so striking about them? The seriousness of her expression, and the divine simplicity of effect. At her side Adrienne, loveliness itself, is just a touch more laced-up, strapped-in . . . whereas it is quite literally impossible not to feel a determination in the body of Gabrielle to permit only that which glides.

One need only think of what these pictures do not show: the other women, the Casino *élégantes*, women with deep-arched backs and rounded rumps and hats like crushing burdens, to measure how much promise lies in the figure of Gabrielle.

She was already saved, by a miracle, from the absurdities of the day.

A SEASON AT VICHY

Varennes is forgotten. Another page is turned:

Vichy marks an essential phase in the singular destiny that was hers. Here she made the acquaintance not of the summit of society nor even of cosmopolitan elegance – Vichy was not a "king's barnyard"[2] like Cannes, nor a summer branch office of the Paris upper crust like Deauville – but of one image of France of which Moulins had shown her only a fragment.

In truth, it was a great leap forward, from the unassuming shade of the garden of La Rotonde to the splendors of the park at Vichy, adorned by shops that sedate ex-courtesans owed to the gratitude of pashas stimulated by them as much as by the healing waters; businesswomen who had now become so proper, so respectable, that their clientele was composed of the whole little world of the Hundred Years' War – all the châtelaines of the region, all the crenellated duchesses by whom the good people of the rue de l'Horloge were so intimidated. What was new to Gabrielle? The long rank of barouches with their graceful canopies, their teams with white-gloved ears, the striking stage set of the Vichy pump rooms decorated with ironwork in the purest "style Métro." Their glazed panels like huge butterflies with wings outspread, sheltering mournful second thoughts: those of senior civil servants whose complexions had been permanently ruined by too many copious dinners, of replete ministers and statesmen vanquished by the weight of official menus and the length of their banquets. And then, the officers . . . victims of their duty and the Ouled Naïl, a nomadic Algerian tribe which supplied dancers to the Moorish cafés of Algiers and prostitutes to the brothels of the Casbah.

If France overate literally in those days, what is one to think of its appetite for conquest? The superabundance of repasts and the colonizing fantasy in all its forms shared equally in providing an endless stream of new customers for Vichy. The heat, desert living, brief encounters in the Moorish cafés, and exotic love affairs wreaked havoc among the family scions. They returned to the mainland in ruins. No remedy but to send them to the waters for treatment. They went to Vichy, where the season lasted six months. You took your waters along with your wife or mistress. The main thing was to get well again and have a good time doing it.

Few Russians, but many Orientals . . . Lebanese, Egyptians. Foreign diplomats turned up with their retinues; one guessed their place of origin by the color of their lackeys. If a servant chanced to be dismissed he would be seen wandering the streets, making the best use he could of what French he had picked up to find another situation. Southern French types – oil or soap kings, merchants or shipbuilders, all old hands at exoticism – would jump at the chance. They could be heard congratulating themselves: "My dear fellow, I've snapped up the darky of Ambassador So-and-So . . ." And they went back to Provence with a Nubian sitting up by the coachman, or a Fatima sprawling in her veils.

Such were the patients Gabrielle watched going by, the people she met out walking.

She had rented a very modest little room, which she shared with Adrienne. Neither a cul-de-sac nor yet a passageway, but a bit of both, it was on one of those streets that exist only in Vichy: a street of bachelor flats, ground-floor apartments where women of easy virtue nested alongside penniless white-collar workers and touring third-rate actors.

According to friends from those days, women who were also striving to escape up into the world and who also dreaded the risk, always great, of a first or second step back into the proletariat, Gabrielle's beginnings in Vichy were arduous, her first steps up unpromising. The confidences of these onetime intimates had a unique quality. They were women still surprisingly attractive despite their great age – one could imagine how compelling they might have been fifty years before.

Often they had been admired, flattered, sometimes sincerely loved, but always deemed unmarriageable, and they died alone, without money or friends, in wretched little hotels. One sensed now that they felt too much envy for the resounding success of Coco to be ready to magnify it even more. So they indulged in scant exaggeration. They confined themselves to essentials, and what they told, in simple and straightforward language, seemed to merit full belief. From a subconscious reflex of self-protection or feminine solidarity, they had surprisingly little to say on the subject of love affairs – not one word about that. They merely described what, from their own point of view, would compromise nobody: the fierce struggle to "make it," the grandeur and misery of their younger days . . . But for the rest, having suffered all their lives from the indiscretion and nastiness to which kept women were subjected, and having also struggled, always and in every way, to appear respectable in the eyes of their contemporaries, they kept silent and thus gave support to the hypothesis of a blameless life where the heart alone mattered. They knew silence was their best weapon: not only did it drape a modest veil over their private emotions, but it hid the love life of a milieu as well, their own milieu, of which, fifty years later, Adrienne and Gabrielle were still part.

We will believe them when they intimated that it was not as easy to get an engagement in Vichy as it had been in a Moulins *beuglant*.

The programs there were in a different class altogether.

Nothing but noted artists, touring Parisians. And no chance of getting a start as a *poseuse*. Theater managers had long since done away with a custom deemed degrading and no longer in conformity with middle-class aesthetics. Those poor girls – offered as bait, huddled like a flock of frightened sheep behind the star – now called forth damning comment: "the vicious circle." They wanted no more of that in Vichy.

But nothing was going to stop Gabrielle. She never hesitated, never thought, "I'm backing the wrong horse." She wanted a career in singing. She just plunged straight ahead.

The more obstacles piled up in front of her, the more ardently she set about burning them down. This will to succeed left her contemporaries – Adrienne, especially – a little dazed and weak in the knees.

The whole question was which door to knock at. The Grand Casino was out of the question; its reputation put it miles beyond reach. Where, then? The Eden Théâtre, where the café was in a lovely cool garden? Tempting. The Eden went in for operettas. The Restauration? The show was lively, but the public too stiff. The Alcazar, temple of variety shows? With its *a giorno* lighting, tables scattered around the stage, naturalistic stage shows, special room for souvenir photographs, Tunisian concert and authentic almehs for the belly dance, the Alcazar tried to equal the Jardin de Paris on the Champs Elysées, which attracted the most "in" circles in the capital. Patients, affluent businessmen, summering cabinet ministers, sprightly foreign ladies, and "true Parisian figures" thronged in for their share of the entertainment at the Vichy Alcazar. But would they want Gabrielle?

She managed to get an audition.

It took place in a cellar under the café. A pianist with pretensions as a composer thumped out old tunes for famished applicants. He ran a little business with a wardrobe dealer on the side. Whenever one of the girls trying out showed signs of talent he suggested that she hire a costume, at her expense. He then notified the manager.

Sometimes impresario slave traders from Paris sat in on auditions. They were always in need of new crumbs to throw to the lions, so they came and sat, listened and judged.

The caf'conc' was essentially a question of specialization. What was the right way to handle this bashful apprentice girl or gangling youth? What type of number should she work up? Should that girl be a *gambilleuse* ("leg shaker") or a romantic, and that boy a monologuist or an "eccentric"? And what style should they adopt? Should they be advised to try for realism or pantomime?

The results of Gabrielle's audition were disheartening. She had presence and an acid charm which might find a buyer, but of voice she had none. Well, the merest thread.

She was told she might have a chance as a *gommeuse*, a type of which Polaire's growing celebrity had produced innumerable imitations. (Judy Garland might be descended from this line.) But first, she would have to work. It all depended on how she progressed. Actually, no one could make any promises.

Adrienne was stripped of her last illusions. Her well-bred look was not suited to this type of work. In no uncertain terms she was advised to seek her fortune elsewhere. She went back to Moulins.

Coco set to work.

The house pianist offered his services. He transposed Paris hit songs for her, to help her place her voice. As a *gommeuse*, of course, she would have to do some hipwork, a few twists and twirls. The whole trick to this was in the skirt, the "pins" and the "windmill." But one also had to be able to sing. Coco whispered, *"Moi j' suis pas méchante, j'suis bien patiente, mais quand je me fâche, v'lan, je lui rent' dedans"* ("I'm not mean and nasty, I'm the patient kind, But when I lose my temper, Bif! I knock out all his wind") in a strained voice. She also sang Max Dearly's *Tra-la-la-la-la, v'la les English,* in which she was slightly more convincing.

Her coach was not sparing in his criticism.

"You've got a voice like a crow, you've got no gestures, you're stiff as a board, and besides your bones stick out – have some ruffles put on the top of that dress."

Coco stuck at it doggedly and without self-indulgence. But she made heavy work of it.

The lessons were not free, and trying out this style and that, *gommeuse* and *gigolette*, feeling her way – fiddling, they called it – cost a lot of money. The ever-greedy wardrobe dealers always found some pretext for cheating the neophyte. They were one long wail of reproach, pointing to imaginary rips, burns, and stains. The costumes had to be mended, ironed, freshened up, remade. Otherwise, my girl . . .

Gabrielle spent her nights needle in hand.

Usually, the *gommeuse* wore a sequined gown. Nothing showed to better effect in the footlights. But what a lot of work they were! The trouble was that at the smallest snag, the sequins ran like a stitch in a stocking. Down went the girls on all fours in a panic, chasing after them, one by one: "My sequins!" Onlookers expressed sympathy. Meanwhile, the implacable wardrobe dealer bore down upon them and slapped another extra charge on the bill.

But Coco stuck it out. She couldn't see herself anywhere else. What was her hope? To follow in the footsteps of Zulma Bouffar at Ems? To meet an Offenbach taking the waters at Vichy, who would launch her on her career?

Whatever else she may have been, she was happy. She was learning how to use makeup, how to dance and sing. She was living in the wings of her dream.

In the past, red sequins had been the fashion for the *gommeuse*. The public adored them. But in Paris Madame d'Alma had risked orchid. Everybody was calling her the *mauve gommeuse*. Even her sequined hat. Unheard-of. Provincial *gommeuses* immediately turned out in mauve. Next, back in Paris again, some kid from the country, not pretty, with a slit of a mouth, had made a small sensation by working the *gommeuse* vein in black sequins. Black! That took some nerve! The color black, a rose pinned to the bodice, and a pair of legs, had been enough. Her first successes dated from six years or so earlier, and she was already beginning to be hailed as a star. Her friends called her Jeanne, but show business people knew her only by her stage name, Mistinguett . . . They were positively incoherent about her. Café-concerts in the provinces hastened to adopt her costume, with the result that Coco had hired a black sequined gown in the traditional *gommeuse* style – short, close-fitting over the hips, very low cut, the bodice molding the figure, and the skirt, edged with ruffled tulle, flaring to mid-calf.

A gown that belonged to no family, no country, no past, but whose grace was to haunt Gabrielle for the rest of her days. However, she didn't know it yet . . .

A day came in the 1930s when women, guided by Chanel, began wearing the sequined gown of the *gommeuse*. Whenever one of them appeared, whether in a drawing room or under the blazing lights of a theater marquee – the simple garment inexplicably dominating all others by sheer force of attraction, gleaming like a black mirror – perhaps Gabrielle Chanel alone knew what that dress meant. Perhaps she saw between the sequins the blurred reflection of a long-gone past.

Finding the money was the hard part.

After the wardrobe dealers' strident demands had been met and the pianist paid and the rent and the food taken care of, what would be left of Gabrielle's savings? Money . . . money. How much could one earn in Paris? Was it as hard to get a break there as people said? She longed to go. But according to the show business people, before reaching the top all the idols of the day, without exception, had lived in blackest poverty. Two francs a day had been given to an unknown girl from Normandy, for a curtain raiser: Yvette Guilbert. Three francs to make a houseful of traveling salesmen laugh: the day's earnings of a thirteen-year-old kid, the young Chevalier. Now he had grown up and people were beginning to talk about him. And Polin, back from America? Rolling in it, so they said. Back in the days when he had been trying to wring a handclap out of an audience of coachmen and cooks for his first songs, he had been paid with a boot in the behind. But was that any consolation? A reason for going on any longer? And could Gabrielle promise herself she would have the same fate as the rest?

Even back in 1906 she thought that since money took up such a large part of conversation – money was the only word music-hall people ever spoke – then the best thing to do was to make sure she got some.

That she performed more than one job at Vichy there can be no doubt. On that point all witnesses agree.

She managed to occupy her time. But with what?

Not mending, as certain of her customers disdainfully implied later on. The picture of the dismal garret in which the poor girl patches and darns resort patients' bed linen in order to eat and satisfy her ambitions is far too contrived and would seem to belong to the realm of invention, together with the assertion (emanating from the same source) that she lived a life of shame . . . of which no shred of proof can be advanced. These must be taken as pure petty jealousy.

"The American press has me arriving in Paris in wooden clogs," Gabrielle would say with a sarcastic laugh. "And why not as a lady's maid?"

These fantasies are categorically refuted by photographs of Gabrielle Chanel taken in 1906 – neither loose woman nor starving seamstress: too modestly attired for the former, and too well-dressed to be subsisting as the latter. That she saw more of Etienne Balsan in Vichy than of anyone else, however, and that he continued to assist her but without making it unnecessary for her to work at all: that seems more likely. Can one imagine Gabrielle Chanel giving up so strong an ambition? Let us rather believe those foul-weather friends when they insisted that despite all her efforts and hopes, Gabrielle found herself at the end of several months exactly as she had been when she left Moulins, a private seamstress refurbishing the gowns of former customers from the rue de l'Horloge who had come to take the waters at Vichy. Still failing to get any engagement at the Alcazar, although backed by a recommendation from an officer of the 10th Light Horse who had connections, she applied to the municipal baths, who hired her as water giver at the Grande Grille. Then, dressed in white, her feet kept dry in curiously proportioned little boots – also white, short, forming part of the uniform – Gabrielle became the person standing down in a pit who chose a glass from the odd-looking garland hanging on the wall in straw holders. In the middle, under a crystal globe, the spring gushed forth, precious and hot. Gabrielle went over and, with solemn air and clinical gesture, filled the glass, then checked the level with a critical eye. She was popular. Hands reached out to her. Compliments rained down from heaven. What was she thinking about? Those boots, which instantly struck her as the essence of comfort? Or the music? Both, perhaps.

In the distance the town band was giving its recital of "potpourri" on the terrace of the Grand Casino. *Madame l'Archiduc* and *Fingal's Cave* forever.

Her impatience was making life unbearable. But we must not regret what she saw as wasted time. Thanks to that time, unconsciously, she was acquiring new ideas. One day, like the dancing *gommeuse* gown, the water girl's little boots would also come back to life on the rue Cambon. On Chanel's feet. Her boots for days of battle . . .

When, in the tenuous mid-October sun, the Vichy season drew to a close, the streets gradually recovered their provincial quiet. The migratory stream of colonials began to thin. The hansom drivers resumed those tranquil dialogues with their horses, now seldom interrupted by hailing grooms.

Then came November and the last traces of frivolity were removed from their harnesses. The fringed canopies were folded up, the ear protectors packed away in camphor. A few shops hung signs in their windows announcing their Paris addresses and the café-concerts rang down their annual curtain in a clatter of planks, hammers, and nails.

It was over.

Success would not come, Coco had lost the match.

TEA AT MAUD'S

When Gabrielle returned to Moulins, Adrienne was no longer there; she was living near Souvigny where her friend Maud Mazuel owned a villa and had invited her to stay indefinitely.

Fantastically practical, Maud's house was: a stone's throw from the little station of Coulandon-Marigny, quite a roomy place, which the natives, familiar with her style of living, called "the château."

Maud entertained a great deal.

In 1973 a retired baker who remembered Maud was still living in Souvigny. A stripling delivery boy when she lived there, he used to take numerous loaves of bread and croissants to her house every morning.

Without extracting Adrienne from the exclusively "horsey" set of her début, her friend Maud had introduced her to some local gentry, who were older than the officers of the 10th Light Horse and had more funds and more freedom than they. But as gentry and officers belonged to the same world and were guided by the same tastes, enjoying equal infallibility in essential matters – i.e., everything to do with horses, women, dress, shooting, and wine – the week never went by without the garrison branch-line railway's bringing its bag of habitués, both military and civilian, out to Souvigny-sur-Orge. They went everywhere together and traveled in a group to the races at Vichy and to garden parties at the municipal baths that were attended by the most elegant society ladies as well as by strangers who slipped in on the strength of their good looks, and one or two notorious fallen women.

Maud Mazuel came of a middle-class family. She had a keen social appetite and a strong desire to get ahead. Born into a different class, she would have kept a salon, but because of her undistinguished origins she had to content herself with arranging meetings and possibly promoting liaisons. Her house was always full. What did she live on? If any couple became acquainted through her and came to love each other "for real," she made sure that, however moon-eyed they might be, the young people should not forget what they owed to her, their friend Maud.

Plump, with no great intellectual capacities, she knew she lacked allure; but she did have a strong sense of fun, self-confidence and, when it suited her, an air of dignity derived principally from the historical allusions expressed in her hats, topped by a musketeer-evoking plume standing stiff as a standard, in the jabots of her Louis XV-style bodices, or in the cut of her tailor-mades, with their Directoire-inspired notched peplums which quite failed to disguise the amazingly high relief of the contours of her capacious person.

She had two contradictory callings: life-of-the-party and chaperone. She managed to be both at once.

Tea at Maud's was a sort of lunch-and-snack.

In her home one met neighboring provincial women who had dropped in to chat, or the *irrégulières* of the gentlemen officers of the Moulins garrison (and the much-admired ballerina of the Théâtre de la Monnaie on whom the young comte d'Espous was dancing attendance more assiduously than ever), but never a legitimate wife.

Flesh and food were good at Maud's, and the style was informal. Nibblers gathered in the garden. Chaises longues were pulled under the shade of the trees; cakes, chocolate and pitchers of cream passed from hand to hand, the bread was arranged in baskets. The great joke on bright sunny days, though, was to don a black straw boater, of which there were masses at Maud's, no matter what else you might be wearing. Then the discipline of the officers' coats began to relax, their collars somehow came unhooked. That was the moment when the gentlemen officers would be arguing about promotion and "having a quick snack" while the local gentry, cigars in mouth, would be conducting agricultural disquisitions and the stud men would be expressing their anxiety, with all the seriousness they could muster, about the future of the Société d'Encouragement, an association to promote thoroughbred breeding and racing. Hadn't the committee begun to let in people "who weren't in the Jockey"? What was the world coming to?

Meanwhile, the fair ladies languished.

There was not one among them, however pretty she might be, who had Adrienne's carriage, bearing, regal posture. More attractive than ever, she was the priceless jewel of Maud's tea parties.

On those days, Maud tried to give herself a rustic air. She stuck daisies in her hat and let the ribbons hang loose under her chin. She disported herself in one of her twill "tea gowns" in which, she said, she felt as comfortable as in a nightshirt. But whenever a public appearance was in order, the members of her clan found, in the duly whaleboned and hatted person of their hostess, the irreplaceable screen they required. Maud made it possible for young women in search of a profitable love affair to move about under the protection of a duenna, and for the others, provincial ladies looking for lovers, to reassure jealous suitors, or worried or suspicious families . . . because they were with Maud.

The little tea parties at Souvigny-sur-Orge enabled Gabrielle to join the clan.

At Moulins, the routine was the same as before: cups of chocolate drunk in a group at À la Tentation, long scarlet legs in the streets and merry pranksters at La Rotonde.

None of Gabrielle's admirers had returned to civilian life.

In appearance, then, everything was as before.

But she soon realized the damage done by her Vichy experiment: it made this homecoming intolerable. Was she aware that her second stay at Moulins would be only a pause? One more year of uncertainty. It made the tea parties at Maud's all the more appreciated, although she was sorry Etienne Balsan would not attend them with her. He had a prejudice against the Souvigny ladies – he found them boring.

Gabrielle was not far from sharing his opinion. Nevertheless, being curious about everything, she faithfully attended the gatherings at Maud's house.

There are many photographs dating from 1905 in which Etienne Balsan does not appear, and in them Gabrielle wears an expression of insolent indifference. Is one to conclude that her experience in Vichy had also separated her from him? Or ought we, for once, to credit the statements of the aging Chanel, who said that for a long time he was "just a good friend"? Sensing that for the present she could not achieve the only ambition she really cherished – to become a singer – Gabrielle was doing at Souvigny, if we can judge by these pictures, what she had done in the cellar of the Alcazar: she was "fiddling" again, looking for the right path to take.

Here is Gabrielle in a crucial hour of her life. Here she is on Sunday at the Vichy race track, seated not in the members' enclosure but purely and simply among the local bourgeois, for whom "going to the races" added a new facet to their self-importance. Here she is, made more different than ever by some quality of alertness totally lacking in the opulent figures around her, the bold simplicity of her attire contradicting Adrienne's ultra refinement: the latter, in full gala, had treated herself to an orgy of ruching and Chantilly lace. Here is Gabrielle, making her debut in high society leisure pursuits while, seated between the Mlles Chanel, officiating majestically, and overtopping Gabrielle by the full height of her plume, we see friend Maud in her role as duenna.

Did Gabrielle lose patience with a way of life that left no room for her private ambitions? Or did she weary of having to assume airs whose sole object was to secure a situation as kept mistress?

Perhaps her lassitude was due also in some measure to a fear that she might not carry off the part as brilliantly as Adrienne.

Because Adrienne had an official beau.

The comte de Beynac was one of those aristocrats with solid landowning foundations and a luxuriant moustache; a hunting fanatic with an added touch of extravagance which, while making him a "character," also formed the chief attribute of his prestige among his intimates. You never heard a word about the wit, the collections, or even the chateaux of the comte de Beynac, and still less about his fortune, but tomes about his accent and his originality. Any anecdote that went round concerning him was told to show off his picturesqueness: Monsieur de Beynac was that Nimrod whose hounds had just brought to bay not a stag, but a wolf, the last to be seen in the Limousin; Monsieur de Beynac was that gambler who with one throw of the dice had won four Casino de Paris dancers from four of his comrades and who, to celebrate his victory, had packed the young women into his shooting brake and then, singing in patois at the top of his lungs, had driven the whole shebang up the Champs Elysées with his four Anglo-Normans at full gallop; Monsieur de Beynac was also that mad devil who, a short time later, having wagered his horses and lost them too, found himself compelled to return to his native province on foot . . . which he did, as though it were nothing.

Such was the man who had become infatuated with Adrienne.

More than three-quarters ruined, he had found a sort of backer in the person of his best friend, the marquis de Jumilhac, who was always willing to finance de Beynac's escapades, provided he could take part in them. Both of them, while paying court to Adrienne, also acted as mentors to the son of a local landowner. This extremely good-looking young chap was already a crack shot and first-rate horseman: in those fields they had little to teach him. Their main aim was to cure him of his provincial seriousness. Capitalizing on his tutors' experience, the young man speedily became a "clubman" of rakish elegance.

Thus there was a trio of admirers jockeying for position at Adrienne's side.

Although the title of protector-in-chief went, no doubt, to the comte de Beynac as eldest of the three, it seems less clear that he was the favorite. Hence, the plan that they should all three go off together for a tour of Egypt. Adrienne would go with them, and the pretty ballerina too, along with her lover, the comte d'Espous – all the more openly, in the latter case, since the comte had decided that it would do to take life a shade more seriously, and was talking of *marrying* his mistress, a most unusual procedure in that society.

Maud was jubilant.

Alas, d'Espous's parents, when apprised of his intention, decreed from the depths of their Languedocian domains that no commoner should ever bear their name and that they would sooner break off relations with their son forever than permit him to dishonor himself. He, the finest name in the region? Had he taken leave of his senses? Slut, trollop, jezebel, hussy, wanton were the mildest expletives they applied to their son's mistress. The terrified lovers decided to wait, locked in each other's arms, for the cherished parents to die.

That, however, would not prevent them from having a foretaste of a honeymoon by traveling up the Nile together.

Gabrielle alone, oddly enough, declared that the pyramids, the Pharaohs, the desert, Khartoum, the temples, and the rest of it did not interest her. She must be made to come, however; Maud Mazuel undertook to persuade her, and failed. Gabrielle maintained that she couldn't see what there could be for her to do in Egypt. "But you'll see the Sphinx," she was told. Clearly, she couldn't care less.

Matters had reached this point, and Adrienne was already choosing her wardrobe for the trip, matching veils to hats and dusters to suits, when Balsan's term of duty ended and he was discharged. Apart from his satisfaction at returning to civilian life, there was now nothing to keep him at Châteauroux. His father had died, his mother too. By chance an estate had come up for sale at Royallieu, near Compiègne. He bought it, from a trainer's widow, in December 1904, just after coming into his inheritance.

Everything about Royallieu suited Balsan's purposes, both pasture and buildings, the latter including acres of stabling. He wanted to set up a stud there, and also try his luck in competition – to run the steeplechase at Pau and "have a go at Aintree." Etienne dreamed of a double life, breeder and gentleman rider.

These plans made him considerably more interesting to Gabrielle.

The first time he mentioned them to her, she was delighted. She professed a boundless admiration for jockeys. The traditional weighing-in ceremony, when the bell rang over the weighing room, the slow procession around the paddock followed by the instant of excitement when the horse moved off capering and curvetting, becoming one with its jockey in his blazing silks – she adored it all. She even had a "routine" which her friends were constantly clamoring for: Gabrielle could mime the moment of truth when the little men in white breeches were hoisted into the saddle. Her admirers would intone in a body, *"Les courses, les courses, ah, il n 'ya que cela"* ("The races, the races, ah, there's nothing like 'em"), the refrain from a revue which had just been presented by the members of the Jockey Club; that was the signal for her to begin. Coco "gave a leg up" and her audience collapsed in fits of laughter; then she caricatured the stern gestures of trainers checking girths.

Most often it was the comte de Beynac who played the part of the horse.

Upon hearing Balsan's plans Gabrielle asked him, "Don't you need an apprentice?"

He took her at her word.

"Ah, the little Coco wants to learn how to ride, does she, she wants to come along; well, we'll just take her along."

This was a far cry from a romantic abduction, a far cry from the language of passion. But Etienne was putting Paris within her grasp. She flung her arms around him.

A GOOD MATCH

Everything at Royallieu was anomalous, not excepting Etienne Balsan's presence there. What was most peculiar of all was that he should have chosen to live in the country. That did not enter into the practices of good society, for which the phrase "getting a place to live" was restricted exclusively to Paris. Getting a place to live meant being compelled to rent, in Paris and for a term of nine years, premises that must instantly be adorned with Louis XV passementerie and hung with fabrics "that would last forever." To consider "doing up a place" more than once in a lifetime was one of those hazardous projects that a decent sort of man would never undertake.

As for "doing up" a chateau, that was inconceivable. You came into possession of a family estate which you maintained in the condition in which you inherited it, and all initiative ended there. The family paintings hung where they were, the armchairs sat in their former places, water closets remained as scarce as before. Only the Rothschilds broke the rule, but few followed their example. And the Faubourg* set, far from judging it chic of Baron Alphonse to have a telephone put in connecting his chateau at Ferrières with his bank on the rue Laffitte – an unheard-of undertaking which necessitated the laying of fifty-four miles of double cable – decreed that the baron's main object had been to impress people. Château proprietors whose residences sported more than one bathroom per floor continued to be looked at askance. What was the point? The motive for such luxuries escaped a society too imbued with its own superiority to admit progress. For it, elegance was defined by criteria other than comfort or cleanliness.[3] The reason was that they would rather confine their ablutions to the contents of one teakettle than be forced, by such ill-advised expenditure, to skimp on the quality, number, or livery of their footmen.

As a result, people found it hard to understand Etienne Balsan.

What was he trying to achieve by renovating a structure unknown to his ancestors? He was an orphan, rich and unmarried. He was supposed to be

---

* The Faubourg denotes the Faubourg St Germain, the most aristocratic part of Paris in those days.

paying assiduous attention to all marriageable virgins. Instead of which, he was holing himself up miles away from the balls. What was the meaning of it? A liaison?

Like many another wealthy young man, Balsan had attracted notice in various fashionable places whenever he turned up on leave. And the Balsans, hearing of his successes, had not failed to exhibit pride and terror in equal proportions. But because of the very brevity of his infatuations, Etienne was looked upon as a tough nut to crack. For example, it was no small feat to have managed to offload Emilienne d'Alençon after a lightning affair.

Emilienne, otherwise the dearest girl in the world although tolerably greedy, was alleged to have claimed innumerable victims. Hadn't the young duc d'Uzès ruined himself for her? And then, unable to think of any other way to keep her, he had given her first one tiara, then another, until every one of the family jewels had followed suit. His mother's only device for putting a stop to so costly a liaison had been to ship him off to the Congo, where, immediately upon arrival, he had died – of dysentery.

With the result that Etienne Balsan, who had succeeded in unhooking himself before it was too late, passed as both something of a hero and a very good match in the eyes of all aristocratic mothers.

But what was he doing at Compiègne?

Royallieu was situated in the heart of a province dedicated to the supremacy of the horse. It was generally accepted that in order to achieve greatness, a thoroughbred must be trained there and nowhere else. This was the quality that had drawn Balsan to the place.

Whole dynasties of trainers had come over from Great Britain and settled there. Chantilly and Maisons-Laffitte were English villages, where the Bartholomews, Cunningtons, and Carters in their red brick bungalows were treated with a degree of esteem echoed by the press of those days. There were no fewer than ten specialized publications, plus a full page in every daily paper, wholly devoted to turf events – a world in which the slightest irregularity assumed the proportions of a scandal. If the rumor was confirmed that some owners, trying to size up their rivals' chances, had secured the services of spies, *L'Illustration* immediately gave the story front-page coverage.

Almost upon her arrival, Gabrielle Chanel was caught up in the toils of this passion.

Could she have imagined that her situation at Royallieu would differ so little from the one she had thought she was escaping by leaving Moulins?

She was going to share the private life of a man who was a perfect example of the "sportsman" type, cut off from every world but the racecourse, seeing only a few intimate friends and some demimondaines.

Etienne Balsan knew nothing of Paris, its artists, men of letters and painters, or of the snobberies of a society of which he shared neither the tastes nor the preoccupations. He cared no more for the travels of the great of this earth than for their pious works. The women he entertained were never those whose summer smartness and labors on behalf of charity bazaars were praised in social columns. They were not philanthropists.

To be invited to Royallieu, you had to be gay, always in boots, and prepared to gallop through the forest for days on end.

Royallieu? A merry band of mates. Apart from horses, laughter, and pleasure – nothing.

IV

The Keepers and the Kept 1906–1914

"Whenever Madame de Villeparisis paced through the hall, the chief magistrate's wife, who scented irrégulières *everywhere, would raise her nose from her sewing and look at her in a way that made her friends expire with laughter."*

— MARCEL PROUST, *Within a Budding Grove*

THE EASY LIFE

Royallieu had been a monastery, founded nearly as long ago as Aubazine. But what remained of its original austerity when Gabrielle got there? Only the tiled corridor, the steep staircase, and the rather feudal-looking portals which still bore traces of the days when the chaplains of Philippe le Bel, and sometimes the king himself, came to make their devotions at Royallieu. The remainder of the structure had gained in grace and lost in discipline during the seventeenth and eighteenth centuries. The monks had been superseded by an order of nuns, Benedictines of St Jean du Bois, and the improvements they wrought were in the image of the century that was *par excellence* the age of French charm. Royallieu owed its resemblance to a handsome provincial stately home to its first abbesses.

Gabrielle was miles from imagining that she would one day wish to own one like it.

That day came only twenty-five years later when she built a villa at Roquebrune, on the shore of the Mediterranean, on a scale befitting her conquests: La Pausa, the domain of stone and sky of the autocrat she had become, but also a habitation whose sobriety derived from what she had retained of the qualities of Aubazine and Royallieu.

A facade cut all tall windows; huge, luminous rooms whose handsome paneling needed only a coat of paint to recover its first freshness: that was Royallieu when Balsan began to "do it up." Ancient basins and Romanesque capitals, the sole vestiges of shattered columns, were to complete the decor of the grounds. A few fragments survived of the severe wrought-iron railing: Etienne Balsan had a facsimile made.

The work continued until his return from Moulins.

When the house was finally ready, he found a painting that had been hidden in the attic to escape destruction when the Benedictines were driven out by the Revolution. It was the portrait, gray with dust, of a cloistered nun. Who was she? Investigations were made. Her name was Gabrielle: the canvas portrayed the first abbess, who had restored a lost luster to Royallieu. Whereupon the effigy of the very devout Gabrielle de Laubespine was returned to its place at the top of the stairs. But significantly, it was not in her room, the largest and handsomest of the house, that Gabrielle Chanel slept. She was given more modest appointments.

Did Balsan think it would be attaching too much importance to her to put her in that room?

He treated her as a lesser guest. After all, she was not a woman to publicize, and still less one to marry, the nice little Coco from La Rotonde . . . No longer an infant, either. She was nearing her twenty-third birthday.

Gabrielle contented herself with a condition which, while assigning her no specific tasks, left her some measure of freedom.

Her resignation was based on the impossibility that things should be otherwise.

Etienne had made her his mistress, that was one thing. But he did not expect her to take on the role of mistress of the house.

In this area, in which so many Parisian women – so many of Etienne's friends – excelled, Gabrielle was the most inexperienced of females. Her incompetence showed when one least expected it. The truth was that she was out of her depth, and everything at Royallieu left her gaping: the comfort, the unaccustomed luxury of the bathrooms; ovens in the kitchens whose likes she had never seen; and built onto the outside of the house, a funny little building where Balsan played a game of which she had never heard – squash. The grooms and stable lads were the only people who spoke a language familiar to her. She felt at ease with them.

Not until later, after she had lost her illusions about a theatrical career for good, did she begin to think of becoming a permanent fixture at Royallieu. But what would Etienne say about that? He would never take it seriously. He was simply offering her a roof, and had no desire for his gesture to be interpreted as love.

Out of natural unsociability and inexperience, as well as her delight in the novelty of it all, Gabrielle passed her first months at Royallieu without ever leaving the place. She adhered scrupulously to Balsan's requirements: she was to be entertaining and idle.

Devoting all his time, energy, and resources to maintaining his position among the top French riders, and despairing when he failed – between 1904 and 1908 he wavered between first and thirteenth place among steeplechasers and his activities cost him more than they brought in – Balsan no longer had time to worry about promoting Gabrielle's ambitions. Coming from that class which understands idleness better than anything else, he would have found it truly peculiar of her to insist on trying to work. But he could not help being amazed at how thoroughly she took advantage of "château life."

Etienne had never met anyone with her capacity for lolling in bed. "She would lie in bed until noon, drinking coffee and milk and reading cheap novels. The laziest woman in the world," he admitted some thirty years later. But when a morning outing was planned, this sloth was the first up and ready.

If Etienne seemed to be seeing Gabrielle for the first time, it was because he had lived without needing to learn that security, suddenly achieved, could be a source of happiness, whereas Coco had never been able to "take advantage" of anything before. At Royallieu her demands were reasonable enough, but she wanted satisfaction of them all and right away: to be able to sleep as long as she liked, to become the best horsewoman at any price, to have to think as little as possible, to grasp the mechanics of insouciance; in short, to beat Etienne's friends at their own game. What was life, after all? A perpetual game of "wait and see."

In her success she saw proof that she was not mistaken.

Nevertheless, it is hard to understand how, with his money, Etienne Balsan could have permitted Gabrielle to be dressed by a local tailor whose only clients were stable lads and huntsmen. Had he come of noble family, this might have been seen as the well-known sign of traditional stinginess; one could believe it was a hereditary trait and blame some ancestor who shared the parsimonious notions of economy of that prince de Beauvau who, possessing substantial properties and waited on by a hundred domestics, served only the cheapest wine at table; or that prince de Broglie who had his daughter dressed by the same tailor that made his footmen's livery. But there was nothing of the kind in Balsan's lineage. This streak of economy in a young man whose friends all boasted of his prodigality reveals the true nature of his feelings for Gabrielle: she was only a protégé, on whom one does not spend. And just as the abbess's vast sleeping chamber was not allotted to her, so she also went without the riding habit from Redfern that no woman kept in style, loved and treated with respect, would have dreamed of forgoing.

As in the days when she went to make her purchases in the shop of the good people of the rue de l'Horloge with a pittance in her pocket, at Royallieu, too, Gabrielle remained one of those who are casually sent to the shop around the corner to get what they need.

Thus everything was exactly as it had been at Moulins.

Did she mind? Far from it. Gabrielle remained grateful to Etienne throughout her life: he had treated her as a young woman from a good family who happened to dress inexpensively.

Her reaction can be explained by the fact that Royallieu was frequented only by the unmarried. All that Gabrielle could learn of the far-off city named Paris was, of necessity, what Etienne's young guests said about it. And because what they liked best was talking about their own escapades, the only echoes that came to her ears were those of the demimonde. For a long time, therefore, she believed that a certain type of ostentation, all things flashy, showy, and "ruinous," living high and driving in carriages from the Accacias to the Tir au Pigeon, drinking at Armenonville, frequenting the Palais de Glace and supping at Maxim's, were attributes of nobody but those "cocottes" whom she would rather die than resemble. Provincial illusion.

The amazing thing is that this attitude, in which it is hard to separate her desire for liberation from her apprehensions and shyness, should have been the starting point of a career, and through that career, of a fashion.

By dressing according to her own ideas, endeavoring in every respect to be the opposite of what those around her saw as luxury, Gabrielle hoped to avoid the fate she dreaded most: being known as a kept woman.

She already believed so strongly in the *costume* that she imagined all she had to do was not wear it to avoid being cast in the *role*.

She had no idea how fast the gears of social gossip begin to grind.

How could she, who knew nobody and never went out, have guessed at the curiosity she aroused? The mere fact that she had been given a home at Royallieu was more than enough to earn her the reputation she so feared.

To all who saw Etienne's removal from the capital as proof that he had something to hide, she was already his *irrégulière*.

A TAILOR IN THE FOREST

So she went to this obscure tailor whose shop was planted at La Croix St Ouen as in the middle of a forest clearing. Past his front door streamed four-in-hands on their way to picnic luncheons, a fashion that had been brought from England and was fast spreading through a class afflicted with anglo-phobia in politics and anglomania in manners. Everyone going to the forest to chase the stag with the marquis de l'Aigle's hounds, or to follow the hunt from a distance, also went by: dog carts snappily driven by young men in boots and trappings, already dressed to ride to the hounds – gray-blue coat, red velvet waistcoat, collar and lapels, hunting stripes, white breeches; game-keepers going to beat the woods; shooting brakes piled high with little girls and boys accompanied by their French governesses, English nannies, German maids and priests; buggies and governess carts behind ponies transporting Italian wet nurses in beribboned bonnets and their cargo of infants. There was a ceaseless traffic of well-turned-out vehicles and well-groomed horses, with glossy coats and tails set just so, jogging along to the meet.

An occasional electric carriage was also seen, and an even more occasional automobile, the latest Rochet-Schneiders; but in height and shape, with their curtains and their little lanterns like those on stagecoaches, they looked so much like horse-drawn vehicles that one could easily mistake them. The blasts issuing from their enormous trumpet horns made horses rear and pedestrians run for cover. Their drivers, former coachmen, had not yet given up their heavy side-whiskers. Crammed in behind, the footmen in charge of the picnic hampers stood, as always, with rigid backs and arms folded over their waistcoats.

On this sight respectful eyes were cast by the modest craftsman who, after serving his time in the 5th Dragoons at Compiègne and winning renown, scissors in hand, in the service of Colonel Granier de Cassagnac, had opened up a business here on his return to civilian life.

His choice was a wise one.

For over a century the Francport hounds had been chasing in the forest of Compiègne. But how many changes of dress! Garbed in red in 1790, the Francport changed to green in 1848 and remained so until Napoleon III had the regrettable idea of adopting green for his own hunt, when they were forced to abandon that color for the current gray-blue. And whenever the masters had to change, so did their men. This was the matter of principal concern to the former tailor of the 5th Dragoons, for his chosen occupation was to clothe not the occupants of these glittering carriages in wide-skirted redingotes and multiple-reflecting top hats, nor the fair ladies depicted by Boldini, nor yet the side-saddle riders in three-cornered hats, but their servants, huntsmen, whippers-in, and liveried grooms.

Gabrielle Chanel remembered it all.

She often spoke of the tailor's confusion when he saw her come in. She would give a detailed description of the shop, the customers in leggings and soft hats, the vague smell compounded of English varnish and horse manure that emanated from their clothes; and told it all so vividly that one supposed she was speaking the truth.

She even said that sometime back in the thirties the tailor recognized her from a photograph and wrote to ask if he might call on her, and she had seen him on the rue Cambon, "a very ordinary little old man" whose

features rang no bell but about whose aroma there could be no mistake . . .
"He still smelled of the same thing, horses."

They corresponded until the war. After that, nothing . . . She seemed
less grieved than offended by his negligence. The idea that he might be
dead never occurred to her.

On the first warm days of that spring of 1907, then, the open-air fanatics
clambered into four-in-hands and rolled off behind superb steeds to nests
of greenery where they emptied their picnic hampers "simply, without ceremony." The women, however, wore the same clothes in the country as in
town. That was how their menfolk liked them.

The fashion was, nevertheless, disastrous for such purposes.

A sort of madness had begun with the century, and its effects were still
being felt. The "Belle Epoque" was nothing but reminiscences. It began by
wallowing in pure Louis XVI, after which one had to drag out and refur-
bish taffeta for round-the-clock wear, shepherdess hats, and the floral patterns
in favor at the court of Louis le Bien-Aimè. Nothing, neither furniture nor
literature, theater nor social distractions, escaped this frenzy. At one improvised garden party the great names of the Faubourg had gathered in the
home of the marquise de Sommery to disport themselves under the trees
in Pompadour hats and white-powdered hair. Even Sarah Bernhardt had let
herself be dragged into it. She put on the worst play of her career for the
sole pleasure of acting the part of Marie Antoinette, in the lamentable *Varennes*
by Lavedan and Lenotre.

Long skirts, cumbersome hats, tight shoes, high heels, everything that
fettered a woman's movements and made it necessary for a man to assist
her, was balm to her husband's conscience in so far as he saw it as a sign
of submissiveness. So long as his wife could not manage without him, the
disturbing freedom of open-air activities did not endanger his authority.
And as far as the women were concerned, the necessity to dress and act
wherever they were as fragile, precious objects requiring care and protection was an obligation that betokened a privilege rather than a fashion, a
sign of caste rather than a refinement of costume, as revealing to the mob
as the deformed feet of the women of Old China or the distended lips of
the disk-wearing Ubangis, and consequently all the more difficult to reject.
The toilettes of the elegant women of the age showed clear proof of their
membership in a circle in which the freedom granted to the fair sex had
limits; proof, too, that with their hair dressed as it was, beplumed and
bedecked with those costly catafalques in which reposed, with outstretched
wings, so many innocent wild fowl, they would never be seen among those

who, under pretext of trying out the latest novelty, permitted themselves to be gawked at in bathing costumes, or exhibited themselves on the decks of motor-powered omnibuses, which made their first appearance in Paris in December 1905, at the Fifth Automobile Show, or pedaled down the paths of the Bois de Boulogne on bicycles.

The horse, nothing but the horse.

Was any exercise more dignified than horsemanship; did any sport guard the feminine mystery more closely? The clubmen all agreed that it was positively indecent to require a female to clamber onto the bench of an automobile when she could enter a closed carriage without uncovering an inch of ankle. And what added to the pleasure of seeing her on horseback, what made a sidesaddle lady yet more desirable, was her long skirt flopping over her heels.

Many affirmed that the motor would be only a passing fad.

Although a large number of more or less experimental vehicles had begun to clutter the courtyards of town houses, and the garage had made such inroads into stabling space that in Paris estate-settlement sales could be held composed entirely of the tricycles, fuel-powered quadricycles, velocipedes, electric cars and traps used by one prince of the Empire,[1] all this nevertheless did not alter the fact that no woman of quality would ever venture to drive such contraptions. Along the paths of the grounds of a private house, sheltered from indiscreet eyes, perhaps . . . but in public? How could one show oneself in cycling knickers, the calf visible clear up to the knee: a condition that, if a decree of the ministry of the interior were enforced, would render it virtually impossible to set foot on the ground. Two young foreigners, the Misses Basquez de la Maya, had only lately fallen victims to it for having dared to deposit their cycles at the foot of a tree and take a few steps in their bloomers in the Bois de St Gratien. The commissioner of police of the Eure had instantly reported them to the director of the national police.[2] What were they doing in France, those little half-castes, daughters of vulgar foreign pirates?

Both knickers and those who wore them were highly suspect.

How powerful must be the ignorance of those who, by nature, are able to dare! The simplest way to brave opinion has always been to brave it unwittingly.

Gabrielle Chanel assuredly had no idea how outlandish her decision was that day she went to the tailor of La Croix St Ouen to order a pair of custom-made breeches the likes of which he had never dreamed a woman could wear. From his first encounter with the modest customer who was asking him to make a copy of some jodhpurs borrowed from an English groom, he must have realized how very different she was from anything he had ever encountered before.

The stranger had no hesitations about the advantages of this garment, because it would save her the cost of a pair of boots and yet enable her to ride astride.

It did not seem conceivable, but it was so.

So dressing her became for the little tailor as preposterous an undertaking as that experienced forty years earlier by a young seamstress of the rue Louis-le-Grand, when she saw two immense crinolines squeeze their way panting into her garret . . . the comtesse de Pourtalès and the princesse de Metternich were about to reveal an unknown designer to the court of the Tuileries: Caroline Reboux.

But at La Croix St Ouen, the story had a different ending.

The little tailor was never to emerge from obscurity.

This is an early expression of one of the traits of Chanel's personality: her determined refusal to recognize any merit or put forward any name but her own.

Nothing daunted Gabrielle.

She tackled her riding lessons in rain or wind, at all hours and in every weather. Her endurance was in direct proportion to the size of her ambition: she wanted to amaze. She succeeded – proudly, angrily.

Etienne Balsan was no less surprised than the rest of her audience.

All the witnesses of those years agreed: Gabrielle was more than commonly gifted.

She had no other instructor but Etienne. He taught her how to manage a horse in training, going off with the apprentices in the early dawn, then changing out of her groom's gear during the day and, after transforming herself into a severe and dignified sidesaddle lady, riding with Etienne and his set.

At the age of eighty-one and a bit, Gabrielle explained the secret of a good seat and how you should hold yourself when riding astride, in most unseemly terms and gestures.

"To do it properly," she said, "there's one way and only one: you've got to imagine you're carrying a precious pair of balls [gesture] and under no circumstances can you put an ounce of weight on them. Good. You understand?"

The horseman's language flowed naturally back to her tongue; that is how they talked in the stables at Royallieu.

*

Etienne never tried to have Gabrielle accepted by society.

Perhaps he knew he wouldn't succeed.

But once her superior horsemanship had made its mark, he took pride in her, and as there was a touch of P. T. Barnum in him and he had not wholly given up the idea of launching her in some form or another, he put a term to her seclusion.

Gabrielle was becoming showable.

But to whom?

Not to the aristocracy of the turf, to the "greats," the Stud Book stewards or course directors of Deauville or Longchamp but, judging from photos, to the highly restricted circle of his buddies, however irregular their circumstances. For the young men were very soon joined by young women of relatively inferior station, their mistresses of the moment.

Balsan's hospitality had, among other advantages, that of being exempt from any form of snobbery. So it was not only the pleasure of seeing old Etienne and taking advantage of his wealth that attracted his jolly crew of horsemen: it was also the rare pleasure of being able to appear in public with a mistress and without a care.

Etienne had banished the coterie of virtuous spouses and intimidating dowagers from his premises and lived sheltered from the "pitiless glare of lorgnettes."[3] Had he seen the futility and absurdity of the social comedy, or was his distaste for drawing rooms only a result of boredom? In any case, an illustrious name held less appeal for him than the blaze of a great sporting career.

Whom did he entertain? First and foremost, the turf stars.

Breeders and trainers seem to have been the only regular visitors during those years, and Balsan also seemed to seek out their least aristocratic exponents. It was an amazingly democratic company for the day, especially if one remembers that until 1914 "running" was the exclusive prerogative of the purest bluebloods.

But Etienne Balsan did not trouble himself about rules, and since he judged men only according to the depths of their equestrian wisdom, it was not surprising to find a man like Maurice Caillaut among his friends – of modest background, with an inelegant moustache and the look of a staid family man; yet he was so infallible in sizing up yearlings that, in partnership with the comte de Pourtalès, he had succeeded in outdistancing the most illustrious breeders on their own ground. Caillaut had won the Grand Prix twice.

Etienne's friends all joined in their host's other major activity, which was playing practical jokes. The favorite consisted in asking the ladies to don their very best finery for the races at Compiègne, and then taking them there on donkeyback along the forest trails. The emptiness and isolation of the long bridle paths gave scope for all manner of larking about. In one famous event, Gabrielle Chanel raced against Suzanne Orlandi, a delicious person with almond-shaped eyes who was then the baron Foy's *irrégulière*. The ladies' instructions were to run the race at full gallop. Some of the men bet on Suzanne, others on Gabrielle; but it was Mademoiselle Forchemer, Maurice Caillaut's lady friend, who won, to his evident satisfaction.

Gabrielle's rather surprising familiarity with the psychological idiosyncracies of these animals may have been acquired on this occasion. To see her face when she said, "You know what it's like, eh, when one of those blasted burros has got it into his nut that he wants to walk. It takes a strong man to make him change his pace," one would swear she was referring to a specific recollection. But it was useless to try to make her say more. And if one speculated about the meaning of the remark, she would retort that it was just a childhood memory, dating from the time when she lived with her father in his horse-breeding days. Lies sprang to life so naturally! She added, "We each had our own donkey, you know." Meaning, presumably, her brothers and sisters.

Of the larks in the forest of Compiègne, never a word.

And how natural her reaction becomes when one first sees the picture in which the full company from these cavalcades stands assembled at Robinson before the lens of a roving photographer. Such discontent in the depths of the fine eyes of the Gabrielle of that period! The delicate face beneath the huge hat bears traces of unfathomable bitterness. Her reserve is patent, and her irony as well. That smile that isn't a smile, that angry mouth, that nervous poise disconcerting as a disguise, designed to hide the secret thoughts she harbored. The only thing clearly and openly expressed by this image of a proud horsewoman is the will to freedom coursing through her veins.

One can already sense the essence . . . The inimitable cheek of a little butterfly knot that converts the woman wearing it into a marvel of uniqueness. In comparison with the pretty girls beside her, she belongs to a different race.

Chanel's entire costuming technique, as developed fifteen years later, is summed up in the outfit she wore that day, undoubtedly the work of the humble tailor of La Croix St Ouen.

In the jacket with narrow lapels, devoid of decoration, allowing the white shirtwaist to show; in the turned-down collar that set up a sort of male simplicity as a foil to the frothy provocation of the Henri II ruffs smothering the throats of the other members of this ride of phantom-horsewomen and making them look as though they were about to canter into a museum of costume in their great-grandmothers' gowns; in the jet-black hat, already obeying the laws of a different perspective and making the headdresses of Mlles Forchemer and Orlandi, so overloaded with veiling and organdy and ribbons, look like anachronisms – in these lie the foundations of what, by challenging tradition, was to distinguish Gabrielle Chanel from all other women, and what would soon bring about her emergence from obscurity.

Monday at St Cloud, Tuesday at Enghien, Wednesday at Tremblay, Thursday at Auteuil, Friday at Maisons-Laffitte, Saturday at Vincennes, and Sunday at Longchamp: that was the week with Etienne, going the round from racecourse to racecourse.

Three years went by, in a world in which the joys and woes of the turf were presumed to satisfy every need. No rows of pearls, no lace, always dressed *en jeune fille* in strict tailor-made and boater – for in her dread of being taken for an improper woman, she rather exaggerated the image of respectability – Gabrielle was living like a garden perennial, stretched out toward the void of racing records. The only resources she had to occupy her leisure time were Etienne's friends, their noses eternally buried in horse racing weeklies, who put up with her teasing and thieving of their clothes (Gabrielle had a mania for borrowing ties and coats), and then the evenings filled with surprises: a good meal, then short-sheeted beds, and, in the shadows of the hallway, spying on the guests to watch their indignant reactions – oh! the fury of the ladies when they found their mules nailed to the floor: "My slippers! My slippers!" – and pillow fights and daubings of shaving cream under the serene eye of that other Gabrielle, the one who hung on the wall, the good abbess. In short, the full gamut of schoolboy humor to which Coco lent her adolescent's half-changed voice, an unvarying circus which, although it might take her to the racetracks or into provincial sunlight five or six times a year, soon brought her back again to the sylvan scents of Royallieu, and sometimes to the curiosity aroused when newcomers were expected.

A few celebrities were served up, as in a dream, to the provincial she remained. Among them, Emilienne d'Alençon and her most recent conquest, Alec Carter, idol of the grandstand.

Emilienne's star was slightly on the wane by 1907. Gone the days of her literary aspirations, and by that time no one ever mentioned the *Temple de l'Amour*, a collection of verse which she claimed to have written. Gone, too, her days of glory when eight members of the Jockey Club formed a company to provide her with an income, horses and paintings, thereby earning the right to visit her "for tea," each in turn.

But she still qualified as a tourist attraction.

She was pointed out to strangers as the *pièce de résistance* of Paris-perversity and her name was known to playboys from Bucharest to London, as well as to the workingmen of Mésnières-Charleville.

With her little upturned nose, full round cheeks, wide hips and ample thighs, Emilienne suggested something voluminous and authentic, something the army used to toast when it needed cheering up.

A good score in the Conservatoire entrance examination, walk-on parts in this and that, including a turn as a white-rabbit tamer in the ring at the Summer Circus: Emilienne's beginnings, at the age of fifteen, had coincided with the dismayed cries of the Parisians at the sight of their capital disfigured by deep trenches. People began talking about her at about the same time as the Métro. But that was all finished now, and when she first came to Royallieu there was no longer any question of bending the knees of young dukes and aging sovereigns – only of having a good time. She was thirty-three. She had salted away her nest egg and her life thereafter was dedicated solely to fulltime skylarking, an occupation for which she showed considerable aptitude and an enthusiasm that combined to form the essence of her charm.

Even the society snobs had ceased to fear competition from a seductress who had become too common to be dangerous.

Born in a concierge's room on the rue des Martyrs, Emilienne was a favorite with the street-corner loiterers, who recognized her as one of themselves. They viewed her with sympathy and a tinge of approbation.

Because now she had begun fraternizing with jockeys.

The previous year the papers had announced her engagement to Percy Woodland, and now she was treating herself to Alec Carter, the man with four hundred wins to his credit. For she was doing the treating . . . The contrary would not have been possible, given Emilienne's financial appetites and the ultimately limited means of this trainer's son.

Less talked about, but shortly to do her reputation no good, were her increasingly frequent appearances in places patronized by an all-female clientele: the cafes for unaccompanied women.

To tell the truth, Emilienne was becoming slightly disappointing. Not only were there the jockeys; she had also treated herself to a lady violinist.

Gabrielle scrutinized the woman who had said *tu* to the King of the

Belgians while arguing that the French, always provided they came from the upper strata, were the only men who knew how to make love properly; but she never felt the smallest twinge of jealousy for this onetime mistress of Etienne's who had so briefly shared his rooms on the boulevard Malesherbes five years before and who came to Royallieu only to be with Carter. Emilienne wore a tucked-front shirt, a wing collar, occasionally a monocle or a white carnation in her buttonhole, and, always, a tie in the style of the nationalist clubmen – dark, sober, held in place by a pin.

Speaking of her, Gabrielle said only that she "smelled clean" – in her mouth, a throbbing paean. She was always an olfactory person, and the tales of Etienne's friends, who claimed that the *bals blancs* (dances for young débutantes) were "reeking bake ovens," positively turned her stomach.

And Carter? Gabrielle did more than scrutinize him; she devoured him with her eyes.

He was a charmer who, beginning that year, bore the impressive title of "unvanquished." Product of a dynasty of English trainers who had settled at Chantilly, he had acquired a sort of preeminence by breaking with tradition and becoming a jockey. The turf public, who couldn't understand how anyone could prefer running risks to administering certainties, took it as a noble gesture and adored him, and when Carter began winning, enthusiasm ran rampant.

To the connoisseur, he personified the equestrian arts carried to the very summit of perfection.

"The best hands you ever saw, and the best companion in the world," said members of the Jockey Club who remembered him sixty years later. The women were all crazy about him, and openly pursued him.

It is not insignificant that a "priceless" cocotte and a jockey – an English one into the bargain – should have been the first people in Gabrielle's life to give her access to celebrity.

With his manners of a prince hailing from some kingdom in which the gods would all be horses, Alec Carter turned up like a signpost at one of the crossroads of Gabrielle's destiny, pointing both back to her origins, the dark ages of her birth in Saumur and the hard-working days of her Moulins apprenticeship peering out at the scarlet breeches, and ahead to her future; for Alec Carter anticipated Gabrielle's other life – that is, her third or fourth life – when, at the age of seventy-eight, she announced without comment that she intended to buy a "pony," give it to the most famous French jockey – Yves Saint Martin – to ride, and go to the races every Sunday. No sooner said than done. In 1961.

The pathos of that new beginning . . . a dialogue of ghosts.

How all things are transformed by time! Now she was the one who was surrounded, bowed to, sought-after, quoted in every gossip column. To the press she was "la Grande Mademoiselle." For her contemporaries Gabrielle was a magician, who needed only a pair of scissors and a few patient passes over some shapeless substance for there to fly from her hands one of those inexplicable objects that had made her what she was: sheer luxury.

Was she going to the races just to enjoy herself? Or was it to get even with that long-ago bevy of ladies in mother-of-pearl binoculars, feathered hats, and skirts that swept the grass at every stroke of the bell ringing to call them back to their seats in the members' enclosure . . . the seats that Balsan's *irrégulière* could never occupy?

For years Gabrielle had been entitled only to the company of dressed-up butchers, shopkeepers, street hawkers, urchins, bookmakers, girls of easy virtue, bullies, and pickpockets; all the Parisian guys and dolls of the turf. One had to be careful, you know, not to run into this or that person whom the sight of the young women of Etienne's circle might offend.

At Longchamp all manner of detours were necessary to avoid the fair Anita Foy née Porgès, the so-legitimate wife of Max, comte Foy, who owned the Barbeville stud in the Calvados and would no more have spoken to his brother's girl friend – little Orlandi with the huge almond-shaped eyes – than would his wife. They accused her of having "debauched him."

And at the Montpellier course . . .

Similar tactics there, but this time deployed in order not to be seen by d'Espous's father and his formidable mother, that comtesse d'Espous who wrote in every letter to her son, "Your slut will be the death of me."

And at Vichy . . .

How many zigzags were made at Vichy so that Adrienne should not cross the path of the family of that nobleman's son whose mistress she had become.

For upon her return from Egypt, Adrienne had made her choice.

Of the three faithful swains who had clubbed together to pay for her cruise on the Nile, two had voluntarily withdrawn – de Jumilhac and de Beynac – in favor of the youngest of the group and protégé of the other two, and to him Adrienne had granted her favors, for all time. Predictable, perhaps? But what was less so was that they too were talking marriage.

The parents made their position clear without delay.

Floods of maternal tears: "Over my dead body." Definitive statements from the father: "She must be a drunken chambermaid."

So from zigzag to zigzag the lovers of Vichy, like the lovers of Montpellier, waited. Time would tell.

Can all that be forgotten? The eyes turning away, the shrugging shoulders – does one forget? It was a cruel time, their "Belle Epoque," a paradoxical past that Gabrielle savored anew with a bitter taste when, fifty years later at Tremblay, surrounded by every possible mark of consideration and respect, she watched her pony, Romantica, gallop and her jockey, Yves Saint Martin, in scarlet jersey and cap, win the race.

WHOSE "BELLE EPOQUE"?

At twenty-six, Gabrielle was almost a stranger to Paris.

Can one know a city one has seen only going in and out of it? Horse races, military parades, and cyclists whizzing round the Vel' d'Hiver: these formed the bulk of Etienne's offerings in the way of entertainment. And if we add a few department stores, the most amazing of which, the Printemps, she mightily admired – a building all in iron and glass which was exactly as old as herself – then we know approximately as much about Paris as Gabrielle did in those days.

There had been a few automobile experiences, it is true. Léon de Laborde, Etienne's best friend, sometimes lent his little car to the "horsey set." It was a red coupé, carriage work by Charron, whose radiator required continual refilling. But it never took Gabrielle where she wanted to go: to the Palais de Glace, or to the Bois on a day when the *élégantes* were competing, or to the Tir aux Pigeons – the places where, according to the gossip columns, it was all happening.

Always rushing to reach the racecourses where their duties were calling them, Etienne and his friends merely skimmed through the suburbs and then bypassed the capital, of which Gabrielle saw only the least impressive aspects: the porte de Vincennes, the porte de Saint Cloud, the Place de la République, which they circled long enough to see an absurd lion that looked like a poodle standing guard over the deplorable statue and, mournful as a chamber pot standing open at the hefty lady's feet, the urn of Universal Suffrage. Gabrielle found it hard to believe that this was Paris.

Most often, they traveled by train. To Etienne's vindictive, chauvinistic, and flag-waving friends it was a sacred duty to watch the annual July 14 parade.

That was a traditional distraction.

If Général Picquart, the minister of war, fell off his horse while passing the troops in review, the event seemed infinitely graver and more deserving . of discussion to Etienne and his friends than Clemenceau's fall from power: he ceased to govern France that same year, almost without the little equestrian group's being aware of the fact.

In the carriage coming home, Etienne and his companions spread out a blanket and proceeded to play cards on their knees until the train steamed into Compiègne. They possessed something like a relentless determination to show contempt for the customs and life-style of the previous generation. Soft hats shoved back on their heads, handsome English tweeds, an air of studied casualness: in these ways they proclaimed their dissension from the starched elegance of their fathers, who were rigid figures in detached collars and four-in-hands, with monocles, walking sticks, and carnations in their buttonholes. They had nothing in common.

Meanwhile, the young women of the group recapitulated the day's excitements, discussing fashion, and, above all, hats. Family, children, love, jewels – none of these aroused as much concern as the question of hats, and not only in their circle! (Remember Aunt Julia?) An infatuation dating from the early years of the Second Empire, and one which had never faded. Recalling the stupefaction so frequently expressed by all who, finding themselves in the presence of Empress Eugenie and the princesse de Metternich, waited to hear those ladies exchange deathless asseverations only to learn that all they ever talked about was "the most attractive manner of placing their hats," or the amazement of that solemn goose Alice B. Toklas alias Gertrude Stein, who, according to her "autobiography," could not conceive, when she met Picasso's mistress (then Fernande Olivier) how she could be loved by so great a genius when the only things she was genuinely interested in were her designer's creations; remembering them, how can one fail to see something disturbing in this permanent passion for adornment?

There is nothing surprising, therefore, in the fact that for the present Gabrielle Chanel's erudition was confined to the names of a few generals and one or two dress designers. For the rest . . . had she even heard of Diaghilev? It is doubtful.

Diaghilev first came to Paris in 1906, with an exhibition of Russian art at the Salon d'Automne; he returned in 1907 with Glazunov, Rimsky-Korsakov, and Rachmaninov, who conducted their own works at the Opera. In 1908 he introduced a singer, Chaliapin, to the Parisian public, in an admirable production of *Boris Godunov*; and it was not until 1909 that he brought the Ballets Russes for their first season, at the Châtelet.

Nevertheless, during the previous seasons he had revealed to the Parisian

public a world of sound and color compared with which people's recollec-
tions of the World's Fair's gilded pasteboard domes and costume-jewelry
Slavism seemed mere picture-postcard aesthetics. But what did the recluse
of Royallieu know of Serge the Magnificent? Or of Chaliapin and *Boris?*
Nothing, no doubt.

She owed the bulk of her learning to the *Excelsior*, a daily to be seen
lying about on every table at Royallieu. In other words, the only Serges and
Borises she knew of were the grand dukes, and then only through the press.

They were front-page items, those two.

A special column was devoted to their loves at Nice, and their unsuc-
cessful incognitos. Let some imperial princess refuse to speak after one of
them had taken the liberty of whistling in the direction of her window as a
means of asking her to come downstairs, and every gossip-monger was
instantly informed. This Serge and this Boris certainly did some strange
things, though. They beat their servants, and in order to keep them "on
hand," they made their aides-de-camp sleep in the bathtub. How could one
fail to hear about it? It happened at the Negresco . . .

And after all, if the grand dukes were dabbling in the dubious affairs of
the demimonde, demi-stage-stars and "princesses of love," it may have been
in order to forget that other Serges and Borises – their brothers, uncles, and
cousins back in St Petersburg – were being used by the nihilists for target
practice. The fleet had been totally destroyed. The Russia of the tsars was
disintegrating and crumbling away; in Poland, in the Caucasus, on the shores
of the Black Sea, even in Moscow, there were nothing but strikes, raids,
uprisings, and massacres. The imperial army was reaping defeat after defeat.
The tsarina looked dreadful. The tsar himself seemed preoccupied . . . That
was enough to pardon the Romanovs' winter escapades at Nice or elsewhere.

And of course, the press had no respect for anything.

Paris was discovering Debussy, Proust, Renoir, Bonnard, a new form of
art in the theater, and the poets who put out *La Revue Blanche.*

But at Royallieu, the only relief from horses was games.

No one there cared about music or painting, and even less about the
avant-garde. Sarah Bernhardt was the only artist whose name was ever
uttered, and with some reservations: after all, she was Jewish.

Adrienne had come to Paris, still engaged to her young suitor and still
escorted by their duenna; she invited Gabrielle to applaud "Madame Sarah"
at a poetry recital. Adrienne was ecstatic with admiration, Maud Mazuel declared
she nearly wept; so is one to believe Chanel when she said, in her old age, that
she had *always* found Sarah hopelessly grotesque, "side-splitting . . . an old

clown"? (Perhaps the antipathy derived primarily from the fact that Sarah Bernhardt had immortalized the white uniform – the close-fitting trousers and arrogant coat of the due de Reichstadt – designed by Paul Poiret.) And what is one to make of her disdain for the theater of the early years of the century?

In February 1964, at a performance of *Cyrano de Bergerac* at the Théâtre Français, the violence of her disapproval shocked those sitting near her. What is still regarded as Edmond Rostand's masterpiece has been vener-ated, of course, for nearly eighty years now, and in France *Cyrano* is the favorite food of a large public. But far from letting herself be moved by the resounding "hushes!" and exasperated protests raining down upon her, Chanel, the center of attention of the whole house, continued to scoff, and it was impossible to make her be quiet. People overheard her devastating gibes at actors and author alike.

"Really, what an affliction! . . . Poetry for publicity jingles . . . What revolting bad taste! How pretentious! Ghastly age. And what an imbecilic notion, the French swagger! Charwoman patriotism."

At the most moving point of the play a stinging "cock-a-doodle-do!" was heard to issue clearly from between her teeth. She was fuming.

What private pain, what resentment, was this hostility protecting or revealing? At whom was her mockery directed? Was it at Rostand? Or, possibly, at herself, and a past whose shabbiness became all the more distressing as she came to measure it more accurately? Moulins, the patriotic songs of the music halls, the "scarlet breeches" attitude . . . was she angry with herself for remaining too long a prisoner of the pleasures and tastes of one caste – the very one which, after discovering her, had relegated her to the lower orders? Was she also regretting the "Royallieu days" as so much wasted time? Too long she had been content to ride a horse and take part in Etienne's foolishness and jaunts and idling about in places all so much alike they scarcely seemed to belong to the towns in which they were located . . . At Pau there were those furnished rooms on top of Old England, where all the sportsmen met after five o'clock but where, as at Souvigny, as at Royallieu, their wives never came . . . And at Nice and Deauville? Those bachelor flats they lived in – always borrowed from one of Etienne's friends and always furnished so identically that when she woke up in the morning she had to ask herself where she was.

Among the other expressions of her anger, the cry "Ghastly age!" at least, is significant. No doubt she was lying when she swore that she had always thought that it was. No doubt that cry was the fruit of a later process. But that didn't make it any less heartfelt.

Ghastly age! The age in which, for fear of being classed among the "unfastened" (i.e., undressed), she had been compelled to adopt a style that was pure imitation, excessive and constrained. Ghastly age! The age that forced her to wear whalebone stiff as an iron collar. Ghastly people, whose power prevented her from being one of the first to witness that radiant dawn that seemed to be simultaneously inspiring all the musicians, painters, and poets of those years.

Tightly corseted, wearing everything it was proper to wear if one wished to be thought proper – muff, huge black velvet hat, long loose jacket tapping the calves, and half veil – Gabrielle strolled beneath the palm trees on the Promenade des Anglais with her coterie of admirers.

That same year, a few miles away, Colette was writing to a friend from the sun of St Tropez: "I am in the sand with six female dogs and two horses. And what fishing! No shoes, no stockings, no hat, no skirt, no corset, no gloves. You can say what you like about Cabourg in comparison with this life, but I'll only shrug my shoulders!"[4]

No, Gabrielle was not the first, and she never forgave the "ghastly age" whose fault she thought it was.

THE QUEST FOR FREEDOM

Etienne's friends all noticed that a new member of their board kept turning up at Royallieu in the spring of 1908. The "set" had been enlarged to include an Englishman with darkish skin and straight brown hair.

An attractive but unusual physique.

What was known of him? That he had spent most of his youth in good boarding schools – first at Beaumont, a Jesuit school for the sons of Catholic gentlemen, then at Downside, an equally fashionable institution run by Benedictines. Consequently that he was of good family, but there was some mystery surrounding his birth. He was not in *Who's Who*. His name was Arthur Capel. Everybody called him Boy. He never spoke of his mother. Some said he was the illegitimate offspring of a Frenchman who had died shortly before Boy finished school. A name was mentioned: allegedly, he was the son of a Pereire. A banker's bastard . . . But no one held that against him, any more than that touch of Jewish blood; for upon inquiry, it was established that he frequented the most elegant places in London. So, because the English appreciated his rare qualities as a polo player and found it quaint or droll of the chap actually to seem to enjoy working and making money, the Parisians good-naturedly consented to do as much, until in the end nobody bothered about the peculiarities of his birth anymore. And his gifts as a lady killer were much praised, together with the fact that he had caused his inherited interests in Newcastle coal to prosper and multiply.

But it was clear that although he had become intimate with men of the most glittering worlds – and among them Armand de Gramont, duc de Guiche – Arthur Capel shared neither their opinions nor their ways of thinking. To him, nothing was more important than work, and he acted accordingly; so much so that he often felt annoyance, although he never expressed it, with those who had most warmly welcomed him into their midst. Was it because he could not fail to see that he would never be wholly accepted? If so, this attitude would explain many things about his life, and one in particular: Gabrielle Chanel was to find in him a depth of under-standing she had previously sought in vain.

When she and Etienne had their first arguments on the subject of her desire to alter her life, Arthur Capel was the only one to take her side. She was tired of living in seclusion at Royallieu? She confessed that she was bored? What was wrong with that? She ought to get out and do something. It was natural.

She spoke of taking up singing again. But there, nobody agreed with her.

Her previous attempts had been fruitless and her younger sister, Antoinette, fresh from a convent, had also tried for success in that field, with no better results than Gabrielle. Having relied too heavily on her fresh good looks and slender waist, Antoinette was now lingering in Vichy without resources or engagements of any description. Adrienne, who had moved there in order to be near her young nobleman, was as "family-minded" as ever, and looking after Antoinette, giving her money and trying to find her jobs.

Wasn't one victim of the voice enough in the family?

Gabrielle let herself be convinced. Better try some other way. Then, encouraged by Boy, she accepted a suggestion of Etienne's.

In Balsan's mind this was only a hobby, not an occupation. To make hats for her friends, wouldn't that be a nice idea? Weren't people already asking for them? And she did so enjoy having the guests at Royallieu secretly come to her room to try on the hats they had admired on her head. Her cupboards were full of them. Even Emilienne . . . She had liked one of Coco's boaters so much that she had kept it and had her picture taken wearing it. Since then, Emilienne wore nothing but boaters. Overdecorated, it is true, and uglified by a thousand little touches of her own, but at least . . . In this instance, Gabrielle's influence was undeniable.

The truth was that she had a really impressive talent, whether or not she owed it to her holidays at Varennes and the sunny days spent smartening up Aunt Julia's hats. In the ease with which she contrived to impart elegance to any scrap of straw picked up on a department-store tour, one felt there was more than taste or ingenuity: one felt, above all, the hereditary ability of those tillers of the soil who had been her ancestors for generations to "make something out of nothing."

What she created was often absurdly simple, and it was curious to see how some of her friends reacted to this sparseness as a new form of eccentricity. Put a wide waving brim with an almost invisible crown supporting nothing at all on one's head and call it a hat? A few women liked the idea, were amused by the little air of defiance about it, and then, it made conversation.

Because, after all, a hat that had no crown of ostrich feathers on it no vertical plumes, or cabbages of crumpled tulle, or floods of streamers – who could have been responsible for such a thing?

Suppositions were made, questions asked. One heard: "Whoever makes your hats?" Ignorance was assuaged by guessing. Rue de la Paix, rue Royale, all around the Opéra – there was no shortage of milliners in those days. They were legion. So what about this hat? Was it by Camille Marchais, or Charlotte Enard, or Carlier, or Georgette, or Suzanne Talbot? But no . . . none of the designers then in fashion could take credit for this adornment that possessed such accomplished grace.

Adopting one of Gabrielle's creations was like crowning yourself with a riddle, and it also involved learning to be attractive by going against the stream.

Moving Gabrielle to Paris created difficulties for Etienne. Should he buy her a business? Take a lease in her name? He had thumbed his nose at censure so long as the stranger from Moulins lived in seclusion at Royallieu, but he attached a great deal of importance to the opinions of the gentlemen in the Jockey Club. To have a mistress, to keep her, to live with her – among them, all that could pass as an essential part of one's prestige. But to make a woman work? That was the unacceptable thing, and Etienne could anticipate severe criticism.

Then too, like many men of his kind, Etienne did not really like to spend money on anything but horses.

So, on this or some other pretext, insisting that he wanted to help his friend without offending her, he simply offered her his ground-floor apartment

at 160 boulevard Malesherbes, convinced that Gabrielle's efforts at emancipation would fit into that setting perfectly naturally.

He was correct.

To set her up in a bachelor's rooms, to give her as an address the one
where he had sown his wild oats with his high-society girl friends, was a
highly original way of launching her. His former liaisons would feel quite
a little thrill discussing hats where, a few years before, they had yielded to
Etienne – and after braving such incalculable dangers! "Losing" the coach
and driver without one's husband finding out, simplifying a costume that
was complexity personified without one's maid knowing, getting undressed
– an undertaking which, as Jean Cocteau remarked in *Portraits-souvenirs* had
"to be planned in advance like moving house" – actually taking a lover at
last, accomplishing the tour de force . . . And here was that same bachelor
flat being put to an avowable use. One no longer went there to take one's
clothes off, one went to do one's shopping.

How novel it all was! Even without the added allure of the hats, the idea
alone would have sufficed.

Success came almost at once.

Etienne's friends, each dragging the next, crowded in.

Boy dropped by for a neighborly chat. He lived nearby, and was lavish
in his encouragement. Charming as she could be when she liked, and still
dressed like a boarding-school pupil on parade, Gabrielle drank in his words.
Here was a man showing respect for her. That had never happened to her
before.

Soon Boy was also sending his lady friends along.

All of turf society paraded in and out of her shop.

Gabrielle never lacked ideas. But she did lack experience and, a more
serious shortcoming, technical knowledge. She had eloquence in plenty and
to spare. Like her father and grandfather, she was a good salesman. But for
her new clientele, even that was not enough. Nobody was more fussy and
demanding than those particular Frenchwomen. If they were disappointed,
they could go away as quickly as they had come.

Once more, Etienne was called upon to help. Although the game was
becoming a touch too serious for his liking, he recommended acquiring technical assistance. There was no time to lose. A meeting took place with a
woman three years younger than Gabrielle: Lucienne Rabaté. Everyone they
consulted was categorical on that point: Lucienne and Lucienne alone was
the person for the job. Which would seem to indicate that in 1909 Lucienne
Rabaté at Maison Lewis was something in the nature of a stock as yet

unlisted but already being watched by the sharpest tacticians of the rue de la Paix.*

Gabrielle hurried to see her.

The thing was to persuade her to come.

It looked possible. Lucienne was trying to build up a clientele. Some actresses and society women swore by her already. She accepted Gabrielle's offer and took advantage of her departure from Lewis to entice two of his best hands away with her.

That was more than enough to begin with.

One day, under pressure of success, it became necessary to enlist Antoinette too. Gabrielle assigned to her younger sister the task of receiving customers and looking after the salon, to which she was no disgrace. The little girl had become quite a pretty young woman. Dressed decently, she was not without charm, although the lower part of her face might be a shade heavy and the overall aspect exude a certain impression of silliness. She had all of Gabrielle's boldness and none of her talent. But, encouraged by Adrienne, who insisted that "the little one is one hundred per cent employable," Gabrielle allowed herself to be persuaded: she would "protect" her.

Moreover, Antoinette had inherited one or two of the traditional family virtues. She was a hard worker. She never protested. As the only person to sleep on the premises, she stayed up after Lucienne had left and Gabrielle too, who was still living at Royallieu. And the following morning at opening time the work would be finished. Good little Antoinette, who would also take around late deliveries.

Adrienne, from her far-off province, applauded; she liked to think that two of the three Chanel sisters were reunited at last and, as in the Varennes days, busy ruffling, lining, covering, pinking, pearling, and cutting out.

She was hoping more than ever that those stinging allusions to her family might now die away. She was the simplest and most straightforward of the three, but in addition to her good heart she had a fervid desire for respectability,

---

* Later, around 1912, she went to work for Caroline Reboux, at the request of the three forewomen to whom the famous designer had just ceded her establishment. The social spirit reigning there was virtually unique for that day: employees of the Reboux firm shared in the profits! It is true that the great lady of hats had been the friend not only of Reynaldo Hahn, Jean Cocteau, and Philippe Berthelot, but of Léon Blum, the socialist statesman, as well. Lucienne was to remain with that firm for forty years, later becoming director of it. She was rightly regarded as the top milliner in Paris during the "roaring twenties."

which had been forced upon her by the reactions of the circle she aspired to join. The intractable parents of her young aristocrat continued to proclaim that they did not want, at any price, what they called "a barracks marriage."

Adrienne was still not *accepted*.

She never was.

And yet, so much love . . . A moment's pause is in order here, to reflect upon the cruel fate of this beautiful young woman who waited more than twenty years for marriage to crown a devotion as sincere as it was tenacious.

HOW TO BECOME A MILLINER

February 1910. Gabrielle had been camping in Balsan's bachelor flat for almost a year, watching her clientele grow day by day.

She was cramped for space.

Turf society had now been replaced by society in general, by the pretty women one knew to be customers of Worth, Redfern, and Doucet. The ladies did not always place an order, but they dropped in, prompted by curiosity.

Antoinette had to move out so that her room could be converted into a workroom. Where to put her? Another problem.

The horsemen of Royallieu were alerted, flew to the aid of the poor homeless waif, and found a ground-floor flat to lend her, tiny but attractive and handy to the workroom.

It was the right sort of district for that type of accommodation.

Recent buildings in the buffet-table style, with vast entrance halls sheathed in marble whose maroon harmonies and complicated contrasts of facing irresistibly reminded one of enormous displays of galantines or garlands of sausages: the tall houses of the Malesherbes district had all been designed to contain, in addition to the spacious apartments occupied by bourgeois families, discreet little ground-floor flats in which the annual crop of seducers might indulge their "habits" out of sight of their wives.

Of course, it was nice for them to be in the same quarter within a few streets of one another – the workroom at 160 boulevard Malesherbes, Arthur Capel's flat at 138, Antoinette's at 8 avenue du Parc Monceau – but the problem remained: working space was inadequate, and the address hardly had a professional sound.

So Gabrielle asked Balsan for a loan. She wanted to rent a shop and open a business in her own name.

He flatly refused. He had just spent a lot of money on some pastureland adjoining his Royallieu estate. His horses were costing him quite enough as it was. He couldn't do any more.

She kept at him.

She said there were too many hazards involved in working in her present circumstances, without a license and in unsuitable premises. That was true. So true that her partnership with Lucienne had not survived. Perhaps she hadn't liked the style of the house? There was considerable confusion, what with Boy coming in and out, and the handsome Léon de Laborde, and Etienne. Lucienne had never dreamed a milliner could be courted by so many men at once. And what was one to think of young men who affected such shocking casualness of dress? Was this some new form of dandyism?

Subjected at an early age to the instruction of exacting forewomen, trained in the merciless school of the Parisian workrooms, Lucienne was a true professional. Rung by rung, she had mounted the ladder of an art in which she had grown from a young errand girl in her smock, assigned to the most lowly tasks, into a "second cutter," her bowl of pins in hand, scurrying nonstop from the workroom to the salon where the wealthy customer one was struggling to satisfy sat enthroned, and finally into a "fitter," a member of the human race at last, entitled to observe the fitting ceremony as a silent witness and even, on occasion, to reach into the huge accessories basket and present, to the officiating holinesses, a spray of aigrette plumes and stuffed birds of paradise intended further to enhance those game bags that were the hats of the day.

This is the stage Lucienne's career had reached the year she gave up her former job to follow Coco.

At first the idea of fashion in a bachelor flat had struck her as hilarious. Both Antoinette and Gabrielle were mad about singing. The moment a customer's back was turned, the Chanel sisters swung into one of their refrains. The workroom rang with song. Sometimes they alternated lines in a more or less highly improper dialogue. Excruciating, those Chanels. So much more fun than the people at Lewis' . . .

But Lucienne soon realized the dangers of the partnership.

Gabrielle did not like to share. She was beginning to have confidence in her own ability and, although she knew infinitely less than Lucienne, paid scant heed to her advice.

Certain secrets of society, according to Lucienne, had to be taken into account if one intended to do one's job properly. They formed an unwritten but scrupulously respected code, which the greenest apprentice on the rue de la Paix learned after a few months at work. Whereas Gabrielle . . . How could she have mastered the fine points of an etiquette that forbade one to give an appointment to baronne Henri de Rothschild at the same hour as to the lovely Gilda Darthy – the two ladies must on no account be allowed to meet, although the bills of both were sent to baron Henri – and how could she know there were two Princess Pignatellis who must be treated very differently, one being a great lady who made special trips from Naples to buy her clothes in Paris, while the other was a bawdy creature who had exposed herself, in her younger years, on the stage of La Scala in a less than scanty costume? Such details were utterly beyond her.

Why struggle? Lucienne had had enough experience of the fashion world to know most of these women. She labored to convince Gabrielle that it could sometimes be advantageous to drop one group of customers in order to acquire another. It was necessary, she said, to adopt a scale of values, and one could not give the same treatment to Réjane and Bartet as to the latest little ingenue from the Odéon. Moreover, the consideration Gabrielle showed for a certain Claire Gambetta – a tall, olive-skinned, outrageously made-up woman, whose name had a magical effect upon her – was quite inappropriate. Gabrielle circled round her repeating "Mademoiselle Gambetta" as though she were singing a hymn. One more faux pas . . . For if there was one customer who should not be let in the door it was that actress, or so-called actress, who had earned universal opprobrium by trying to capitalize on her name. She had sung *T'as cassé ta pipe, ta pipe, ta pipe* ("You've kicked the bucket, the bucket, the bucket") on the night her uncle Léon Gambetta, the orator, the man of the lost provinces, the idol of Alsace-Lorraine, lay dying on the heights of Ville d'Avray.

It was madness. This universally condemned woman must not come back.

But upon learning what Mademoiselle Gambetta's crime had been, Gabrielle had hooted with laughter. To her, such a gaffe was a long way from providing grounds for scorn or hostility.

"She was doing her job," she retorted harshly.

Conflict ensued.

Lucienne leaped at the first opportunity to go elsewhere, leaving Gabrielle to her own devices.

That's where amateurism got you.

But how was she to convince Etienne?

Gabrielle tried again. Lucienne had left her: that was an argument which might sway Balsan. The fact that Arthur Capel was encouraging her added ardor to her efforts to bring Balsan round. Capel believed firmly in Gabrielle's talent, and he too thought the time had come to set her up in different surroundings. He took her side on every occasion.

Balsan was surprised and rather annoyed at his best friend's treason. Here was Arthur Capel taking "work" seriously, Gabrielle's "work," which, like Etienne, he had at first treated only as a game. What was the meaning of that?

In due course the reason for his inexplicable shift became clear: Capel was in love. He admitted it, moreover. With Coco.

The honeymoon for three was over.

In order to understand Etienne, one must remember that mercenary mistresses, encountered too young had made him suspicious of love. But the fact that other people could still believe in it touched him more deeply than anything else.

So, Boy and Gabrielle . . .

Being a decent chap, Etienne continued to lend her his bachelor flat, although he knew perfectly well she was sleeping elsewhere.

The change of régime took place without tears or scenes. It was a switch-about in the best tradition of French philandering. When Arthur Capel replaced Balsan, as a matter of course it was he who advanced the money to buy the shop.

In the last months of 1910, Gabrielle found herself working in a mezzanine at number 21 of a street whose name, for more than half a century, was linked with hers: the rue Cambon.

Royallieu was still the regular meeting place, and on the surface nothing had changed.

A few variations in detail, however.

Balsan, forsaken, became jealous. Seeing how lightly Gabrielle accepted the break had wounded his pride. He began to miss her.

Gabrielle returned to Royallieu as a guest, with Arthur Capel. For visits restricted to weekends. One would have said she was a different woman. Her pearl-gray riding habit made it suddenly plain that her life had changed.

By the quality of the cloth, the smart catching-up of the bias-cut skirt, the long weighted jacket, deliberately asymmetrical in front so that, once in the saddle, it would be full enough amply to cover the knee bent around the horn; and by the high spirits in which Gabrielle joined her friends every morning in this attire, one would have had to be blind not to see that her long-cherished dream had come true. She was now dressed by one of the grand masters of the field – one of those Englishmen frequented by the beautiful horsewomen in top hats and false-front waistcoats whose flashy elegance made the heart of the young Marcel Proust skip a beat.

But whoever her tailor was, and however much respect he inspired in Gabrielle, she had nevertheless imposed one or two of her own ideas upon him that revealed certain secret links with her youth. Who cared what he kept telling her – that it was inconceivable, under any circumstances whatsoever, for a lady rider to abandon the strict white shirt and triple-knotted white piqué stock which, once pinned in place, produced the same impression of impeccable stiffness as a detachable collar? What did such stiffness have to do with her? Perhaps in other circumstances . . . but at Royallieu?

"We just hack, among friends," she explained.

The way of life there permitted certain relaxations of the rules.

That was not the view of the tailor, who expressed his disapproval and almost his grief at seeing a pretty young woman coolly contemplating his dishonor. What was it she wanted? To ride sidesaddle but without a stock, and wearing an open-collared shirt? Sheer madness. And what else? To wear, with a severely cut tailor-made, a blouse with a round collar and a loosely tied chiffon scarf? What an idea! . . . She ought really to leave that sort of thing to schoolgirls.

The tailor was apoplectic.

And Gabrielle was scarcely less accommodating in other matters: she turned down his suggestion that she should go to Motsch and order a black plush top hat with a monocle fastened to the band, such as the princesse Murat wore. That was no more to her taste than the little black tricorne garnished with a few ostrich feathers that had just been made fashionable by the princesse de Caraman Chimay.

She would have none of such headpieces.

She intended to wear a piqué headband which, fastened under her chignon, would be quite enough to keep her hair in place.

The tailor asked her to repeat what she had said.

"A headband?" he queried incredulously. "Did you say a headband? Something like what the tennis women wear?"

"No," she snapped back. "Narrower . . . neat . . . more like a nun's headband. You see what I mean? Worn just off the forehead."

This affirmation only added to the tailor's misgivings.

It was certainly a rare privilege to be Arthur Capel's special friend, but it was not sufficient grounds for setting oneself up as an arbiter of elegance. The young woman would not go far. She was mixing her styles.

NEW WOMEN FRIENDS

On numerous occasions Gabrielle Chanel maintained that she had never loved but once, and had known only one man who was right for her: Arthur

Capel. And it is more or less certain that, for once, she was telling the truth.

Capel's foreign accent, the pace of her new life, all the prestige attaching to a busy, considerate man, the large dark eyes that looked at her with authority; the hair, also black, so deep a black that it threw a jet shadow around his head; all that created a new atmosphere.

The days of the merry "set" were over, and the gallops through the forest too. In order to act, to build, one needed a solid companion by one's side, someone one could lean on. Arthur Capel was that companion.

She had always longed to break out of the subservient role in which friv-olous officers and blasé sportsmen had cast her. Here was a human being showing her affection, confidence, esteem. Was it a new life? Really a new life?

Capel had had innumerable mistresses. He abandoned them. They tried to get him back. He was determined to ignore them. Was that proof of a lasting love? With hope facing her, doubts poured into Gabrielle. Could she trust this Capel? Weren't his tastes more or less the same as Balsan's? Another sportsman; sportsmen forever and always in her life . . . But he was more than that. He was interested in everything, he cared about politics, history, he read quantities of strange books. The works of a socialist like Proudhon – *Du principe fédératif*; of a scatterbrained scholar like Fabre d'Alivet – *Histoire du genre humain*; of a visionary like Saint-Yves d'Alveydre – *La Mission des souverains*: they were his bedside books. But one also found thrust into his bookshelves works by people like Nietzsche, Voltaire, the Church Fathers, Spencer's *Political Essays*, and the memoirs of Sully, which he was most anxious that Chanel should read. Gabrielle discovered that one could be a champion polo player and an ardent reader at the same time. Surprise, surprise!

Then one of those reactions set in which life knows so well how to orches-trate. Chanel was forced to admit that work held less allure for her when she was in love than when she wasn't. She was becoming acquainted with happiness and she found, to her wonderment, that it was a condition suffi-cient unto itself.

However, she had to carry on and keep her business moving ahead.

She tried to persuade Lucienne to come back, and succeeded, for a short time.

Then, reassured on that score, Gabrielle abandoned herself to the current: first, she could not bear the thought of leaving the house, so that the loved one should never need to wait for her; then came a violent reaction: she didn't want to live in a cloister; then, an equally violent remorse. So, sitting tight in Boy's flat, she dreamed of living only for him. But that was no life . . . so what next?

She had lost interest in café-concerts. Yet as soon as she heard the women in Boy's set talking about their visit to Isadora Duncan, Gabrielle was immediately bitten by the show-business bug again.

Curiosity alone had attracted her customers to the American's studio. They were hoping that a visit to the woman who preached freedom of the senses through the dance would give them some mysterious revelation. But that was not what Gabrielle was looking for. Eurhythmics was all the rage – more than a style of dancing, it was becoming a system of education, and people of all ages were setting out as upon pilgrimages to the institute which the master of the method, Jacques Dalcroze, had just opened in Dresden. So Gabrielle wanted to learn to dance. Informed of her desire, Arthur Capel encouraged it. What harm could there be in his friend making up dances along with her hats? Why not give it a try? He dreaded nothing so much as an idle female.

It was, nevertheless, in the company of such idle females that Gabrielle made an expedition to the avenue de Villiers one "at home" day.

Isadora lived in a commune, surrounded by frivolous and uninhibited artists of every description. She entertained her guests with bared breasts beneath a peplum. A remarkably thin young man wearing a faun's beard never left her side. Alcoholic mixtures, most novel, were handed round. There was much laughter and chatter, the young women enjoyed themselves enormously. Gabrielle listened. The long-awaited moment came, Isadora announced that she was about to improvise; she was observed to fling herself forward with upraised arms as though all the gods of Olympus had come to roost in the glass panes of the ceiling. Her attitudes carried such conviction that one forgot the meagerness of her props: one garland of crumpled paper roses.

The effect of her dancing was to thrust the young beard-wearer into the middle of the studio with a single leap, which, in Gabrielle's opinion, spoiled everything. Urged on by strong spirits, the young man – who was Kees Van Dongen – began playing the satyr. He seized the high priestess' buttocks in both hands without her showing the least sign of displeasure.

Isadora continued her improvisation to the end, still addressing her magnificent movements to the ceiling.

Artistic circles might applaud, if only out of a desire to flout convention. But not Gabrielle. Nothing had prepared her for such extravagant behavior, not even the heavy-footed heartiness of her *beuglant* days. She had had experience with smutty talk, but this, at Isadora's, was licentiousness.

She found this form of exuberance nasty. Respectful of the proprieties? Chanel? And how. What else could one expect from a pupil of the nuns? Or from a demimondaine? And she was both.

In the last years of her life she seemed to retain no memory of the vicissitudes of this occasion. But when, speaking of Isadora, she said, "Whenever I saw her she was tipsy. A small-town muse," one felt she was packing into that condemnation all the embarrassment and perplexity she had experienced on that long-ago day.

Giving up the idea of becoming a pupil of the Duncan school did not mean giving up the dance altogether. Gabrielle went on looking and finally found a teacher to her taste: Caryathis, a specialist in character dancing. A high proportion of peasant blood, a seamstress mother from Auvergne, a pauper's childhood spent largely in a convent where the first communions were more ceremonious than anywhere else because Monseigneur de Dreux-Brézé in person came to preside over them – so many points in common between Caryathis' past and Gabrielle's. And the father? A twin of the senior Chanel. His children called him "Monsieur le Saltimbanque . . ." A peddler of small wares, he tramped the roads of France barefoot with a pack on his back. A baker's assistant in the home of a baronial Périgourdine at the time of his marriage, he subsequently earned some renown in the kitchens of Chez Larue before taking off forever, first as chef cuisinier on board the Trans-Siberian train, then as lover of a Russian lady, then as nothing. His forsaken spouse found a situation with a richly kept singer, and there little Caryathis, while helping her mother cut out *gommeuse* gowns in the sumptuous wardrobe room resounding with arpeggios, awaited her fourteenth birthday, when she was turned into an apprentice at Paquin's. Was that what appealed to Gabrielle, or was it the dancer's style? – a mixture of classical ballet and Dalcroze's eurhythmic methods.

This extravagant character, whose name remains linked with such strange choreographic concoctions as the dance of the Green Serpentine in Ravel's *Mother Goose* and Eric Satie's *Belle excentrique*, and who, until she parted company with the dance, lived the wildest of existences, was, beginning in 1929 and for forty years thereafter, the wife of Marcel Jouhandeau, introducing into both his work and his life the echo of permanent conjugal discord. (Jouhandeau was a refined, sentimental, risqué, and rather private author. Deeply religious until his marriage with Caryathis – whose real name was Elise Toulemon – Jouhandeau shrank from seeing himself as the homosexual he was.) Thus, the muse of the cafés of Montmartre, the indomitable female at whose side so many and such varied companions had succeeded one another amidst fire and tears, married her way into literary legend.

Elise Jouhandeau remembered perfectly clearly Gabrielle's coming to her studio on the rue Lamarck, which at that time was also accommodating her tumultuous love affair with Charles Dullin, founder of the Vieux Colombier. As both actor and producer he had considerable influence on French theater from 1913 until his death in 1949. Without her testimony we should know nothing of Gabrielle's matutinal appearances on the heights of Montmartre in 1911, or of her choreographic aspirations, or of the subterfuges she resorted to in order to obtain admission to Caryathis' classes. She claimed she had come to keep her best friend company. "A celebrated cocotte," asserted Caryathis. But although Caryathis had done, seen, and said all in the course of her life, she never disclosed the name of that friend of Chanel – who had since "become somebody," she added to explain her reticence.

Gabrielle did not fare much better on the rue Lamarck than she had done in the cellars of the café at Vichy eight years earlier. She was not gifted. But it was not for want of perseverance. Caryathis saw her almost daily. After several months had passed, Gabrielle faced the fact: she should quit.

This was her last attempt.

After that, she continued to attend "Carya's" classes just to keep fit, and sometimes took over from the "beater," making everyone roar with laughter.

How did she remember her first experience of a part of town where people lived with empty pockets, but happy as on a country farm? Montmartre was a word Chanel never pronounced, a place in which she apparently had never set foot. Yet what could have been more exciting, in 1911, than the Butte, a village that welcomed wanderers of every description – painter, poet, or anarchist? A few steps from the studio on the rue Lamarck was the boulevard Clichy where Picasso had just moved, and Van Dongen's studio on the rue Caulaincourt, and the Bâteau Lavoir where Juan Gris lived, and number 12, rue Cortot where Utrillo, Valadon, Reverdy, and the libertarians surrounding the alarming Almereyda dwelled. Almereyda, whose real name was Bonventure Vigo, was Chanel's exact contemporary. Born at Béziers in 1883, he became, as Almereyda, editor-in-chief of *Bonnet Rouge*, the anarchist daily. Arrested in 1917, he died in Fresnes prison, almost certainly assassinated by order of the three ministers, then in office, who were his financial backers. The mystery of his death, occurring as it did in the middle of the war, was never solved.

All the Bohemians knew Caryathis and she knew all of them. But Gabrielle never woke up to their existence, and went sedately back to the heart of the big city in which, unsuspected by her, so many memorable events were about to take place. What did she know of the Châtelet and the series of new productions there? *The Firebird* came in 1910, *Petrushka* in 1911. And Nijinsky in *Specter of the Rose*. The world of the ballet was as foreign to her as Montmartre.

All she cared about were her love affairs, her business, and a missed calling which marked her for life.

As for her choreographic endeavors, her hopes in this field had been shorter-lived and less burning. And yet there is no scarcity of photographs in which we see an aging Chanel trying to execute rather pathetic entrechats in the arms of Serge Lifar. She was still dreaming.

After 1911, however, Gabrielle ceased to neglect the reality at hand: an increasingly fervent clientele who, in their efforts to appropriate everything Chanel invented, encouraged her to enlarge her field of action. Knitted shirts, such as Arthur Capel wore playing polo or on the beach – that is what she would have liked to see her customers wearing. And then, sweaters and blazers. Why did nobody make them except in England?

At that point, the idea did not get beyond the drawing board.

It seemed to her that women were not as ready to accept her innovations as they said they were. There were still too many frills and furbelows *à la* Doucet in the air, too many Turkish notes from Poiret. For the present, it would be best to stick to hats. The time for innovations would come later.

She had a few more illusions to lose before work became her one object in life.

She loved, she was loved. She was twenty-eight. She was beautiful, and what was more important, she was unique. Slender, dark, bursting with vitality, supple beyond words and possessing a disconcerting charm, Gabrielle was already applying to herself what would one day become the secret of everyone's attractiveness-according-to-St Chanel: she looked ten years younger than her age. Her shop? For the moment, it was just a hobby, commissioned by Arthur Capel. Her only reason for caring about it was that she didn't want to disappoint the person in whom she had placed all her hopes: Boy.

That she ardently longed to marry him is also beyond all doubt. Happiness, respectability, the good opinion of society; those, along with a fortune, were what this marriage would have brought her. But it was never even remotely in the cards.

SUNDAYS AT ROYALLIEU

However, there was no condescension in Arthur Capel's feelings for Gabrielle. He abandoned himself to them completely; he took her around, introduced her to his friends as a man who is welcome wherever he goes. Gabrielle's spontaneity and sharp tongue being the qualities he most admired in her, Boy insisted that she take part in conversations. In the first days of their affair, this was agony for her. "What have you got to say?" he would ask. Nothing worth hearing . . . The extent of Gabrielle's ignorance was beyond belief. Once outside the subjects of the records set by a few fashionable man killers and a few thoroughbreds and jockeys, what did she have to say? What was said by the girl friends of the Don Juans of Royallieu? That Liane de Lancy's flame-colored boa was the longest, "La Belle Otéro's" corset the tightest, Louise Balthy's tongue the sharpest, and that Cléo de Mérode was the fairest of the fair . . . Records and more records. The sempiternal chatter of cocottes.

Gabrielle owed her release from the narrow interests of society romance to Arthur Capel. Nobody could erase the damage her past had done to her – and for which she had to suffer on more than one occasion in her life – but at least her circle of friends was no longer limited to demimondaines.

The year of this turning point was 1911, a year of happiness like few others in Gabrielle's life.

Boy introduced her to his favorite sister, Bertha, a very young girl dazzled by her brother. Bertha's one desire was to escape from England and live freely, frankly, and passionately. She responded warmly to Gabrielle, which incited the latter to seek out Bertha's company. A foreigner . . . wasn't that something new to look at? She had no cause to regret it, for Bertha had more than one surprise in store for her.

And it was also Arthur Capel who introduced Gabrielle to the theater – a highly unconventional milieu whose prime quality was not, by any means, moral uprightness, but which nevertheless offered a vastly different range of attractions from Gabrielle's habitual entourage. And then, too, in that world the ability to seduce was not considered to be a woman's only weapon. According to the actresses, talent was actually what counted most. It was all very novel.

The Sundays at Royallieu assumed a new form. Not that one had less fun – the gags followed faster than ever – but Capel and Balsan had now united their groups of friends. Balsan's were still horsemen, one and all, and Capel's were artists; the quality of the group was much the better for the merger.

In the company of artists whose beginnings had in many cases been as arduous as hers, Gabrielle's marginal status went unnoticed. Nobody asked her who she was or where she came from. Released from such pressures, she could at last be herself.

A second Gabrielle made her appearance, a young actress already distinguished by a rare gift of presence: Gabrielle Dorziat, who was born in 1880 and reigned over the Paris stage uninterruptedly from 1908 until recently. She acted at Sarah Bernhardt's theater during the latter's lifetime, in Paul Bourget's plays with Lucien Guitry, in Molière and Giraudoux with Jouvet, and in Cocteau's theater under the author's direction. She made some sixty films between 1922 and 1962, including *Little Boy Lost* with Bing Crosby, in 1952. *Prix de cinéma* for the best French actress in 1949, *Prix "Elle"* for the best-dressed artist both on stage and off, in 1957.

Then, in the person of a soprano, Marthe Davelli, who had just made a brilliant début at the Opéra Comique but who, offstage, lived only for fun and games, the group found its life-of-the-party, and Gabrielle a double. The two women accentuated their resemblance by doing their hair the same way and wearing the same clothes. A friendship grew up between them, the real basis for which was that neither could resign herself to not being the other. Gabrielle would have given the world to be able to sing like Davelli, whereas the other, a slave to the harsh discipline of her art, envied nothing so much as Gabrielle's freedom and sentimental successes. Also among the new recruits at Royallieu was a young, exquisitely romantic creature who might easily have inspired the painters and writers of the nineteenth century. She had done some acting, minor elegant-lady parts – without much talent, it must be admitted – at the Gymnase. She went by the name of Jeanne Léry.

The daughter of a woman of somewhat dubious morals, Jeanne Léry had fallen victim to her own passion. She left Paris to hide her affair with one of her mother's many lovers: Grand Duke Boris.* As he forbade her to remain in the capital, Jeanne abandoned her obvious course together with her career in the theater. Then she gave birth to a boy, whereupon her lover abandoned her. Jeanne Léry then went straight back to Paris, and to her friends in the theater. No one could resist the valiant girl who, having staked all she had on one throw, watched her dream disappear.

---

*   Grand Duke Boris, born May 2, 1879, was the son of Grand Duke Vladimir, brother of Tsar Alexander II, and the first patron of Serge Diaghilev. His mother, Maria Pavlovna, née Duchess of Mecklenburg, was widowed in 1909; she remained Diaghilev's friend and continued seeing him in exile. On her husband's death she became president of the Academy of Fine Arts; she was openly hostile to Rasputin and unsparing in her criticism of the empress' blindness and Nicholas II's shilly-shallying, even advocating his abdication. Maria Pavlovna was one of the few women of value in the last years of the tsarist regime.

She was among the young women visitors to Royallieu who spent their time devising new pranks to amuse Etienne Balsan. For instance, there was that memorable May night when Capel and his friends decided to make an entrance at Etienne's in disguise. But its nature was to be kept a close secret until the last moment.

Responsibility for organizing this event fell to Gabrielle. She improvised a "country wedding."

Here, perhaps, we can grasp the reality of a theme that expressed, at second hand, both what she had been and what she hoped to become. Her "wedding" joined together the garments of the past – peasants in their Sunday best – and the wedding gown that was her secret longing.

Bride, groom, and attendants had been dressed in the department stores. Etienne, more surprised and possibly more deeply touched than he cared to admit, opened the door to a virginal bride in white lawn, her bodice intriguingly garnished with a bouquet of mandarin oranges – that was Jeanne Léry; an old lady in gray twill who proved to be Arthur Capel; a baby in an amazing bonnet – Léon de Laborde; and the two Gabrielles, arm-in-arm.

Gabrielle Dorziat was dressed as a slightly retarded village girl, in socks that were too short and a dress that was too long. Gabrielle Chanel acted as her escort. She was dressed as a shy adolescent, a village Fortunio, the lovelorn swain from Musset's comedy *Le Chandelin*, whose little self-weave jacket worn over a white waistcoat, a freshly starched shirt with turned-down collar, clumsily tied loose cravat, white turned-up trousers, and high button boots had been bought in the junior boys' department at La Samaritaine.

Nothing could have been more fetching than this page girl, and one would do well here to inquire into the nature of her magnetism.

Essentially, it lay in the skill with which Gabrielle had donned a man's costume while carefully accentuating all that was most feminine about her, whence the impression that she was not in disguise, but about to pose for a painter.

Nothing could be more revealing than this rough outline of a process she subsequently perfected: the feminizing of masculine fashion. Then, beyond the costume itself was what it suggested: an ambiguity, a dandyism that belonged to the world of Marivaux and Musset, and perhaps, in the dreamy mournfulness of the model, to that of Watteau. One is again forced, therefore, to posit heredity as the only possible explanation for a grace so very French in character.

But who can tell us what also made that figure so modern? Detached from the page of an album, here is the yellowed photograph that, although dating from an age in which the "style Métro" reigned supreme, had already flung wide the doors to our own era.

Success, fun, conquests, and an impression, sometimes, that life was beginning for her; yes, some chains were being shed, but Gabrielle would have been unable to say what was making her free.

For many a long day she remained the little "dolly" from the Moulins *beuglant* who trusted only women from her own station in life. And it is curious to note that although she chose a cocotte as go-between when she wished to be accepted by a woman of notorious misconduct – Caryathis – it was Jeanne Léry and not Gabrielle Dorziat who became her friend.

It was Jeanne whom Gabrielle asked to approach Gabrielle Dorziat. For what purpose? She wanted to make Dorziat's hats for the play she was rehearsing at the Vaudeville. It was a chance worth taking. Gabrielle Dorziat was playing the lead (Madeleine Forestier) in an adaptation of Maupassant's *Bel Ami*. She was to be dressed by Doucet, the most famous designer of the rue de la Paix. But from whom would she order her hats? Dorziat was persuaded. The hats were signed Chanel. The two straw hats she wore in the play, with wide brims turned up on one side and no plumes or trimmings, set off the celebrated actress' gowns to perfection.

That was Gabrielle's first job in the theater – a widely acclaimed first job. A new era in fashion was dawning, and its simplicity portended the death of the opulence of the "Belle Epoque."

DEAUVILLE, OR THE PARTY WAS A WASH-OUT

The spring of 1913 had been chaotic.

In May there had been the earthquake of *Le Sacre du Printemps*, from which people were still recovering. Several persons had felt themselves directly implicated by the composer Florent Schmitt's apostrophe: "Silence, sluts of the sixteenth!"*

People in the audience marveled to see the powerful Madame Muhlfeld, in whose drawing room congregated everybody who was anybody among critics, unmoved by the insult and continuing to set the tone for the rest of high society by uttering loud peals of laughter.

---

* The sixteenth arrondissement of Paris is, *par excellence*, the district of conservative bourgeois and wealthy families.

"To go to *Le Sacre*" nevertheless became everyone's top priority project in the ensuing weeks – a craze that could be explained by the allure of a new theater, the Champs-Elysées, of the choreographer, who was none other than Nijinsky, and finally, of his assistant, a disciple of Jacques Dalcroze: Marie Rambert. Was this to be the official consecration of the "earthy" school? It seemed likely. Diaghilev himself had just come back from a pilgrimage to Dresden.

On that first night all the stars in the Paris social firmament had gone to the theater hoping to see the Russians performing a sort of elegant gymnastics in ballet form, composed largely of graceful poses and timid improvisations. It was an illusion cruelly shattered by the black mass that exploded on the stage.

One flabbergasted provincial was there too to witness this tumult: Gabrielle Chanel. She owed the privilege to Caryathis, who was herself the guest of von Reklinghausen, her rich German lover, and was sharing her good fortune with Charles Dullin, his French – but poor – counterpart. It had thus been necessary to invite Gabrielle, to appease Dullin's sensitivity: he could not bear the idea of a *ménage à trois*.

The chance meeting between Dullin and Chanel was to bear fruit in later years.

Imagine Gabrielle's stupefaction at the scene that night. What were the little rows of a provincial music hall compared to the paroxysms of the capital? She could never have imagined the wealthy clients of Messieurs Doucet and Poiret, silk-packaged, swathed in turbans and aigrettes, becoming involved in such a spectacle.

But fashion too was at a turning point. People were hesitating.

One or two young beauties, by abandoning the "style Scheherazade," had already heralded the decline of both the turban and the house of Poiret. Judging by *Comoedia*, the comb ("complement of soft waves") was now the rage: "At these sumptuous gala occasions, the performances of the Ballets Russes, Mlle Gabrielle Dorziat, who is in some degree the modern Petronius of our feminine elegance, was one of the first to join in this renovation. Now one sees nothing but heads becomingly dressed with blond or brindle tortoise-shell." All in white, a huge ostrich boa falling from her shoulders, Dorziat, crony from the Royallieu gallops, sat enthroned in the stalls with a cascade of hair frothing at the back of her head. She had become a star.

And how could one describe Caryathis' hair? A short time before, she had cut off her thick tresses in a fit of pique, tied a ribbon round them, and left them hanging from a nail in the home of a man whose ardor she had failed to arouse. Consequently she came as Joan of Arc, with a fringe across her forehead. The sight offended spectators' eyes almost as much as the turned-in feet, crude postures, and collective hysteria of Diaghilev's Russians responding to the barbarous dissonances of Stravinsky's score.

There is no doubt that this theatrical evening gave Gabrielle the idea of cutting off her hair too, but she did so only three years later, after long and careful deliberation. Back around 1925, when she was rightly being hailed as the woman responsible for this revolution, she appropriated the reaction of the Parisian public to Caryathis' entrance that evening at *Le Sacre* to embellish her own tale. She invented a little news item which she often repeated in later days and which has been faithfully transcribed by the pens of innumerable journalists: the exploding gas ring that set fire to her hair just as she was about to leave for a gala performance, then the quick scissorwork to hide the damage, the sacrifice of her long locks, and the invention of the coiffure which was to become hers and that of all her contemporaries. There followed her entrance at the Opéra, where her appearance created a sensation among the first-night public. Let us believe the sensation. But of the rest, not a word. Rather than an accident, we should imagine a deliberate act, a calculated decision worthy of the cool-headed businesswoman she had, in the meantime, become.

For Gabrielle, that evening with Caryathis marked the beginning of a certain knowledge of Paris. Was it to deepen? Unfortunately the summer did not look promising. The press was filled with echoes of an increasingly widespread idea, that of some inevitable conflict.

Scornfully irrational, Parisian high society, infinitely more troubled by rumors of a state-imposed income tax than by any threat of war, behaved like an ostrich in the desert: it went to Deauville and buried itself in the sand. And Gabrielle went with it. There was nothing novel in this state of mind, the country had acquired the habit: this was the second time in less than forty years that people had gone to Deauville to avoid facing perils which always seemed more threatening in summer.

Back in 1870, the duc de Gramont, then minister for foreign affairs, had had to mount the speaker's platform in the House on July 15 to read France's declaration of war upon Germany, and so was of necessity "stuck in Paris." According to his granddaughter's memoirs, "the fashionable world was at Deauville." We see the full horror of her worthy ancestor's predicament. There was the war, yes. But, equally afflicting, there was the fact that the duc de Gramont would be deprived of his August at Deauville that summer.

In 1913, gone was the Empire in France, and gone was the eagle on the escutcheon, but nothing in the Normandy summering habits, and nothing in people's minds, had altered. At Deauville the Second Empire absurdity danced on. Enormous hotels, on whose facades the rustic Norman half-timbering had been combined with all manner of contemporary refinements, and splendid villas striving to look like cottage, castle, and Swiss chalet at once continued to attract their contingents of purest Parisian frivolity. The holiday spirit authorized certain liberties, but they had to be exercised with discretion, and only at times and places in which one was certain to encounter nobody who was not of one's own world. For side by side with the "fashionable" people were the *irrégulières* and theater women – those women one must be careful never to address – capering about more freely and hence more dangerously than in Paris.

For the morning walk, only the pier was permissible. The fashion for bathing had not really caught on. A few pioneers – Chanel among them – ventured forth. One observed their movements through a lorgnette, disapprovingly. The sea was there to be looked at, not bathed in. One left the beach to maids, nannies, and children, with permission to build sand castles.

Certain fashion trends began to be discernible, but how timidly! "Something is happening to the Faubourg" was the dowagers' alarmed comment, referring to the comtesse de Chabrillan, who had just displayed her rebelliousness in three spectacular acts: she had had her jewels reset and her town house redecorated, to the shocked dismay of her mother, madame de Lévis-Mirepoix, and she had begun to wear silk stockings.

The appearance, one windy day, of two English girls in berets had provoked divers reactions. "A kind of headgear which gives the wearer a casual and countrified air, an art-student quality," noted the local columnist in her weekly report, while the rival daily judged it an eccentricity best left to the "misses." The debate was considered trivial in any event by the aristocrats' wives and summering Parisians who would not have been seen dead out of doors on a windy day and performed their *footing* solely within the precincts of their own gardens, and who were, in any case, protected from this sort of aberration by their way of life.

They spent long afternoons visiting neighboring residences, taking tea at the polo club, making stunning appearances at the races, which they attended in white lawn – those gowns, satin-stitch embroidered and worked with Valenciennes lace inserts, which were a lady's maid's nightmare. Elegance also required pointed slippers with four straps over the instep, which could be fastened only with the greatest difficulty and the aid of a buttonhook; a triple row of pearls cascading over the bodice; a parasol in the hand; and the transportation, on hats of Brussels lace, of everything in the way of ostrich plumes and chiffon roses that was needed to maintain their standing.

That was the fashion in 1913, when Gabrielle Chanel, encouraged and financed by Arthur Capel, opened a shop on the rue Gontaut Biron, the nerve center of Deauville, the quintessence of a smart street, where tango dancers, fashion setters, and horsemen forgathered, and which still separates the Normandy, superluxury hotel, from the Casino, where stakes run high. Gabrielle hired two husky girls, red-cheeked country wenches hardly sixteen years old, who only just knew how to sew. Never mind, it was enough to begin with. Then, because her shop was on the right side of the street – the sunny side – she added a wide white awning on which her name stood out in black, for the first time.

One can imagine the effect she produced, bustling around town in a tailor-made of masculine cut and comfortable shoes with rounded toes – as disconcerting on foot as on horseback, having given up none of the idiosyncrasies that the arbiters of elegance had so earnestly exhorted her to forswear. She showed herself at the polo club in an open-necked shirt and a most peculiar hat, a sort of flattened melon or panama of her own devising. And then finally, to top it all off, she was openly flaunting one love affair but not dismissing the coterie of admirers that continually surrounded her. Léon de Laborde, Miguel de Yturbe, and even Etienne Balsan spelled one another as her escorts whenever business kept Arthur Capel away from Deauville.

Her friendships were no longer confined to the young men of Royallieu, however. Everything in Deauville conspired in her favor, the success of her shop no less than her association with a polo player whose match had seldom been seen in the Normandy plains.

Boy was something of a star. He conducted his business like a man in a hurry, unencumbered by the sacrosanct principles of bourgeois prudence. There was no one he had to humor, no feelings he had to spare among sensitive members of a family board of directors. Being his own master, he followed his own nose. And instinctively, Arthur Capel's nose led him to the hottest points. His coal-shipping fleet was growing steadily.

Even though a series of incidents had taken place in Morocco, provoking violent collisions between the chancelleries of Paris and Berlin, Boy had his eye on that apple of discord, that "wasps' nest" as Jaurès put it. Anyone else would have hesitated. Not Boy. France's colonial conquests, he had a presentiment, were going to open up new markets for him.

Before Lyautey's troops had been in Fez a year, Boy Capel was already investing in Casablanca and talking about turning it into the port for English coal imports to the whole of North Africa.

Bankers of various nationalities, barons both Erlanger and Rothschild, statesmen and politicians, financiers whose activities no one could define, journalists on the look-out for scandals (which were increasing along with the influence of industrial circles), press magnates – Edwards, Hebrard, and Bailby – high-society couples, international beauties followed by husbands whose morals were as questionable as their quarterings (such as the disturbing Olga de Meyer, who was said to be a daughter of the king of England, and her recently created baron of a husband, who was a pioneer fashion photographer): henceforth it was among these that Arthur Capel was piloting his craft.

He carried Gabrielle along in his wake.

The first houses whose thresholds they crossed together were English. Summering lords – less circumspect than their French fellows – showed little concern for the lineage of the pretty person Boy Chapel was in love with. The fact alone was enough, in their view, for the two to be received together.

Gabrielle never forgot that.

The vehement sympathy she displayed throughout her life for all things British, her conviction of England's superiority in every respect, had no other cause or origin.

As a couple, Arthur Capel and Gabrielle also caught the fancy of Sem.

The famous caricaturist had changed hunting grounds more than three years earlier. Paris had formerly been his favorite spot, and more particularly the allée des Acacias where he posted himself every morning at ten with his friend Boldini. Sem always dressed in the latest fashion, suits with short jackets in bold checked tweed. He was built like a jockey and always impeccably turned out in public, while Boldini was as broad as he was high, with an enormous head on which a minute hat perched uneasily. The two companions on the prowl were not inconspicuous, to say the least. In the evenings, their base camp was Maxim's. But those days were over for Sem; his irony was now venting itself upon Deauville.

The pitiless penciler, so dreaded by people seeking to avoid this form of celebrity while there were others who would gladly have paid him to notice them, portrayed the handsome Boy as a centaur wearing a polo cap and abducting at full gallop a woman recognizable among thousands: Gabrielle. On the end of a mallet brandished like a lance swayed a feathered toque. The allusion was clear, but to make it more so, and to ensure that everyone should know that the centaur might be the lover but that he was the backer as well, Boy was holding, in addition to his prey, a hatbox on which was written the single word "Coco." That was more than enough to remove any lingering doubts in the minds of the "Tout-Deauville." It also provided unprecedented promotion: Gabrielle was beginning to *be something* in the eyes of the world. Adding to this the fact that Sem himself began to display a tenacious affection for her – the little man with the marmoset face, the mischievous eyes, and the boater raked over one ear was often seen at her side – and that, at the other extreme, she maintained infrequent but friendly relations with a creature as intransigent and explosively gifted as Charles Dullin, one is forced to admit that the milliner from the rue Gontaut Biron had a most singular circle of acquaintances.

Boy was often away. His business required it. And she: absorbed as she was by her success, which was sometimes more than she could cope with – the shop was continually full of customers and she had had to enlist her sister Antoinette again – did Gabrielle realize what was going on in Paris? There, other conquests were being attributed to Boy, other affairs, with foreigners, real ladies with fine names, a breakneck parade of liaisons. Could Gabrielle believe that professional obligations alone kept him away so much of the time?

She had no inkling of what was to come, and if the gossip had reached her ears she would have been inclined to discount it. Every time he turned up, after all, Capel was as devoted as before. Yet she had lost. But she didn't know it: too many things, some happy and mad, others sad, conspired to keep her from guessing.

There had been the death of her older sister, Julia the hapless, who left a son. The fate of this nephew whom Gabrielle had never known, consigned as he was to solitude in the depths of the country, was sobering enough to touch Capel as well as Gabrielle. They assumed responsibility for the orphan and sent him to the English boarding school at Beaumont that Boy himself had attended. Without their help what would he have become? In all probability a Hospice child, like Julien and Alphonse Chanel. Only young Bertha Capel, her head always awhirl with wild ideas, refused to believe the child was not Gabrielle's. Some years later, by dint of intimation and veiled allusion, she gave rise to an enduring myth: he was Boy's son, or Chanel's false nephew.

Then there had been Adrienne's arrival, lovelier and more in love than ever. She came to the shop, borrowed hats, bought other hats, wore a different one every day, and caused so much comment as she went about the town that Gabrielle's clientele doubled. Thereupon Chanel, who had just unwittingly discovered the utility of the live model, pressed Antoinette into service as well. Arm-in-arm the two elegant women were sent off to the pier at the smart hour. They returned triumphant: every eye had been fixed upon them. Then, retreating to the back room of the shop, the room they called "the confessional," the three pupils of the canonesses of St Augustine, united at last, treated themselves to a giggle of complicity. Back in the days of Varennes or Moulins, who could have predicted the turn their lives were to take? Sometimes, at the day's end, Maud Mazuel would join them there, for she still appeared at Adrienne's side, although now in a different role. She was no longer the chaperone giving Adrienne the advantage of her connections. Now the tables were turned: Maud had become the friend whom Adrienne, invested with a firm fiancé of unwaveringly honorable intentions, carried in tow. They were hoping, with the help of a trip or two, to turn up a husband for dear old Maud.

The one least sure of the future was still Gabrielle. She had thought life with Capel would be different, but she was beginning to see that in many respects he remained a prisoner of his circle and his ambitions, and this was all the harder to understand because in so many fields he was strikingly open-minded.

The reason for it was that Boy, too, had an account to settle with society. The secret wound of his unknown paternity nagged at him. France was becoming increasingly anti-Semitic and chauvinist, and showing it with unprecedented violence; and the enemies of many a prominent person had tried to bring about their victim's downfall by discovering, among other flaws, that of dubious origins. Arthur Capel's conviction – so surprising in a man of his stamp – his certainty that in order to outwit his tenacious foes and get the upper hand of them at last, he must ally himself with some great name, can only be explained by the political and social climate of the day.

This was not the only change in Boy's character. He was acquiring an incomprehensible lust for power. Was it social climbing? He was being seen in strange company. What, for example, could he be doing with Clemenceau? The former premier was not a man to be so easily seduced. So? How to explain his interest in Chanel's lover?

Here was something the clubmen did not like at all.

In those days, as far as the conservatives were concerned, Clemenceau was just a dubious and foul-mouthed individual. Hadn't he turned his newspaper into a sort of war machine, firing off red cannonballs at the respectable Monsieur Poincaré? What was he up to? Did the chief of state need his permission to make an official visit to St Petersburg? In the eyes of traditional society, which believed only in convention, Clemenceau had every possible drawback, the worst of all being that he believed in neither the strength of the tsar nor the sovereignty of the pope. Doubt the tsar, doubt the pope? And it was a man like that whom Arthur Capel was frequenting, a nonbeliever in sloppy clothes who had dared to expel the apostolic nuncio.

Clemenceau's hat, which he wore shoved over one ear, his gloves of a kind seen only on dressed-up farmers and house servants, aroused the sarcasm of all right-minded people. Barrès, who was a *gentleman*, at least, was quite right when he wrote that "Clemenceau is one of these coachmen of whom we are seeing all too many . . ." That hit the nail on the head: a coachman. The handsome Boy had taken a fancy to a man who never took off his gloves, not even in a drawing room, a peasant who ate his breakfast in dreadful slippers and a checkered cap, and who, thus attired, concocted some frightful brew, a thick soup reeking of onions. Was that a friendship worthy of a young shipbuilder, a prince of industry? And why should one put up with behavior from Clemenceau that in anyone else would have been judged a moral offense? Could one forget that in reply to a shepherd from the Var who called him a spy and traitor and accused him of selling out to Great Britain, Clemenceau had found nothing funnier to do than open his trousers? Then, adding obscenity to vulgarity, he had exclaimed, "I can't help it, my friend, the Queen of England is mad about this little toy. She won't have any other." Was that to be countenanced? And it was Arthur Capel, an Englishman and Roman Catholic to boot, who saw wit in this lout? There was something almost obscene in it, something nobody could explain.

The only effect of these misgivings about Arthur Capel was to confirm his idea. Like Clemenceau, and perhaps because of him, he no longer believed that peace could be saved. The terrible deadline was approaching, and it showed plainly what might be done with Newcastle coal, Boy's fleet, and his knowledge of the world of business. Coal would be the key to everything, no? Therefore, trying to render himself invulnerable, his thoughts turned more than ever to the idea of settling down.

He wanted Gabrielle to be his sole confidante. He always came back to her. Perhaps it would have been wiser to see this as a sign that he loved her alone; but he did nothing of the sort, and the truth did not become plain to him until after he had made his mistake . . . until after he was married.

As for Gabrielle, her illusions were shattered; he would not marry her. The great love she had dreamed of looked doomed. Make a break? Lose Boy? Not possible. So all she could do was tolerate the intolerable, resign herself to an imperfect love and accept another marginal place, the only place she had ever known.

After 1913 Chanel hoped no more. She had never looked in better spirits, but jealousy was gnawing within. She did not let it show, although the first signs appeared then of the bitterness that was ultimately to engulf her.

Thereafter her revenge took the form of making independence her sole aim in life. She wanted to be free. Free from everything, from society, men, love – an aspiration that was to give a new direction to her life, for to satisfy it she had only her work. From then on, that was the only real thing, the only source of satisfaction. She approached it grimly, with all the super-abundant energy left unconsumed by her failure to gain happiness.

The strange thing is that in a society in which achievement and work were the least esteemed of all virtues, she had succeeded in finding, if not happiness, at least a man who shared her predilection for them. Perhaps it was this that bound them together at the deepest level. Whatever obstacles they faced – first the war, then Boy's marriage – they never abandoned each other, nor did they ever abandon their efforts to found the Chanel empire, together.

A beautiful month, that June of 1914. The Deauville season had never looked more promising. A record crowd for the period. English, children, sportsmen, everybody was there and all the villas were opened up and occupied by armies of domestics making sure that gardens, kitchens; and drawing rooms were all in good order, when a shot was fired in Bosnia-Herzegovina and its echo traveled all the way to Paris.

But not to Deauville, where it made no more noise than a dud firecracker.

Gabrielle Chanel had recently added some illustrious names to her clientele. Her success left her no respite. She owed it to a Rothschild who, as the victim of an unprecedented affront, had sworn to destroy Paul Poiret, thereby increasing her readiness to launch Chanel. Poiret had dared to order her out of his rooms, and in the presence of a crowd of customers.

On the whole, the fury of the sultan of *haute couture* seemed fully justified.

This Rothschild was said to be mad for fine clothes and male admirers. No one, it is true, bought more than she did and no one claimed a longer list of lovers. And the young men continued to frequent her home long after being ousted from her bed, thus providing her with a sort of permanent escort. On the pretext of a sudden illness, she had requested Poiret, whose best client she was, to send his collection to her at home and insisted that it be shown her by his most attractive models; she then proceeded to have them parade past her in circumstances which they judged unacceptable. The baroness, her hair hanging loose, in an orange "tea gown" with multiple ruchings, reclined on a chaise longue in the center of a ring of ribald gigolos who paid no attention to the gowns but a great deal to the mannequins modeling them. Poiret, seeing his young ladies return as rampaging furies, swore revenge.

Gabrielle Chanel was the beneficiary of this exemplary vengeance.

Banned from Poiret's, the baroness hastened to Chanel, accompanied by her most exalted friends, the owners of boxes at the races – the very same whom Gabrielle had been forever running away from in her Balsan period: the comtesse de Pracomtal, the princesse de Faucigny-Lucinge . . . One young St Sauveur, who was considered a good match, no longer bought her hats anywhere else. From "pretty enough," she grew to be extremely beautiful. A few years later Léon de Laborde, the habitué of the Sundays at Royallieu and Gabrielle's accomplice and most fervent admirer, suddenly lost his head over this person he had never looked at before, and married her. A decision which must have prompted bitter reflections in Chanel's mind. Her position was ungratifying enough. Was she sorry, that day, that she had made such good use of her bag of tricks?

At last, the baronne de Rothschild brought round the inevitable Cécile Sorel, who, no longer content with having the opulence of her toilettes applauded on stage, had begun to entertain so lavishly that Rolls Royces, Panhards, and Levassors were causing traffic jams outside her residence on the Quai Voltaire. This meeting was not insignificant, because although the luminaries of high society looked upon Gabrielle as merely a young milliner of talent, Sorel, more perceptive, recognized her as a true personality. She ordered some hats and made Gabrielle promise to call on her in Paris.

Came the month of July, and days of leaden heat. Gabrielle decided that the time was ripe for innovations. It was not impossible, with the help of a sweltering summer over which so many dangers loomed, that women would consent to wear loose, casual clothing. Chanel put into action a plan she had long nursed in her head. She ordered lengths of two textiles characteristic of the British locker room: the knit of sweaters and the flannel of blazers. Both were, of course, borrowed from Boy. She often repeated such raids in later years, poking about in her lovers' cupboards for new ideas.

In this way her first original was born, reminiscent in form of the sailor blouse and in fabric of the jockey's pullover. The line was loose, requiring no corset. It did not call attention to the curves of hips or breasts. The body was merely suggested.

A fashion whose sole object was *not* to accentuate the female charms – sometimes to the point of caricature – was in direct opposition to the style of the day. Gabrielle took her chance. She was convinced that by respecting the natural she would subtract nothing from the feminine: on the contrary. She was right. The response she received proved it.

This was her first success as a dress designer. But almost immediately afterward came the mobilization. War? Nobody at Deauville believed in it. Nevertheless, the end had come for a certain type of easy life. The compulsory display of riches, amusement given the status of a sacred duty by the "haves," and the manners and fashions of French high society, were all about to go under. In reality, it was the beginning of the death agony of the apparently indestructible nineteenth century, fourteen years late. But nobody in Deauville troubled himself about that, either.

The French nobility went off to its rendezvous with death the way they might have rushed to meet a mistress neglected too long. War, if that was what was coming, had a meaning. No one was unaware of it. When the pre-1870 frontier was restored the nation would regain its two lost provinces. War? It was coming. Could anyone still doubt it? The enemy armies were on the march.

In a few hours brothers, husbands, and servants were gone. "A fraternal handshake for all, no tears, no kisses."[5] The ladies fell back limp upon their chintz-covered sofas while their German chambermaids, in fits of anguish and with cries of "Jésus, Maria!" on their lips, retching and hiccuping, hastily removed from their garret walls the lithographs glorifying a Kaiser who, with fixed eyes and clenched jaw, had already become a slave to his role.

A second shot was fired on August 4 and its reverberations also were unheard, but this time they were drowned in the noise of departures. Jaurès had been assassinated. The voice of the bearded man in the bowler who had cried out to the French, "Do we want to be a nation of war or a nation of peace?" was stilled while crowds of young men were pouring into the Gare de l'Est singing, *"Vive la tombe! La mort n'est rien"* ("Long live the tomb! Death is nothing").

Thus, war emptied Deauville once again.

The family villas standing proudly at attention on the horizon looked down upon spaces increasingly invaded by emptiness and silence. No more light gowns or parasols *à la Potinière* and no more nannies on the beach. The shops had lost their holiday air. The Royal was closing and the Normandy, by staying open, seemed out of place and time.

With the exception of Mrs Moore,* a tenacious American resolved not to abandon the theater of her most brilliant campaigns, the foreigners had left. Then all automobiles were requisitioned, the price of gasoline went up, and horses came back into their own. At that point, the holidays seemed so patently compromised that even Mrs Moore gave up. But where was one to go next? Biarritz? She had a very clear memory of the place, for it was there she had cunningly contrived to be presented to the king of England. Edward VII's chauffeur was bribed and faked engine trouble, so that Mrs Moore, happening by, might humbly offer His Majesty the services of her own vehicle. Charming . . . the king had deigned to accept. But what was the Basque coast like now? They said people at Biarritz still believed in the ritual of dining out. So Mrs Moore went back; a large number of foreigners living in France did too – a migration the consequences of which Gabrielle Chanel might meditate upon at her leisure, as she listened to the long sigh of the Channel surf.

For she wasn't budging.

Boy, mobilized in due course, had advised her: "Wait. Don't close. We'll see." She obeyed. She waited on the beach that seemed abruptly cut off, she couldn't tell why, from the huge world now beginning to throb with the rising mutter of conflict.

Among the foreigners leaving Deauville, there was one who was Russian in nationality and Polish in name. Too impecunious to pay for his holiday himself, he had relied on journalism to treat him to one. *Comoedia* had assigned him to cover the seaside festivities at the "queen of beaches." Arriving at Deauville on July 26, he was taken by surprise by the news of the mobilization while observing the habitués of the Grand Casino around the baize-topped table. Inside the huge receptacle, all high windows and electric pallor, half the musicians scurried off the stand within seconds, the crowds at the tables thinned, and the uncertain notes of a last tango displayed a strange unwillingness to die.

Comoedia's special correspondent was called Wilhelm de Kostrowitsky. He might have called himself Flugi d'Aspermont like the Italian who had

---

* Kate Moore was an old lady whose character as an American snob was almost unique in Parisian annals. She managed to inveigle her way into the most exclusive circles through sheer weeping and lamentation. Commenting on her death in 1917, Paul Morand observed that she disappeared "just when the Americans were finally about to have a position in Europe!" Proust's remark in *Le Temps retrouvé*, "For the American woman, dinners and social events were a sort of Berlitz School," defines her perfectly.

fathered him, if that gentleman had recognized him, which was not the case. So it was as Guillaume Apollinaire that this particular foreigner became first a French gunner and then a French casualty.

He entitled his story *La Fête manquée* ("The Party Was a Wash-Out") and in it he recounted, in bitter-sweet terms, Deauville's farewell to the good old days.

The story possesses a unique reality: here is the opulence of fashionable summering, as told by Apollinaire with all his love of mystification and the fantastic. As, for instance, when the free-lance journalist reports that on the morning of July 31, 1914, he saw "a wondrous Negro in a cymar of changing hues . . ." pedaling through the streets of Deauville on a bicycle; then, coming to the sea, he proceeded to ride into it, his green turban slowly dwindling to a speck on the surface of the water. But apart from such flights Apollinaire was a conscientious reporter. He missed nothing, neither Mrs Moore encrusted in her snobbery nor the boomerang-shaped nose of Monsieur Henri Letellier. He observes, he notes: "Few tangers for the tango." He confesses: "We do not believe in the war." He sees everything, the panic of the German servants and the emptiness of the streets. We read: "The rue Gontaut Biron presented, every day between noon and one o'clock, the bleak aspect of a thoroughfare in Pompeii . . ." And the poet left too. "An automobile carried him off, making an enormous impression on the increasingly sparse population."

Those were the days when his cubist friends were littering their canvases with letters and scraps of newspapers while Apollinaire, guilty of similar experimentation in the field of poetry – the introduction of blocks of illustrations set into pages of type, and the first picture poems – was being relieved of his position as art critic for *L'Intransigeant*. "You have obstinately persisted in defending only one school, the most advanced, with a partiality and exclusiveness inappropriate to our independent newspaper," the director wrote him in the letter of dismissal.[6]

His return trip, that night in 1914, inspired a poem that he wrote in the shape of a little motorcar: "I shall never forget that nocturnal voyage when none of us spoke a word . . ." He was going to Paris. Abandoning Deauville, the Pompeii in which, in the rue Gontaut Biron, Gabrielle Chanel remained, clinging to her shop like a shipwrecked man to his buoy.

V

The Foundations of an Empire 1914–1919

"We were of that generation which, at eighteen, when spring came in the year 1915 and it was understood that the men would not be dug out of their trenches for a long while yet, of that generation which had the extraordinary good fortune, for the first time since, since, I don't know, since people were eighteen in France-times-fifty, to see a woman's ankles in the street."

— LOUIS ARAGON, *Henri Matisse*

AN ODOR OF GANGRENE

Gabrielle's days were passing ever more emptily when, on August 23, 1914, at the price of the battle of Charleroi, Boy's advice – "Wait!" – became acutely relevant.

Deauville was filling up again.

On the twenty-seventh, German troops entered St Quentin; on the twenty-eighth, a dramatic communiqué, "From the Somme to the Vosges . . ." revealed the extent of the invasion. At Deauville the Royal was hastily reopened for use as a hospital, while into the family villas and neighborhood estates poured, not the common people, but the lords of the manor from the Meuse, the Ardennes, the Aisne, all those who, seeing their stately homes occupied or threatened, were fleeing to their summer residences.

"We shall show you what kind of barbarians we are, all right," was the proclamation von Kluck had just hurled at the population. Then, because the finest châteaux of France were going down like ninepins – the comte d'Hinnisdal's Tilleloy, a fifteenth-century gem, burned; the marquis d'Aramon's Anizay destroyed; the princesse de Poix's Pinon razed to the ground – Deauville became the aristocratic town of the "rear."

Ladies arrived "having lost everything," they said. And it was true. Except the money to buy a new wardrobe. They went to the only shop in town that was open: Chanel's.

In return, she offered them what she was wearing herself. A straight skirt just off the ground, showing only a glimpse of the foot, a sailor blouse, a shirt, boot-heeled shoes, a hat barren of decoration, nothing but a plain straw shape: that was her wartime attire. It was right for moving about on foot, for walking fast, for going places without problems, which is all anybody needed. The Chanel look became the look of the day.

Then came the first casualties: men with greenish skin lying on the straw of train carriages. The road from Deauville to Charleroi was long. Visions of horror . . . the Royal began to smell of gangrene.

Since it wasn't the season for distributing mulled wine in train stations, the ladies offered their services to the physician in charge, who accepted them. But their ardor had to be cooled. They rushed about, they talked too much. They were ordered to dress in white. Where to find blouses, aprons, caps? The hotel linen cupboards afforded only leftover chambermaids' outfits, wide gathered sleeves and long-pocketed aprons like those worn by the waitresses in the Bouillon Duvals, a chain of inexpensive restaurants whose peculiarity lay in the fact, very rare at the time, that the serving was all done by women. These stocks were promptly handed out by the doctor. That same evening, after a great hustle and bustle of ineffectually manipulated pins and vain tryings-on and hopeless exchanges between one and another of the ladies, after fits of anguish weirdly reminiscent of those they had experienced on costume-ball nights, they had nowhere to turn but to Chanel.

Gone were the days when Elisabeth Greffulhe would order a nurse's outfit in Cluny lace from Worth to assist during her daughter's confinement. Nevertheless, when they asked Chanel to alter the hotel blouses to fit them, the volunteers also begged her to try to give them some little note of elegance. Gabrielle consented: she would "make something" of these uniforms.

First of all, get rid of those chambermaids' lace caps, an accessory far too symbolic of the job of those for whom it had been intended; yes, *that* must be replaced. With what, asked the nurses-to-be? With something neat and dignified. The rest, she said, would take care of itself.

She was a good milliner, the ladies knew that. They trusted her.

The results surpassed their wildest hopes.

But her new clients were gravely mistaken if they thought the miracle had been wrought by a Parisian designer. It owed far more to the child of Aubazine and Sundays at Aunt Julia's.

Help was needed. Antoinette raced off to fetch Adrienne, and came back empty-handed. Adrienne couldn't bear the thought of stirring. She was in agonies. With no news from her "adored," she had become a weeping statue. Antoinette had found her prostrated, leaning upon her faithful followers: Maud Mazuel and the former prima ballerina of the Théâtre de la Monnaie, the eternal fiancée of the comte d'Espous. Fuming, Gabrielle issued an ultimatum: the fate of Adrienne's "adored" was that of every "adored" in France; and army postal services left much to be desired, she added, more peremptory than consoling. Besides, there was nothing like work to take your mind off your troubles. Adrienne gave in. They sewed all night.

It was the old Moulins guild, reborn in the wispy steam of irons, the smell of hot metal and starch sticking to the fingers. Fingers flying. Few words. Everyone working until she dropped. It was starting all over again. Virtually monastic headbands flew from hand to hand and, while the long scarlet legs of the cavalry made war, the Chanel girls sewed once more.

This, these hastily produced nurses' uniforms, represented Gabrielle's sole contribution to the national effort. She was never seen among the wounded at the Royal, she was never a nurse. Later, the warriors – at least those who escaped – expressed their surprise. Balsan in particular: "We didn't see much of you, Coco." Why hadn't she been a nurse, too? "Not my cup of tea," she replied. And never a visit, not even when "going to the front" became almost a fashion among lovers, married or not. "Not my department," said Gabrielle.

She had an answer for everything. But she never disclosed the deeper reason for this refusal.

The truth was that she would pay any price to get away from her past, and the only way to do it was to avoid those who had witnessed it: the military.

In the first days of September, the front was sagging everywhere, people weren't saying "the Germans" anymore, but "the Huns," and the government of France had moved to Bordeaux. Deauville received a second wave of refugees: more gentry, mostly from Seine-et-Oise. Gabrielle knew this lot, she had glimpsed them from afar – handsome huntsmen in white stocks and ladies in sidesaddle habits and tricornes – in the days of her anonymity at Balsan's.

But her budding renown meant that they now looked upon her as "knowable." Besides, it was wartime. And these ladies also needed to replenish their wardrobes. So, she was acknowledged. A few cool words were exchanged. Gabrielle learned that Etienne's estate had been occupied by German staff officers. How that hurt! Soldiers and military clutter in the house that had welcomed her, in the garden which for a time she had thought the fairest in the land; Royallieu disfigured, invaded, was another facet of the general wreckage.

Outside events had the most unforeseeable effects on Chanel's professional life. In one way, they served her. And she had perforce to realize that what was stripping others of their past, was helping to forge her future. A curious fate, in which the enemy's every step closer to Paris was a step toward freedom for her.

When the German forces were within twenty miles of the capital, Gallieni ringed the city with barbed wire, called up forty thousand civilians, and set them to work digging trenches. The theaters were all posted as "closed." Actors, actresses, authors, and critics left town. Deauville was overrun with them.

They were the last to come.

There weren't enough rooms for everyone. But, "except for gaiety, the lobby of the Normandy had resumed its customary aspect."

Gabrielle had nowhere to seat her clients so she moved tables and chairs onto the sidewalk and the ladies sat and chatted outside the door, in the shade of her broad white awning. Idleness. Anxious gossip. Contradictory rumors. "The mayor of Deauville was hard pressed to curb defeatist talk and ordered people to keep silent."[1]

The newcomers intimated that something was being planned on the French side. Was it likely? Everybody knew that Gallieni's forces were dropping where they stood. The French, still reeling from the battle of Charleroi, had been joined by the exhausted units of Sir John French. Then began a period of feverish suspense for Gabrielle. At last she understood what Adrienne was going through. Because one of the liaison officers on Sir John French's staff was Lieutenant Arthur Capel.

What happened on September 6 was unexpected enough: herds of cattle came plodding into Deauville. They filled the racecourse under the watchful eyes of their guards, improvised cowherds neither young nor old and, judging by their clothes, neither civilian nor military. They were in fact a detachment of the territorial army, sent out from Paris to keep the beef reserves grazing.

Since the beginning of the war, no common man's voice had been heard in Deauville. Now, into this setting so opulent as to be almost unreal, came sounds of the speech, full of banter, sometimes resigned and expressing a millennial patience, of street dwellers and tillers of the soil, hansom cab drivers and carters, all manner of representatives of a solid, seemingly infallible mankind. They had witnessed the transformation of the capital: shops shut, civilians drilling on the esplanades, newspapers reduced to a single page and their copy restricted to the official communiqué, taxis and automobiles requisitioned. They were assailed with questions. Through them, people heard the tale of the war. They went to listen to them on the grass, like Arab storytellers.

Thus the queen of the beaches, the essence of frivolity, became aware of what lay in store for it: Joffre with his fagged-out "poilus" and "tommies" was about to take the offensive. The commander-in-chief did not mince words. His order came: "Stand and be killed rather than retreat." The anguished anticipation of the long-skirted ladies redoubled. Then, loaded with reinforcements, lurching down the road to the front, the taxis of Paris drove off into legend. The Marne: Paris was saved.

The cattle and their guards went away. They left a void. People missed them. But the soldiers had to be fed. And so Deauville was restored to the privileged.

Then the highest-born ladies dared what they could never have conceived of doing two months before: they went bathing.

Gabrielle Chanel devised extremely chaste bathing costumes for them, with wide bloomers reaching to the knee.

THE SPIELERS

It was mid-October that year when Gabrielle heard from her brother Alphonse. The handwriting – the perfectly closed circles she knew so well, with proper little *a*'s and *o*'s lined up like eggs in a basket, and every letter penned with all the necessary broad strokes and tie-overs – was that of all people who, like Alphonse, had learned to write under the ferule of a country priest.

Alphonse had been drafted and was about to depart. He was joining the 97th Infantry, leaving behind him a pregnant woman and a little boy, penniless, in a hamlet in the Cévennes. That was all the letter said. But Gabrielle could not doubt that this needy sister-in-law was Madeleine Boursarie, a silkworker whose marriage had been celebrated on November 17, 1910, at Valence and announced to the members of the clan on fancy notepaper framed in waffled lace, such as was sold at country fairs. Gabrielle, then making her début as a milliner, had promptly congratulated her dear Alphonse.

Jeanne Devolle's four children always kept in touch. In the past Gabrielle had been unable to do more than write to Alphonse, following him through his various adventures, which were also those of Lucien, and sending him her good wishes when he married. She knew that as soon as they reached working age both the tougher Alphonse and the gentle Lucien had been placed as apprentices with an itinerant, and that a few years later they had been picking bark on the slopes of Mont Aigoual, and later digging coal down a Cévennes mine. The Chanel brothers had not parted until 1907, when Lucien had enlisted in the infantry. He was eighteen years old then and, although temperamentally a pacifist, he wanted a career in the army. At the end of a year, however, he was discharged and found himself back on the street.

There were two alternatives open to him: to go north and join his father, who had settled in Brittany, or to go back on the road with Alphonse, who had become a traveling newspaper agent in the Gard. He opted for the former. He bore no grudges; just turning up at his father's would prove that.

Albert Chanel had abandoned the innkeeper's place he had when his wife died and turned itinerant again. This progenitor – whom Gabrielle made into a winegrower and then a "dear departed," after attributing to him a life of travels of all kinds and sending him off to make a fortune in the United States – actually now officiated solely on the fairground at Quimper. Everyone in the clan knew it. They also knew he had gone back to woman-chasing and had conceived a liking for hard drink. They would not have ostracized him on any or all of these counts, if there had not been something else.

In the first place, there was his caring no more about his parents than about his children. It was Aunt Julia, always and forever, who, with Adrienne's help, looked after them.

Henri-Adrien Chanel was approaching his eightieth birthday. He was living on the avenue de la Gare at Varennes, not far from the Costiers'. Upon reaching retirement age, the former peasant had gone back to his roots. The people of Varennes, who only saw him digging in his garden, burning weeds and fishing for frogs, could not imagine he had ever been an itinerant. For them, the old man was a Cévennes mountaineer, ending his days in dignity with his wife and daughter, the respectable Madame Costier who was married to an employee of the SNCF, the French national railroad company.

Adrienne, scrounging little sums here and there, did her best to lighten their declining days. She visited them at Varennes regularly, and the Costiers' neighbors found her excessively elegant for a peasant's daughter. There was something odd about it – but how beautiful she was! And how much her father liked the fact that even in her glory she continued to think of him. Of the ten children he had fathered, she was always his "little girl," his favorite. Adrienne would take the train from Vichy, magnificently dressed, with a basket of provisions on her arm. That day Aunt Julia would get out her white tablecloth and there would be a feast. For one day, the house at Varennes was the chosen place again, where the scattered members of the roving clan could reconvene.

But what made the Costiers break off relations with Albert Chanel for good was Lucien's trip to Quimper in 1909. He had found his father living with a woman who was younger than he but drank just as much.

Although he had not a penny to his name, Albert Chanel welcomed his son most warmly, lodged him in the furnished rooms he shared with his companion, and offered to hire him too. Thereupon, taking advantage of this unexpected increase in his staff, he vanished. "Touring," he said.

Lucien learned from his father's concubine what these "tours" consisted of. Albert would hire a fine team on credit, stick plumes on the horses' heads, and travel through the region announcing, with many a verbal flourish, that he would soon be back, with the china dinner service of a nobleman whose trusted agent he was. The nobleman was in difficulties, he said. He was parting with his plates and platters, putting them up for sale the following day, and nobody could miss such an opportunity.

The next day, Albert did indeed come back . . .

Using his best line of patter, he would persuade the villagers to buy sets of dreary cheap market china, assuring them it was one of the treasures of his master, the marquis de Barrucan. He seldom came a cropper. The marquis's name worked on his audience like a charm. Needless to say, there never was a marquis de Barrucan. Even the name was invented – Albert made it up from the word *barrique* (a large barrel or cask). As we see, even at this low point, which showed every promise of being permanent, Albert Chanel was still haunted by his old vintner's dream. It makes his daughter Gabrielle all the easier to understand, when, in her efforts to disguise her origins, she stubbornly revived the paternal fairy tale and conferred upon him, in the eyes of the world, that dignity to which he had so longed to accede. She made him a winegrower. She was taking her revenge upon life, as well as avenging her father: albeit posthumously, Albert Chanel got his wish.

But Lucien also learned that, according to Albert's woman, on at least one occasion Albert had been forced to decamp in a hurry. It had happened several years earlier, she didn't know exactly where. But it was for no good reason that Albert had come all the way to Quimper, where he knew nobody and nobody knew him. The woman thought, although she wasn't sure, that before coming to Brittany Albert had had a little run-in with the gendarmerie.

And that was not all. Lucien also discovered to his chagrin that his father's companion was a woman of evil ways. Taking advantage of Albert's absence, she threatened the young man's virtue. Fleeing this Phaedra in rags, Lucien left Quimper without waiting for his father's return.

He sought refuge at Varennes. There, the family tribunal was merciless. Drunkenness, dishonesty, depravity, it was too much. Albert was stricken from the records. His name was never pronounced again.

But Lucien found work elsewhere. Like his father and grandfather, he became a market trader. Once again there was a Chanel, selling shoes this time, in the shadow of the cathedral at Clermont-Ferrand. His stall occupied a prominent position in the market, between the rue des Gras and the rue des Chaussetiers. He built up a faithful following of country people.

Then he decided to take a wife – and did, in 1915. Almost immediately, the army remembered him. Lucien pointed out that he had been discharged against his will, and definitively. He was nonetheless sent to an infantry regiment, the 92nd.

More timid than Alphonse, Lucien did not dare ask anything of this far-off sister who, according to members of the clan, "had made a fortune." He simply announced that he was going off to be a soldier, as, a few months previously, he had announced his marriage. But every time he was on leave from duty, he stopped in Paris. Gabrielle welcomed him cordially although she carefully refrained from mentioning the monthly stipend she was sending to Alphonse. Was she afraid he would ask for one too? One of Gabrielle's employees, Mme Aubert, an accomplice from the Moulins days and a superb redhead who in due course became directress of her salons, sent a monthly postal order for three thousand francs, a considerable sum at that time, to the bugler Alphonse Chanel. But why did the money have to be sent to Alphonse's postal sector? Wouldn't it have been simpler to send it directly to his wife? There was a reason for that: the mother of Alphonse Chanel's children was not his legal wife. When and how did Gabrielle learn this? She certainly had not remained ignorant of her brother's irregular position for long. But she did not hold it against him. Alphonse was living in concubinage? He wasn't the first man in the family to whom that had happened. She herself had been born out of wedlock. For twenty-five years Alphonse Chanel benefited from her generosity, with never a delay or omission.

When, in 1911, Alphonse had met a Mlle Causse in the Gard, an angular young woman with a small holding near Vigan, he neglected to tell her he had already married the previous year. So, when she found herself pregnant, she was surprised that he didn't marry her. Jeanne Causse's family was highly respectable, and therefore her condition had to be kept secret. She ran away from home and went to Nîmes, got a situation as a house servant and, in due course, gave birth at the hospital to a child whom she declared to be nameless – with one or two variations in detail, the same procedure followed by Jeanne Devolle a quarter of a century earlier.

At the time, Alphonse was a mechanic at St Laurent-le-Minier. He serviced the mine trucks, learned about the early automobile motors, and led a gay life. Occasionally he went to Nîmes, where Jeanne Causse, loving and willing, waited for him. Three years later they were still together, and Jeanne was pregnant again, at the time Alphonse was mobilized. Jeanne lost her job and went to live with a relative at Florae, where she gave birth to a little girl, who, in gratitude for the miraculous monthly allowance, was named Gabrielle.

In the meantime, the marriage between Alphonse and Madeleine Boursarie – of which Jeanne still had no inkling – had been dissolved. The divorce decree was filed by the civil court of Valence a month before war was declared.

Suddenly stricken by a sense of responsibility – owing solely, no doubt, to the fact that a conscripted father had certain advantages, not least among which were furloughs – Alphonse Chanel decided to recognize his two children. He did not mention the fact that he was divorced, and on the act of recognition he is described as a bachelor.

Thus another Gabrielle Chanel came to be recognized after some delay. In 1919 a third child was born at Ganges in the Gard, and named Antoinette.

Alphonse Chanel and Jeanne Causse settled down to a permanent arrangement which lasted forty years. Not until 1953, when their father died, did Alphonse's children learn that their parents had never been married.

Like Jeanne Devolle, Jeanne Causse was a thoroughly miserable wife. Alphonse was a perfect replica of his father. Whether rolling drunk or in debt up to his ears, he kept coming back to Jeanne again and again.

"God in the streets, the devil at home," she used to say.

The local saying accurately described the man whose destiny she had elected to share.

She was a brave girl.

At the time of her daughter Gabrielle's birth, there was nothing left of the land she had owned at Vigan. Alphonse had speedily consumed her property and savings. But whatever he did, Jeanne never despaired of seeing him settle down one day.

In 1919, foot-soldier Chanel came back from the wars. Gabrielle's allowance guaranteed him an undeniable degree of comfort. He decided to settle at Valleraugue, a little Cévennes village at the bottom of a deep valley: hard by, the snowy summits of the Aigoual, pine forests, mountain streams and, when berrying time came around, baskets and baskets of blueberries and raspberries.

A few years ago the local people, the old folk of Valleraugue, could still recall the arrival over fifty years earlier, in 1919, of a sharp-witted fellow on a cycle, a moustachioed father who seemed to have a nose for business. The first thing Alphonse did was to buy a market gardener's cart and a horse, and make a daily trip to Ganges to buy enough vegetables to stock his wife's little stand. But this occupation was too humble and he soon wearied of it. Then he managed to get hold of the only tobacco shop in Valleraugue. Proof that Alphonse had a long arm . . . for the previous licensee had to be evicted.

How had he done it? He tried everything, visits and political string-pulling
– but also, by dint of sounding the charge in the 97th Infantry, he had
acquired chronic bronchitis. No flies on our Alphonse.

During the twenties tobacconist Chanel was observed at the wheel of a
smart car, and people learned at the same time – through the postman –
that he had a dress-designer sister in Paris who showered largesse upon him.
Thereafter the open-handed shopkeeper, who liked to buy people drinks
and lose money gambling, and who said himself that he had never saved a
penny, was treated with the most cordial respect. Along with the mayor, the
pastor, and the priest, he was the best-known person in the village.

"THOSE ENGLISH BLIGHTERS"

In the last months of 1914 the Parisians, judging the capital to be once again
at a safe remove from the front, returned home. Aristocrats and bourgeoises,
no longer having their "day," their servants or their coal, or even an open
pastryshop where they could meet for tea, suddenly discovered the advantages of hotels. The Ritz, because it was the most central and best heated,
became the favorite meeting place of the ladies who had all been taught in
the same convents, danced at the same balls, and been subjected to the same
restrictions at the hands of frowning husbands.

For them, in the past, hotels had existed only as places to stay in during
the summer and, in all other circumstances, as places for sin. Left to their
own devices, the abandoned spouses discovered that they could actually
forgo their husband's permission and dare to show themselves at the Ritz.
They advanced as far as the bar, access to which had been rigorously forbidden
them in peacetime. The great novelty was that a lady of quality could now
speak directly to a barman, knowingly rub elbows with an atheist politician,
share a seat with a parvenu, and overhear a discussion between speculators.

Nothing could stop what the war was bringing women closer to, what
had always been beyond their reach: freedom.

Once again, it was the war that gave Gabrielle Chanel a boost. Her Paris
shop, located by sheer chance at 21 rue Cambon, nothing else at the time
being available, was now along the daily route of these women who were
learning what goes on in a city – because, for the first time, they were
traversing the streets of Paris alone and on foot.

So, like her ancestor, that Henri-Adrien Chanel who, back in the 1860s,
followed the age-old tides of the religious pilgrimages, Gabrielle, gifted with
the same sharp nose and the same mobility, judged that it was time to pull

up stakes in Deauville. A chance to take. She would have to leave a sales-woman in charge of her business there until the following spring; she would have to pack her trunks and go back to Paris . . . which she did, and Antoinette with her. Pure luxury in the eyes of those who thought they knew her best; in fact she was pure peasant, always aware, since childhood, that making a living meant being hauled about indefinitely from town to town.

By December 1914 the Chanel sisters had moved back into their respective bachelor quarters in the Malesherbes district. Adrienne had returned to Vichy where she had a sad duty to perform. Her parents had died: Angelina while visiting Adrienne, Henri-Adrien a year later, at Varennes. It was for Adrienne to provide both with a decent last resting place. She had them buried together at Vichy.

So many to mourn! The names of the deceased stood out like milestones in people's letters. First it was Adrienne telling Gabrielle about the death of one of the high-spirited officers who had had such an appetite for laughter at La Rotonde; later it was Gabrielle's turn to inform Adrienne she had lost one or another of her admirers, one of those handsome youths who had gone to take tea with Maud and break hearts. And then, the Royallieu group lost its most illustrious horseman: Alec Carter, the British jockey, was one of the first to be killed. He had joined the 23rd Dragoons in order to be with his French friends, and was immediately made a sergeant, to his great delight. A week later he was dead, as though it profited a man of arms nothing to have personified all equestrian art and science in time of peace.

The soldiers were beginning their long entombment in the mud of the trenches. In Paris, the businessmen were active. Cloth and coal had become rare commodities, objects of frantic speculation. Boy, while performing his military duties, took advantage of every opportunity to dash back to town and look after his interests. For Gabrielle, relocating in Paris meant being closer to him.

His friend Clemenceau, now head of the Army Commission, was the most formidable politician in France. He harried ministers, denounced the inadequate supply of munitions, the delays in arming, the impotence of the health services. The wounded – it was a crime. They were being evacuated amidst horse dung and urine, on the straw bedding used to transport cavalry remounts. Was that to be countenanced? He also attacked profiteers, draft dodgers, and especially his archenemy Malvy, a minister of the interior who was caught at Arcachon in an intimate tête-à-tête at the home of Nelly Beryl, a demimondaine, while elsewhere men were fighting and dying. Seizure, suspension, censorship – all were useless, and Clemenceau's paper was more widely read than any other. One hundred thousand copies . . .

But this kind of action was no longer enough for him. He began a new form of inquiry, which he was to continue until the end of the war. Why confine himself to quarrels between desk officers? He wanted to seek the truth on the spot, in the very trenches.

Dressed as for a sitting in the Senate, apart from the fact that he now wore boots and had traded his bowler for a comical felt number so old it had become a mere ghost of a hat – he had a lifelong affection for unlikely lids – Clemenceau made trip after trip to the front.

During one of these tours of inspection he went through a village near the front lines where an English unit was encamped, the men at ease. In one group of horsemen, Clemenceau recognized a familiar figure: Arthur Capel. He was playing polo, in the presence of Sir John French.[2] Behind Clemenceau, a quaking delegation stood dreading the worst: sneers, an avalanche of sarcastic comment, verbal body blows aimed at the English. With one gesture Clemenceau swept away their fears. "Those English blighters" delighted him. Playing chukkers in front of tottering houses and shattered walls, what cool! He insisted on stopping, he wanted to congratulate them personally.

Was this proof of bias, or irresponsibility?

Had Arthur Capel bewitched him, as some people claimed?

No; it was something very different: a friendly nod to his youth. How could Clemenceau have failed to love Boy? Thirty years earlier the Frenchman too had crossed from one world to another with staggering boldness, snatching up everything that came his way – society women, actresses, just plain girls – gleefully courting scandal and swindles as though deliberately trying to make his head spin. Hadn't he been sufficiently taxed with it, after he became famous? Hadn't his opponents rubbed his nose deep enough in his mistresses, his debts, his horses? Yes, indeed, his horses . . . because riding had been his passion. He had even earned a living from it in the United States when he was a penniless youth in search of a job. In Stamford, Connecticut, where he taught French and riding at a girls' school, he too had been a "masher"; his pupils were all mad about him. And in the same vein, the insults hurled at him . . . What about Mary Plumer, that pastor's daughter he had divorced, and why? Let him explain himself. Such questions were instantly trampled underfoot by his anger. And then, he spoke English far too well, didn't he? But that was another story. There had always been something shady about Clemenceau's anglophilia.

To whom did Arthur Capel owe his nomination to the Franco-English War Coal Commission? It seems unlikely that Clemenceau was uninvolved in the decision.

While in that year 1915 the fighting men watched the tragic panoply of instruments of daily death grow larger and larger without a single voice being raised in protest – the sudden roar of the first airplanes in the sky over battlefields, and the first tank attacks, and also for the first time asphyxiating gas, the poison for which there was no antidote – Boy Capel was having visions of a world few men dared think of yet. Living between Paris and London, far from the battle zones, becoming not just another officer but one of those who select one alternative among many, and impose it: that too was enough to make one's head spin.

This should be seen as the dream of the ideal man of ambition.

Which Arthur Capel most assuredly was.

He was going back to England, to negotiate as an equal with the scions of noble houses.

But before going, he was given a summer leave. Just a few days – enough for a short holiday. He took Gabrielle to Biarritz.

There was a new division of classes in France: at the front the sufferers, in Paris the talkers, at Deauville the waiters, at Biarritz the profiteers.

The Miramar wore its peacetime aspect. There was dancing every night. Soldiers on leave, their ears still ringing with a very different music, found their feet again on the waxed dance floor. The tango was their antidote. In what key did the orchestra play "Under the Argentine sky . . ."? Back there, where the sky was all explosions, the shells were whistling in E-flat. It was against the memory of that song they now had to defend themselves.

From across the border arrived a faithful clientele of dark men with carefully waved hair and cackling Spanish women animated by a highly developed sense of elegance and a great appetite for pleasure. They threw tantrums outside the doors of closed pastryshops. What was happening? Biarritz was no longer "quite the thing." And the Russians, where had the Russians gone? No more police cordon to protect the nautical capers of Prince Yusupov and Grand Duke Dmitri. How beloved those two had been! So divinely handsome. The women had flocked around. In the end, the divinities lost patience: could they never be left in peace? The local authorities were alarmed. Hence the cordon. But Biarritz had a shortage of gendarmes. So the aides-de-camp made a bulwark of their own bodies and quickly thrust out beach robes. Wasted effort. Nobody could be grander than the grand dukes, their heads always towered above their bodyguards.

Those days were over now, well and truly over. The Felixes and Dmitris had flown, and unless one wanted to travel with one's own pastry cook and flour – expedients to which some resorted, despite the complications involved – no more *gâteaux* either. Shocking, was it? Between us, Gabrielle couldn't have cared less. Nor could Boy. So there were profiteers and dodgers? Well, that's life. There were. The shame of it lay rather in the fact that wars always spawned them, no?

When all was said and done the really stupid thing would have been to refuse to exploit such people, in the name of heaven knew what fine principle. Did the rich declare themselves disposed to buy *anything*? In wartime, "anything" had one very specific meaning: luxury. So one gave it to them. Both Boy and Gabrielle had the idea of repeating in Biarritz the experiment which had had such felicitous results the previous year in Deauville. What was his purpose? Did he want to revive the atmosphere of their first love? Or add another feather to Gabrielle's cap? Why? To make up for present infidelities, or as a protection against those to come? Unless, unconsciously, he wanted Gabrielle out of Paris just when he was going to be there more often.

Such ulterior motives may have flitted through Boy's mind. But what dominated it was the penchant he shared with Gabrielle for taking risks and doing things. That was the deciding factor. A few days before he left, Arthur Capel advanced the money and Gabrielle opened, not just a shop this time, but a real live *maison de couture* in Biarritz, with a collection of dresses selling for 3,000 francs.*

The town of Biarritz had never seen a designer set herself up in such magnificence. Not in a shop: in the Villa Larralde on rue Gardères; the villa belonged to the widow of comte Tristan de L'Hermite, née de Larralde-Dieusteguy and was located across from the Casino on the way down to the beach. A dwelling that tried to pass itself off as a castle, with a tower on the street, a huge inner courtyard and high stone walls. Gabrielle began by renting it and filling the courtyard with hydrangeas.

A lot of money laid out; now all she had to do was make a go of it.

At first she tried to prize Adrienne, the only woman she trusted, out of her retreat. But there was nothing to be done with her. It never occurred to Gabrielle that anyone could resist her; she offered superb gowns and gay

* About 2,000 euros today.

holidays, but Adrienne still refused. The 25th Dragoons was resting, she was about to receive permission to spend a few days with her "adored." She was living in anticipation. But later . . . She promised, later . . .

When she did come, the implacable Gabrielle delivered herself of one of those pronouncements of which all her life she possessed the secret:

"From now on your later is too late."

It was because Antoinette – as always – a fool but such a willing one, had come running, and had already set up a convoy of seamstresses shuttling between Paris and Biarritz, so that newly recruited apprentices could be trained.

Adrienne therefore got a cool reception.

Gabrielle was beginning to be hugely irritated by this inamorata who froze into an attitude of petrified waiting at the drop of a hat. What could there be to worry about when a man was so infatuated with you that his sole aim in life was to marry you? And, worst of all, Adrienne did not even seem content with what would have made Gabrielle's cup overflow, and was forever imagining her *respectability* to be in danger.

As a result she made a great fuss over what then appeared and long remained for Gabrielle a subject for gleeful needling. Adrienne returned from her trip to the front mortified and bewildered. The man checking visitors' permits had asked, "You are not the wife of Lieutenant X?" and she had confessed that she was not, whereupon he added, with a frankness more ingenuous than disrespectful, "That's all right, then, I'll let you through. The colonel would rather see girl friends than wives. He says, like, a wife softens a soldier, but a girl friend . . ." Any tendency to tearfulness was forestalled by Gabrielle's curt last word: all she wanted to hear about was what concerned her work. She added that the remark Adrienne had found so offensive wasn't as silly as it sounded; besides, if she was so upset by the way soldiers talked she had better not venture into the fighting zones.

This was the first chill between them, and also foreshadowed Gabrielle's new face, that of a woman in whom the signs of ill-contained animosity would unexpectedly flash out. Visions of shared love and simple happiness depressed her. She lashed out against something she had never known. But if frostbitten dreams lived inside her, they were cleverly concealed. She disguised this seedling bitterness by refusing to weigh love against the urgency of her need to succeed.

Gabrielle had drawn up her plan of campaign. Biarritz? A sort of outpost bringing Spain within reach: a "neutral" country, close at hand, with everything the phrase implied in the way of supplies of raw materials and customers. She had to get a firm foothold, as though from behind a half-open door. And then? Snap up everything that passed, sewing cotton, fabric or female.

Once this conquest was certain, her stratagem was to return to rue Cambon and set up headquarters there. She was in a hurry to get back. Boy was in Paris without her. Could she count on Adrienne? Forget it. She would leave Antoinette at Biarritz with full powers. Let her stay there for good. That was all one asked of her. Gabrielle undertook to convince her that her future would be made in Biarritz and nowhere else.

Antoinette was slightly on the shrill side, as women go. She feigned reluctance. But Gabrielle was adamant. Her intensity suddenly overpowered her need for affection. She grew heated. She used all her weapons, threats, intimidation. Was Antoinette a moron, or what? Would she ever meet an attractive, wealthy foreigner who was willing to marry her except at Biarritz? And what was the main thing after all? To get married. Antoinette had no time to lose.

As far as the fittings were concerned, Antoinette could relax: that's what the forewomen were there for. All she would have to do was run the salons and greet customers. And what more could the conceited creature ask? She would be living on equal terms with great ladies, international beauties and society belles, a species universally threatened with extinction. Paris, as she well knew, was no longer the garden of elegance. Opulence? It was still worshipped at Biarritz, at Biarritz alone. There was nothing foolish in wanting to clothe this last outpost. One day, when peace had come again, the ghost of elegances past would be seen creeping out from under the ruins and swelling like sails in the wind. It was in anticipation of this day that Antoinette must do as Gabrielle told her. To hold Biarritz, that was the Chanel sisters' battle plan. It was time she got it into her head. The last lace, the last embroideries, the last crepe de chine: Antoinette alone would be able to use them. Come now, no more dithering. It would be madness to get out of practice.

The idea was first discussed in July 1915. By September everything was ready.

Gabrielle was soon able to see how profitable her idea had been. But could she have known in advance? Orders from the Spanish court, from the "Tout-Madrid," San Sebastien, Bilbao; the Biarritz house was working to full capacity with more than sixty employees.

By the end of the year, fortified by this victory which was hers alone, Gabrielle was back in Paris, where for the first time her staff were to see her true colors: she was impulsive, capricious, authoritarian, caustic. She bore herself as an absolute master, assuming personal responsibility for liaison between her outposts. She supplied Antoinette direct from Paris, where one of her ateliers worked on Spanish orders alone. Then, as a general deploys his strategic reinforcements according to the shifting fortunes of the war, Gabrielle shipped personnel from Paris when they were required in the Basque country and, a more hazardous undertaking, performed the opposite maneuver successfully as well. She badgered appalled families who didn't want "their little girl going up to Paris," she argued with them and persuaded them it was their duty to let her go. But what about the dangers of the big city, the war, the soldiers on the loose, the Zeppelins? "Humph!" sniffed Gabrielle angrily. Were they patriots or were they not? The vanquished families bowed their heads and submitted.

Thus, while a pitiless battle was being waged at Verdun, Gabrielle Chanel consolidated her empire. That year the winter was glacial in Paris. For want of coal, children were freezing to death. The war industries were permanently threatened by a shortage. Victory depended on coal. His personal interests coincided so closely with the general interest that he could devote himself to them without the smallest scruple.

By the beginning of 1916 Gabrielle Chanel had full authority over three hundred workers. Her independence was ensured.

For anyone who was still able to think about elegance, that acute dilemma "Chanel or Poiret?" had ceased to exist. Gabrielle's formidable rival was devoting all his talents to the armed forces. Drafted into the quartermaster corps, he had succeeded, by standardizing the cut of army overcoats, in saving twenty-four inches of cloth per soldier and four hours of labor per finished garment.[3]

That left Gabrielle Chanel as the only starter in the race. In those years, it was a distinct advantage to be a woman.

She didn't realize it until, to her surprise, she found herself able to repay Arthur Capel. Which, guided by a very sure instinct, she hastened to do, without asking his advice. She knew he would be amazed to learn that the decisions taken gaily and lightly on a holiday evening had so speedily turned into an enterprise from which she would earn her living. She also dimly sensed that repaying her debt would alter the terms of their problem – the best proof being that Boy was suddenly madly jealous again. How gladly he would have let her keep every penny of profit on her success! But what he had to do now was accept her independence. A surprise for which the times had ill prepared him.

That profound change in Gabrielle was to cause Boy keenly to regret every pleasure he tasted without her.

In 1916, trying to duplicate in Paris the style that had made her success in Deauville, wanting to remain true to herself, she had to find the closest possible approximation to knitwear. The choice alone says much. Knitting: the eternal occupation of country folk. But all such products of needle gymnastics were out of the question at a time when wool was scarce and used only to knit balaclava helmets for fighting men.

In those lean days, having been born into poverty became an advantage. Would it be wrong to add that this was a most fragile asset, one that a few years of close proximity with luxury – that is, with the true governor of fashion and all the contagion it implies – would ordinarily have been enough to destroy? Not the least of the temptations facing Gabrielle was to yield to the fascination of the Ballets Russes, to conceive a feminine allure swathed in orgies of fabric and loaded down with silks and gold, a type of charm respectful of every clause in the canons of beauty-according-to-Bakst. As we know, this did not happen. The germs carried by that "great wind from the steppe" spared Gabrielle. Give up *ornamentation?* Long familiarity with a clientele for whom sumptuousness equaled elegance might have made this impossible for a Paul Poiret, a Worth, or a Doucet. But Chanel? Initiated from earliest childhood into the art of using what other people didn't want, she had neither to change herself nor give up anything. Therefore, when a textile manufacturer named Rodier, having nothing better to offer, showed her a line which had never been used and which he believed unusable, he was greatly surprised at the interest he aroused.

The cloth had been an experiment.

Its inventor, designing it for use in lingerie, had hoped to strike a responsive chord among sportsmen. Rodier imagined that the young, so enamored of the outdoor life and the *style anglais*, would appreciate a woolen material called jersey, and would justify its creation by wearing it in long monogrammed underpants, nightshirts with long tails, and made-to-order suits of underclothes.

Nothing of the kind.

When presented, the fabric was judged too dry by some, too scratchy by others, "not amusing," and then, what kind of texture was that? A mechanical knit? Come, come, now, the most prodigious advances of technology will never prevent it from *rucking up*, from *bagging* – don't try to tell me! The color was equally unpopular. A beige that good wholesalers found "indigent," it made one think of engine drivers, manual laborers, overalls. In short, nobody wanted it. Then the war came along. Rodier had other things to think about, and his stock of jersey was left on his hands.

Gabrielle bought it.

It was exactly what she was looking for – a knit, but machine-made. She told Rodier that its very soberness would make a place for this fabric in a realm hitherto ruled by custom-made goods. He didn't believe a word she said, thinking it unlikely she would be able to convert women to a material that men had found too unpleasant for their own use. She took no notice of his exhortations and ordered more of the stuff. He refused, not wanting to go back into production at the risk of wasting his scarce raw material. Let her try it out first, they could see later.

An argument ensued. Bitter words were exchanged. She called Rodier a coward and a cad. He was adamant. A small sample of what Chanel's relations were to be, for half a century, with manufacturers and sellers of all sorts, and also with her associates. However great the services rendered or risks shared, she always managed to see herself as her own sole supplier; she schemed to do away with the others, to squeeze them out and take their places. Sometimes it would end in farce, sometimes in melodrama, with proceedings, lawsuits, reconciliations, slammed doors, cries of "I've had enough," announcements of divorces without appeal . . . and fresh starts. We may as well note, once and for all, that it always proved impossible for her to remain on good terms with those on whom, by the very nature of her work, she *depended*. It was not a question of personalities; it was the very idea of dependence that had become abhorrent to her.

Proof that Gabrielle was right came immediately to allay Rodier's fears. First of all, there was what she made out of his cloth and began wearing herself. An unfitted redingote ending midway down the skirt, with no decoration of any kind and so severe as to be almost masculine.

Even someone less canny than Jean Rodier, someone who knew nothing of technicalities but could see what made a woman elegant, would have sensed at first glance that this garment possessed some unknown strength.

What had prevailed in the past? The demands of a clientele entitled to everything: exclusive rights to the ornamentation, to the fabric, and sometimes to the model as well. You altered and transformed to suit the wishes of society celebrities, so that what they wore was "a synthesis of their personal tastes and those of their designer."[4] And woe unto him, if the fair overprivileged chanced to notice a gown bearing some faint resemblance to her own on some other female!

But now, with Chanel, ornamentation was suddenly giving way to "line"; a garment had appeared that was determined solely by the logic of a creator grappling with necessity.

Women's fashion owed to Poiret such major innovations as the lightening of the corset and an attempt to shorten the skirt – novelties that Chanel's fans have all too often attributed to her without, moreover, provoking the slightest denial on her part – and Poiret also had a sense of color that has never been equaled. But it was nevertheless Gabrielle Chanel, in 1916, who made such decisive changes in fashion that she compelled it to change centuries: women had the right to be comfortable, to move about freely in their clothes; style became more important, to the detriment of adornment; and lastly, "poor" materials were suddenly ennobled, which automatically made possible the rapid growth of fashion within reach of the majority.

Then, too, she aimed at what nobody before her had dared so openly: women moving tall and straight in clothes that no longer sculpted waists or curved backs, women wearing radically shortened skirts. Poiret allowed the foot to show? Gabrielle Chanel increased the climb, amply disengaging the ankle. Poiret's waists were no longer pinched to choking point? Chanel did him one better: she removed the waist altogether. Did she do it on purpose? Or was it only, as some say, because of the inferior quality of her jersey? There can be no doubt on this point: she had no choice. And for the first time a revolution in feminine attire, far from following any whims or caprices, consisted essentially and unavoidably in abolishing them.

Because you couldn't do a thing with that material. One dart, the slightest tension, and the threads, too loosely worked, would unravel. Anyone else would have given up. Gabrielle dug in her heels. Simplify, that was the only way. The shirtwaist dress stopped well above the ankle.

With one stroke Gabrielle annihilated the centuries-old gesture so many men had breathlessly awaited as a woman prepared to mount a step: the discreet lifting of the skirt. A certain form of femininity was ending – that of the thousand-pleated bodice and the cascades of veiling on the hat, the era of Vichy, of Souvigny-sur-Orge, the era of Adrienne's conquests.

By rubbing out her own past, Gabrielle changed the look of the street scene forever.

The woman who "allowed the long train of her mauve gown to spread behind her"[5] had had her day. One now had to guard against the tolerably distracting allure of a free-striding body which could dress itself without assistance and undress itself in the twinkling of an eye. And the nostalgics, those who yearned for the fair departed – they were like so many Orpheuses lamenting in vain. Proust redoubled his "Alases!" and "How ghastlys!"; but neither his moans at the sight of these gowns that were "not even made of cloth" nor his sorrow at beholding such "undistinguished" women would ever bring Madame Swann to life again.

Commentators were understandably discouraged by the newcomer. She bore no resemblance to anything, having – at least in their eyes – no memory and no tradition. She was an absolutely new woman, a woman whose dress was *without allusion*. Pointless to interrogate her. The rules of the game had been deliberately muddled.

What attitude was one to take toward a fashion the key to which could not be found in any museum? However much erudition one might deploy, this woman was beyond belief. And who could have dreamed of looking for her sources in the depths of the most forsaken of French provinces? No one ever heard it said that the refinements of fashion could have their roots in a gravelly highland.

THE "CHARMING CHEMISE DRESS"

The disappearance of the fashion magazines *La Gazette du bon ton* and the *Journal des dames et des modes*, which ceased publication in 1914, explains why the display of a little more than the ankle remained, until the end of the first World War, an exclusive attribute of the Parisians. Cut off from the rest of the world, they did not realize until 1919 that their low waists and straight coats would come as something of a shock to foreign visitors.

What they were wearing was promptly to become Fashion.

It is not the least paradoxical aspect of the history of these particular Frenchwomen to have shown, in an era of black disaster, the image of the future. Although they didn't know it, they forecast the brash and noisy youth of the coming peacetime. No leg was visible in the streets of America in 1916, where skirts still trailed the ground. Clear evidence, if needed, is provided by a photograph taken in 1917 of the assembled members of the Cosmopolitan Club parading in New York. Hardly the beginning of an ankle curve to be seen.

There is a contradiction here though, for Chanel's name first appeared in print in the American press.

The first Chanel model ever reproduced appeared in 1916 in *Harper's Bazaar*. It defied description. In words, this garment could only be approached by a series of negatives. But it lent itself admirably to a sketch pad, being all of a piece and pure in line.

It was a dress from the Biarritz collection. Intended for Antoinette's clients, it was undeniably alluring, but possessed not a single prewar note. No violets on the bodice of this dress, much less cattleyas, for the good reason that there was no bodice. Neither ruching nor ruffle at the throat, for there was no more throat than bodice. The garment split in a V like a saber slash and opened onto a waistcoat of masculine cut which, between its lapels – oh, audacity! – showed glimpses of a bare throat, and even more than throat. No puffing in the sleeves, or any of the "kimono" cut so dear to Poiret, but a sheath covering the arm from shoulder to wrist like a stocking. No veils or parasols, just a broad-brimmed hat whose close-fitting crown made the head appear small and which bore none of the things that had previously constituted the essence of a hat. No knives of partridge feathers poking skyward, no swirls or draperies of chevalric ostrich plumes, because no ostrich. A flat, narrow twist, however, garnished one side of the crown like a ribbon . . . but the difference was that this twist was made of sable, not ribbon, and whatever one thought of this detail, call it one thing or another, a discreet echo of the muff or an indispensable softening, the fact remained that nobody had ever seen a woman wear fur in such a way. As for the waist . . . But who can talk of waists where there is no belt at all? Gliding around the hips, a long scarf in the same colors as the dress floated like a general's sash.

Disheartened, no doubt, by the loss of so much, but nonetheless admiring, the American editors had produced a brief caption in homage to this dress. They called it "Chanel's charming chemise dress."

Gabrielle had to wait four years before she obtained as much from the French press. Enough years for a country to recover its love of frivolity.

Not one word about Chanel, not one model reproduced until 1920.

It is hard to imagine what effect this early transatlantic fame had upon Gabrielle. Did she even know about it? Nothing is less certain. "The charming chemise dress" . . . news of such official recognition would not have displeased her. But America, crouching in its neutrality, was becoming increasingly remote.

What were the United States for Gabrielle in 1916? Her views were very decided: since she loved Boy, she had to share his opinions on all matters. And in this matter, Boy shared the opinion of Monsieur Clemenceau, which is to say that his type of diehard took a dim view of President Wilson and his dreams of peace without victory. Boy and his circle were sufficiently concerned to forget the "charming chemise dress" and Gabrielle's laurels. Especially when, regardless of the fulminations of the French Foreign Ministry in Paris, Clemenceau began directing his attacks against President Wilson in person.[6] Then, from all shades of opinion, sharp criticism arose. This was no way to hasten the United States' entry into the war, and Clemenceau was doing more harm than good. Whereas Sarah Bernhardt, at the same age, was proving vastly more effective with her triumphant tours. She was all the rage in New York. Wasn't she promising to persuade the Americans to come in?

Clemenceau's was a curious position. The rear guard loathed him. The only group he was popular with were the soldiers. So then he did what he always did in such circumstances. As others immerse themselves in crowds,* he went for a mud bath – in the trenches.

It was October. To his everyday attire he added the baroque touch of a wide hand-knit scarf, and one is again forcibly reminded of the similarities between him and the man who, twenty-five years later but in comparable circumstances, showed proof of a sartorial imagination at least as singular: Churchill. Who can forget the vision of Sir Winston's top hat and stick, when he came to inspect the English coastal defenses in 1940, the "zip siren-suit" in which he greeted Eisenhower in 1944; or better still, the silhouette of the old man at El Alamein in 1942, passing the British troops in review with a white parasol in his hand?

So it was a mufflered Clemenceau who went to put heart into those who elected him long before the rest of France: the men at the front. They treated him as a soldier, this senator who used his walking stick like a pick-ax to clamber out to the outposts and satisfy himself that the men had sufficient bread and weapons. They affectionately dubbed him the "Old Man." They even went so far as to forget the respect they owed him, as, for instance, that sentry in the Commercy sector who, hearing himself hailed by some-body in a moustache who was a weird-looking sort and no mistake, and inca-pable of imagining that the fellow who had turned up so suddenly in the trench next to his was a venerable senator, shut him up with a "Cut it out! Can't you hear the Hun coughing?" Clemenceau was jubilant. That October, he also went to visit Sir Douglas Haig in the British zone. He proclaimed the organization there "admirable." Ah, those English . . . you could count on them.

Clemenceau returned from the front and plunged into the thick of a

---

* Allusion to a quirk of General de Gaulle, who sometimes liked to leave an official procession and mingle with the crowd, which was known as taking a *bain de foule* (crowd bath).

diplomatic upheaval. The President of the United States had once again taken the initiative, expressing his hope that the parties to the war might consent to negotiate. With 874,000 dead in the French ranks, 634,000 among the British, wasn't it time to put an end to the slaughter? Whereupon he judged it expedient to send a long pacifist letter to the French Senate. Clemenceau took it as a personal attack. He was being bearded in his very den.

He mounted the platform and, once more, the Quai d'Orsay hid its face in its hands.

"We are being assassinated, sir; this is no time for speechmaking."

That was the close of his furious diatribe. Was that really any way to talk to a President of the United States?

At that point there came a rumor that revolution had reached the tsar's palace gates and the image of the "Russian colossus" was just a big bag of nonsense flung in the face of the French soldier to deceive him. And then people were also saying, although nobody could quite swear to it, that the handsome bathers with the white hands and pretty eyes, the princes' sons whose nautical frolics at Biarritz had so enthralled their admirers, Grand Duke Dmitri and Prince Felix Yusupov, had suddenly turned into formidable avenging angels. Killers, those two? They were suspected of having arranged a sort of ambush–surprise party in St Petersburg, of spiking the port with cyanide and offering pink and poisoned petits-fours with one hand, holding loaded revolvers behind their backs with the other – all to assassinate Efim Novy, the depraved monk, the intimate adviser of their most sinister cousin Alexandra, empress of all the Russias. Was it conceivable? But if they weren't guilty, why had the tsar sent the beautiful Dmitri off to the depths of Persia under a general's guard and relegated the irresistible Felix to his estate at Khomsk? The incident was hushed up. But the monk Rasputin? Dead or not? Nobody talked of anything else.

And so no one in Paris was more sought after, that December 1916, than the princesse Lucien Murat. The reason was that she got a letter from Russia every week. The comte Charles de Chambrun, then first secretary at the French Embassy in St Petersburg, would have written to his Marie every day if he could have. But . . . there was a "but." Prince Lucien, you know? Chambrun waited for Marie Murat to be widowed, and married her in 1934. In the past the princess had been more lampooned for her neglect of costume than lauded for her wit. But suddenly Parisian society, forgetting that one could always see her petticoat, discovered every virtue in the young woman: she was vivacious, she was droll and – why not? – she had a "certain chic."

Among those letters from Russia was one Princess Marie was able to read aloud. People invited her in order to hear it. It was the Parisian post-prandial letter that winter. One could hear it at Cecile Sorel's, as at Philippe Berthelot's. Berthelot was deputy Director of Political Affairs at the Quai d'Orsay, and from 1917 he was regarded as the most influential person in the ministry. Gabrielle Chanel became acquainted with its contents at both tables.

"I am just back from the Yacht Club where Grand Duke Dmitri was finishing his dinner as I was starting mine," the letter said. "He waved me over. The fourteen persons at the next table were all talking at once and with incredible vehemence. Suddenly, the voice of [Grand Duke] Nicholas Mikhailovich [nephew of Tsar Alexander II] rose above the din:

" 'And I tell you he is not dead.'

"I turned to my neighbor, Grand Duke Dmitri. He was white as the tablecloth. His bloodshot eye betrayed anxiety. Sitting down beside him I had the impression that the hand he was holding out to me with a pale smile had been soaked in tragedy. An indefinable sensation.

" 'And you, Your Grace,' I asked in a very low voice, 'do you believe Rasputin is dead?'

" 'Yes,' he murmured.

" 'Are the murderers' names known?'

" 'They may be the first names in Russia,' was his almost inaudible reply.

"Then Lorenzaccio rose, jangled his spurs and made a cavalier bow:

" 'Good-by, gentlemen. Today is Saturday, I'm going to look in at the Michael Theatre.' "[7]

That was what the letter from Russia said.

So what with one incident and another, Chanel's "charming chemise dress" and the drawing in *Harper's Bazaar* – really, one could hardly keep one's mind on it.

A few days more, May 1917, the last days when Gabrielle was, briefly, a happy woman.

Arthur Capel and she celebrated in Paris the publication of the book* on which he had been working for over a year, and which had just been

---

* *Reflections on Victory and a Project for the Federation of Governments*, by Arthur Capel, Werner Laurie, London. Fifty years later, a big crystal-headed pin was still holding together a few crumpled sheets of the manuscript. It was a relic lovingly preserved by Gabrielle, brought out only in the presence of a few privileged friends.

published in London. For between two trips he had undertaken a most unlikely task: he had written a book. When asked what its title was to be Boy would answer, *"Reflections on Victory."* It took an uncommon degree of confidence in the outcome of the war and an uncommon nerve to indulge in reflections of that nature in 1916. Clemenceau, when he heard about the scheme, announced that he would supply all the necessary documentation. Then, to his *Reflections on Victory* Boy had appended *A Project for the Federation of Governments* and a foreword in which he explained that he was English but had lived long enough in France to love that country and to think in French. It was a sort of confession of the double allegiance that was tearing him apart. He added that it was in France and nowhere else that the foundations for the union of nations must rise – which, coming from an Englishman, was startling, to say the least.

Arthur Capel bolstered his theses with quotations that revealed his rather eclectic taste in reading. He quoted at once Bismarck and Napoleon, Plutarch and Hermes Trismegistus, William the Silent (William I of Orange) and Balzac; but he preferred, of all the others, Sully's *Mémoires*.

A curious mind and a strange book, in which there is no want of contradictions. Speaking of victory as though it were imminent, whereas despite the Americans' entrance into the war the Allies' position had never been more precarious since 1914, the author set out his belief in the construction of a future City that would respect democratic tradition. Yet he rejected its component part – "one of the most unreal and damaging innovations of the last hundred and thirty years" – the citizen. He drew a bleak portrait of the centralizing State, a "deplorable businessman, disagreeable purveyor, bad employer, bad administrator," which he hoped to see disappear and be replaced by a Europe-wide federation, giving full autonomy to every corporate body, region, people, and race. This would incline one to see Arthur Capel as not only a premature "European," favoring total decentralization and wholly condemning any "Europe of nations," but also as a corporatist nourished on principles he thought modeled on those of a Proudhon – although the latter saw no solution to the injustices of the world except in the abolition of capital, a reform which would assuredly not have been to Arthur Capel's liking.

Another paradox: the work was a vibrant plea for youth. "In our civilized society," he wrote, "it is the old who devour the young by making them languish in subordinate jobs . . ." He pointed out that the French Revolution had been accomplished by men under thirty and reproached King Louis XVI for having been, at twenty, "old with all the age of the

Monarchy." Statements one would hardly expect from one of His Britannic Majesty's loyal subjects and a Conservative to boot. He held the gerontocracy responsible for the "slaughter" into which European nations had been plunged. To avoid repetition of such crimes, there was only one way: "liberate the young," give them the right to speak out and give them power. Amazing language when one reflects that in France, Arthur Capel was betting everything he had on the return to power of seventy-six-year-old Clemenceau.

The essential quality of Capel's book derives from the time of its writing. Seen in this light, the author's anguish regarding postwar problems and his intense longing for a durable peace assume their true meaning. It is also surprising to discover, at a time when revenge was the dominant emotion, a young man doubting that peace could be established on a firm basis if it was achieved by crushing all the aspirations of the German people and administered as a punishment. That sort of peace, according to him, would do nothing but stir up fresh longings for revenge.

The book came out on May 10. Five days later, one of the darkest periods of the war began. Over 107 regiments affected. Men refusing to go up to the front. In the railway stations, soldiers on leave attacking gendarmes and insulting them. What was happening? Was it the "Russian movement" taking over?

On the Senate platform, Clemenceau analyzed the causes of the affliction with his customary vehemence. The mutinies? They were nothing but legitimate lassitude and the consequences of shameful propaganda. The morale of the troops must be boosted and the defeatists throttled. He threatened and, once again, he denounced:

"Minister of the Interior, I accuse you of betraying the interests of France."

If the epidemic was to be stopped, the germs swarming around Malvy and Caillaux would have to be neutralized. Fifteen people in prison, no other remedy.

One can imagine that a book confident of victory and devoted to the postwar period, appearing in this atmosphere of horror, would arouse a good deal of comment. People were amazed that a dandy should have so many ideas in his head, and in future Boy was no longer cited for his polo wins or his business acumen, but for the space devoted to his book in the columns of the London *Times*.[8] The literary supplement's critic commented at length on the author's vision of the future: "Mr Capel's notion is to form *at once* a federation of the British Empire and the Allies which should be used as an instrument for bringing about and preserving peace by inviting neutrals to join in and eventually including *those of our enemies* who really desire peace." The *Times* found particularly audacious the idea of detaching from the German bloc those enemy countries which seemed most ready to break their alliance. He nevertheless regretted the author's failure to go more deeply into the practical aspect of things, especially the means of making the federation a reality.

After his recognition by the English press, Arthur Capel began spending more and more time in London. He was still in love with Gabrielle but he was following his ambition and made no secret of his intentions. Even in Paris he had dabbled in pretty widows. In London he met more of them. One group of young Englishwomen of the highest ranks had welcomed him with unexpected warmth. He was going to try to marry into that aristocracy. On her side Gabrielle, who cared deeply about nothing except her love for Boy, succeeded in willing herself to believe that he was now going to be less important to her. She was beginning to develop defenses against his line of action. She had believed in eternal love, and she had been wrong again. She felt spurned, even by Boy's very reliance upon her. Let him marry whomever he pleased, but let him cease needing to tell her about it all the time. The gulf between her and Boy's new friends was decidedly too wide to be crossed. He was living and spending all his time among people she didn't know, never would know, no doubt, and that was where they had got to, *her* Boy and herself . . .

She cared a little less, however, now that she too was being accepted by intelligent men, beautiful and brilliant women. But in a very different society. At Cecile Sorel's, Gabrielle had met a remarkable woman, muse to many artists and destined to be her only close friend: Misia Sert. The event is recorded in Paul Morand's diary, on May 30, 1917. "In the last few days the fashion has become for women to wear their hair short. They're all doing it: Madame Letellier and Coco Chanel in the lead, then Madeleine de Foucault, Jeanne de Salverte, etc.

"Cocteau tells of a preposterous dinner party at Cecile Sorel's the day before yesterday. The Berthelots were there, Sert and Misia, Coco Chanel who is definitely becoming quite a personage."[9]

When the echo of the successes of this short-haired Gabrielle reached London, it was Boy's turn to react. There was *his* Gabrielle making her way into a circle in which he, Boy, was nothing; that is where they had got to after so many vows and promises. Maybe she had had enough of him, now that she was independent and almost rich. Arthur Capel found the thought all the more disturbing as it had never occurred to him that Gabrielle might be able to live without him.

THE IRRESISTIBLE RISE
OF FAIR ARTHUR

Paris was strange, that November 1917. Hotel life was at its gayest, morals and manners were considerably relaxed, it had become the thing to sport a lover, and airmen were by far the most in demand. The city was a crossroads for soldiers of every nationality on leave. People were doing their best to amuse the Americans. But the unfortunate Mrs Moore was no longer around to welcome her compatriots. A vase of ashes in the columbarium at Biarritz was all that was left of her. She had died at the Hotel Crillon after a last, "not even very smart" dinner party. The demise of this snob as the consequence of a literal faux pas (she fell down the stairs) took on a symbolic value. The whole wartime social pretense followed her nose dive into the void.

The difficulty of obtaining food made people forget that a few traitors had been jugged and the beautiful Mata Hari shot notwithstanding the tears of her lawyer, who happened also to be her lover. One less spy. What difference did that make? The Allies were on the brink of disaster. In Italy it was the time of Caporetto, the rout, an entire army overwhelmed and the Allies' right flank, the Italian defense, annihilated. In Russia no more tsar and no more army – first chaos, then Lenin. The Russian colossus was deflating like a balloon; one guarantee of strength on which so many French had relied was brutally withdrawn. The public felt it had been duped. Here was rebellion in a country whose glories everyone had smugly extolled, but never its tragedies or its poverty. The curtain had fallen on a stage set "of a splendor no court in the world could equal."[10] No more red escorts of hairy, bearded, haughty Cossacks, no more galloping emperor "followed by the glittering squadron of grand dukes and aides-de-camp";[11] and the white-canopied dais on which mournful empresses and their innocent daughters had sat enthroned to receive Poincaré was empty. "The unbelievable trail of accidents and miscalculations which for nineteen years marked the reign of Nicholas II"[12] was ending in abdication, and the fatal salvo of Yekaterinburg was to resound incongruously in the ears of the French bourgeois, like the slam of a pretty picture book being snapped shut in their faces. No more tsar? They were speechless with amazement. But not fools enough to suppose that Vladimir Ilich would honor the commitments of Nicholas II. So, like Leporello mourning his master's death while crying out on all sides, "My wages! My wages!" the little investor cried out, "My shares! My shares!" and vainly bemoaned the loan* to which, his head turned by the pretty pictures, he had subscribed eleven years earlier.

The military prospects were even worse. There would be no miracles: the Russians were going to lay down their arms, there would be an immediate peace. The formidable Ludendorff, supreme commander of the German army, would withdraw from a henceforth innocuous front and hurl one hundred and eighty divisions at France; maybe more, maybe two hundred. And the Germans' numerical superiority was far from offset by the United States' entry into the war. True, Pershing's men were there – a decisive asset, but one that couldn't be used, for the American army was not yet in fighting condition.

That was the situation when Clemenceau was called upon to govern France. "War, nothing but war" was his platform. No doubt the hour would come when Paris would welcome home her victorious troops. But that great moment could only be achieved through "blood and tears."[13] The men ceased calling him the Old Man, and the "Tiger" now roared through their tongues, in drawings and cartoons.

The moment Clemenceau took office Arthur Capel went to see him.[14] Going over the heads of ministers, ignoring his closest associates, thumbing his nose at the all-powerful Mandel (the young head of Clemenceau's private office) and walking straight up, at thirty-five years of age, to the head of the government: nothing could please Clemenceau more than this way of getting things done. He, meanwhile, was juggling ambassadors and restoring commands to disgraced generals without even consulting the president of the Republic. But what did Capel want with him? His fleet . . . he was placing it at the service of France and, despite the threat of submarine warfare, undertaking to keep French factories supplied with coal. Clemenceau accepted, sang Boy's praises on every side, and began treating him like an old school chum, while Boy went back to London, where more than ever he was seen in the wings of power. He now moved on from merely important circles to governing circles.

In the early months of 1918 Capel took advantage of a trip to France to call on the Duchess of Sutherland. Tall, erect, of regal bearing, she was Millicent (1867–1957), daughter of the fourth Earl of Rosslyn. On her

* In the spring of 1906 Russia, ruined by the disastrous war with Japan, negotiated a loan from the western countries, which was bitterly opposed in the French press by Maxim Gorky. The banks, encouraged by the government of the day, made available to the Russians large sums which were never repaid.

seventeenth birthday, she had married the Duke of Sutherland, a childhood friend of Winston Churchill's. Churchill described her as the most beautiful woman who ever lived – and now the Duchess of Sutherland was in charge of an ambulance corps in the army zone. Lady Dudley, the Duchess of Westminster – a large number of great English ladies, followed by their daughters, nieces, and various young friends, were doing as much.[15] The Duchess of Sutherland, thus, was no exception. But was it for Millicent that Boy made the trip, or for one of her nurses? Among them was a young person who had already caught his eye in London. She was the youngest daughter of that fourth and final Baron Ribblesdale, whose portrait by Sargent is one of the jewels of the Tate Gallery. All the Ribblesdales looked like the portrait: in other words, they were all exceptionally beautiful. How could one resist the temptation to ask for the young woman's hand? The daughter and daughter-in-law of lords, widowed almost before she was wed, she was a fragile, candid, sweet-tempered, and bewildered creature. War had taken away everything she had. First her husband, then her childhood friends, "who stood for something very precious to me, for an England of my dreams, made of honest, brave and tender men . . ."[16] as her brother Charles Lister wrote before he was killed in turn. In her presence Boy felt guardian-angel wings sprouting on his shoulders, and cultivated the feeling until he could mistake it for true love. Still, he hesitated. There were other possibilities. Some in France, some in Belgium . . . There was no shortage of pretty widows. And then, before anything else, Gabrielle must be told.

As soon as he got to Paris, he began to regret having to announce such sad news. Success becomes women, and Gabrielle was looking finer than ever. Her Biarritz branch was flourishing. That year she had purchased the Villa Larralde outright and paid 300,000 francs cash (about $150,000 today) for it. She was popular, admired, animated, asking no one for help and without attachments. Dynamic, that Gabrielle, stimulating . . . Was Boy as touched by damsels in distress as he had thought?

He invented a thousand excuses to put off the fatal moment. A kind of intimacy was reestablished between them. All of a sudden love, passion, it all began again. Boy admitted to her that for him what was being revived had never died. They started living together again. But the bad news still hung there in the air. At last, unable to endure it any longer, Gabrielle precipitated the confession. Boy had something to say to her. Let him get it over with. She was ready, ready to hear it, had been for a long time. She had been walking alongside unhappiness for years now, trying not to look at it too closely. Here it was. There was nothing to do but stare it in the face.

A few more days passed, with Boy still unable to make up his mind. He could, no he couldn't . . . The worst part of it was his fear of losing Gabrielle. That was the danger, he saw no other. But she kept insisting. Then he told her: Diana Wyndham, ambulance driver and daughter of a peer, was the one he hoped to marry.

Gabrielle heard him out without a tear. Boy was allying himself with everything she was not.

A little while later, Arthur Capel's trips between Paris and London became more frequent. He had just been appointed political secretary to the British delegation to the Supreme Interallied Council at Versailles.

To Gabrielle that meant only one thing: Boy was going to be in France more often, and stay longer.

He was and did, and although officially engaged to Diana Wyndham, he went on seeing Gabrielle as before.

Then arose the question of where she was to go. Gabrielle couldn't continue living under his roof on the boulevard Malesherbes, after all. To move out . . . another torment. Possibly the worst of all. Arthur Capel urged her to take a house in the suburbs. Why so insistent, and why the suburbs? She became suspicious. Was he trying to get rid of her again? Gabrielle surmised that it was partly that, but something else as well. In preparation for the impending change in his life, he wanted her established as an *irrégulière* in some discreet place where he could come to be with her.

In short, she was losing Boy and not losing him.

Those were the days when Paris was under the diabolical fire of a newly invented weapon, a long-range cannon, and the walls of St Gervais fell in upon the faithful on Good Friday; those were the days when graceful silhouettes glided from the Ritz to Chanel's in quest of a nocturnal attire that would enable them to show themselves in the lobby, and later in the cellar, in something other than their nightgowns. She put them in pajamas. A first and hasty hint of the trousers that were to appear four years later on women with razored necks wearing ambivalent felt hats and manipulating matchbooks and cigars: the emancipated, dressed like pretty young men, whom some people looked upon as a moral outrage.

So while Boy continued to be disobeyed – living in the suburbs meant living far from him and she was not about to do that – Gabrielle sent the "happy few" to shelter in the cellars in scarlet pajamas. The color was rather startling. "Why red?" she was asked. She replied, "Why not?" People weren't going to start wanting explanations, she hoped. She had slammed the door on her past and never liked to be asked to reopen it. But anyone who found the key was free to use it. Would the costume have been conceivable without her memory of the long scarlet legs? Consciously or not, Gabrielle, facing the threat of Big Bertha, turned back to Moulins and the 10th Light Horse. Strange parallel. Unwittingly, the clientele of the Ritz was taking over from the jolly horsemen of the *beuglant*.

Then came the dreadful fresh outbreak, as though four years of fighting had meant nothing. Again the German breakthrough, the British 6th Army outflanked and, galloping up from Pontoise, from Lyons, Nevers, and Moulins, the Light Horse, those same ones Gabrielle was trying to forget, who had been wrestling with factory strikers for the past four weeks, and the dragoons, and Adrienne's beloved among them, all hurled in as reinforcements, but too late, and with a break in the front over fourteen miles long it was impossible to connect with the English; then came the retreat of Douglas Haig's men, and Clemenceau toiling indefatigably from one headquarters to another, creeping within 300 yards of the enemy positions like some aged tragic gnome, decamping from one end of villages under machine-gun fire while the Germans poured in at the other, never leaving the front, haranguing the Australian troops in English and singing songs with the Senegalese, summoning the Japanese to join the war, insulting Count Czernin, Emperor Charles, and all that remained of the Dual Monarchy, stirring up the rest of the world and clamping down at home; then came the flushing of the anarchists out of their Montmartre dens, death penalties pronounced against Almereyda's accomplices, the Tiger, enraged, roaring in parliament: "Domestic policy? I am fighting a war. Foreign policy? I am fighting a war. I am still fighting a war . . . I shall go on fighting until the last quarter of an hour, for the last quarter of an hour will be ours"; Clemenceau pushing out Pétain in favor of Foch, *that radium-filled bastard*, putting him in charge of military operations, all the French reserves called up but those reserves couldn't hold the line any better than the British; and then came the second Chemin des Dames battle, disaster, 700 cannon lost, 80,000 prisoners, Compiègne bombed again, the enemy at the gates of Paris, Big Bertha busier than ever, the panic, concierges quitting their doorways, cooks refusing to go to market, scandalized dowagers replacing their cowering servants, deserted streets, overcrowded trains, proper ladies and people with cars fleeing the explosion-racked city, heading as fast as they could for Biarritz, for Deauville, where the proud villas and chintz-covered sofas offered themselves once more to weeping ladies but not the same ladies because now you could see their ankles. So many dead! Nobody was spared. Gabrielle's beautiful customers counted their losses . . . Lieutenant Prince Alexandre de Wagram,

Lieutenant Prince Jocelyn de Rohan; Captain Prince de Polignac, Lieutenant Comte Jean du Breuil de Saint-Germain, Captain Adrien de Gramont-Lesparre, Lieutenant Airman Sanche de Gramont, Charles de Chevreuse, Henri d'Origny, and all that remained of the 10th Light Horse was transferred to the infantry.

Gabrielle's freedom consisted in being different. No family, no husband, no children, no dead to mourn, nothing forcing her to leave Paris.

Four years before, at Deauville during the battle of the Marne, she had seen the numbers of her clients swell. What could she hope from the Chemin des Dames? Atrocious as it was, this defeat too did her no disservice. For one thing, it kept Boy in France. At Versailles, the Supreme Interallied Council was meeting day and night. How could he get married in England? All leaves had been canceled. A reprieve? It was Boy's marriage momentarily delayed.

A chance apartment rented in the confusion of the threatened city was, despite its peculiar atmosphere and a laughable alcove, the scene of her last happy hours. A powerful aroma emanated from the walls – a smell of cocoa. Fear of running out of opium was what had driven the previous tenant away. He had decamped, leaving a collection of kimonos in his cupboards and giving Misia Sert the job of finding him a tenant – an opportunity Coco immediately seized.

It was a ground floor on the Quai de Tokio, its windows designed to receive light from the Seine on one side and the Trocadéro hill on the other. But, having been covered over with opaque silk, they had the benefit of neither view. A dim twilight glow. The first thing one noticed upon entering was the discrepancy between the floor-level furniture and a monstrous Buddha. The alcove was completely lined with mirrors. More walls of mirror at the entrance, and a black lacquered ceiling. Details that were to remain deeply imprinted upon Gabrielle's mind. Tirelessly transposed, reworked, personalized, they recur again and again in her subsequent dwellings like obsessive leitmotivs. They recreated a decor outside which she would have felt unbearably foreign.

"*Qui qu'a vu Coco dans le Trocadéro?*" Did the woman traversing her season in despair ever remember that other Gabrielle, the one who had dreamed of being crowned queen of the music hall? "*Qui qu'a vu Coco . . .*" There she was, at the Trocadéro, having "arrived," as they say. But arrived where? Love, security, everything was still out of reach. What little she possessed had cost her so much in effort, had meant so many obstacles. She had been offered nothing except a part to play, always the same, the part of offstage lover, the eternal extra. Extra let her be, then. She was inclined to give up the fight and accept her part – but only on condition that what had made her happy these last years would endure. She imagined what her life would be without the daily surprise of Boy's visits. Without him she would have nothing at all. More than ever, she wanted to keep him.

Warmer weather came, and the American army was ready. By September the end was in sight. A few more ordeals, the battles of the Argonne, and it was October. Arthur Capel had gone back to England. News of his marriage reached his French friends just as victory became assured.

An Invernesshire mansion had been the setting for his wedding: Beaufort Castle, standing on a rise above a landscape in which fields, streams, moors, and lochs were so arbitrarily entangled that one knew in an instant this could only be the heart of Scotland. The ceremony took place in the private chapel of Lord Lovat, the bride's brother-in-law and fourteenth baron of the name. Did any thought for the daughter of the Cévennes market traders cloud Boy's satisfaction as he was received, not in the guise of raiding commando but as full-fledged member, into a family noted for its versatility no less than its lineage? To be sure, Lord Lovat owed the prestige he enjoyed in the House of Lords not only to his exceptional command of Scottish domestic affairs but also to the fact that the folkways of the grouse were an open book to him. One should add that in the Boer wars he had commanded the Lovat Scouts, a private regiment formed of the men of his own clan levied on his own land by himself. His children and servants filled every nook and cranny of a dwelling in which draped tables, Oriental vases, fireplaces, screens, shades, racks, and stands crushed by hangings and festoons and so many other accretions of the Victorian age had gradually softened the asperities of a primitive stronghold. Lovat hospitality could be compared to no other. They could make anyone believe the family had been born without a trace of partisan passion and they agreed with everything. Warring politicians, Tories and Liberals alike, young men down from Oxford exhibiting the tempered socialism which upper-class students of the day so proudly affected, preachers and poets – such as Ronald Knox and Maurice Baring – streamed in and out all summer long, and the main danger to which guests at Beaufort Castle were exposed was that of coming away a papist, victim of a shotgun conversion, for the most intriguing thing about Lord Lovat as a Scottish peer was his militant Roman Catholicism.

Kind souls complacently treated Gabrielle to a description of this distinguished home which, because of Lady Lovat's affection for her sister, the young Mrs Capel, opened wide its doors to Boy. By marriage, he had now acquired what he most desired: a solid connection.

Arthur Capel had changed camp.

Gabrielle Chanel thought that freedom for her would now consist in offering herself a garden filled with lilacs and roses, in which she could relax after the work that provided the only certainty in her world. Lilacs, roses, and a view, something expansive and restful to contemplate with the kind of affection she no longer felt for Boy. She imagined this state of mind would be permanent, and for it rented a villa named La Milanaise at St Cucufa, where she went to spend lonely days. She chose it for the lilacs and the roses, and the view of a festive Paris chanting its victory, where people were singing and crying in the same breath and a delirious crowd cheered Clemenceau in the streets – all that enthusiasm she did not share. But was it only for that? Wasn't the isolation of the house at St Cucufa an answer to Boy's wish? A quiet, discreet place where she could live *out of the way*. The gentle air of St Cucufa could not help Gabrielle bear the pain she was enduring, however. A gnawing resentment.

Then, men came to the house, the men of her revenge, her spite; men, to prove to herself that she was free; men, too, to prove that she could have them richer, more famous, more handsome and more noble than the loftiest of the young women Boy had ever toyed with . . . Gabrielle took to men as she might have taken to alcohol, gambling, drugs, night roaming, the danger of unspeakable places, to death.

She intoxicated herself with something else, too: the discovery of a new world, Misia's. She plunged into that world like a person drowning.

ON THE MAKING OF GOOD MATCHES

Gabrielle's woes all began in 1919. Arthur Capel was back, though, and evidently could not resign himself to being parted from her. He was rich and married, and had achieved everything he needed to further his ambition, but he could not help missing what he had given up in exchange: a more varied life, the "bachelor life" in which Gabrielle had occupied first place. With her he had freed himself from many a prejudice, successfully managed his career, and endured the horrors of a war from which the world was just emerging in ruins. Gabrielle was identified for him with the war. She was his campaign, his action . . . How could he help it? Shared activities which seemed secondary to him at the time – such as the various phases of Gabrielle's launching, and his underwriting of her first efforts – assumed a different value after his marriage. They loomed larger and larger every day until they became confused in his mind with noble and exalting deeds. In fact, it was as though Boy had to have Gabrielle's love in order to succeed in the hazardous undertaking of his marriage to somebody else.

Gabrielle watched this process taking place. But unlike Adrienne or other *irrégulières* whose fate she had too long shared, she was not a woman for dark corners and eternal sacrifice. She felt a sort of exasperated disappointment in Boy.

Not that she loved him any less. But those self-blinding faculties without which love is eviscerated, like it or not, were wearing thin in her. These were the seeds of a disenchantment whose fruits she was to harvest until her dying day. Because in losing respect for the style of loving of what was called the elite, she soon came to regard the class as a whole without indulgence. And from there to criticizing it and then to challenging its primacy – the elite? what elite? – was only a step. Taking that step was one freedom still open to her. Gabrielle did not deny herself it. A curious attitude in one who was called upon by her work to associate daily with that same so-called elite.

Nothing confirmed Gabrielle's suspicions more than the absurd contract into which Bertha Capel entered soon afterward; of her own accord, she chose to be married without so being. A decision that can be explained only as a touch of lunacy, a sort of bravado *à l'anglaise*.

Wasn't Boy's recent experience proof that the institution of marriage functioned poorly and ought to be abandoned altogether, at least in its traditional form? Wasn't it tempting to unmask the whole comedy of the arranged or social marriage? To make no pretense of physical harmony, to show the world a marriage of pure interest in which there was no actual contact between the partners: that was Arthur's sister's choice.

While a guest in a villa in Deauville, Bertha became the pawn in a bargain of a type one might suppose no longer existed.

Weighing in at more than two hundred pounds, with a fortune that passed for one of the largest in England and a revealing soubriquet – she was known as Cupid – Lady M. put one in mind of an evil genie escaped from the *Thousand and One Nights*. Every summer brought her to Deauville with her husband and two young men, only one of whom, the younger, was her son. The other was the issue of Lord M.'s first marriage, and it was on his behalf that Cupid was now exerting herself in Bertha's direction. The boy was only nineteen, but it was essential to marry him off. She found endless pretexts for bringing the two young people together. They didn't seem to mind. So then, like the wicked fairy in the stories, Lady M. swore to Bertha that if she agreed to marry her stepson, "she would have no cause to regret it." For Lady M. was prepared to award her future daughter-in-law an annual income of a million pounds. There was one proviso, however: no children. What about the fiancé? Lady M. would vouch for him. At the first rebuff he would desist. It was more than likely that a reluctant bride would be exactly to his taste.

Apart from that, Bertha was free to live as she pleased. The young wife might have as many lovers as she could take, as long as it wasn't talked about. Lady M.'s requirements, thus, boiled down to two: no scandal and no kids.

Was this, as many people claimed, Lady M.'s revenge? Some say Bertha was the lady's husband's greatly beloved mistress. But even more people guessed that Lady M. was merely earning her nickname again. By depriving her stepson of legitimate offspring she was making her own son the sole heir to Lord M.'s title and prodigious fortune.

To be rich and to live freed of any of the formalities of marriage: it was the answer to Bertha's prayers. She accepted the deal and, the wedding over, so ably permitted her husband to forget about her that forty years later, reunited around a roulette table, they failed to recognize each other. The stranger's features did, however, arouse a fleeting sense of *déjà-vu* in the husband. "That face rings a bell," he whispered to the maître d'hôtel. "Who is that old woman?" Which earned him the reply:

"That is Milady, Milord."

Eye witnesses saw Lord M. back away from the baize-topped table and take his leave as precipitously as propriety would permit.

Next it was Antoinette's turn to marry, also in 1919.

Aviators, as we know, were much in demand. The one she selected was of the most popular breed: a well-educated Canadian who had abandoned family and fatherland to enlist in the British Royal Air Force.

Oscar Edward Fleming was twenty-three when he came over from Brighton to Paris. Training for the hard task of piloting airplanes had not prevented him from leading a life he must have found singularly different from that for which his youth had prepared him. His father, a lawyer, had eleven children to bring up and no money. With four sisters preceding him in the genealogy, Oscar was the oldest boy. Sisters, mother and father, everybody was thrilled by his decision to enlist and become an airman, and the Flemings' natural austerity yielded, along with their natural parsimony, to the obvious fact that Oscar deserved some help. He took advantage of it to spend more than his pay and live in the European style, or in other words, well beyond his means and in the company of young men infinitely wealthier than he.

No mask is more deceptive than the uniform, and no time more muddled than that immediately following a war. Antoinette fell victim to a very common misapprehension: she thought he was rich. It was not only out of cool calculation that she encouraged him, however, but also in order to succeed where Gabrielle had failed: to marry for love. She fancied this Oscar. Oh, the infinite mendacity of costume! She imagined a flattering rank, a perpetual shuttle back and forth from Canada to France, and herself as an ambassadress of Parisian elegance presiding over all Ontario.

They became engaged.

The anxious Flemings dispatched their eldest daughter, Gussie, to Paris with instructions to investigate and report. But Gussie too succumbed to the allure of Europe and, after sending her parents a few vague but enthusiastic letters, informed them that she would not be back for a year. In her exalted state it was hard to make out exactly what her plans were, apart from the fact that on Gabrielle Chanel's advice she intended to devote herself to interior decorating. She had always been fond of antiques and bric-a-brac. It seems that it was also Gabrielle who sent Gussie to Spain bearing highly flattering recommendations to persons with resounding names. Gussie was going to a country spared by the war to collect Renaissance furniture. Ought they to pursue the investigation, dispatch another informer to Europe? The Flemings thought it wiser to let well enough alone. Bertha, their second girl, volunteered; but her application was rejected. If she went too, could they be certain she would ever come back?

Oscar was married in Paris on November 11, 1919. Antoinette's witnesses were a captain of the Light Horse who was none other than Adrienne's adored, and Arthur Capel – shipowner and chevalier of the Legion of Honor. Since the bride's father could not be left totally unidentified he was declared a merchant and, to make things simpler, a resident of Varennes, which, although untrue, sounded good.

After a brief stay in Brighton to complete his training. Oscar Fleming announced he was returning to the vast family residence at Windsor. Antoinette, his bride, came with him. She traveled with a chambermaid, seventeen trunks, and a crate containing a silver tea service, the work of a renowned goldsmith, whose urn-shaped samovar took up an enormous amount of space. At home, Oscar's brothers and sisters were studying for examinations and there was nothing light or gay about the atmosphere. In addition to his legal activities, Mr Fleming senior took a great interest in his country's political affairs. He specialized in navigable waterways and devoted his spare time to a study of the course of the St Lawrence.

Antoinette never had a chance to don the sumptuous outfits Gabrielle had given her or, since no one entertained, to use the samovar, which remained in its crate. Speaking no English, she had great difficulty in making herself understood by her new family. One of her young sisters-in-law called her maid a *singe* ("monkey"), that being the only word of French she knew, so the outraged domestic turned in her apron almost upon arrival, and had to be repatriated at the Flemings' expense. Mrs Fleming senior took a dim view of her daughter-in-law, whose exaggerated fondness for finery was turning the heads of all the girls in the house. Relations with Antoinette grew still more strained when Mrs Fleming found her youngest daughter smoking in the toilet. Antoinette, who smoked in public, which was contrary to the canons of good Ontario society, was accused of having given her a craving for tobacco. At that point, Oscar was sent to Toronto to study law. It was felt that he would work better alone. Antoinette, left by herself in Windsor, was bored out of her mind.

In every letter from Paris, Gabrielle and Adrienne doled out sensible advice, playing for time. They urged Antoinette to make herself useful. Gabrielle appointed her Canadian agent for Chanel fashions, hoping that might lengthen her patience and also put her costly trousseau to some use.

The arrow-straight dresses, some fringed with pearls and others with plumes,[17] were extracted from the trunks. Antoinette took them to some Detroit department stores, but the buyers wanted none of them. Such dresses did not seem acceptable, they did not conform to the tastes of the local clientele. Antoinette tried again. No use. Then, discouraged, she gave up. She had married a penniless student and been relegated to the depths of a province ruled, as far as fashion was concerned, by the very quintessence of banality. It was finished. She swore an oath of allegiance to Gabrielle and asked for a return ticket. The sooner the better. Then, whether innocently or as another delaying tactic, Gabrielle wrote to her sister telling her to wait and to her brother-in-law saying how nice of him it would be if, during the holidays, he would entertain a young Latin American desirous of familiarizing himself with the Ontarian way of life before returning to his homeland. The Flemings offered him their hospitality. The young man was a nineteen-year-old Argentinian who wore his hair plastered down with brilliantine, an eternal carnation in his buttonhole, peculiar belted jackets, and white spats over short blond leather boots. He had an amiable personality and was very rich. In his luggage he transported a gramophone with detachable handle and folding trumpet, on which he played, for his private delectation, all the latest Paris dances: the bear-step and the crab. He tried to teach them to the young Canadians, insisting that they were American dances; but they wouldn't believe him because nothing like that had ever been danced in Ontario. And then the tempo was deemed excessively fast, and the postures shocking. Whereas Antoinette . . . Whenever the gramophone was wound up she positively left the ground. She would put on one of her fine outfits and, head and blond curls tossing, swirl from Oscar's arms to those of the young Argentinian, bending and swaying in every direction. Once again, she was severely criticized. The Fleming parents wondered. Why had this Latin American been wished upon them and what was he doing in Windsor? They decided he must be Gabrielle's son who had been sent to Canada solely to entertain and amuse Antoinette. Would he ever go away?

He left as he had arrived, without the Flemings ever figuring out what he had come for in the first place.

Shortly thereafter, Antoinette followed him.

Did she tell them she was leaving for good? The fact that she took nothing with her, neither feathered gowns nor urn-shaped samovar, suggests that she did not.

The duration of her marriage had been a brief fling at Brighton followed by a dreary term in Windsor: less than one year. But that did not prevent Oscar from pining for his Parisian conquest. His infatuation with the little French girl, so lively, so gay, who sang and danced so well, had been sincere. He had, in short, loved her. The family avoided her name. In due course, he got over her and found someone to comfort him in his affliction.

Some months after her departure, Oscar informed his father that he had become a widower. He did not seem particularly chagrined by the fact. Antoinette had died in Argentina. Mr Fleming, not one to fool around with morality, suspected a trick on his son's part to enable him to remarry. He ordered an inquiry, which was duly carried out by the Royal Bank of Canada. Confirmation was not long in coming. The complications of a case of Spanish flu hd carried Antoinette off in the course of "a prospecting tour" of South America on behalf of the Chanel firm.

Who would have believed that two of the three orphans of Aubazine would disappear so soon? First Julia, now Antoinette.

We have no light on the subject of Gabrielle's grief. But it is very probable that the pain she was then suffering had rendered her impervious to all other woes. Boy . . . Boy . . . Gabrielle was alone.

THAT NIGHT BEFORE CHRISTMAS

All we know of Arthur Capel's last trip is what can be gleaned from the conflicting accounts of his contemporaries. He set out in his car with Mansfield, his mechanic. Some interpret this departure in the first chill of winter as a desire to break with Gabrielle. His young wife was awaiting him at Cannes, where they were to spend Christmas together. Boy was heading for the Mediterranean coast, they say, because he hoped to put an end to this madness of his love for Gabrielle by removing himself from Paris. Others put a very different construction on the journey. According to them, Boy was going off in search of some remote house in which he could spend a quiet moment with Chanel.

Choose whichever version you prefer.

The motives differ, but not the result.

It hardly matters whether his dream house was white or pink, or stood in the shade of cypresses or laburnum . . . It hardly matters what made Arthur Capel leave, since he was not to find the peaceful haven he was seeking. Only death was waiting for him.

A few traces of the event can be found in the English daily papers of the period.

Under the headline "English motorist killed in France," the *Times* of December 24, 1919, published this: "Lord Rosslyn, telegraphing last night from St Raphael, stated that Captain Arthur Capel, who was killed in an automobile accident on Monday, is being buried today at 2:30 P.M. at Fréjus with full military honors."

A Reuters telegram supplies a few additional details: "Captain Capel was driving from Paris in the direction of Cannes when one of his tires burst." The faithful Mansfield was seriously injured.

Lastly, in the *Times* of December 29, 1919, this: "Captain Capel's death is a great blow to his many friends in Paris. He was probably one of the best-known Englishmen living in France where he had important coal interests. During the war, he did excellent liaison work both officially and unofficially, and was a great favorite with Clemenceau. He was a thorough sportsman and at the same time a lover of books."

In addition to the traditional work of a liaison officer, thus, "that blighter" of an Arthur was performing what the English language chastely terms "unofficial work." . . . How much *all things are costume!*

Finally, in February 1920, with a forthrightness of which only the British press is capable, the *Times* published the last will and testament of Arthur Capel, "of Boulevard Malesherbes, Paris, and of Cheyne Walk, Chelsea, S.W., lately liaison officer at the Versailles Conference." One hundred words, written in his own hand, apportioned his entire fortune of 700,000 pounds among his official and unofficial heirs. Illusions fell. The deceased's philanderings stood revealed to every eye and one is struck by something like a posthumous shrug – "Since I'm dead, the devil take the lot of you!" – clearly expressed in the document.

The executors for England were Lord Ribblesdale and Lord Lovat; for France, Armand Antoine August Agénor de Gramont, due de Guiche. The *Times* published the document *in extenso* and the names of the two *irrégulières* mentioned in it were not abbreviated. Equal sums, forty thousand pounds each, went to a Frenchwoman, Gabrielle Chanel, and an Italian countess, a young widow whose husband had been killed at Verdun. The remainder, apart from various bequests to his sisters, became the property of his English wife and, after her, of "our child."

For Arthur Capel had a daughter, born in April 1919. Presumably unaware of the fiercely anticlerical convictions of Georges Clemenceau, and ignorant of the torment to which the statesman had previously subjected his American fiancée, a pastor's niece – "You have to choose between God and me" – Lord Lovat, whose devoutness made him somewhat shortsighted, thought to honor both Arthur Capel's daughter and Clemenceau by asking him to act as her godfather. This was not the first time he had received such a request. Peasants from the Vendée, army privates and civil servants had often tried, and all in vain. Him, a godfather? His secretaries transmitted his indignant refusals. But in this one instance, Georges Clemenceau relented. It is true that the ceremony was to take place in England and he had no intention of attending. He who was no longer either "Old Man" or "Tiger" in the hearts of his countrymen, but "Father Victory," sent a delegate to represent him. And Arthur Capel's firstborn had the rare distinction of being the one and only goddaughter of the fiercely anticlerical Georges Clemenceau.

At the time of Boy's death, his wife was pregnant again. And it is with the birth in 1920 of a posthumous child, a second little girl, that we reach the end of the earthly career of this Don Juan who carried within him a permanent contradiction between what he was and his desire for what he could not be.

*

When, on December 22, 1919, the news of Boy's death reached Paris, a few friends from the Royallieu set happened to hear it together. One of them undertook to notify Gabrielle. Léon de Laborde set off for St Cucufa in the middle of the night. There, his ring woke the butler. Joseph Leclerc* hesitated to admit a caller he knew so little at such an hour. But Captain Capel he knew very well. An accident? He was dead! . . . Léon de Laborde recalled how hard it was to persuade Joseph to wake Gabrielle. The butler knew better than anyone else what a plunge in the abyss it would mean. "Wait until tomorrow," he kept saying. But Laborde insisted. Joseph went. Then Gabrielle came down, in white pajamas, her short hair in a bushy tangle around her head. "The silhouette of an adolescent, a youth in satin," said M. de Laborde. For the first time then, he saw her powerless to hide an emotion, her face torn by a mute grimace, her expression betraying a world of agony.

But not one tear.

He also recalled how he struggled not to say it all at once, talking only of a very serious injury. And the butler saying, "There is no need for that, sir, Mademoiselle has understood," and then how Joseph hurried away to make her a cup of tea. After which they had to wait for her to emerge from her silence, not long, just a few minutes during which she never removed those stricken eyes from her visitor's face. "The worst of it," Laborde said, "was this woman crying with dry eyes." Then she stood up and, without a word, disappeared into her room only to return almost at once, fully dressed, an overnight bag in her hand. It was almost dawn. She wanted to leave right away. They drove until late the following night.

From Cannes to Monte Carlo, all the big hotels were getting ready for the big day. In winter the coast was English, and as there were no proper Christmas trees around, paper stars were stuck on windows and revolving doors, to make the winter visitors feel "at home."

Despite Laborde's pleas, Gabrielle refused to get out of the car in Cannes. He wanted her to rest. She wouldn't. She had a horror of the hotel, all hotels. They were parked, she still with the same frozen face, having sat in

---

* Joseph Leclerc entered Gabrielle Chanel's service in 1917, recommended by Misia Edwards, for whom he had worked since 1912. She had just changed husbands, and in becoming Misia Sert she thought it expedient to change servants as well. So the priceless Joseph, a domestic of Chekhovian demeanor, passed from Misia to Gabrielle, where he remained until 1934. The testimony of his daughter, Madame Suzanne Leclerc-Gaudin, who lived with Chanel from the age of twelve until she was twenty-two, has been by far the most sensitive and clearly observed encountered by the author.

the same position since the previous night – and at this point the comte de Laborde became a little confused in his recital, because it had all happened such a long time ago and he wasn't sure anymore whether Gabrielle had suddenly begun to look like a ghost or whether it was "as if she had seen a ghost."

But he suddenly realized that he had parked his car only a few yards from the spot where, ten years previously, a photographer who was "doing" the Croisette, had immortalized them all with his camera, Gabrielle admirable with her mournful expression under the big black velvet hat, and behind her, in rows, the college of her admirers (from which only Boy was missing, because that had been "before his time" as they say, but as soon as the picture had come back they had sent it on to him in the form of a postcard because everybody knew only too well that Boy already loved no one but her). So, that night in Cannes, Léon de Laborde skillfully began to put the car into reverse to move it before . . . But Gabrielle's hand came to rest on his arm: "Never mind, go on," and he left her curled in a corner of the car awaiting his return while he went to find out what was happening, even though it was three o'clock in the morning.

In other circumstances, the comte de Laborde would have telephoned the Casino in Monte Carlo, sure of finding Sutherland there, and Rosslyn and the rest of his English cronies, and Lady M. especially, for it was Bertha he was looking for. Finally, going from doorman to doorman and hotel to hotel, he tracked her down. Bertha was beside herself, but asked them both to come up right away. They must come, she had a suite of rooms and could put them up. Mad, but a good-hearted girl. And then, just before he hung up, another piece of dreadful news: they had come too late. The body had been sealed in its coffin that evening. Another blow for Gabrielle, after driving all day and all night, she would never see Boy again.

Gabrielle swallowed it like the rest.

Lady M. greeted them in floods of tears. Gabrielle returned her kisses, dry-eyed.

She waited for dawn sitting on a chaise longue, refusing to undress despite the supplications of Bertha, who was offering her a bed, mauve crepe de chine sheets, a swansdown coverlet, and heaven knows what else. But it was no. A reaction which the comte de Laborde still could not understand forty years later. Having spent all his life as a dandy in Paris, he was out of touch with the peasant world. In Lady M.'s elegant suite at Cannes it was as though somewhere, not very far away and very present although invisible, a body lay stretched out between two candles, with the boxwood branch and the jar of holy water and the crucifix on the chest and the sheet pulled up to the chin. However sophisticated she might have become, however beautiful and alluring, the atavism of the Cévennes rose up in Gabrielle then beneath the deceptive surface. She was that lean peasant woman whom grief petrifies, nails bolt upright to her chair, stiffens so that she cannot even let go of her handbag. Can you imagine a peasant from Ponteils, Alès, or anywhere else, in such a situation, *taking off her clothes?*

The next day, again . . . She informed Bertha that she would not go to Fréjus. How could that be? No use arguing. She would not go. But the funeral? No. She wanted to see the scene of the accident. Bertha offered her car. Gabrielle wanted no one to come with her. Not even Laborde? Not even. Bertha gave in.

Bertha could judge what happened from the account her chauffeur gave her afterward. He had driven the young lady to the place where Milady had sent him the previous day. The captain's car was still there, on the shoulder, half-carbonized, unsalvageable. The young lady had walked around it, feeling it with her hands like a blind person. Then she had sat down on a mile-stone and there, turning her back to the road, head down, not moving an inch, she had cried horribly. Horribly. For several hours, the chauffeur added. He had kept at a discreet distance.

So Gabrielle could cry; she knew how. But only with her face to the earth.

That night, in a fairyland Cannes, all a forest of parasol pine and euca-lyptus where a few vast villas emerged from endless gardens, there was more noise than usual. It was Christmas. So in the rooms next to Bertha's there was a party, with an orchestra and Negroes playing blues.

French, English, Americans were burying the war, hurling themselves after pleasure. All they could think about was jazz.

VI

The Slavic Period 1920-1925

"Every new fashion is a refusal to inherit, an act of sabotage against the oppression of the previous fashion; fashion sees itself as a right, the natural right of the present over the past . . ."

— ROLAND BARTHES, *Système de la mode*

BLACK SHUTTERS

It had probably been decided between them. Three months before Boy died Gabrielle moved from number 21, rue Cambon, where she had been licensed as a milliner since 1910, to number 31, where she was registered as a couturière and remained for the rest of her life. Three months after Boy died, she signed the deed of purchase of a villa which had been repainted according to her instructions and was now ready for occupation. She moved into it, yielding to the lure of remoteness which seems to have been one of her major desires in those years. Thus she exchanged the woods of St Cucufa for the slopes of Garches, one villa for a larger and better-situated one, La Milanaise for Bel Respiro – two names, fit titles for a short story by Colette; two gardens, as well, of the kind Colette best knew how to describe, especially the garden of Bel Respiro, laden with scents and song and copiously enveloped by trees, the whole expressing Chanel's very definite choice: to live hidden, not to be in Paris.

The first months of 1920 had brought some trying moments at La Milanaise for the servants of the young woman whose grief occasionally assumed alarming forms. On Saturdays, at the end of her working week, she would arrive to weep in secret.

Her butler told how she had had her bedroom done all in black – walls, ceiling, and carpet, even the sheets on the bed were black; it was all in rather dubious taste, reminiscent of the funeral fantasies of Charles V at Yuste and Sarah Bernhardt exhibiting herself in her quilted coffin.

However, Gabrielle spent but a single night in that room. No sooner had she gone to bed than the bell rang: "Quick, Joseph, get me out of this tomb and tell Marie to make me up a bed somewhere else. I shall go mad." And Marie, Joseph's wife, obeyed. She installed her mistress according to her wishes and spent the rest of the night at her bedside. The next day the black hangings were removed and an upholsterer was ordered to "do the bedroom in pink."

This anecdote is worth recounting less on its merits than for the passion implied in it, of a type no longer current in those early postwar years: a sickness that turns everything inside out, that can grow into frenzy, insanity, a passion *à la* Mathilde de la Mole, the heroine of Stendhal's *The Red and the Black*.

In Chanel's growing predilection for black there is yet another link with the peasant world. Everyone knows how important the garments of mourning are in the country. Also, it is not too farfetched to see in this story the signs of a language that is beginning to be influenced by professional mannerisms.

When she gave orders for her bedroom to be, first, "dressed in black" and then "done in pink," Gabrielle was using shoptalk. She presumably hoped her heart would be as docile as the strangers who made up her clientele, that it too would follow the fashion for pink, and that sorrow, once she had made her palace fresh, light, and luminous, would subside.

In short, she was telling her pain what to wear. Oh, costume!

Anyone who wishes to see this as trivial is free to do so. But for the others, Roland Barthes has written a book, *Système de la mode*, that gives a sense to this decoration of a private place, suddenly veering from black to pink. What was Gabrielle looking for? Release from the vise of her memories. Not an easy task. She began by giving way to the night, indulging in it, letting herself be devoured. Her imagination became so distorted that it led her to the bizarre. An edict covered the walls not in gray or mauve but in the heaviest thing she could think of, the thing closest to the clothes she would have worn if she had been a lawfully wedded spouse and widow: in black. Barthes says, "As a substitute for the body, clothing, by its weight, partakes of man's basic dreams, heaven and cavern, sublime and sordid, flight and slumber; by its weight a garment becomes wing or shroud, enchantment or authority."[1]

Gabrielle's first grief was all darkness; but then she shook herself, wrote "forbidden" across black and, tackling the bedroom again, tried to exorcise it by forcing it into pink. She trusted to the efficacy of the simplest possible charm, a direct descendant of those in the almanacs her ancestors used to peddle, a sort of proverb: "For a pink room, a happy heart," she seemed to be saying. She knew no other system. Another comment by Barthes is in order here: "Fashion can be told in proverbs, too, and can follow the laws of objects rather than of men, as it does for the oldest man in human history – the peasant with whom nature converses by means of repetitions: bright coat wants a white dress; simple accessories for rich fabrics."

It was not until March that Gabrielle, more vulnerable than a girl of thirteen facing her first heartbreak but bearing within her a second Gabrielle, sublime and ready for anything, finally left La Milanaise, and the curtain fell on the black/pink bedroom. She took Joseph and Marie with her, and the whole menagerie: two formidable German shepherds, Soleil and Lune, and their five puppies – her "Big Dipper" as she called them – and the two little terriers on whom she doted, Pita and Poppée – Boy's last present.

To Garches she was an extravagant curiosity before it ever saw her. She had had her villa stuccoed in beige and its shutters lacquered in black – two hues which made the entire neighborhood frown. Another instance of her faith in black . . . It was considered a wrong note. That black stroke repeated in the four windows of the facade was pretty, however, and went well with the paler gray harmony of a curiously concave slate roof. But Garches was wholly dedicated to the Norman manner. Bel Respiro opened a dubious parenthesis in the series of bourgeois residences – luxury cottages and rich men's bungalows that were like little temples to matrimony, displaying their half-timbering like so many proofs of social success. Whereas those black shutters . . . The occasional passerby would stop and stare between the branches at this villa that looked like nothing on earth. What could he make of it? The house resembled a painted canvas, trompe-l'oeil in 1920s colors, a stage setting turned to the future despite the fact that it stood at the junction of the rue Alphonse de Neuville and the rue Edouard Detaille.* Intriguing, to think that a luxury suburb dedicated to the memory of two of the worst daubers of the nineteenth century would be transformed, the moment Gabrielle arrived, into a meeting place for artists considered downright scandalous by the official arbiters of the twentieth, those latter-day Detailles and Neuvilles. First came Stravinsky, then Cocteau. And then Reverdy, then Juan Gris, then Laurens. The gulf makes one's head spin . . .

But just as Gabrielle moved with a single bound from the artistic desert in which her condition had previously kept her prisoner to the best that her century had to offer in painting and music, so she disdained the ordinary commercial theater almost as soon as she met it and, following Cocteau and Dullin, discovered Sophocles instead.

---

* Alphonse Marie de Neuville (1835–85). Pupil of Delacroix; a specifically academic, middle-class, and national phenomenon. Neuville painted scenes from the Franco-Prussian War with demoniacal minutia. His paintings were hailed as major events in official art shows. *Les dernières cartouches* was one of his most famous color prints.

Jean-Baptiste Detaille (1848–1912). Pupil of Meissonier; it is a far cry from Goya's *Horrors of War* to Detaille's "war-as-if-you-were-watching-it." A military painter, Detaille was one of the major exponents of the official art of his time. His *Le rêve* jerked more tears from his contemporaries than all his other allegories.

Of course Misia Sert was the initiator, but it would also be an arbitrary oversimplification of Gabrielle's new life, to reduce it to that one influence. Even without her, Gabrielle might have found a remedy for her afflictions in that singular passion: the sheer joy of understanding the artist, the creator, with no thought of collecting. For although overcurious about life, Gabrielle never troubled to covet.

Paintings? Drawings?

One is staggered to think how little she possessed.

Objects, yes. A perfect jungle of them. As mysterious as possible, objects seen nowhere else. Objects to capture and contain a breath of the unknown, a perfume of the Orient, an echo of a faraway world. Many books, too, some of them extremely rare. But apart from a pair of andirons by Lipchitz and one minute oil by Dali, no signed objects, not one portrait, and not a single painting by a master.

Thus, she loved the artists beyond their work. She loved them but desired only to be dazzled by them, and took pride only in having known them intimately and having discovered them better than some collector itching to carry their work home with him. The difference between a certain breed of amateur – for example, a collector of Gertrude Stein's ilk – and Gabrielle Chanel lies in their notion of creativity. Gabrielle was more than ordinarily sensitive to the mysteries of style. She fell readily under its spell, a penchant explained by her vast respect for anything handmade. Here again we would need to dismantle the mechanism of her attitude and look for its hidden springs, and we would undoubtedly find moments she herself had forgotten, by the millrace at Issoire in the craftsmen's part of town, or in Aunt Julia's house at Varennes, or in the garden where nice Uncle Augustin was raking, carting, weeding, and still others, many more, of which she could not be conscious, accumulating in the lowly hovels of her Cévennes ancestors, and forming her heritage.

In any event, she never lost her child's sense of the enchantment that can come from the gesture of a creating hand. The event itself was enough for her, the enthralling instant when . . . An eternal orphan contemplating the miraculous. With the qualification implied by her upbringing – namely that a miracle enlightens you, is not to be confused with an object of everyday manufacture such as a dress, and is to a large extent the work of God – and until further notice, any child brought up by nuns knows that God is not for sale. In this, the influence of the Aubazine orphanage and the convent at Moulins is self-evident.

Gabrielle's contempt for people who insisted on possessing everything they admired was phenomenal. And it was not want of money that gave it to her. Hers was a concept of art she had fashioned for herself with no reference to her pocketbook; it was something she had experienced, that was all. For anyone who knew Misia Sert – she, too, extravagant and rolling in possessions in those days – there would seem to have been a true resemblance between them, at the outset, that lay in their equal contempt for all people for whom a painting was just a painting. To be two, each confirmed in her notion that she was right – two of us, at last! Now Gabrielle had found a guide. For thirty years, she was associated with the thoughts, judgments, and tastes of a woman known to have had a share in every artistic activity of her age.

One can never say enough about how fascinating this encounter was.

Every day the granddaughter of the market traders of Ponteils was to see that Misia who, like Gabrielle herself, left nothing behind – no diary, no correspondence, not even a note – nothing; yet both made their mark on the first twenty years of the century. A light, insolent mark, the mark of muses, inspirers, and mistresses.

Now began the age of Misia.

PICTURES OF A YOUNG POLISHWOMAN

With her, you have the feeling that putting her life into words serves no purpose at all, the image having so long preceded and so far excelled any texts subsequently devoted to her. Legendary Misia . . . that way she had of refusing herself to anything *written*.

She tried to tell her own story but never found herself. As a result, even her memoirs do not give us a key. In *Misia par Misia*[2] Misia is not. One page by Paul Morand, who knew her well from 1914 on, tells us more than the entire book in which he too had sought her in vain: "Misia," he wrote, "not as her feeble memoirs re-create her but as she really was . . ."[3] A thumbnail sketch follows. No text approaches her more nearly; in fact, it is an abduction. Morand kidnaps his model at full gallop because "with her," as he said, "you had to work fast." Misia is there, all of her: the Misia of twenty, "a beautiful panther, imperious, bloodthirsty and superficial," admired by a few painters and one or two poets – the "Misia of symbolist and fauve Paris"; then the perfidious Misia, of whom Philippe Berthelot said you must never give her anything you cared about – "Here comes the cat, hide your birds" – the Misia who had "arrived," devourer of millions, the "Misia of World War Paris"; and finally, that "Misia of the Versailles Peace Paris," who was already Gabrielle's inseparable friend, the friend of 1919 and 1920, the dark years, the Misia who saved Gabrielle from the black/pink room by giving her Italy to look at. With her, Gabrielle. left France for the first time and discovered Venice.

We will pause here. Let us make it clear that writing on this theme means using words like "sketch" and "outline" and that we are talking about not one but a good dozen different drawings.

And after all, why not tell Misia in pictures? Découpage, collage, montage? Spread out the portraits she posed for, choose among the letters she received and the poems she inspired, add a few graphics, and make an assemblage of the whole that will leave the reader with an impression of a beautiful and rare enigma? Alive, she would have joined in the game, glad to be presented to posterity as a riddle in flesh and blood, oil, canvas, and paper. In other words, this is the only language Misia could adapt to.

Misia's heart. Images by Vuillard. 1895–1900.

First of all, her photographs.

The ones Vuillard took of her. Vuillard, who dressed in "ready-made" clothes from La Belle Jardinière and was so proud of his shutter camera. Click! His camera went "Click!" and immortalized, in a drawing room on the rue St Florentin, the ample curves of a young bride, her plump fresh cheeks, her hair dressed in the fashion of the day, upswept and bouffant. A fresh picked fruit, still sun-gilded, was Misia,* daughter of a sculptor, a jack-of-all-trades, quite worldly, and very much a Pole: Cyprien Godebski. Thadée Natanson had fallen head over heels in love with his young cousin, who lived alone in a modest apartment in the eighteenth arrondissement, rue du Printemps. He married her, although she was hoping to become a concert pianist and earned her living giving lessons to pupils her own professor wouldn't take. A man of great talent, that professor. He predicted a brilliant career for the girl. Musicianship, sensitivity, speed – he said she had all the qualities. When she announced, "You know that Natanson who has been courting me, well, I'm going to marry him," the master dissolved in tears. His darling pupil couldn't do that to him . . . Hold it, click! That was Fauré, the first famous heart the cruel one broke.

---

* Misia Sophie Olga Zenaïde Godebska, born in St Petersburg on March 30, 1872, died in Paris in 1950.

A few years later she made Vuillard weep, and then Thadée, the bearded groom at her side in the photo taken in the chintz-decorated drawing room on the rue St Florentin. The drawing room with the small floral print covering armchairs and walls, sheathing mirrors, draping the potted phoenix, which already, unknown to anyone, was a Vuillard. And Misia, too, was a Vuillard, and what about her bearded Thadée . . .

Here another photograph, again from Vuillard's Kodak: Misia one summer day, dressed in a full, soft tunic gliding to the ground – a "tea-gown," but one that bore no remotest resemblance to Maud Mazuel's provocations in the garden at Souvigny-sur-Orge; on the contrary, impeccably chaste was that teagown, with a sort of peplum held between the breasts by a velvet knot which one imagines red and whose mere presence on this swelling, sedate bodice was wildly exciting. Her expression? That of a well-fed, ruthless cat, fixed upon the face of a puny sister-in-law as though to say, "Ah, may I never, never look like her!" For contrast, place across from this silhouette of sublime plenitude another face, that of Misia's last years, Misia after opium had turned her into a skeletal old woman, still royally insolent and extreme in everything, but nevertheless pathetic and somehow defeated. Useless to seek there any trace of the woman Thadée had loved. What had happened to his cruel young Pole?

Then, in case some might be misled by the collage, we will group together, mount, and compose in the form of a monument, like an arrow stuck in the ground in the center of a maze to show the way out, all the paintings Vuillard made of her: *Misia aux Champs*, 1896; *Misia au corsage à pois*, 1897; *Misia à la tenture fleurie*, 1898; *Misia à la partie de dames*, 1899; and then, for one last look at the gentle Vuillard, let an end of his scarf peep out, cut out a piece of his eternal bowler hat, a fragment from his short boots, put in his bald forehead (from Bonnard's study drawn in 1908), and include a scrap of his writing snipped from a letter to Misia; throw it into a corner first, though, for that is undoubtedly what she did with it – no, better, assemble all the letters he sent her and show them like that, crumpled and blotted, first of all the one in which he thanked her for a recording she had just made (here, profile of Ludwig van), and circle these words: "Through you, I should owe this other joy to old Beethoven, melancholic as all else that comes to me from him. But he also makes one think so strongly of sweet reason and health, like you, Misia, who have so great a share of them," and this bit too: ". . . I have always been very shy with you," and finally, on a torn scrap these scarcely legible words which explain all the rest: ". . . happiness was that you were there."

Misia's spirit.
Texts by Verlaine. Mallarmé. Diaghilev. 1896–98, and 1914.

Like a wind blowing over her, the incessant rustling of talent. So many artists! A garland of beards of many colors: Lautrec's bushy collar, Fénéon's little tuft, Roussel's flowing mane, Renoir's trim white patch, Valloton's goatee, the straight black Assyrian square-cut of the young brothers-in-law, the young husband, all the Natansons, the broad side-whiskers of Misia's half brother Cipa Godebski, friend of musicians, to whom Ravel dedicated *Les Contes de ma mère l'Oye* on which the flamboyant Caryathis had had the effrontery to improvise a few years before. And let not this hairy coterie be taken as an irrelevance designed to throw us off the track. There is no other way to measure what separated Gabrielle and Misia than to observe Thadée's young wife at home in her country house surrounded by her friends. This shows the arresting contrast between their pasts, one living at Villeneuve-sur-Yonne in an unassuming low white house with a pediment like a circumflex accent, a former posting station; and the other at Royallieu among the tall stones of the abbey Etienne Balsan had turned into his château.

In the one, horses and sportsmen and young women thinking only of lovers, success, and money.

In the other, painters and poets, and first of all, Verlaine.

Show him as he is in Valloton's woodcut, his eyes narrowed by an inexplicable shadow, his spheroid brow, and Misia in a photograph of that time, no frills or fuss, apparently dressed in a simple twill gown. But as the poem he dedicated to her, those few lines in which Verlaine compared her to a rose, has somehow been mislaid – Misia lost everything – put a manuscript, a title in its place: *Invectives*, or any other of the poet's works published in that review which now belongs to a legendary past, *La Revue blanche*. The review was founded by Thadée Natanson; Proust and Gide were among its contributors. It appeared from 1891 to 1903 and it was to the impressionists what *Nord-Sud* was to the cubists fifteen years later. And Misia was the heart of it, the spirit, the body. And who else was its publicity and its poster? Does any other document give a better idea of her influence? For on newsstands, in shop windows, and on booksellers' shelves, it was she, so easily recognizable under the heavy mask of her veils, who personified it. Include at this point, then, the best of *La Revue blanche* posters, the one signed Lautrec.

Another contemporary document: here, one sunny September Sunday, are Misia and her friends, and among them, Renoir. That was the day painters and poets followed Mallarmé's funeral cortège to the Samoreau cemetery. The friend who used to walk over for a visit, their Saturday evening caller, had left them. Here, in violent contrast, frankly invading the rest: a pair of clogs, the ones Mallarmé used to put on before setting out for the Natansons'. And the label from one great wine, too: a claret he brought along every time. And finally, a heavy lined cloak: the one he threw over his shoulders before returning home again late at night. And then, somewhere, in very big letters, the words, "Ha, ha! Such a sweet girl," because that is what Mallarmé used to say when Misia sat down at the piano to play, and because the famous quatrain he gave her, written on a fan, has been quoted too often.

In 1933 Cocteau claimed that Misia still had the fan, he had seen it in her hands: "Her fan bore Mallarmé's famous quatrain and I do believe that of all her marriage contracts and all her residence permits, this is beyond any doubt the only identification paper ever preserved by this admirably muddled Polishwoman . . ."[4] Ten years later she confessed that she had no idea where she had put it . . . Whatever became of Misia's fan?

Consent to produce the fan only if enlightened amateurs, not seeing it, should feel themselves cheated:

Aile que du papier déploie
Bats toute si t'initia
Naguère à l'orage et la joie
De son piano Misia.

(Wing by paper spread: / Beat wide, if ever / Misia from her piano initiated thee / To storm and joy.)

Keep that quatrain, ever about to fly away; pin it down with a wooden clog and let one edge of the cloak drift across the final words.

In case you still have some blanks, some white spaces left to fill in, "to make it hold together" as the painters used to say, think of the word "sorceress" applied to Misia. That is what Eric Satie called her. "Aren't you something of a sorceress?" he wrote her. And the recluse of Arcueil was no man to importune the ladies. Rather unforthcoming type. But not with her. In the same letter he told her his "bit" was ready. The "bit" was *Parade*. He never called his ballet anything else. Lastly, let us add this, *mezza voce*, as one would use a confession: "Remember, if you please, that a long time ago we very seriously reached agreement upon the fact that you were the *only woman*

I could love." By adding a monocle on a ribbon, a top hat, a white toupee or any other idea on the same principle – opera glasses, anything, an original score, model stage set, page from a treatise on choreography – contrive to make this declaration of love summon up its author as accurately as possible: Serge Diaghilev.

Misia's body. Images by Renoir and Bonnard. 1898, 1906, 1917.

Misia leaning against the in-curved back of a bench, her admirable arms raised above her head: photograph of 1898. The only value of this vision of her, in a pose fit to damn a saint, with Bonnard standing in front of her and Renoir seated at her side, is as an intimation of the documents it evokes – the portraits, the masses of portraits. How many did she sit for for Renoir? Seven? Eight? She couldn't remember. So place here, as a piece of partial evidence, a letter from Renoir: "Come. I promise that I shall make you even more beautiful in the fourth portrait . . ." Essential, the final phrase of the message: "WE SHALL EAT AS WELL AS POSSIBLE." Put that in very big letters. Isn't that a predilection shared by so many French painters? Braque, Derain . . . A good meal, the fee painters paid their models in gratitude for that other offering, their presence. Remember the date of the letter, also essential: 1906. Misia was divorced from Thadée and had remarried. To make it clearer, place here one correctly folded copy of the *Matin*, a mass-circulation daily. That way everyone will understand that Alfred Edwards, its owner, had taken his place in Misia's life, with his millions, his political connections, his influence, his big belly, and his mistresses.

Misia had hesitated. What did Edwards' rich friends, the luminaries of the "Tout-Paris," have in common with the habitués of her Villeneuve-sur-Yonne Sundays, with Renoir the clogmaker's son or Vuillard the corsetmaker's boy or Bonnard and his wife who, before calling herself Marthe de Meligny, had been plain Marie Boursin, a little clerk stringing beads in the funeral wreath shop on the corner of the rue Pasquier? And what did Edwards want with her?

To get away from him, Misia leaped onto the Orient Express heading for Vienna. He booked the compartment next to hers. Still trying to escape, she hid in a little hotel. He reserved every room in it. Then she called for help. Vuillard first, then Thadée. Both came running. Thadée was the first to leave, tolerably disgusted by what he had seen, and even more by what he had done: Edwards offered him a job running a mining

Chanel in 1907, aged twenty-four.

Chanel in Paris in 1909,
unadorned by pearls or lace.
Beneath her silk dress she wears
an undergarment emphatically
braided in black.

early photograph of Chanel (undated).

anel with the ballet dancer and
reographer Serge Lifar in 1910.

Chanel with the Duke of Westminster at the
Grand National in 1925.

Chanel with Winston Churchill and his son, Randolph, at a meet of the Duke of Westminster's boar hounds, in 1928.

A drawing of a woman in a Chanel suit, c. 1925.

Chanel in Paris in 1931. The Parisian press always called her "the best brain the fashion business ever had".

A drawing of a model wearing a knee-length Chanel dress, which appeared in French *Vogue* in 1925. At this moment of the twentieth century, women were putting their faith in Chanel's new rule: simplicity.

A model wearing a Chanel dress, 1928.

Chanel in Paris in 1936. Despite once laying down that only artificial jewels should be worn, she decided to launch a new collection made only of real stones. Rumour had it that the idea and the jewels too were Iribe's. It was at the time of this exhibition that his liaison with Chanel became official and that he moved into her quarters in the Faubourg Saint-Honoré.

Chanel with Cecil Beaton in 1930.

Chanel in 1932.

Chanel on the mirrored staircase of her couture house in Paris in 1954.

Chanel with Jeanne Moreau, whom she called "the unmatchable", in her private quarters in 1960.

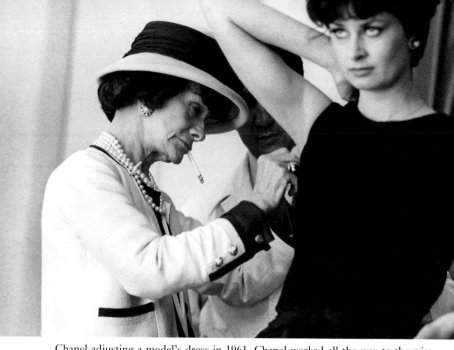

Chanel adjusting a model's dress in 1961. Chanel worked all the way to the wire.

Chanel models wearing "two impossibly lacey evening gowns", as depicted in *Harper's Bazaar* magazine, 1938.

concern somewhere in Poland, and he accepted. Vuillard stayed on, doing his best to play the bodyguard, with his sad eyes, floppy cravat and natty little suit. Without much conviction. Between a ruined Thadée and the powerful owner of the *Matin*, Misia's choice was made. Edwards the ogre appropriated her. Here, a photograph of an *irrégulière* who made the headlines that year: Lanthelme. Unbelievably beautiful . . . something in the style of Emilienne d'Alençon but a hundred times more seductive: Edwards' Emilienne. For it is practically certain that she was still his mistress some time after he began courting Misia. Accident? Lanthelme fell into the Rhine and drowned. Was she pushed? . . . On February 24, 1905, Edwards married Misia at the Batignolles town hall.*

All this in order to show the painters' friend and inspiration of the greatest poets of her day setting out to discover the world of money and light women, suddenly embarking upon a course which Gabrielle Chanel had traveled in the opposite direction ten years before when she wrenched herself loose from the fate and the circle of the Royallieu Emiliennes.

There were not only dissimilarities, thus, between the two friends. They joined hands across their secrets. One couldn't help thinking that Misia's attitude toward Edwards, her way of trying to eradicate him by refusing to talk about him, was like Gabrielle pretending never to have lived in Moulins. She would repeat, "Moulins? . . . Moulins? . . ." looking vague, as though you had asked her for the moon.

After she became rich Misia went on posing for *her* painters, more than ever. But how could Bonnard have supposed, contemplating her with the eye of a connoisseur as she sat on that bench at Villeneuve-sur-Yonne in a pose fit to damn the saint he wasn't, that one day the bench would become a divan and the garden a boudoir, mingling the glitter of mirrors and the

---

* One might like to muse over *Le Foyer*, the play Thadée Natanson wrote the following year with his friend Octave Mirabeau. How much did he actually contribute to this work, which was a comedy "of plot, social satire and character all at once," as Léon Blum wrote in a review in *Comoedia*? Was this Thadée's delayed revenge? *Le Foyer* was first produced at the Comédie Française in December 1908, three years after the Natansons' divorce. One can't help finding a parallel between the eternal triangle of wife, husband, and lover in the play, and the dramatic conditions of the real-life separation. The lover, "a man of money, brutal, cynical" and "a great financier," whom Blum also called "a scoundrel," is not wholly unlike Edwards; and the heroine, Thérèse, first acted by Madame Bartet, was like a Misia seen in black. "Box-office receipts were enormous. Paris shivered," says Pierre Brisson in *Le Théâtre des années folles* (Editions du Milieu du Monde).

satin on the walls? Portrait, please: *Misia* by Bonnard, 1908 – *Misia au boudoir.*

Imagine Bonnard at his easel, slightly overwhelmed, thinking back through laughter and joy to the other Misia, the one of 1898, and not far from her Lautrec, after heaven knows what wild night with one or another of his *Madames*, Lautrec snoring, his huge-lipped mouth half-open and one button at the top of his trousers undone for comfort, but having removed neither his linen hat nor his pince-nez, and with one chunky pear from the orchard within reach of his hand. There's a bite out of the pear, you can see the tooth marks . . . click! A snapshot. The camera of Alfred Natanson, Thadée's brother, went Click! immobilizing forever this image of the sleeping Lautrec. Another time, nearsighted under his silly hat – a Sunday at the Relais when everybody had gone for a walk – Bonnard had stumbled upon Misia and Thadée in the grass. Click! Alfred, with his newest-model camera, strolled that way too. The shouting! The photograph! They all wanted it. "It's a Renoir!" they cried. But he, Bonnard, although he said not a word, modestly thought, "It's a Bonnard." They were lying down, Thadée and she, Misia light against his legs, her head on . . . Ah, no! During working hours, one really must not remember how those two had been lying there then, him with his boater shoved back on his head, her with that lost gaze of a little girl to whom love has just been revealed. And her head on . . . Enough, for God's sake! Stop thinking about that, and especially during a sitting in front of that divan which was bad enough, what with all this silk, and evoked heaven knows what pose *à la* Miss O'Murphy, this divan on which a young woman in a lavish satin gown sat looking at Bonnard and smiling. Madame Edwards . . . Who would have thought it? Bonnard had just painted a portrait of the rich Madame Edwards.

Leave nothing out of that portrait, when you come to it. Make sure that the pale roses on the console mean what they did to the painter that day. So wide open, those roses . . . Not so much a bouquet as an excuse to look away from Misia and her breasts like an invitation, pearly and themselves almost too full-blown.

To tie it all up, stick in the Legion of Honor. The one all of Misia's friends, without exception, refused. Vuillard, Bonnard, Valloton . . . What could official recognition do for those who spent their congenial Sundays at Villeneuve-sur-Yonne? As for the pursuit of medals . . . give that Legion of Honor the place and significance of the exclamation points in an interview with Renoir: "Do we need protection? We are men. We are more than men: we are artists! Let them leave us alone! Let them leave us completely, thoroughly, and definitively alone! That is all we ask!"[5]

HEALTH IN VENICE

Misia was simply offering Gabrielle the same cure she had taken herself many and many a time, after a storm. A life, she thought, was something you whipped like cream, something you wound up and spun like a top, something you kneaded with both arms like dough; otherwise, it took over and lived *you*.

Gabrielle let herself be led. At first, like an automaton. There had been a brief Parisian period before that, in the first months of 1920, when she was seen at Misia's heels everywhere she went, present but silent. At gatherings in her home Misia enchanted her audience, at the piano or in speech. The word is not too strong: "She enchanted us in the literal sense of the word," wrote Jean Cocteau.[6] Her "open house" hospitality was very different from anything Gabrielle had known in the past; and there was also a style, a mixture of dreaminess and demand, a longing to be understood belied by a permanent "have your fling and be damned" – Misia's style, the style of Chopin himself. Misia, queen of Paris, in her heart of hearts was Polish.

She had her private universe, like no other. When Pascin, Soutine, and Modigliani were living in Montparnasse and Montmartre's stock was going down, that was where Misia's poets and painters still lived, still in Montmartre, the Parisian home of Bonnard, Juan Gris, Reverdy. Le Dome had become the meeting place of the literary avant-garde, but Misia's writers and musicians, Jean Cocteau and Radiguet, Auric and Poulenc, forgathered at the Boeuf sur le toit, nocturnal antechamber of the Ballets Russes. There was a reason for that: she was more than ever involved with The Dance. And there was another reason: her marriage with the ogre had ended. Edwards' millions had not made up for the fact that Misia's artist friends and Misia herself felt ill at ease with him. She was divorced. But her third matrimonial venture brought her to grips with another nabob. At least this one was a nabob of painting.

To have both the Spanish clergy and the Wendels as customers was not, obviously, in the line of a Bonnard or a Juan Gris, and it was possible to laugh at José-Maria Sert. Absurd, a painter using powdered gold, and working in the same manner for the twenty-year labor of monumental frescoes of the Catalonian cathedral vaults at Vich, the walls of the League of Nations, the salons of the Waldorf-Astoria in New York, and the boudoirs of the

Parisian bourgeoisie. One could be witty at his expense, and Cocteau never missed a chance. In his letters to Misia he called Sert "Monsieur Jojo" or said, "the falling shells meowed like big wicked Monsieur-Sert-style cats." Of course . . . But there was one fact nobody tried to dispute: one evening when he and Misia were having dinner together at Prunier's, at the very beginning of their relationship, José-Maria Sert had introduced her to Diaghilev, and on that account he earned the undying gratitude of the artists in Misia's circle. To work for Diaghilev was what they all longed for. And then, their muse's third spouse undeniably possessed a sense of theater that had been lacking in both his predecessors. And lastly, we must grant him a sort of genius with objects, a sense for extremes, and for creating alliances between contradictory periods, all done to a very high degree. Through him, Misia found her true decor. That was not negligible. The fair-play artist friends were the first to acknowledge it: "Monsieur Jojo was a talented decorator." In short, they did not loathe him. They found him "very Ballets Russes."

The big event that year was Igor Stravinsky's return. The composer had decided to opt for French citizenship. His stay in Switzerland, where he had settled in 1914, was ending; and everyone was predicting that the man who had already given the Ballets Russes *The Firebird, Petrushka*, and *Le Sacre du Printemps* would now resume his post at the side of the inspired impresario whose favorite composer he had been. And so it happened; Diaghilev immediately asked him to do *Pulcinella*. The idea was to work some themes by Pergolesi around the scenario for an Italian comedy which Diaghilev himself had unearthed in a library in Naples. Picasso was going to do the sets and Massine the choreography.

Gabrielle Chanel, who was almost unconsciously acquiring a taste for this luxurious Bohemia, watched the preparations for the ballet in Misia's shadow. Nobody knew her. She was hardly even introduced. Nobody heard her speak. She watched and listened. She had never been to such a wonderful party. For once, nobody was asking her anything. They didn't even bother to find out where she came from or what she was doing there. No more past. A great freedom descended upon Gabrielle. Without knowing it, she was entering what might be called her Slavic period.

Not long afterward, Gabrielle began paying more attention to what Misia kept telling her, and finally consented to her plan. After talking to Gabrielle's friends and questioning Joseph whenever she went to Garches, Misia decided that what her friend needed was to be removed from Bel Respiro and from her work, her routine; she kept saying that they were what was making life such hell for her, they were what kept her grief so keen. Go away? Get out? Gabrielle agreed.

So she went to Venice with the Serts.

Of her many trips, this was one of the few she would consent to talk about. She acknowledged that "the Serts had saved her." She didn't say from what, but that burst of confidence, brief as it was, showed the depth of her gratitude.

Who can ever tell what her first sight of Venice meant to her? José-Maria Sert, with his luxuriant beard, was her guide. It was he who taught her Venice as only he knew how to do it, he who made her love it. In his fashion. For to hear him talk the secret of the town did not lie only in its palaces, churches, and public buildings, in the splendors of statues and the apotheoses of ceilings. Gabrielle learned his lesson. Between museums and life her choice was soon made: she chose life, indifferent to the past that lay revealed in the Venetian museums, marvelously ignorant of everything it implied. La Serenissima? The what? She had hardly heard of it. But the Venice of the "roaring twenties," where Harry's Bar had just opened, the town stretched out upon the water where the gondoliers were masters of the canals, "the most brilliant town of Europe"[7] where everything was happening – she knew that Venice, all right. She always cared less for works of art on exhibition than for those on location, still in the sites they were designed for. And she never lost her soft spot – not for Italy, which she disliked – but for Venice.

Apart from this and London, she was seldom heard to extol the virtues of any foreign city. Berlin? She said she had never been there, which was false; but as we will see there was a reason why she never spoke of it. New York she was forever mocking; she spoke of Madrid as a remote provincial backwater; Venice alone, in her mind, attained the rank of a foreign capital. Perhaps it was her way of acknowledging the power of a setting unreal enough to force her outside herself, or perhaps, every time she said "Venice" she could relive the period when she was just emerging from anonymity, becoming known and, within a few months, Misia's equal. For that was the big event: Diaghilev, even more than Venice – the meeting with Tsar Serge.

Serge Diaghilev was on holiday. He was lunching alone that day with Grand Duchess Maria Pavlovna when the Sert-Chanel trio happened past, having arrived the night before. Exclamations. Effusions. Misia was a friend of Maria Pavlovna as well as of Serge. Three chairs were brought up and they all had lunch together. What conversation had the newcomers interrupted? What memories were the exiles exchanging as they sat face to face in the foreign splendor of Venice? During her husband's lifetime the grand duchess had sponsored Diaghilev's first efforts at the Imperial Theater. He had been one of those privileged persons for whom "the uncrossable barrier between the third lady of the empire and the rest of the world"[8] had never existed. She had received him in her St Petersburg drawing room, "where the armchairs had ruffles, the lampshades had ruffles, and even the brush braids on the ladies-in-waiting's skirts had ruffles."[9] When this world came to an end, Maria Pavlovna, by some miracle, survived. Her daughter, her three sons, all alive . . . To be among the living mattered far more to her, no doubt, than the loss of everything else, and Maria Pavlovna was one of those good-hearted women who, although no longer possessing a matchstick herself, could still contemplate with equanimity the successes of others.

After their tête-à-tête was interrupted, conversation turned upon the financial straits in which Diaghilev was floundering again. Massine was rehearsing a new production of *Le Sacre du Printemps* and Serge wanted to include it in his opening program in Paris. He was certain of success, even though the controversial work remained faithful in every respect to the spirit in which Nijinsky had conceived it; according to him, *Le Sacre* had become his box-office bread-and-butter. But he had to have money. The cost of this revival was phenomenal. Diaghilev paid no attention to the thin dark-haired woman with Misia. Although he saw her almost daily during the Serts' stay in Venice, Diaghilev did not even try to remember her name. But one can easily imagine what sort of specters were haunting Gabrielle during this memorable luncheon.

So this was the mother of that grand duke whose name the young people at Royallieu never pronounced above a whisper in order not to upset poor Jeanne Léry by stirring up bitter memories! So this was the mother of that Boris who had made her friend of Royallieu Sundays pregnant, the little vaudeville walk-on, the best heart in the whole scatter-brained bunch of them, Jeanne Léry who had gone to see Dorziat and got Gabrielle her first costume commission for hats. And Diaghilev . . . At last she was looking at the man Misia so admired, the magician . . . And the ballet whose revival these new friends were talking about would be the only one she had ever seen. That wild scene back in 1913, the turbaned ladies purple with rage, the old comtesse de Pourtalès bellowing her lungs out, her tiara all askew, the shouting and confusion and that crazy Carya with her hair cut so peculiarly that people turned around to stare at her – all of that rising to the surface of Gabrielle's memory. Why did it have to be that particular ballet they were talking about in Venice?

The trip to Italy accomplished more than one thing. First of all, Gabrielle's friends, starting with Misia, decided she was better. Boy was forgotten. The irrefutable proof? She was no longer just a spectator, she was beginning to participate. Hadn't she invited Igor Stravinsky to live in her home? He and his wife and four children were going to stay at Bel Respiro. Wasn't that a sign? And then, she had stopped crying. When we see women who are not crying, we readily pronounce them cured, ignoring everything they do not say, everything they hide, the secret wounds ready to bleed at the first bruise . . . In short, Gabrielle had recovered the strength to keep her feelings to herself, and so people considered her to have reached that degree of indifference which they tend to mistake for emotional health. She looked happy. They took her at her word.

A little while later Diaghilev, back in Paris but still without money to produce *Le Sacre*, was about to give up hope when the doorman of his hotel announced that a woman whose name was unfamiliar to him was asking to see him. He hesitated. He was busy. Then he sighed and went to meet her. At first glance Serge Diaghilev knew there was something wonderfully familiar about his caller. It was Misia's friend, it was she, Gabrielle Chanel, bringing him money to put on *Le Sacre*. "And she handed Diaghilev a check exceeding his wildest hopes"[10] and made only one condition: he was never to speak of it. That was understood, yes? Never, to anyone.

Diaghilev spoke. To Boris Kochno, a young Ukrainian poet whom Diaghilev hired as his private secretary in 1921. Kochno later composed numerous ballet scenarios and then, from 1925 until Diaghilev's death, played a dominant part in the artistic direction of the company. His works on ballet are regarded as authoritative.

It took a long time, half a century, for Gabrielle's gift to become public knowledge. In his handsome book on Diaghilev, Kochno related this incident in her life which might otherwise never have been known.

"THAT VIRTUE OF LUXURY . . ."

As far as her friendship with Diaghilev and Stravinsky is concerned, no confusion is possible. But what about Grand Duke Dmitri? In what circumstances did they meet? It is hard to imagine exactly how things were between them.

Some say this was another consequence of the trip to Venice; according to them, Grand Duchess Maria Pavlovna's nephew was there too, and she introduced him to Gabrielle one day in the summer of 1920. On the other hand, the event might have taken place at Biarritz, where "the grand dukes were being kept by women and drinking to forget the Revolution,"[11] where people from countries with a high rate of exchange – North and South America, Spain, England, Egypt and the British Indies – came pouring in, where the price of land was soaring, villas were building, and everybody speculating. Where the Chanel empire stood firmly on the foundations laid by Capel. Business at the Biarritz branch was booming. So it is not surprising that Gabrielle should have been there too. Nor is it surprising that a few of the Romanovs should have reassembled on the Basque coast where they used to frolic in their days of glory. A few of them still owned villas in the region.

According to Dorziat, it was definitely in Biarritz that the Dmitri-Gabrielle meeting took place, but in much plainer circumstances. No grand duchess to make the presentations, only Marthe Davelli. Since the days of the gay giddy weekends at Royallieu and her stage début, the lovely soprano had risen to the top at the Opéra Comique. She had been cheered in *Butterfly* and *Carmen* and was preparing, that year, to tackle the difficult role of Papagena in *The Magic Flute*. She still assiduously cultivated her resemblance to Gabrielle, so successfully that they were sometimes taken for each other. And nobody ever saw her dressed in anything but "Chanel."

Dorziat insists that it was at a party attended by at least three Royallieu alumnae – Gabrielle Dorziat, Gabrielle Chanel, and Marthe Davelli – that the latter introduced Grand Duke Dmitri to her friends and made it very plain that they were lovers. Davelli's love of fun had not lessened with fame: an incorrigible party girl. Whatever the hour of the night, she could always produce some nightclub pianist, or sometimes a sax player to listen to, some pretext or other for not going to bed. That summer, at the end of one such outing, she noticed that her companion was showing rather more than polite interest in Gabrielle, and is alleged to have seized the opportunity to tell Chanel, "If you're interested I'll let you have him, he really is a little expensive for me." However fantastic they might be as dancing partners, grand dukes were no longer the ideal life companions, poor things, for town painters of her type. Not a penny . . . everybody knew it. So going around with them meant paying, inviting . . . and what with the price of champagne and nightclubs . . . But that was just where Davelli and Gabrielle differed. She passionately wanted to please, did Gabrielle, but cared not a whit for partying and still less for the nightly merry-go-round. And Grand Duke Dmitri, in this respect very much unlike his uncles, cousins, and friends who had also escaped by the skin of their teeth, wasn't much of a go-go boy either. No wild oats in that young man's life. The eccentricities in which his cousin Yusupov* had become so proficient, the pranks which had earned him something of an aura of celebrity because he alone could make the tsarina smile, had never been Dmitri's cup of tea. Marked by both a miserable childhood and a severe upbringing, Dmitri hardly even bore a family resemblance to the other exiled Romanovs. The long legs, yes. Could anyone be a Romanov without those stork stilts? The height, too, the small head, and a fine-looking man, to be sure, but there the similarity ended. For the rest, not one thing in common. He may have had no idea what fate would do to him next, but Dmitri knew well enough what he had suffered throughout his youth. That was the truth. He was twenty-nine years old and sure of nothing else.

As soon as summer ended, Dmitri Pavlovich went to live at Bel Respiro. His man came with him. Ever since that dark night in January 1917 when the prince had been placed under arrest in his St Petersburg palace, Piotr had never left his master's side. He went with him when General Maximovich announced the tsar's decision: immediate deportation. That was the price of taking part in the murder of Rasputin – he was exiled. At the Nicholas railway station Piotr had seen Dmitri surrounded by police, "all approving of the crime – O Russia!" He had seen him tear himself away from the arms of Grand Duchess Maria, "his shivering, desperate sister,"[12] and the glacial cold and the whirling snow and everyone thinking the two travelers were headed for certain death, whereas in fact the imperial decree had saved their lives. It was simple: Piotr, the six-foot-six, broad-shouldered hulk with the long hair on top, the friendly giant, had always been there. Way back in 1905 at Tsarskoe Selo, yes, even then. In those days, only a few months after the assassination of Grand Duke Serge, Piotr was already looking after little Dmitri. Piotr, who understood without being told, who sensed the adolescent's anxiety as he helped him into his dress uniform. But what a year that was! And why dress parades? With everything else that was going on . . . But by order of the tsar, Dmitri Pavlovich had to present his new regiment to the sovereign. What was the point? He was already commander of the 11th Grenadiers and here they were making him head of the 4th Imperial Household Fusiliers. At fourteen . . . Was it because the heir apparent's

---

* Prince Felix Yusupov, who married a daughter of Grand Duke Alexander Mikhailovich, was Grand Duke Dmitri's accomplice in the assassination of Rasputin, and the prime instigator of the murder.

health was so uncertain, was that why the tsar was treating Dmitri like a son? People often said so. Anyway, Piotr had dressed Dmitri, helped him to buckle on his shoulder belt and sword, then to tighten the cheek strap of an enormous helmet topped by a fierce eagle hunched over its claws, its wings nearly full-spread. A fourteen-year-old boy with that thing on his head . . . Monsieur Bergamasco, court photographer, had insisted on taking his picture. After which, Piotr had watched while Dmitri, somewhat over-shadowed by his gigantic fusiliers, paraded past the emperor. The following year . . . What a lot Piotr had been through! The following year, at the annual ceremony of the blessing of the waters, Dmitri, again in dress uniform, was on duty beside the tsar while Piotr stood in the front row of the battalion of footmen, grooms, gardeners, cooks, and bottlewashers. Ridiculous ceremony. Instead of being held, as usual, opposite the Winter Palace in St Petersburg in front of a large crowd, and instead of blessing the water of the Neva, the tsar, who was almost living in hiding in Tsarskoe Selo, had blessed some water in a basin. And the only people there were a few grand dukes, the palace guards, his servants, and some gold-garbed popes. And the flickering censers and language of the Gospels had risen above the still waters of the palace grounds through which a shoal of goldfish sedately swam.

So many tragedies, Lord, Lord . . . Piotr often wondered how they had ever managed to get through them alive. And especially him, Dmitri. Because people had hardly tried to spare the lad. The minute the war began he had been sent to the Prussian front with the Horse Guards, and there Piotr and he had rubbed up against the Germans. Nasty business . . . sixteen of the twenty-four officers in their squadron had remained on the battlefield. Dead . . . After that . . . well, after that, they had not had too easy a time of it surviving Russia's domestic troubles. They had fled. They groped their way to the west like blind men. The exile in Persia had saved them. Sure and certain that if Dmitri had not incurred Alexandra Fedorovna's hatred he would have been slaughtered with the rest.

And here they were today, when all they had left in the world, the pair of them, was this house in the country where a Parisian dress designer had taken them in, and an infinitely tactful butler who pretended not to notice their threadbare suits or the newspaper lining the soles of their shoes to cover the holes.

She was eleven years older than he, they were together day and night for a year, the relationship meant far more to him than to her, they remained friends forever after, and that is all anyone will ever know about, the Gabrielle–Dmitri episode. Thus the interest of the testimony of the grand duke's son, who now lives in Ohio under the name of Paul Romanov Ilyinsky, when he states that the memory of Chanel never faded from his father's mind, that he never spoke of any other woman as he did of her, and that she was actually the one great love of his life.

It was no coincidence that 1921 was a good year for Gabrielle, too. There is more than one way of being happy. This was nothing like the wild joy she had known with Boy – but at least, in the smiling glow of her affair with Dmitri, she recovered a degree of serenity that helped her to complete one of the most important undertakings of her life: the invention of a perfume that would guarantee her freedom forever. Nineteen-twenty was the birth date of No. 5, upon which, over the years, her prodigious fortune was built. Some fifteen million dollars[13] of it, if the figures published at her death are accurate.

One thing is certain: Gabrielle was more active that year than ever before. The first point to establish is that the development of a scent combining natural animal or plant essences with synthetic products for the first time demanded an impressive creative effort. The shattered female Misia Sert was dragging at her heels less than a year before, that Gabrielle always on the point of breaking down, would have been quite incapable of it. Which implies a radical change in her personality, and something or someone must have brought it about. The support she found in Dmitri Pavlovich, for sure. Otherwise, what? Once again, although nothing allows us to affirm that she was living in total bliss, everything seems to indicate that she was regaining confidence.

Other designers before Gabrielle, and Paul Poiret in particular, had sensed that fashion and perfume had too many points in common not to lend themselves to a profitable conjunction, and had sought to branch out into the perfume industry. But nobody before Chanel had dared to move away from floral scents. Until 1920, a woman's only choice was to adopt the smell of one flower or a few easily identified flowers in combination. Luxury meant that you reeked of heliotrope, gardenia, jasmine, or roses, for although the product was highly concentrated, it faded quickly. Therefore you had to be overperfumed at the beginning of the evening if you wanted to be scented at all a few hours later. This explains those outrageously perfumed men and women who people the memoirs and chronicles of the opening years of the twentieth century. "A fat taciturn man with sensual features, Thibaud de Broc wore a shocking amount of scent . . . ," we read in the memoirs of Elisabeth de Gramont. Or again, "The duc de Mouchy was our nearest neighbor. I always knew when he had walked past on the pavement, because he left it reeking . . ."

Gabrielle Chanel was about to change all that. By creating a stable formula, she made it possible to use smaller amounts of it. In addition, she replaced perfumes having identifiable scents with one that smelled like nothing you could name. There are some eighty ingredients in No. 5, and although it may smell fresh as a garden, it is nothing like any garden you were ever in. It was in this way that she was making perfume history: No. 5 had the arresting quality of an abstract creation.

It would be too much to see Dmitri as Gabrielle's sole source of inspiration that year. But a close link between what she created in 1920–21 and what he gave her seems undeniable. To begin with, there was that mania for scent. Who can forget that no European court had a passion for perfume like the Russian, and had had it for centuries?

Which of Dmitri's phrases, which anecdotes made Gabrielle aware that a perfume was more than the instrument of deceit she had always mistrusted, readily suspecting overperfumed women of having "bad smells to hide"? In the Royallieu days her only favorable comment about Emilienne d'Alençon had been that she "smelled clean." Rather, perfume was an object of supernatural power, a mixture to be patiently experimented with and perfected until it acquired "that quality not yet understood by men, that *virtue of luxury* for which there will need to be yet other upheavals in the world before we comprehend it . . ."[14] One would also point out that coincidence alone can hardly be blamed for the meeting between Gabrielle and Ernest Beaux, in whose Grasse laboratories No. 5 was perfected. Coincidence, also, that this eminent perfume chemist was the son of an employee of the court of the tsars; and coincidence, of course, that he spent most of his youth in St Petersburg? That's asking a lot of coincidence . . . unless we make the effort to call it by its rightful name: Dmitri.

The invention of No. 5 was ostensibly a very straightforward affair, a piece of research conducted jointly by Ernest Beaux and Gabrielle, each putting his vast knowledge at the other's disposal. The leading role, of course, was given to Gabrielle by those whose interest it was and still is to manufacture evidence for a legend. Nothing boosts perfume sales like a legend. All you need is a fairy tale in which a beautiful sorceress and an alchemist lean together over their alembics, presiding at the birth of the mysterious liquid; then everything becomes possible. The sorceress knows just as much as the alchemist, of course; she decides, commands, gives orders and, where necessary, drops in a touch of this or orders a little less of that with her sovereign hand. The legend is then used for publicity and that's what you call good promotion.

But in fact, far from being plain and simple, the development of No. 5, for which Ernest Beaux alone was responsible – Gabrielle had the last word, but he only gave her four or five samples to choose from – proceeded in a rather heavy atmosphere reminiscent of the whispered machinations that herald a palace revolution, the fact that the subject was a perfume merely adding a touch of *Thousand and One Nights* to the suspense. Plenty of intrigue, sudden reversals and secret alliances. Nothing was missing from the script, not even the spectacular disappearance of one of Coty's top chemists. The deserter fled, clutching to his bosom the fruit of long years of research: the formula for a perfume Coty could not make up its mind to put on the market because it cost so much to produce. That was one reason why this chemist went over to the enemy: he was afraid his invention would never be made available to the public. It is more than likely he promptly handed it to Gabrielle. Who was he? Did he leave on his own initiative or was he bought? Was his name Ernest Beaux? All queries being met by the impenetrable silence of those who know, we must be content to leave this point in darkness. But one thing is certain: about seven years later, Coty was producing a perfume that was almost exactly the same as No. 5. But although it sold tolerably well, Aimant never made a dent in the Chanel market. No. 5 had been launched.

Yet the Chanel container absolutely contradicted the convoluted presentations favored by its rivals – the cupid-shaped flasks and lace- or flower-etched urns – because the other perfume makers still believed that such affectations were an effective sales device. The noteworthy feature of the sharp-cornered cube Gabrielle put on the market was that it transferred the imagination to a different dimension. It was no longer the container that aroused desire, but its contents. It was no longer the object that decided the sale; the emphasis shifted to the one faculty really concerned: the sense of smell, brought into confrontation with this golden fluid imprisoned in a crystal cube and made visible solely in order to be desired.

Much might also be said of the trim graphics of the label, which rendered obsolete all the curves and curlicues adorning perfumes of the past; and of the stark harmony of this presentation which relied solely on the contrast of black and white – black, black forever; and of the title, lastly, composed of the single word "Chanel" joined to one dry number and tossed into shop windows like a tip; "Play the five."

What was the meaning of this numerical language? It left shoppers as under a spell. And in the seal on the neck of the flask, what was the purpose of this initial all alone in the middle of a black circle? A "C"? Julia and Antoinette alone could have told . . . With them gone, who knew what lay behind those signs? Who else knew about Gabrielle's past, her ancestors? Who else could have alluded to the monogramming mania of her peasant forebears or the occult floor-mosaic at Aubazine? Nobody tried. Besides, the die was cast. Even if Chanel's rivals had launched more Nuits de Chine or Borgia, what could they have changed? No. 5 inflicted upon its competitors' headiest concoctions "the dishonoring stigma of the outmoded."[15]

The following summer Gabrielle went neither to Monte Carlo nor to Biarritz, but to a villa at Moulleau, near Arcachon, which she rented for the season. Ama Tikia was the name of this white house. The sea thundered against the garden wall.

Few visitors came during the two months she stayed here; Dmitri and Gabrielle were seldom disturbed. A fisher's pinnace took them out to swim every morning. They came back late, long past lunchtime. The faithful Joseph and his wife Marie looked after the house, Piotr was there too, of course, and Gabrielle had also brought along her kennelful of dogs.

Sun, sea, strolls through the countryside, and what more? A brief visit from a few close friends of Dmitri – Count Kutuzov and his wife and two daughters, who had also spent the winter at Bel Respiro. Gabrielle found a job for Kutuzov, who was to become one of the mainstays of her business staff for over fifteen years. But apart from that, apart from the sea and swimming, nothing, or next to nothing, else.

This holiday was so little like Gabrielle that its singularity is worth mentioning. It was the longest she ever took, and the only one she spent in this way. Thereafter she was seen only in the most fashionable summer resorts, and the houses she occupied, wherever they were, remained permanently full.

It seems clear that that summer beneath the Moulleau sun, Gabrielle and Dmitri were sufficient unto themselves. Can one imagine a stranger intimacy? She, the daughter of a market trader who was still haranguing housewives somewhere in France and hawking, from the top of his rickety wagon, suspenders, handkerchiefs at two francs a dozen, apron strings, and linen-cotton fabrics; and he, grandson of Alexander II, nephew of Alexander III, cousin of Tsar Nicholas II, he whose physical weaknesses and charms were displayed on every stamp, banknote, or coin of the countries over which his relatives still reigned. Dmitri's only resemblances were to royalty.

Did they ever try to tell each other everything? Did she confess her wretched childhood to him, her mother's death, her father's rejection? And he, whose mother died giving birth to him, what could he have told her in reply except that he understood, having gone through similar experiences at the same age? His childhood had been a unique form of misery – a solid gold misery.

He had posed for his first photograph as a lace-gowned nursling on the knees of an almost centenarian grand duchess, his great-grandmother. The artist executing this portrait, which was to be prominently displayed in the homes of all the Borises, Cyrils, Pauls, and Constantines of the imperial court, had coerced the baby into resting its head against the shoulder of a queen, his grandmother Olga of Greece; and since the infant's mother, although dead, had to appear somewhere in the family group, they had slipped a medallion of the deceased into Dmitri's little fist. Nobody was going to notice the long thread strung through the ring at the top of it and held by an invisible nurse.

Thus, all the Borises and Cyrils of Russia and all the Pauls and Constantines of Greece and elsewhere could tell themselves, when they looked at this document showing a melancholy orphan whose sad eyes were subsequently to trouble women's hearts so deeply, that little Dmitri would be looked after and mothered by three princesses, all dressed identically despite the differences in their ages, and all equally heedless of changes of fashion because no such thing exists where court protocol has taken its place.

But that was not what happened.

Dmitri was mothered by nurses.

He was brought up by young Englishwomen, seconded by silent assistants, also English. They weren't really wicked, only a little too strict. They said St Petersburg was no place for a child. Too many family obligations, royal receptions, too many tea parties in a great confusion of unruly cousins, too many morning-afters of indigestion, and then all those excursions to the Winter Palace in gilded coaches followed by escorts of hussars – it was dreadful. "Don't get overexcited, Dmitri . . ." Dmitri heard hardly a word of Russian before he was five. And then those never-ending Orthodox services . . . With peal after peal of deafening bells, choirs like thunderstorms, moaning and golden gowns, and the bass voices of the celebrants which so intimidated little Dmitri. "Come on, child, behave please . . ." No good, all that, not good for children. But Nanny Fry and her assistant, Lizzie Grove, both said they were fond of Russia even so, and looked as though they meant it. They were fond of it because it had inflicted a memorable humiliation upon that brigand of a Napoleon and also because Russia was the home of the samovar, the secret of good tea.

The St Petersburg palace in which Dmitri grew up was gloomy and architecturally nondescript. The third floor – that reserved for servants and the nursery – looked onto the Neva. Nanny saw to it that the chambermaids' vigorous songs, echoes of their loves and laments, should not distress childish ears. A little of the sound filtered through, though. Dmitri listened hard. He could feel his heart thudding almost the moment he heard a woman's voice. So happy, their voices, and lilting . . . But Nanny said he was not to listen. The nursery was to remain hermetically sealed off from the rest of the world.

Visitors were rare. Dmitri grew up without books or playmates, as Nanny did not consider them indispensable to a healthy childhood. Girl cousins sometimes called briefly, coming from nearby palaces and wearing that air of haughty shyness they were born with, which erected something like an impenetrable barrier between themselves and the rest of mankind. As for Dmitri's father: he would whirl in unannounced in some glittering uniform – Grand Duke Paul was commander of the Imperial Guard – and Nanny hardly had time to begin her curtsey before he was gone again. Nanny said such sudden appearances only upset Dmitri and really, that was not the best kind of surprise . . .

One day when Dmitri was sitting in front of his glass of milk and bread-and-butter with his sister Maria, both of them supervised by Nanny and her assistant sitting very stiff and straight because it was teatime and one does not lean one's elbows on the table or let one's spine sag, one day Grand Duke Paul came in accompanied by a bearded giant in front of whom all the servants had squatted down in weird positions. The children were told that he was Uncle Sasha and they might kiss him. But the servants said it was the tsar and you could only speak to him on your knees. And the children, whose Russian was faulty anyway, were completely at a loss.

There had been more surprises.

A short time later, Nanny Fry had just agreed to dress Dmitri in a blond leather overcoat which was much too elaborate for her taste although the little boy was especially fond of it, when a chambermaid came in in a great state. Nanny ordered her out again. She would not have people rushing in and raising their voices in the nursery. It was dreadful for . . . But on the heels of the chambermaid came an officer whose face was all twisted: undress the children, put them in white. The tsar was dead. Nothing good could come of all these orders and counter-orders, declared Nanny. Which had not saved Dmitri from having to stand through endless fittings while his ceremonial robes were being finished. Cousin Nicky's coronation – he wore a beard too, but he wasn't quite as big as Uncle Sasha – was to be celebrated with full pomp and ceremony. Nanny had said that really . . . But nobody listened to her and she had led a satin-clad Dmitri by the hand up to the platform on which they stood to watch the imperial cortège go by.

So Dmitri never had a mother.

At eleven, he had no father either.

For having become engaged without the consent of Nicholas II, Grand Duke Paul was banished.

One might have supposed that a forty-two-year-old widower who had already given the crown one princess and a sturdy little prince might dispose of his life as he saw fit. Far from it. Olga Valerianovna, whom he proposed to wed, had been born Karanovich. A bit meager, in the way of lineage . . . She was also a divorcée, and that was what shocked the tsarina so much, that was what she could not tolerate. So Grand Duke Paul was separated from his children. He might marry and go to Paris if he pleased, but Dmitri and his sister would remain in Russia, by order of the tsar. What was to be done with them, however? They were handed over to their Aunt Ella and Uncle Serge.

Grand Duke Serge was governor of Moscow. A long-limbed character with a morose expression, passably obtuse. His wife, the tsarina's sister, was extremely devout. They had no children. The home atmosphere was sinister. After that trouble in 1905, the couple had gone to live in an apartment in the Kremlin. Dmitri thought he would die of gloom there. No more nurses, but a pompous tutor with the rank of general. It was while he was inspecting Dmitri's homework one day that a terrific explosion was heard. A bomb had been hurled into Uncle Serge's carriage. Aunt Ella rushed out to pick up the pieces of her husband's dismembered body. After which she was seen no more except in nun's dress. She became abbess of the Martha and Mary Convent of the Sisters of Mercy.

Grand Duke Paul took advantage of these events to try to recover his son and daughter. Appeal rejected. Dmitri and Maria had to stay in revolution-rife Moscow.

Now there was no woman in Dmitri's life, except for his sister who loved him with an all-consuming passion. The two were seen wandering together through the Kremlin, among the palaces, monasteries, chapels, bastions, and arsenals which gave that weird conglomeration the look of "a fortress, a sanctuary, a seraglio, a harem, a necropolis and a prison"[16] all at once. They were inseparable. Then the tsar put an end to this unseemly display of devotion by marrying Maria off to the Swedish crown prince, despite the fact that his sexual affinities had not previously led him to take any interest in women. A few hours before the arrival of King Gustavus, her future father-in-law, and a few days before her wedding, Maria went into one of the Kremlin chapels with Dmitri to pray. They stayed so long that they had to be reprimanded several times. But they paid no attention. They heard nothing. What did people want with them? There they were, hand in hand, acutely aware with every passing second that they were living the last hours of their childhood.

As soon as the holiday ended, there were some changes made at 31, rue Cambon. Tasteful women, very pretty women, were hired, some as saleswomen, others as models. Many, when speaking to Dmitri, said, "Cousin . . ." with amazing accents. Their names were hard to pronounce, they were princesses, countesses, and exquisitely well-mannered, they were Russian and ruined. The cream of Moscow drawing rooms . . . As soon as they started work, a flood of their friends poured in after them – those whom fate had treated more kindly, those who, for a time, still had money to spend. And they spent it. And as these ladies were apparently unable to move an inch without drawing in their wakes everything which the châteaux of Styria or Scotland or the forests of Germany or palazzi of Venice contained in the way of kin, whatever place they happened to be in instantly took on the air of one of those rooms they had abandoned forever, one of those drawing rooms all in cretonne, passementerie and hot-house plants that had so successfully fostered their ignorance.

Leaning over a mezzanine rail, where she could remain invisible and yet dominate the scene, Gabrielle reveled in the success of her stupefying act. Unable to perceive the poignancy of this carnival of has-beens, all she saw was its prestige. Far beyond anything her competitors could offer.

Changes in the sewing staff, too.

Gabrielle was engaging embroiderers.

A news item which did not fail to startle fashion journalists. Embroidered dresses? From Chanel? What had got into her? Was she about to abandon those strict garments, all so much alike that they had inspired Paul Poiret's most famous witticism: "What did Chanel invent? Poverty de luxe."

It was true; Gabrielle had decided to round out her collection with a few embroidered numbers. Just an idea . . . a fancy to interpret that *rubashka*, the belted muzhik blouse, to translate it into her own language, why not? A body-hugging *rubashka* done in thin wool and worn over a straight skirt, with discreetly embroidered bands on collar and cuffs – a garment, in short, whose feel came entirely from the Russian soil but whose form was pure Parisian. Gabrielle could not help thinking it would add another weapon to her arsenal of feminine allure. She was right. Her lovers' pasts had always been a source of enrichment for her. The *rubashka* idea worked so well that she set up an embroidery workshop. Grand Duchess Maria was put in charge of it. After divorcing her Swedish prince, she had gone back to Russia to live. Driven out by the Revolution, she found refuge in Paris with the only man she ever loved, her brother Dmitri.

So it was that in 1921 Bel Respiro became the rendezvous for foreigners. In their native land the people assembled there would never have had occasion to spend a night under the same roof. One wonders at the chance that brought together a descendant of a Cévennes tavern-keeper, the son of a baritone from the St Petersburg Imperial Theater who had come to the west to renovate the music of his time, and a Russian *ci-devant*, son of kings and now a homeless wanderer, one more stateless person among myriads, to cohabit in intimate friendship. What was Dmitri's value as a person? The mind reels trying to imagine what the colonel of eleven, or the youthful conspirator who thought he could deliver the imperial family by killing Rasputin, might have become in other circumstances. As it was, his subsequent destiny was so colorless that once one has said he remained a fine figure of a man until his death in 1942, and Gabrielle's fast friend until the end, one has said it all. This moment of happiness in a villa at Garches, resulting in his ephemeral effect on a detail of Parisian fashion, becomes, although lasting but a season, the main event in his biography. It may seem a small claim to fame, to have brought into Gabrielle's salon that year, to the surprise of one and all, the Russian steppes in the form of a full fur-lined cloak, and the boyars in a dark shimmer of embroidery on a dress. But seeing it as Dmitri's farewell to his past gives a different perspective. How could anyone fail to understand that these embroidered dresses which other people were applauding, and these floor-length skirts that rippled as though the wind were billowing through them, were secretly restoring to him the Russia he had lost forever.

LIFE WITH A COUPLE OF GENIUSES

Gabrielle's parting from Dmitri coincides with her departure from Bel Respiro. No scenes. It was common practice in those days for a prince, when he had nothing else left, to offer his name and title to some young woman who had the rest. Dmitri was no exception. He contracted a rich alliance and married Audrey Emery, an American, in Biarritz.

Gabrielle's reasons for leaving Garches were not sentimental. The death of Marie, wife of her faithful Joseph, weighed far more heavily in her decision. Complications following Spanish flu had deprived the house at Garches of its diligent and highly esteemed manager. Gabrielle decided to move closer to her place of work. Also, the villa was no longer suitable for her purposes. Too small, too far away.

She came to Paris. The spectacular expansion of the Chanel enterprises had put it well within her reach.

After the uneventful suburban drive and weekend domesticities of Bel Respiro came a sterner scene: the Faubourg St Honoré, regular, repetitive facades and tranquil gardens, a history of intrigue, and a town house at number 29, the residence of the comte Pillet-Will. Gabrielle took the best rooms, a ground-floor suite soon supplemented by the second floor as well. High ceilings, a long chain of enormous rooms opening onto greenery that went all the way to the avenue Gabriel; there the eternal Joseph became a sort of agent-with-power-of-attorney, hiring cooks, footmen and kitchen-maids, and there a new life began.

The internal arrangement of the rooms, the distinguished classicism of this new residence, was immediately disrupted. Gabrielle wanted to escape from the overbearing greenish-gilded paneled walls she had loathed almost at first sight. But she was not allowed to make any structural alterations, so camouflage was necessary. José-Maria Sert and Misia were called in. What else could she do?

When Chanel took her place in the grand Parisian parade, the break with classicism had already begun. Architecture, furniture, textiles, colors, fashion, everything was about to be transformed. But the Arts Déco explosion in 1925, which was to consecrate, even in the eyes of the uninitiated, the work of architects and designers to whom Europe would owe a new life-style, had not yet taken place. Apart from a privileged few and the odd connoisseur, it was a rare Parisian who grasped the importance of a Corbusier, Mackintosh, Klimt or Van de Velde, and an even rarer one who commissioned or acquired their works. Consequently, France was in a state of more or less total confusion as regards line and form when Gabrielle instinctively gravitated toward the style most strongly affirmed in her circle: the baroque taste of the Serts. She was initiated by them, and through them she discovered – at the age of forty – the main components of a decor that she patiently made her own, gradually enriching it with familiar objects.

As much gold as at Misia's, and just as much crystal, but more black accents; hardly any marble, even less tortoiseshell, and absolutely none at all of that substance so favored by the tsars, who used to present every passing head of state with the inevitable malachite chimney clock – a Russian affliction that had not spared Misia, whose home sported a massive dining-room table of that aggressive green.

The first piece of fine furniture in Gabrielle's apartment was a piano. No sooner placed than played. By Stravinsky, Diaghilev, Misia, the pianist of the Ballets Russes, and on and on . . . There were complaints. Comte Pillet-Will, who lived upstairs, found the racket unendurable. There was worse: one evening, very late, Spanish singers and guitars. His indignation burst all bounds. Dance-hall music! Artists with a gallows air were seen entering her door, accompanied by an outlandishly dressed female dwarf and a legless cripple in his soapbox, who performed a parody of a bullfight in the middle of the main courtyard.

Once again the ground floor thumbed its nose at the recriminations of the upper level. Stravinsky and Diaghilev had gone together to recruit these dancers in Spain, and treated them like any other full-fledged artists. Among them were Gabrielita del Garrotin, a dwarf and remarkable dancer, and a legless beggar who also came to Paris. Picasso, who was designing the sets for this brief dance concerto, brought them to the Faubourg. It was at this time that he became acquainted with Gabrielle. Excited and amused by his compatriots' presence in Paris, he chose the "theater-within-a-theater" as a setting for them and, rather than placing them in any scene reminiscent of the common cabarets where they usually danced, he conceived a quaint nineteenth-century theater with a heavily gilt-laden black background and a double tier of red-upholstered boxes, and in each box he seated a carica-ture, painted in trompe-l'oeil, of a worthy dignitary in top hat accompanied by beautiful obese ladies. It was a happy time for Picasso, whose high spirits shone forth in this satirical evocation of his native land. A brief and curious phase in his life, when, breaking with the Montmartre bohemians, he frequented the "quality" and, with imperturbable solemnity – his Spanish gloom – played the part of the painter who had "made it." He accepted invitations to luncheons and dinners given in his honor by the vicomte Charles de Noailles or the comte Etienne de Beaumont, and for the occa-sion donned an ensemble in which he had never been seen before: suits cut in the latest fashion, butterfly ties and, ignoring the shrugs of his ex-cronies, a watch chain across his waistcoat. He inhabited this period as temporarily as all his previous residences, but he liked to make people think his reconciliation with society was permanent, and sometimes succeeded in believing it himself. Would he go so far as to accept official honors? Adorn himself with academic distinctions? People began to say so. Juan Gris wrote to his friend Kahnweiler in disgust: "Picasso is still doing beautiful work when he has time . . . between a Ballet Russe and a society portrait."

He became friendly with Gabrielle while working on *Cuadro Flamenco*, and even stayed in her house. Not for long, and only when the vast disorder of the Ballets Russes, where last-minute alterations and improvisation were the rule, kept him in Paris. His fear of loneliness – a dominant trait in him – gave him a sovereign horror of spending the night alone in his apartment at 23, rue La Boétie, of finding the bedroom with the two brass bedsteads empty, the drawing room with the heavy Louis-Philippe divan empty, and the upright piano mute under its inevitable garnishing of candelabra: the conventional setting of his life as the staid family man who was most Orthodoxly wed to Olga Khoklova, an officer's daughter and one of Diaghilev's ballerinas. But that summer he had sent Olga to Fontainebleau, where she was resting after the birth of their first son and where Picasso, who never tired of recording the attitudes of both mother and child, sometimes even added the time of day when dating his sketches: "19-11-1921, at noon" says one sketch of Paulo when he was hardly two weeks old. It was this doting parent who spent the night at Gabrielle's whenever he needed to.

Misia also had her room at the Faubourg, but for less obvious reasons.

On more than one occasion Joseph woke with a start to find a whole houseful gathered in the pantry. This quarrelsome, famished, parched horde? The Ballets Russes in mid-metamorphosis, with Serge Diaghilev, the man who tried everything, abandoning his traditional Russian sources of inspiration and opening up new horizons for the cultural life of the west by becoming the most ardent propagandist of those largely foreign artists who were soon to become the pride of French painting and music.

In short, until the furniture, which was being selected in consultation with Sert, was brought into a home whose style made history in more than one sense, the piano, installed in an otherwise empty room, was Gabrielle's only link with the painters and musicians around Diaghilev. The objects which came after it immediately revealed the character of a house as one in which provision for dreams had been made deliberately.

First of all, there were the Coromandel lacquer screens.

Arranged around the piano to form a rather theatrical sort of alcove, masking the openings through which one could enter, exit and reach other rooms without being seen, it was for this purpose that they began life with her. Joseph played the part of the invisible man with them, setting the table in the library and being careful not to disturb the artists – for whom he had scant affection, considering them all parasites, opportunists, and "characters."

With the screens, which were at one moment like tall, glaze-crackled walls and the next pierced with tracery, allowing light to filter through like a moucharaby, the guiding lines of the Chanel decor were in place by 1921. Often questioned as to the reason for this choice – not one journalist confronted by the mysteries of that setting ever failed to begin diligently digging for the key to it – Gabrielle never confessed who had influenced her. How could anyone have dragged the truth out of her? The staff of her daily life was concocted out of recipes borrowed from the Serts? The very vehemence of her denial gave her away: "What are you making up now?" she would fume. At the age of eighty-odd, when her obsessional imposture had swelled to a frenzy, she unblinkingly informed one of her most faithful followers: "I have loved Chinese screens ever since I was eighteen," and expected to be taken at face value.

The last chance of her prime came while she was living at 29, rue du Faubourg St Honoré; it was there, in that house whose like cannot be found outside Paris, shaded by enormous trees and looking as though nothing had ever disturbed it, that she was loved by a poet, Pierre Reverdy.

Thoughts of marriage certainly did more than cross Gabrielle's mind. Reverdy certainly loved her deeply, too. Would she relieve a poet's poverty? Make a happy man of that unquiet spirit? Not a chance. Could Gabrielle have guessed at the existence of another persona, then unknown to everyone including himself, a Reverdy thirsting for the absolute and drawn to solitude as a martyr to his stake? She had no inkling of it, nor of the somber joy that impelled him to run away: "To run away nowhere, that's what we need, underneath it all . . . There is an inexpressible thrill in running away."[17] From this it will be clear that Gabrielle was resolutely playing a hand she had lost from the start.

A provincial, a transplant . . . "at once somber and solar."[18] His hair was black, that crow-black of gypsy hair, his skin olive, his speech flinty, his voice resonant: Reverdy talked as passionately as she herself. Speech must have been one of the luxuries they refused themselves least, those two. Neither tall nor slender, he was not attractive in the ordinary sense of the word. He was in other ways, though. The striking thing about him was his strange ability to metamorphose anything with a few words. And then, the depth of his eyes. It was that, most of all, that appealed, the black light in Reverdy's eyes.

He was grandson of a craftsman and son of a winegrower – more than enough to tempt Gabrielle into trying to connect past and present. To a degree Reverdy was the speech and skin and hair and, in some vague way, the childhood of the Chanels. Her brothers – Alphonse the bold, who often came to Paris, and Lucien, the gentle Lucien, whom she had just gratified with an allowance as generous as the one earlier bestowed on Alphonse – had the same gift of gab, a sort of rhythm found at the heart of any peasant speech, wherever it may hail from. And like them, Reverdy was never happier than when working with his hands. If we add that he cherished the tyrannous memory of a vineyard at the foot of the Montagne Noire, over-looking the Bas Languedoc, the extreme southern fold of the Cévennes range, a pink earth gray-streaked in winter, green in summer, and utterly detached from the world; if we take into account the keen sorrow he felt when – sometime around 1907 – the wine crisis forced his father to sell the property in which he had invested all he owned, then we are abruptly reminded of the senior Chanel, eternally dreaming of vines he never possessed.

At last Gabrielle was living with a man of her own breed, as deeply marked by the hazards of the soil as her own people. By uprooting the Reverdys from their homestead, the wine slump had first made Pierre into a city boy unable to forget what he had lost, and then into a boarder at a school in Narbonne, a recluse enduring desperate days. His horror of the boarding school scarred him as with a hot poker. If ever Gabrielle told him about Aubazine or Moulins, how easy conversation must have become for them.

Reverdy was extremely proud of the master craftsmen from whom he descended, his wood-carving grandfather and his stonemason uncles, who carved for churches – and Gabrielle claimed to be first and foremost a craftsman. And how he talked about his father! A free-thinker and ardent socialist, Reverdy Senior had brought up his children to be atheists: "I am only a shadow of that man," said his son. "Never have I met a mind so flex-ible or so wide, coupled with such a violent and generous temperament, always breaking out of the frame . . . He was my model" – something else Gabrielle could be more than ordinarily sensitive to. What had she done, from Vichy to Paris, but *break out of frames*? Life would never offer her a man better fitted to understand her.

Later, much later, when the time of loneliness came, and rancor, and lies were hurled in the faces of the people she talked to like an angry refutation of things as they had been, the poet's name alone seemed admissible to her and worthy of being associated with hers. After Boy, Reverdy. Apart from those two, nobody.

Until the last years of her life Chanel liked nothing better than to compare Reverdy, impecunious and unrecognized, with the poets of his generation whose fame or fortune struck her as hideously unjust. What were they all, what was Cocteau? "A fake," she would say in a rage-choked voice, "a fake versifier, a phrasemaker, a nobody. Reverdy: he was a poet, I mean, a clairvoyant." Woe unto anyone who tried to tell her otherwise. Some names simply drove her wild. Valéry . . . She called him everything in the book: "A person who lets himself be covered with honors, the shame of it! They stick them on him everywhere. Like on a Christmas tree. Now they've got him on the front of the Trocadéro. The government takes us for idiots. On the Trocadéro, I ask you! Hollow, pitiful lines. What trash!" To her it was an unpardonable insult that words by Paul Valéry should have the honor of being engraved on a public building – even worse, on *her* Trocadéro. "Don't give me that rot! I tell you it's a scandal." She raged herself hoarse and jerked at her necklaces as though she would break them. She shouted that it was time people learned the truth. That was in 1950. She never got over it. Twenty years later she was attacking the president of the Republic. Someone had better tell him, she said, that he didn't know the first thing about poetry. The anthology[19] he had perpetrated was meaningless, because Reverdy wasn't in it. She would repeat: "Meaningless, you hear me? Absolutely. What was Pompidou trying to get? The Académie? Who's going to read it, anyway? Schoolboy stuff." How to stop her? In the end, people left her to her temper.

She owned the complete works of Pierre Reverdy in their first editions, and nearly all of his manuscripts. Among other treasures, a copy of *Cravates de chanvre*[20] with an original water color on every page, and every stroke at once so spontaneous and so exact that one is immediately aware, leafing through the book, that one is looking at the work of a master. It became impossible to *see* Reverdy except through Picasso's vision of him. For it was he, one evening, who illustrated that unique copy just for fun: "For Reverdy I made the illustrations in this book, with all my heart," says the dedication, and it is signed Picasso. A priceless object, which Chanel sometimes kept locked in her safe but more often left out within reach. When people said, "Some day somebody is going to steal that from you," she would answer, "Of course they are. Beautiful things are meant to change hands." And when she would give some booklover permission to spend a day in her library, he would come away reeling . . . In every one of Reverdy's works, in every manuscript, words of love and affection, year after year from 1921 until 1960, the year of his death. In *Les Epaves du ciel*, "To my very great and dear Coco with all my heart until its last beat," 1924. On the manuscript of *La Peau de l'homme*: "You do not know, dear Coco, that light is best set off by shadow. And in it I have never ceased to cherish the most tender friendship for you," 1926. On a later edition of *Ardoises du toit* (1941):

> *Coco chérie,*
> *j'ajoute un mot à ces mots si durs à relire,*
> *car ce qui est écrit n'est rien,*
> *sauf ce qu'on n'a pas su dire.*
> *D'un coeur qui vous aime si bien.*

(Darling Coco, / I add a word to these words so hard to read over, / for what is written is nothing, except what one didn't know how to say. / From a heart that loves you so well.)

On *Sources du vent:* "Dear and admirable Coco, since you give me joy by finding something to like in these poems, I leave you this book and would like it to be a soft and gentle bedside lamp for you," 1947.

Standing on the shelves of Chanel's library, Reverdy's magnificently bound works read like a confession, punctuated by storms and silences and strung out over the years. Suddenly, there, through these dedications, the story becomes plain to anyone who knows how to read. For once, Gabrielle hid nothing. She cooperated, even anticipated people's questions. Otherwise, why would one find standing alongside Reverdy's works a copy of *Tendres Stocks*[21] which Paul Morand sent them in 1921, joining their names together in the same dedication so that their liaison could be accurately dated.

Reverdy first met Gabrielle not long after Boy's death. It was at Misia Sert's, where he sometimes went, although neither music lover nor balletomane. He was interested only in painters and the company of poets and writers, always provided they were not socialites. Because he never hid his contempt for that sort. So he seldom went out. He had no time to waste on drawing rooms. With the one exception of Misia's, where he was bound by a sense of gratitude.

He had met her in March 1917, the year in which he founded *Nord-Sud*,* a periodical placed under the patronage of Apollinaire and one which,

---

* The literary review so called by Reverdy because it was the name of the underground line connecting Montmartre and Montparnasse, the artists' and writers' headquarters. Through *Nord-Sud* Reverdy wielded an influence which Michel Leiris defined as being "as revolutionary for the poetic sensitivity of our century as that of his cubist painter friends." *Mercure de France*, no. 1181.

with manifestos by Reverdy himself expressing a clear and forceful policy, and illustrations by Juan Gris, Léger, Braque and Derain, became the rallying point of modern poetry for the younger generation of the day.

Reverdy, although released from military service and relentlessly anti-military, enlisted immediately after the declaration of war. He was given a medical discharge in 1916. In his view, *Nord-Sud* was to bring together all those of resolutely modern tendency, French or foreign. To be a liaison among painters or poets who, although still imprisoned in the trenches, were also defending literary cubism: a review to be read in the mud . . .* *Nord-Sud* was his war, the only one he cared about, a war to establish the poetry that was breaking with the past. It was, also, the unexpected help of Halvorsen, a Swedish friend, that at last gave Reverdy a chance to express himself. *Nord-Sud* was his hope, perhaps his victory.

A more than foolhardy campaign, when one thinks of the poverty in which he was floundering.

After being discharged, Reverdy returned to his precarious lodgings at the very top of Montmartre, in the gray glimmer of a strange garden. Number 12, rue Cortot was a dilapidated edifice as famous as the Bateau Lavoir. The other tenants? Suzanne Valadon and Utrillo, Almereyda and a few anarchists who, after trumpeting for years their refusal to bear arms, had let themselves be drafted.

Plenty of empty rooms in the house when Reverdy returned, but the concierge was still there.

Reverdy returned to this formidable guardian angel with no great joy, for his sons were "perfect apaches"[22] and the terror of the entire district. He returned to the same old chill and mist, and the awful emptiness of the Butte studios, the silent streets, and all the things he loved about Montmartre as well as those he hated. An artsy-craftsy style, a belly-aching hirsute bohemianism, the "java" and the accordion – these disgusted him so thoroughly that he affected a completely contrary mannerism. Like Derain who went in for "English chic," or Braque who wore a bowler hat and tried to look like a bookmaker, Reverdy, whose aberrations in dress were confined to a little English cap such as those worn by stable boys, showed his contempt for the artistic crowd by wearing his hair short, a neatly knotted tie, and a

---

*   The painter André Masson, among others, became acquainted with Reverdy's work through *Nord-Sud*, by reading, from camp to camp, a poem of his which Masson found "lovely, lovely as a piece of flint." "Remémoration," *Mercure de France*, no. 1181. Joan Miró entitled a 1917 still-life *Nord-Sud*, although he knew neither Paris nor Reverdy.

double-breasted jacket he had never been known to remove. He is dressed like that, moreover, in the drawings Juan Gris and Picasso made of him in 1918 and 1921.

An early morning walker, he returned to the Butte and its steep flanks, its flights of steps looking as though they were hooked onto the sky. He mounted them slowly at dawn, at the hour when hansom cabs carrying the last nightclub crawlers home met carts coming back from market loaded with vegetables. His prewar job, his one and only source of income – he had no choice but to return to that too. He had been a proofreader, working for the morning papers that were made up during the night, finding short-term jobs here and there in little printing shops tucked away at the back of dark courtyards, until 1921, when necessity compelled him to take a full-time job at the *Intran*, at that time the evening paper with the largest circulation, on the rue du Croissant. And his wife. He returned to her, too. She was waiting for him, patient and dutiful in their icy rooms. Because there was that: two people had to live on what he earned, and keep warm and clothed, even though all his poems were rejected and he had been driven to manufacture his books himself, from the text, which he printed with the obsessive fussiness of a craftsman's grandson, to the binding, which his wife, an expert seamstress, stitched for him, and it was a miracle if one of his slim volumes, printed in editions of one hundred, found more than thirty readers.

The woman who shared his life belonged to the days of his Montmartre début, when Reverdy had only just arrived and Paris seemed like a punishment to him. Her name was Henriette. And the Italian artists, such as Modigliani, who had adopted her, nicknamed her Riotto.

A young woman with large, gentle eyes, she worked as a junior cutter for a fashion designer somewhere around the Place Vendôme. Nobody knew she cared for Reverdy until one day she quit her job, and from then on they were always together. Whenever things became too tough, Reverdy's companion took in sewing at home. She wasn't the only one. Agero's wife,* a little creature who always wore a smock and was often mistaken for a schoolgirl, was also a seamstress and also took in work. Fernande Olivier, who knew them both, remembered that "they spent whole nights sewing to support their great men."[23] There was a marriage, but when? Reverdy never

---

* Who was this Agero, mentioned by no one except Fernande Olivier? Presumably the most obscure of the Spanish painters wandering the streets of Montmartre at Picasso's heels.

confided in anyone. He was so reserved, so terrified of being a bore, he left his closest friends in the dark. Neither Braque, Juan Gris, nor Max Jacob knew exactly when he and Henriette were married.

And then came that year 1916, when Reverdy was discharged and a wild hope was born. *Nord-Sud* . . . a review in which the editor's name would not appear. Only sixteen pages, the first one doing duty as cover. It wasn't much, but enough to start with. At last he was going to be able to give space to young unknowns like Aragon, and to publish Breton and Tzara, to reveal them, win them over to his own cause; and perhaps, at last, the publishers would begin to take some notice of him.

Two women interested themselves in his project: one was Joyce's friend and admirer Adrienne Monnier who, by agreeing to sell in her little book-shop a periodical she considered too expensive – fifty centimes – but that showed, she said, "a serious and consistent spirit," did more than encourage Reverdy: she launched him. And the other was Misia. She helped him in every possible way. She found readers for *Nord-Sud*, made her friends take subscriptions, and, to give him more assistance without being too obvious, bought his first manuscript poems, those slim volumes he had made with his own hands, at the highest price she could persuade him to take for them. "Rare, precious things . . ." And whatever Misia said became law. She circulated them, showed them around, demanded dedicated copies.

"The single copy of this book was written for Misia," he wrote on the manuscript of *Entre les pages*. And ceremoniously signed, "Pierre Reverdy, at Paris, 12 rue Cortot, Montmartre."

That, too, was better than encouragement, and Misia could hardly have done more. But the trouble was that even that was not enough. Despite its modest dimensions, *Nord-Sud* came and went like a summer shower. By the sixteenth issue, lack of money and readers . . . And no one has ever heard of a financier turning up to rekindle a slowly dying fire.

Reverdy's attempt must be seen in the strange light of those years of the great transition from war to peace. Everything had changed; fortunes had changed hands, words had changed mouths. Monopolizers and sharks had taken over, as though the habit of baring one's teeth was now ingrained and that was the only language people understood anymore. Nineteen-eighteen – bullets had stopped killing; now it was the murderous shrapnel of money. So, Reverdy . . . Few authors have been so thoroughly persecuted. Him, bare his teeth? Cry out, perhaps . . . and denounce, and call men to witness. But bare his teeth? That was no more a part of his makeup than whining or buttering up the rich in the hope of extorting a subsidy from them. To use poetry for that – to compromise? Reverdy could never do it. "Life in society is one huge adventure in piracy and cannot be successful without a great deal of conniving,"[24] he later wrote. This author had no knack for parlor games. And besides, patronage was dead – nowadays there was no support except for things that brought a return.

When peace came, Reverdy was about to abandon the pursuit of his fondest dream. The *Nord-Sud* experiment had borne some fruit, undeniably. Breton had dedicated one of the poems in *Clair de terre* to him, and Aragon had done the same for the finest poem in *Feu de joie*. He was better known, more esteemed, better loved, and if only he had been prepared to compromise on certain points the surrealists would quite happily have welcomed Reverdy into their midst. In short, he had gained prestige. He had also found a publisher. That was the most tangible positive result: his poems were being published in editions of three hundred. But can you live on esteem? Having no fondness for complaining and still less for making scenes, Reverdy chose the diffident solution: he kept quiet. He simply estimated the extent of his failure.

In 1918, therefore, *Nord-Sud* became defunct. Reverdy was not going to listen to people who tried to tell him that in one sense he had made headway. What was the point of talking? He had lost, yes, lost. Publisher, prestige, esteem . . . Fat lot of good they were! And even new connections. What could he expect from them? He loved life, though. But his greatest satisfaction came not from pleasure itself but from excessive indulgence in it. Too much drink, too much food, too many cigarettes and everything else to satiety, to revulsion, even to remorse. However unconvinced he was of the existence of happiness, he still liked, heaven knows, to charm and be charmed . . . "Women, that is, women who need but one feature, a single line, a tremor of the figure or a grain of chance in the eye, to become fascinating."[25] In fact, he went after women as after everything else. He was by no means a Don Juan, but they ruled his life. Intermittently, however, and not that particular year. Hence the scant notice he took of Gabrielle, the first time he saw her. And she, still suffering from Boy's death, took little more of him. Which does not imply indifference. They got along well enough. Thus, before they came to love each other, they had already found happiness in friendship, back in 1919. A curious relationship, beginning with the sentiment that ordinarily ushers in the end.

A LOST CAUSE

That she had a hard time adjusting to Reverdy's ambivalences one can readily conceive. Gabrielle could not help feeling that his long sojourns at the Faubourg and sudden escapes to Montmartre, his obsessive interest in her and the dark delight he took in running away from her were somehow contradictory. That habit he had of proclaiming his hatred for all ties. The fascination of silence in this brilliant talker, and of asceticism in this man so sensitive to luxury that he called it "an ambitious spiritual necessity."[26] What was one to make of it all, what really counted for him? A form of unawareness of or indifference to others – was that his true nature? One day when Gabrielle was entertaining, Aimé Maeght (one of the most celebrated art dealers of Paris, and a friend of Braque and Reverdy) saw Reverdy walk down the front steps and, paying not the slightest heed to the guests' startled reactions, head for the lawn with a basket on his arm: he was going snail hunting. One constantly felt a protest rising up within him which he didn't even bother to hide, and saw, in his eyes, that conflagration Aragon had been so struck by, "that fire of anger unlike any I ever saw."[27] It was enough to drive one mad. You never knew which was strongest in him, his contempt for money or his love of good living, his conviction that happiness was a snare and a delusion, "a meaningless word which has become encrusted in the human mind like an inoperable cancer"[28] or his confidence in the human heart that you suddenly tripped over in mid-sentence. One was forced to question whether, with him, love might not have to be joyless. Gabrielle was dazed. As, for example, when Reverdy, wanting to finish with the myth of happiness once and for all, asked, "What would become of dreams if people were happy in their real lives?" A day came, later, when he returned to that thought and expanded it. A day came, later, when he proved that "the most durable and solid link between beings is the barrier."[29] Then she would accuse him of being unhappy *on principle*, and indulging in his disenchantment. If he was not happy, it was because he didn't want to be. Come, now . . . happiness existed. Even though her whole life proved the contrary, everything she had known as a child, the bad blood between her parents, the failure of her life with Boy, and even though she had as little faith in happiness as he, Gabrielle now exerted all her strength to deny it. They tore each other apart, agonizingly. Utterly bewildered, she listened to him repeating that "man understands the force and value of the poetic signal better when he is no longer bound to anything except by a few and feeble roots."[30] She stared at him . . . What was she in his life, a barrier or a root? Both, perhaps. Ah, to understand . . . to understand what she was underneath it all, that was her greatest worry.

But the strange thing is that she should have been so wrong about the nature of the conflict that was gnawing at him. There was more than his aversion to being unfaithful, although that weighed upon him, to be sure, and heavily. But weighing still more heavily, and stronger still, was what was calling him elsewhere. The heroism of purity, that dreadful temptation, a sort of Catharan* folly, a heritage of his native province. Who told Gabrielle the news? Reverdy himself? We will never know. The one sure thing is that nobody in the Montmartre circle of artists was unaware of it: Reverdy had been, in his own words, *struck by lightning*. Suddenly, to this free-thinker's son came God like a heart attack . . . Well, Gabrielle was not to be frightened off by that. Such were still her illusions, and such her conviction that loving and living were a business to be managed like any other, that she rebelled. Was she going to have to do battle with heaven? Wrench Reverdy from its grasp? She was not one to recoil. He loved her, so he would give it up, wouldn't he? Even when she knew the whole truth, Reverdy's conversion and baptism on May 2, 1921, Gabrielle never doubted for one minute that she was strong enough to carry the day.

We again owe our ability to date the beginning of this strange conflict to her library. On a copy of *Fermé la nuit*,[31] this dedication by Paul Morand: "To Coco Chanel, friend of lost causes" and a date, 1923. The exact period when the gulf between Chanel and Reverdy was widening. She loved him, though, and he loved her, but she was forever colliding with this fundamental discontent in him, like a nausea at life and all the cowardice it implied. An obsession which, as the logical extension of a literary crisis she knew nothing about, was all the more incomprehensible to her.

People suppose that at the origin of Reverdy's painful withdrawal into isolation and oblivion there was nothing more than a search for God. But they are ignoring the fact that Reverdy was alone long before the spiritual adventure overtook him. His work, his refusal to compromise, and his intolerance were inducements to isolation at least as powerful as his religious aspirations. They had broken the same bonds and were scarcely distinguishable from one another in his mind. He was already alone when Gabrielle began struggling to keep him, alone between her and Henriette,

---

* Catharism refers to a dualistic (heretical) religious movement of the Middle Ages.

alone with his few remaining friends. And he managed to discourage even the most faithful with his rages and indignations and defiance, his sort of peasant roughness akin to Chanel's own and, worse yet, his peasant intransigence which was not always easy to put up with. The surrealists, for instance: since the time when he was twenty and boiling over with enthusiasm, "the air has never been laden with such heady perfumes. Never have we been guided toward the unknown by such confidence and lightheartedness"[32] – since the advent of the cubists, nothing had appealed to Reverdy so strongly as the explorations of the poets grouped around Breton. As they began to be known, he came to think there were no major obstacles between him and them. He could subscribe to some of their goals. Their manifestos showed it plainly. Suddenly, something broke the spell. He no longer believed in their methods. Surrealist delirium, dream impulses, fantastic visions . . . What a load of nonsense! He tackled Breton and his friends on the need to regard poetic creation as a research into everyday reality conducted in *cold blood*. One had to keep a clear head, resist exaggeration and, above all, shun everything that deranged the senses. Anyway, Breton went too far . . . Reverdy kept saying he would neither kowtow to society nor be part of any literary stratagem whatever. Lucky for them he didn't hurl God at them too, like a slap in the face. The surrealists – without disowning him, however – left him in his rightful place, "at equal distance from dishonor and glory,"[33] and what had once united them quickly dissolved. One disagreement, one fracture, and more to come. He was becoming increasingly alone.

Picasso, Laurens, Braque, and Juan Gris were left. But for how long? Gabrielle went on seeing Juan Gris, Reverdy avoided him. Another quarrel there, which grew progressively worse and remained a mystery to all. Thus most of his first friends, those he could not live without in the early days of his residence in Montmartre, had become strangers to him. Except for one mystic who was also a bit of an astrologist, a poet who dressed one day as butcher's boy and the next in tails and monocle: Max Jacob. He was responsible for Reverdy's conversion.

So long as his impressive appetite for life kept functioning, Reverdy listened to what he took to be the maunderings of an incorrigible madcap without great interest: that is, Max's tales of his various visions, first in 1909 and then in 1914. On the shabby walls of the Bateau Lavoir an apparition of a man "of an elegance of which nothing on earth can give any idea . . . Christ in a pale yellow silk robe bound in blue."[34] Christ between the enameled iron toilet and the mattress on four bricks – and nice, unsuspecting

Max, whose feet were terribly cold that day and who was desperately hunting for his slippers, suddenly stood up and found himself face to face with . . . The next time it was while Jacob was watching a film at the cinema, and a character in a yellow robe invaded the screen: Christ again, but this time, to Max's intense surprise, his ample cloak was shielding the numerous offspring of his concierge! Lastly, during mass one day at Sacré Coeur, the Virgin said to him: "Goodness, what a mess you are, my poor Max!" Whereupon the irate Max retorted, "Not such a mess as all that, my good Holy Virgin!" and stormed out of the church in a complete dither, upsetting the faithful and earning a sharp reprimand from the verger.

Nor had Reverdy been spared a detailed account of Max's baptism and first communion, with Picasso playing godfather – a Pablo Picasso as prayerful as one could wish but still facetious, for he absolutely insisted that his godson should be named Fiacre; but Cyprien (Cypriano della Santissima Trinidad were among the seven names conferred upon Picasso at his baptism) was the name finally given to Max Jacob on February 18, 1915. And as Reverdy was intrigued by the story and had a great desire to know more and to understand, and as he plied Max with questions and Max shrank from no verbal acrobatics where there were friends to be converted, he had given, in his grubby room, a pantomime performance of the passion of Christ. A monologue, in ordinary language, but so enriched by Max's talent and imagination that Reverdy, who was highly emotional, had burst into tears.

That was how it all began.

When it came Reverdy's turn to be baptized, he wanted Max Jacob for his godfather.

But misunderstanding arose between them very quickly.

The literary differences that had separated him from the surrealists were now supplemented by spiritual differences that separated him from the Christians. Where would it end? Gabrielle labored to overcome the solitude into which Reverdy was retreating. She stepped in at every opportunity. She knew Max Jacob very well, he amused her enormously. He used to ask her advice about shirts, worked out her horoscope, and read her palm, described Christ's exquisite hair style to her and advised her to "launch" a similar fashion. Best of all, he made her laugh until she cried the day he told her how he had been simultaneously appointed superstitions consultant on lucky and unlucky colors to Paul Poiret, and spiritual adviser to the princesse Ghika, with whom he spent his holidays. This most pious of ladies was none other than that most beautiful of belles, Liane de Pougy, who had married herself into a princedom.

It was at Misia's, of course, that Gabrielle had met Max Jacob a few years before. And not just any day, either . . . The day he had come to introduce his latest discovery, a child prodigy of fourteen: Raymond Radiguet.

Such strange years, engendering so many different explosions. The fireworks of the Arts Déco, the shock of the first surrealist exhibition, the earthquakes of the Black Revue added to the stupefying nakedness of Josephine Baker, and *The Gold Rush*, creating a permanent alliance between Charlie Chaplin and the French intellectual.

But no one yet seems to have recognized how important a part Gabrielle played in those years – a fleeting and barely outlined image in this theater of the unpredictable.

A long year, a lost battle. Thus can be summed up the final months of Gabrielle's sole literary romance. It was 1924. There were one or two truces with Reverdy but not enough. After that, the temptation of God was decidedly the stronger and there was no more room in the poet's life for anything but exile, solitude, and a sort of supreme heroism of absence, the unique source of his inspiration. "Poetry is in what is not. In what we feel the lack of. In what we would like there to be."[35]

Tisser, interposer entre le monde et soi
le filet mots silencieux
dans tous les coins de la chambre noire.[36]

(Weave and hang between world and self / the net of silent words / in every corner of the black room.)

That was where Pierre Reverdy was heading.
So Gabrielle bowed out.
The attraction of that black room was one of the things she understood best. She was going to lose Reverdy, but in a sense they would come together again in what tormented them both to an equal degree: an inalterable authenticity, and, still more tenacious, their belief in the value of shadow as the best way to highlight the essential. Double heritage of a peasant past which each was to exploit in his own manner: Chanel by making black the instrument of her success – 1925 was the year of women in black, of a fashion that ceased to be seen as a passing accessory in the eyes of posterity and became the expression of an age; and Reverdy by leaving Paris for good.

And there he was, buried in a sort of deliberate death.

On May 30, 1926, after burning a number of manuscripts in front of a few friends who knew nothing of the reasons for this auto-da-fé, he retired to a little house just outside the Abbey of Solesmes,* where he was to live for thirty years – with his wife, but alone, "alone against the skin of the walls."[37]

It was inevitable that Reverdy should do this, and inevitable that Gabrielle, after struggling grimly, should find strength to accept defeat without burning all the bridges between her world and his. Leaving her, Reverdy lost neither her trust nor her admiration. In the final analysis, that would seem to be the essence of the feeling that bound her to him: boundless gratitude. Until Reverdy's death the memory of an attraction that neither age nor time had eroded crackled through her like lightning.

With what amazement we observe the similarity between this woman and this man who found their fulfillment – she by mingling ever more intimately with what was most superficial in her century, he by becoming ever more isolated and remote from it – "on the threshold of oblivion like a night passenger."[38] A day would come when Gabrielle would be remembered solely for her courage in insisting that it was the purity and plainness of a style that made it lasting, and in fighting, discriminating colorist that she was, against "the inconceivable and tenacious prejudice" of centuries ". . . which had abolished black, the negation of all colors."[39] In other words, she survived herself because of what she had in common with him: black, the hue of both their achievements; and the simplicity of tone, the "surgical sparseness"[40] that had so long been viewed as shocking. And then, whether one likes it or not, the fact will also remain that every time his poems are mentioned, his own song "like a splendid subterranean vein of quartz,"[41] it will be impossible to avoid mentioning her name too, for the strength she gave him, the confidence and the material assistance. No one can conceive how generously and tactfully she helped him, secretly buying up his manuscripts, approaching his publishers personally, paying annuities to them which they then paid out to him. So for those who come after, Gabrielle's lovely name will always remain linked with that of the hermit of Solesmes.

---

* Solesmes, located southwest of Paris, near Le Mans, is a village of six hundred souls built around a Benedictine abbey whose facade towers above the slow current of the Sarthe. Once a simple monastery founded in the ninth century, it was reopened in 1833 by Dom Guéranges (1805–1875). One hundred monks of the Order of St Benedict live there permanently, making Solesmes a center of study and especially of prayer comparable only to Montecassino in Italy.

CONCERNING ONE KIND OF THEATER
AND TWO AGENTS-PROVOCATEURS

"Chanel goes Greek" – a headline seen in one or two Parisian periodicals at the end of 1922.

This had nothing to do with fashion trends, however.

The stories were about Chanel and the stage, and were printed on the entertainment page. She was working with artists who would make history ten years later, but in those days they were identified with the avant-garde and merely alarmed people.

Antigone in a free adaptation by Jean Cocteau, with settings by Pablo Picasso, music by Honegger, and costumes by Chanel: so read the December bill posted outside a picturesque edifice suitably reminiscent of Utrillo's countrified Paris: the old Montmartre theater. It was an experimental *Antigone* and, according to some, would be more provocative than satisfying, as those who were producing it were both inexperienced and immature. Gabrielle Chanel was thirty-nine years old and had never made costumes for the theater before. Picasso was forty-one, Cocteau thirty-one, Honegger thirty.

In changing masters that year, the Théâtre de Montmartre changed names and destinies as well. Charles Dullin had just founded the Atelier there. "The company seldom had enough to eat . . . An iron stove in one corner of the house heated an even dozen spectators every evening."[42] But his first production, *The Pleasure of Honesty*, had revealed an unknown author to the French, Luigi Pirandello. The Atelier immediately became the focal point of efforts to enlarge the repertory, to look ahead for a more European theater, and to develop a new acting style. In other words, it had its own public, a public of students, intellectuals, and artists. Beginning in December 1922 Charles Dullin exercised his sovereign talents in the little structure with its peristyle and *pissotière* and its little square scantily shaded by a few trees, equidistant from the cupolas of Montmartre's Sacré Coeur and the fever-flushed facades of the Pigalle nightclubs, where the *Antigone* of Sophocles, revised and amended by Jean Cocteau, was performed. What could already be called a public of habitués received the play more than warmly.* It was a completely unconventional production.

---

* "The applause of a first-night house of young artists and cultivated people was just as loud as the critics' expressions of distaste at the dress rehearsal." Otto von Wätjchen in *Rheinische Blätter*, no. 5, March 1923.

We should note that this exercise achieved far more for Gabrielle than for anyone else. While the journalists, by Cocteau's own admission, classified the settings as a Christmas Holy Family scene and Picasso's masks as "a Mardi Gras shop window," and so on for the rest – the guards' shields, superbly black objects decorated with designs inspired by Delphic vases, had to wait more than thirty years before they came to fruition in certain Vallauris ceramics – Gabrielle's costumes were unanimously praised. They had a good deal in common with the setting and props, however, and faithfully followed the highly restricted palette imposed by Picasso. Brown was the main tone, in combination with a very pale beige and an occasional note of brick red showing off against the sunny background because "the tragedy took place on a bright clear day."

Cocteau gave as much publicity to Gabrielle's share in the production as to Picasso's and Honegger's. "I asked Mademoiselle Chanel for the costumes," he told the press, "because she is the greatest designer of our day and I do not see Oedipus' daughters being badly dressed."[43] And he illustrated the close tie between action and costumes by adding, "Antigone has decided to act. She wears a magnificent cloak. Ismene will not act. She stays in her any-day dress." So, we see, Gabrielle Chanel was receiving tokens of admiration before the curtain ever rose.

Her costumes did the rest.

She never created any more virile or more convincing.

Did she get help from Dullin? There is every reason to suppose so, and also to suppose that the exacting director of the Atelier was as responsible as Cocteau for giving her her chance. Dullin was everywhere at once, and looked after her in particular. But he did not take credit for the production, because he did not want his name on the bill twice.

The excellence of the cast disguised some deficiencies in the text. A Greek actress, Genica Athanasiou, played a shaven-headed Antigone with plucked eyebrows, two Mephistophelean pencil lines scoring her forehead, her faunlike eyes strongly outlined in black and carried out to her temples. Her bare neck emerged from a loosely woven wool cape as from an executioner's block. The costume alone designated her as victim. "Drunk with rage and brute power,"[44] Charles Dullin, the former lover of Caryathis and Gabrielle's companion of a tumultuous evening at the Ballets Russes, played Creon, creating the character of a tyrant which remained marked by the actor's personality for many years. A Creon with straggling beard and long nose, his brow girded by a sort of barbarous metal band – the first jewel signed Chanel, no doubt – an old man clutching an earth-toned mantle around his skinny shoulders, a king deaf to the ominous mutterings of his soothsayer. And in the part of Tiresias, Antonin Artaud* – Genica Athanasiou's offstage lover – replaced the word with the cry and attained summits of fury that left the public gasping. Listening to the imprecations of this man who presented himself "like those martyrs who are burned and make signs on their stake,"[45] in a scene provocative enough to be almost a "happening," one could imagine what the work and long torment of this visionary poet would be like in a few years.

The greatest photographers and best draftsmen haunted the wings of the Atelier during that production. For instance, Man Ray made an amazing portrait of Genica Athanasiou, and Frank Crowninshield (then director of *Vanity Fair* and of the French edition of *Vogue*) commissioned Georges Lepape to make a series of drawings. The French edition of *Vogue*, which enjoyed considerable prestige in the art world at the time, published them in February 1923 with a commentary that was a model of prudence. Mention was made of Sophocles, Cocteau, and Dullin. Picasso's name was omitted, along with Honegger's, and pointedly that of Antonin Artaud. The costumes by Gabrielle Chanel, on the other hand, were enthusiastically described: ". . . these woolen robes in neutral tones giving an impression of garments of antiquity redis-covered after centuries." And still on the subject of the costumes: ". . . this is a fine re-creation performed with an enlightened and intelligent sense of the past." Far wider publicity than Gabrielle could have hoped for.

We should note that in 1922 Gabrielle acquired a hellenistic marble of very fine quality, which thereafter became the focal point of her drawing room. One or two classical draperies were also seen in her collection that year. They were only a passing phenomenon, although singular enough to attract the attention of Cocteau, who made some very lovely drawings of them.

Never wavering in her firm determination to transpose discoveries made in her private domain into her professional work, ancient Greece no sooner existed for her than it became part of Gabrielle's expression. Would it have been quite the same if this experiment had not been made?

*

* Antonin Artaud (born in Marseilles, 1896; died at the Maison de Santé of Ivry-sur-Seine, 1948). First an actor, then the creator of an avant-garde theater. Author of two manifestos in which he presented his theory of the theater of cruelty. Insane and hospitalized on several occasions, he was found dead in the room in which he had been living as a recluse for several years. Long unrecognized, Antonin Artaud has now become an idol for the new generation, who see him as a forerunner of the Living Theater and the Theater Laboratory of Wroclaw, and as a precursor of Jerzy Grotowski.

After *Antigone* came *Le Train Bleu*. That meant switching from Dullin to Diaghilev, from Thebes to the Riviera, abandoning the bleeding world of tragedy for a fantasy realm, a land of operetta where the heroes, instead of Eurydice, Ismene, or Haemon, were named Perlouse and Beau Gosse (Pretty Kid).

For fourteen years, from 1923 to 1937 – after *Le Train Bleu*, came *Orphée, Oedipe Roi*, and *Les Chevaliers de la Table Ronde* – the cycle of Cocteau's creations proceeded as though he could not see his characters except in Chanel costumes. But what about her? Observing how unwillingly she spoke of her theatrical activities after 1926 – even with the most dogged perseverance, one could hardly extort from her the names of productions she was involved in – one cannot help thinking that she was soon content to perform her job as a conscientious craftsman, and not without certain reservations. Was it that Cocteau's flamboyant mixing of disconnected ages, combining classical myths and medieval legends with a modern idiom, seemed arbitrary to her? What did she feel about him? Irritation, even then? Did she already, almost as soon as she knew him, reproach him for being too charming, for not being Reverdy?

"I very soon had enough of his classical salad," she was to say many years later.

This was rejecting a world of metamorphoses which had dazzled her at first, a universe of purple hangings and winged personages, the plethora of statues and plants and talking beasts that Cocteau brought to French dramaturgy. If one thinks of the fervent friendship he displayed for her over so many years, and realizes what she owed to him in the way of connections and experience, then it was also blackest ingratitude. Disappointing Gabrielle . . . Cocteau had a bigger heart, he who could judge and yet describe her, as well as and perhaps better than Colette, with her ". . . tantrums, her spitefulness, her fabulous jewels, her creations, her caprices, her extravagances, the lovable things about her like her humor and generosity, composing a unique character, winning, attractive, hateful, excessive . . . in a word, human."

Was there any justification for Gabrielle's disgraceful attitude? Did she consider, after inviting Cocteau to the Faubourg, sheltering him often there with his drug-smoking friends, convincing him that he should have treatment on at least two occasions and, also twice, helping him to pay for his detoxification, that they were even with each other? The ability to love, with which Cocteau was always so generously endowed, and his true weapons, those of the heart, were gradually beginning to slip from Gabrielle's grasp, as though her hands were infected by some deadly creeping paralysis.

But that was later. Their relations were still unclouded when Cocteau was commissioned to do another work. The order came from Diaghilev. Get to work without delay. This was not actually a ballet but a "choreographed operetta." Another attempt at novelty, typical of the "prodigious agent-provo-cateur"[46] that Diaghilev was. On what occasion had he been charmed by that most French, most "common" music in the world: the tunes of Christiné and Maurice Yvain that were whistled on street corners by people who never went to the theater except "to relax and enjoy themselves," music from a world scorned by critics? And it was those very tunes, and the "powerful charm of the pavement,"[47] that Diaghilev wanted to transpose and rehabil-itate. By freeing the dance from the somewhat cloying delights of the fairy tale, by giving it a flavor of modernity, Diaghilev and Cocteau were creating a niche for a theater that combined dancing, acrobatics, pantomime, and satire, a form of expression not unlike the "musical comedy" that subse-quently conquered the United States.

Did Gabrielle realize that this time she would have to contend with not one but two agents-provocateurs? Diaghilev and Cocteau working together on the same project, one's description of himself fitting the other like a glove: "I am, first of all, a great charlatan – but with style; in the second place, a great charmer; and thirdly, I have no end of cheek . . ."[48] But cheek was something she was plentifully endowed with too. And she weathered all the tempests, backstage scenes, intrigues, disagreements, and hostilities that are the daily bread of the dance.

Once again a brilliant cast united a group of friends. For her first appear-ance in the Ballets Russes program, Gabrielle found herself in even more distinguished company than at the Atelier. The other striking feature about this idea of Diaghilev's was that although he had backed many bigger proj-ects than this, few were as much of a gamble as his *Le Train Bleu*. For the skittish music he wanted, he chose a composer whose Provençal and Jewish origins doubly disposed him to gravity: Darius Milhaud. His reputation was founded on cantatas from biblical themes and melodies for poems by Paul Claudel, whose secretary he had been. As he later confessed, Diaghilev's offer had taken him more than by surprise: "In those days the fashion was for a hedonistic and charming kind of music far removed from what I was composing . . . which didn't at all suit Diaghilev's taste, as I knew. I had never thought of writing an operetta, even one without words. It was a gamble, and I took it."[49] The score of *Le Train Bleu*, begun on February 15, 1924, was completed in twenty days.

For the setting, second gamble. Diaghilev turned to a sculptor who had never built a single stage set, Henri Laurens. Laurens was a French sculptor who began sculpting at thirteen, discovered cubism in 1911, and became friendly with Braque, Reverdy, Modigliani. He died in Paris in 1954. And he was just as "serious" as Reverdy, whose friend and illustrator he was. Diaghilev asked this Parisian from Paris, this laborer's son, to re-create a fashionable beach resort and to visualize the frivolous world of a crowd of idle rich. Henri Laurens also accepted the challenge and set to work. His decor gave a curiously geometrical flavor to the Riviera beach cabins and parasols. Angular, truncated constructions – one might have thought the set was made of pieces of paper stuck together.

To rehearse a Cocteau ballet and give choreographic coherence to a scenario in which bathers disport with tennis players, golf champions, and pretty young things in search of adventure, Diaghilev called upon Bronislava Nijinska.* Third gamble. Long unable to leave Russia, separated from the Ballets Russes throughout the war, she spoke not a word of French. She had been marked by the Revolution and had no inclination for a life of luxury or for pleasures and, moreover, no idea what this *Train Bleu* might be, where it came from or whither it was bound. "The personalities and events from which Cocteau proposed that Nijinska draw her inspiration belonged to the worldly milieu of the day – a milieu that Nijinska, who led a quiet, secluded life, didn't know and, furthermore, detested."[50] One can readily imagine how little assistance these names can have been to Nijinska: "As models, he cited a pair of acrobatic dancers who, that year, were appearing at Ciro's† late in the evening, snapshots of the Prince of Wales playing golf, slow-motion films of foot races, and so forth." Despite the efforts of Diaghilev, who acted as interpreter and mediator, Cocteau's relations with Nijinska "from the outset were tense, if not hostile." Kochno adds: "The atmosphere at rehearsals was highly charged."

Gabrielle made no concessions in her part of the work. She abided by Cocteau's rules and punctiliously followed the principle he had expounded on several occasions: "Rather than seeking to remain on this side of life's

---

* Like her illustrious brother, a "ballet baby" descended from generations of dancers. Admitted to the Imperial School at the same time as he, she applied to have her contract with the Maryinsky Theater terminated out of solidarity with Nijinsky when he was suspended on a charge of indecent dress and inadequately covered private parts, in the absurd incident of 1911. She quickly rejoined him in Diaghilev's Ballets Russes.
† A nightclub fashionable from 1925 to 1937 or so.

ridiculousness, to smooth it over . . . I emphasize it, I push it further, I try to paint *truer than true*."[51] *Le Train Bleu* was accordingly not danced in half-real and half-imaginary costume, but by real barelegged athletes, some in sandals and some in tennis or golf shoes.

The women's costumes were based on those worn by the bathers of the day, who ventured into the water warmly dressed: pullovers made in a rather loose-fitting jersey, and below them a patch of trunks reaching to mid-thigh. Gabrielle had not tried to be picturesque, but to enhance the dancers with the appeal of actuality. And it was certainly not in this guise that Nijinska could conceive of young men or women in hot pursuit of Mediterranean pleasure, or of this *Train Bleu* people kept nagging at her about. What would she have liked? Floating peignoirs? A stylized version of the fashions formerly in vogue on the shores of the Black Sea? Did she think there was any possible similarity or any comparable features between that vanished world and the follies of the Riviera? What people were blaming her for, tacitly or openly, was that she kept trying to "go Russian" on them. The more keenly she felt their misgivings, the more grimly she fought to get her way.

Cocteau labored to make it clear that as passengers on his *Train Bleu* he had selected only the least desirable sort, and it was not by accident that the girls and boys were classified as "*poules*" (chicks, broads, skirts) and "gigolos." "*Poules*"? "Gigolos"? the supremely distinguished ballerinas repeated after him; to them the words were meaningless. "I made a long speech to the company, explaining just what the word 'operetta' means . . . and what is, in my view, the plastic problem that this ballet presents," wrote Diaghilev,[52] and added, "I was listened to with devout attention." But with what results? Between author and choreographer one of those guerrilla wars of the theater was being waged, a mute struggle with no quarter given, inconceivable to anyone who has not been involved in one. Cocteau kept insisting, publicly and during rehearsals, that the choreography had to be altered. He breezily ordered some dance passages to be replaced by pantomime scenes: "I am not asking my name to be put on the programme as director . . . but I do insist on being listened to."[53] He would not budge: what he wanted, he said, was to recreate on stage a hardhearted youth which "pushes us around with impertinent contempt . . . those superb girls who stride sweating past with tennis rackets under their arm and get between us and the sun."[54] Nijinska, meanwhile, defended her principle that stylization was necessary, insisted that it would do nothing to weaken the satire and would on the contrary give the ballet the timeless reality that realism withheld from it. Her confidence in her arguments was increased by the fact that she had triumphed over Diaghilev's misgivings a few months earlier with *Les Biches*,[55] a one-act ballet with songs. After long hesitation he had asked her to choreograph a series of satirical scenes dealing with the same social milieu – that of Chanel's clients, a blasé society of women hankering after emancipation, tomboys with long cigarette holders and ambiguous, even perverse attitudes, countered in Poulenc's libretto and music by a type of masculine partner already very close to the athlete-gigolo of *Le Train Bleu*.

Les Biches had been unanimously praised. Nijinska was therefore qualified to exchange Larionov's isbas in *Renard*,[56] a ballet-burlesque with songs, for the mocking grace of Marie Laurincin's settings in *Les Biches*; the rowdy folklore of Goncharova's *Noces*,[57] choreographic scenes with singing, for the pink and blue world of that philandering party of 1923, than which, "as in certain of Watteau's paintings, one could see or imagine nothing worse."[58] Diaghilev was the first to agree: "Here everything is going along much better than I had expected. Poulenc is enthusiastic about Bronya's choreography and they get along excellently together . . . But then, this good woman, intemperate and antisocial as she is, does belong to the Nijinsky family."[59]

But that is not how it went with *Le Train Bleu*. There were few problems with the four principal dancers, but the rehearsal atmosphere was extremely ill-tempered from start to finish. Everything was late – settings, program, curtain – and only the stars had had costume fittings.

"Beau Gosse" came fresh from London. The part had been given to a young English dancer trained at Astafieva's Russian School and virtually unknown to the French public. Anton Dolin, with his dead center part, black hair glued to his scalp, velvet eyes, and acrobat's jersey, was the living image of a beach Don Juan according to the canons of 1925. He was "Chéri" in his prime, a "Chéri" with muscles.

Also most convincing was the "Golf Player." Diaghilev had brought him from Poland in 1915, a pupil at the Warsaw school of dance. Brilliant, endowed with a virile grace, Woizikowsky was already a favorite with the Parisians. At the time of the break with Nijinsky, he had taken over some of the illustrious soloist's parts and, contrary to all expectations, had occasionally equaled him. An athletic role suited him perfectly, and not even the most fastidious arbiter could have found fault with his costume on the links. Did Chanel owe this success to the photograph of the Prince of Wales? Cocteau was delighted. The heir to the English crown, whose allure and occasional idiosyncrasies of dress gossip columnists never tired of celebrating, would not have hesitated to partner a young man as exquisitely turned out as he. Woizikowsky wore a white collar, tightly knotted tie and, along with his plus fours, a striped sweater with matching socks. "Perfectly smart," was the ruling of one of the prince's close friends, the Duke of Westminster, whose furtive appearances at the Théâtre des Champs Elysées were intriguing and unexplained. Which of the English girls was he after? Misia didn't know him, he was not part of her crowd. People wondered what he was doing there.

No problems with Sokolova either – whose real name was Hilda Munnings. She was the first English dancer engaged by Diaghilev and, after remaining for ten years the only one of her kind in a company composed of exclusively Russian ballerinas, Hilda had become metamorphosed into Lydia. First she changed her name, then her language, then her whole style; from living day and night in the company of defectors from the Maryinsky Theater and Imperial School of St Petersburg, she had become indistinguishable from them, apart from a sense of humor that could only be British.

The role of "Perlouse" gave her a good chance to make use of it.

Anyone but Gabrielle Chanel would have invented opportunities to refer to such a glorious episode in her life. When asked, "What about *Le Train Bleu*? Couldn't you tell us a little . . . the rehearsals, the dancers, all that?" she would answer, "They were in another world. And anyway, I was only there to do the costumes."

In white from head to foot, racket in hand, her hair held by one of those bandeaux which Gabrielle Chanel had worn, to her tailor's deep chagrin, on her canters through the woods at Royallieu thirteen years before, Nijinska herself took the leading woman's role, the "Tennis Player." Small, muscular, and thick-ankled, she was rather low-slung, like Nijinsky, and her face, with a kind of Mongol flattening, heavy chin, fleshy lips, unattractive mouth and slanting eyes, was also reminiscent of her brother. On her, the headband was not wholly becoming. Nijinska lacked that infectious vivacity to which the woman she should have taken as model owed her popularity. Suzanne Lenglen – who, as fifteen-year-old champion of France, had succeeded in raising a laugh from the stands at Wimbledon with her extraordinary leaps – was undoubtedly the wittier of the two, but even so no one could deny that Bronislava Nijinska alone could have given such authority to a performance that compelled attention by sheer unexpectedness. Some woman, as they said . . .

It was at the dress rehearsal that *Le Train Bleu* nearly came off the rails. The company hadn't known whom to obey, Cocteau or Nijinska, and seemed to hesitate at every step. Gabrielle had been present throughout rehearsals, yet everything on her side was wrong too, both skirts and shirts. Caught in the crossfire of the interminable bickering, *poules* and gigolos had had a hard time of it. And now they were being ordered to dance in costumes they had never even tried on! It was a pitiful spectacle, as Boris Kochno, who watched it, well remembers: "The dress rehearsal of *Le Train Bleu* took place . . . before the heat in the theater had been turned on . . . The sight of those bathers shivering on the beach in costumes that did not fit them was both lamentable and laughable. When the curtain rose on this dismaying spectacle, Diaghilev fled to the last row of the balcony. He felt utterly powerless to remedy the disaster, and asked which of the other ballets could be substituted for *Le Train Bleu* at this last moment."[60]

What made the situation even more critical was that the ballet was to open that very night.

Among the gigolos Serge Lifar, a new recruit from Kiev and a beginner of remarkable beauty, doubted that the costumes could be used: "They were not costumes conceived for dancing. When we performed certain movements, they became either too long or too short."[61]

Diaghilev, of course, was accustomed to this sinking-ship atmosphere. He was an old hand at it. But what began that afternoon was a poker game as well as a race against the clock. Not one dancer, not one ballerina in the company, not one dresser, not one stagehand left the theater. Between this calamity and the instant when the forestage curtain would part upon a first-night audience, there were only a few hours left . . . Some handymen of genius set to work.

Picasso whirled in. A month before, in the unbelievable chaos of his studio, Diaghilev had stopped short in front of a painting of two women in white tunics whose torn shoulder drapes exposed their bare breasts – two women like flowers bent by the wind, a distillation of the joy of running. It was a painting from that period of Picasso's called "the Giants." Diaghilev had begged Picasso to let him use it, he wanted it for the curtain for *Le Train Bleu*. Picasso hung back, but finally gave in as everyone always did to Diaghilev. And, reluctantly, Picasso said yes, as he said yes to a commission for a series of sketches to be used as program illustrations, which Boris Kochno had no end of trouble extracting from him. Picasso pretended to have lost the drawings. He would find them, never fear . . . But the mess in his studio was beyond description. And the printer threatened to cancel the job. The publisher demanded that they give it up. A nightmare. As for the curtain, Picasso had lost all interest in it; Diaghilev gave the model to one of his close associates to enlarge – Prince Schervashidze, who was absolutely amazing at this sort of work.

When Picasso first saw his curtain, he was so dumbfounded by the prince-craftsman's rendering that, not knowing how to show his enthusiasm, he dedicated the ecstatic race of the two women to Diaghilev, and wrote across the bottom of a work to which he added not a single brush stroke, "Dedicated to Diaghilev," and signed it "Picasso 24."

This was the one happy event of the afternoon. For the rest . . . the jerseys had to be taken apart and put back together again, and the skirts refitted. Meanwhile Nijinska and Cocteau, who no longer had time to argue, were going over the choreography together. They corrected, tightened up, rehearsed.

Those who saw Gabrielle thirty years later in the frenzy of the nights before collection presentations, scissors in hand and a deep furrow across her brow, can easily imagine her as she was then, on the stage of the Champs Elysées, still young and beautiful and even then silent, kneeling in front of Diaghilev's dancers in the humble posture of the craftsman facing his work. Her fight against time and a recalcitrant medium had not yet become a pretext for soliloquy. Later, only later, with age. Then she acquired that mania for accompanying her work with a long murmur punctuated by sarcastic commentary. "She talks as she works, softly, in a purposely restrained voice," noted Colette in her portrait of Chanel. "She talks, she teaches and corrects with a sort of exasperated patience."[62] The habit grew worse over the years, like a malarial delirium. It fascinated every writer who approached her, and sometimes terrified her friends. But it had to be translated, interpreted, decoded. However obscure, that running commentary retained, until the very last day, all the value of the utterances escaping from the lips of the oracle.

To whom was this torrent addressed? In a sort of half-coma, she who always eluded every question yielded the secret of secrets to people who never asked her anything.

"Always take away, always pare down. Never add . . . There is no beauty without freedom of the body." The only persons to hear her were young women weak with fatigue, whose bodies her dissatisfied hands seemed to be clawing at for nights on end. "Always too much of everything," she kept saying. "Too much of everything . . ."

But back on the stage of the Champs Elysées that afternoon, nobody uttered a word. And for three solid hours there was nothing but the kind of silence and movement that defeat time.

The program, ready at last, with the cover by Picasso and the six studies of dancers which Boris Kochno had had such a struggle obtaining, announced a particularly brilliant season, with settings by Braque and Juan Gris.

On June 13, 1924, when André Messager raised his baton and the first notes of the fanfare rang out – a fanfare Diaghilev had commissioned from Georges Auric in honor of Picasso's curtain – *Le Train Bleu* was back on its rails. The ballet was unrecognizable. The house, a most unlikely mixture of everything France, Italy, and England had to offer in the way of artists, patrons, aristocrats, and rich bourgeois, gave it an ovation. Anton Dolin's hair-raising acrobatic variation was one of the show stoppers of the evening.

A short time later the press published some words of high praise about Nijinska: "In *Les Biches* Madame Nijinska has just attained greatness without premeditation." Jean Cocteau wrote them.[63] The quarrels were buried. And *Le Train Bleu* came in for its share of applause: "Works such as *Les Facheux*, *Les Biches*, and *Le Train Bleu* seem distinctly new and modern because they modify the present and bring the future surging out of it," said the press.[64]

But one could glean no further particulars from Gabrielle.

"Le Train Bleu?"

"What about *Le Train Bleu?*"

"The public? The people?"

If her recollection of the audience that night was so vague, perhaps it was because she was so thrilled to have been part of the event, and her emotion had absorbed everything else. Unless her habit of self-defense, her fear of being "exploited" even by her closest friends, and her mania for caution were already ingrained. Though in this instance she had nothing to hide. One tried again . . . baronne Edouard, baronne Henri, baronne Maurice, baronne Robert, every Rothschild on earth was there, she wasn't going to try to make us believe . . . And then the ghosts of the "Tout-Proust," why, the social columns were full of them, the D'Arenbergs, Caraman-Chimays, Greffulhes, Gramonts and other Orianes, and the comte de Beaumont, the comte Primoli, and all the Charluses and Norpoies of the day: Had she forgotten them? She pretended to remember nobody, neither the Deauville faithful who were present that evening nor the splendid Italians. The duchesse de Camastra? Princess Bassiano? The daily columnists spared their readers no name, and on gala evenings went over every theater audience with a fine-tooth comb. Didn't she read newspapers in those days? But Gabrielle set herself up at the other end of the earth from all that. The Americans in Paris, all those ladies from tsarist Russia who still happened to be solvent, the Spanish señoras from Biarritz and the Englishwomen from Venice, Princess Paley, Lady Cunard, Colonel Balsan and his wife: she didn't remember. These names which formed the backbone of her clientele seemed driven from her mind by her need to be universally contrary.

Not to mention the even heavier silence she draped around certain figures who went back to her Moulins days. The jolly boys who had given up their little girl friends and their scarlet breeches and begun touring the racecourses as gentlemen owners, they were there too in clusters that night, weren't they? With their spouses, weren't they?

Which was enough to make her instantly forget their names. Her whole heart rejected a society that, in the days when she herself had been nothing, had thrust her aside into a category from which she had since broken free. At last she could afford the luxury of refusing to "know" them.

"What did you do after the performance?"

"We all went to Misia's."

"All who?"

"Like after Picasso's marriage. More or less the same people, the painters. It was a little less *Boris Godunov*, though."

"Why?"

"Because of the musicians. All French: Auric, Poulenc, Milhaud . . ."

For her that went without saying: she believed at all times and in every respect that only the artists were worth bothering to name, and her infuriated partiality denied whatever was not them. There was no snobbery about it, moreover, and no trying to give herself equal importance.

One magazine succeeded in persuading her to authorize publication of a selection of notes which she variously called maxims, reflections, and sentences, and there unknowingly revealed the true cause for her unwillingness to talk about designing for the theater.

Let there be no mistake about it, though: few activities in her life gave her such great satisfaction. Her refusal to boast about it was a conscious decision. It derived from the fundamental distinction she drew. Her words: "Costume designers work with a pencil: that's Art. Fashion designers work with scissors and pins: that's a news item."[65]

So rare a combination of pride and modesty reminds us once more of someone else who suffered from it, as acutely as she: Reverdy, also irrationally proud, and irrationally modest. "I was beleaguered by incoercible pride, and the fact that it had no pretensions to support it rendered it all the more troublesome,"[66] he wrote at approximately the same time. Something else they had in common.

VII

A Victorian Illusion and
Its Aftermath 1925-1933

"It all began with a mistake in French."

— LOUIS ARAGON, "Le Fou d'Elsa"

BOGUS BLISS

A quarter of a century after his death the second Duke of Westminster remains as much a victim of his legend as Gabrielle, whose lover he was from 1925 until 1930. To portray him clearly is, first of all, to divest him of the accretions of his coterie of gossip columnists. He was the richest man in England. They glued themselves to his tracks. If we were to take what they wrote as gospel, we could not spare the Duke of Westminster such commonplace qualifications as capricious, lavish, bored . . . He was indeed all of those at once, but more. It would be doing him an injustice to say there was no more to him than a rather muddled amorous greed or a desire to enjoy his fabulous fortune to the full.

Physically, he was a tall, sturdily built blond exhibiting to the highest degree a style summed up in this concise formula: "elegant – in other words, detached."[1] His British upbringing had done its work well, and he showed no outward trace of the fierce temper he in fact possessed. Him, violent? This amiable giant was known only for his passion for gambling, games, and childish pranks: immersing a wrapped lump of sugar in his coffee and calculating with a stopwatch the time it took to dissolve, or hiding diamonds under his mistresses' pillows, or taking advantage of their slumbers to suspend costly pendants like huge pebbles from their hat brims.

The fact that he beat them when they had ceased to amuse him was less generally known.

His likes and dislikes were all matters of public notoriety, and the same anecdotes were endlessly repeated about him. The Duke of Westminster had a great sense of humor; the Duke of Westminster was a most original type; the pockets of the Duke of Westminster were filled with surprises – a little box of water colors, a gold coin – his toys, in short; he smoked cigars in his dressing gown and drank green chartreuse; his man was required to iron his shoelaces every morning, but it didn't bother him that there were holes in the soles of his boots; he distributed kingly tips but was reluctant to waste money on a hat check . . . He was known as a good sailor and praised for loving sports, wild flowers, dogs, ponies, and picnics as much as he did women. All of which implies that he was a product of a good school – Eton – and had served in the Guards.

Churchill himself, when he had occasion to write a few lines in memory of his boyhood friend, began by saying: "He was deeply versed in all forms of animal sport and saw into the heart of them,"[2] a statement that he deemed would pay most fitting tribute. They had become friends in 1900 during what Churchill termed "a somewhat adventurous journey." Adventurous? He could not have chosen a more euphemistic expression for the jaunt, which was the Boer War. The fact that he proved himself on that occasion "fearless, gay, and delightful" as a companion "in danger or sport" was evidently as worthy of note as his hunting abilities, since Churchill made mention of it before going on to add: "Although not good at explaining things or making speeches, he thought deeply on many subjects and had unusual qualities of wisdom and judgment. I always valued his opinion." One might wonder that this aspect of the man is mentioned only at the end if it were not simply a confirmation of the very essence of the British view of the human race: albeit neither a mighty thinker nor a fine talker, any man who proves himself a decent traveling companion, makes it his business to deal straight, and possesses a feeling for social nuances is more than eligible to move among people of quality. The Duke of Westminster met these requirements at all times and in every respect.

But it would still not be enough to call him overwhelmingly English without adding this: he imagined himself a man of his time, but the person now entering Gabrielle's life was in reality every bit as Victorian as his grand-father, the first Duke of Westminster, who brought him up. And therein lay the root of his problem; for since he was unaware of the fact, he could not understand why he did not seem to be the first duke's equal.

For one thing, the 1920s were not an ideal culture medium for a great lord of that vintage. The era when one couldn't count one's servants but knew there had to be sixteen courses to a meal, always described in French on stiff white pasteboard bearing the armorial crest; the era of enormous wardrobe trunks and laced gowns, with soubrettes waiting up until dawn for ladies who were totally incapable of undressing themselves; of wives whose only justification was to procreate and give ease to husbands interested in nothing but their guns, horses, and dogs: those times would undoubtedly have suited Gabrielle's new lover better than the rackety age of the Charleston.

It may seem curious that after Arthur Capel and Grand Duke Dmitri we should find, for the third time, a man at Gabrielle's side whose childhood had been scarred by the absence of a father; but we should take it as no more than a quirk of destiny, its wink, its way of showing that the evil is the same whether the missing parent be godson of a queen, as in this case, or market trader, as in that of Gabrielle – in short, the affliction is absolute.

Gabrielle's lover was born in 1879. He was only four when his father died. The father, although neither a sportsman nor otherwise enterprising, negligent in dress and almost obese, had found a wife and a pretty one at that, a beauty of nineteen. He was also said to suffer from epilepsy. "That poor boy . . ." The letters of Queen Victoria, his royal godmother, never speak of him in any other terms. Thus the only memory he bequeathed to his son was that of his wretched health.

There remained the redoubtable grandfather, to whom the child was entrusted. Hugh Lupus was this old gentleman's name. A name in use in his family since the year 1066, when William the Conqueror disembarked in the British Isles along with one of his great-nephews, a certain Baron Hughes, who displayed such propensities for ferocity that his comrades-at-arms flatteringly dubbed him "Hughes the Wolf." He was also so keen a hunter that he braved the wrath of church and flock and transformed a chapel into a kennel. He sired innumerable bastards, and legitimate sons as well. All alike. All hunters like their father, all possessing, like him, a super-abundance of corpulence and strength. They were designated by the fitting surname of *gros veneurs* (stout huntsmen). The years passed, and the name, given first in jest and then out of habit, stuck to them. But as often happens after a war, when there is commerce of language between peoples, both tongues degenerate and that of the conqueror is often the first to show signs of wear, paying tribute to that of the conquered. Thus the surname of the descendants of Hughes the Wolf was gradually transformed into Grosvenor, and it became that of one of the foremost families of the realm.

For the Grosvenors, then, "it all began with a mistake in French," not to mention a coat of arms, *Azur a Bend'or with plain Bordure Argent* – that mix of two languages sealing a treaty between them as sacred as an exchange of blood between two men.

Also, the history of the Grosvenors was inseparable from the history of their horses. A deliberate mingling, which those responsible for it perceived as highly flattering. One consequence of it was that the ancestors immortalized by Gainsborough and Reynolds could hang along the walls of Eaton Hall in the places of honor, and by their sides hung the cream of their horses, painted by the most skillful genre-painters of the day – those, at least, who had made names on the battlefield or racetrack, such as Copenhagen, a product of the Eaton stud who bore Wellington at Waterloo; or Macaroni, who was spoken of so reverently at table that young Grosvenor, mixing up his ancestors and their horses (this was shortly after his father's death), once asked his nurse:

"And me? Am I descended from Macaroni too?"

After their death, the priceless vertebrae of some of the stars of the duke's stud were exhibited like prize ivories beneath the chandeliers of Eaton Hall, and became the symbolic pillars of those immense galleries in whose centers they were enshrined. You studied them as you walked past. You tried to wrest from them the secret of their supremacy. With the doggedness of the impassioned amateur, the first Duke of Westminster undertook his grandson's education. For the infant Grosvenor, placed under the tutelage of an indulgent old man who spoke as a connoisseur, this consisted in a long, leisurely stroll among skeletons.

"Touchstone by Camel out of Banter," the old man would explain. "He had the hot blood of Eclipse from both sides. Twenty years' service in the stud . . . Three hundred and twenty-three of his sirings produced three hundred and twenty-three winners. He was born the year the eldest Grosvenor was given the title of Marquess of Westminster by William IV. That was 1831. He had only nineteen ribs . . ."

"Who?" queried the child. "The earl?"

"No, no . . . Touchstone. Count them."

The child's errors became all the more readily understandable when we add that a few months after one of his grandfather's greatest Derby triumphs he was nicknamed "Bend'or" in honor of the winning horse – the celebrated Bend'or by Doncaster out of Rose Rouge. The fact that at birth he had been christened Hugh Richard Arthur was utterly forgotten, and it was as Bend'or and Bend'or alone that the second Duke of Westminster was known in both the chronicles of his age and the hearts of his mistresses. Bend'or . . . was Gabrielle taken aback? Not in the slightest. Presumably the idiosyncrasies of Eaton Hall were like a new verse to an old song, by comparison with those of Royallieu – which also rendered the duke's eccentricities more acceptable to Gabrielle than to many another woman.

"Anyway," she used to say, "the English brain isn't made like ours. Can you imagine a Noailles being named after a horse? A Noailles going about calling himself Epinard or Biribi or Jujubier or something like that? But in England . . . Well, these sorts of mixups were more common over there than in France and people didn't think so much of them."

Bend'or had often told her how contemporaries of his grandfather used to sing his praises – how, having been a page at Victoria's coronation, he died thirteen months before her as though out of courtesy; how for forty

years running he sat in his same seat in the Lords, adopting positions sufficiently liberal to startle his peers but doing so with sufficient good-humor
not to lose their esteem; how he intervened effectively both in defense of
the Armenian minorities being massacred by the Turks and in tabling a bill
to ensure that department store clerks could have chairs to sit on without
the seated position being deemed disrespectful to lady customers; and how,
despite the heat of this debate, the duke had carried the day with a comfortable majority . . . all of which did less, in fact, to establish his fame than the
time when, acting on a sort of higher instinct, he took the racing world by
surprise by spending 14,000 guineas, a sum at the time unequaled, to buy
Doncaster, the stallion that was to sire a line of invincible racers in the Eaton
Hall stud. The first duke had also been Master of Horse to Queen Victoria,
and that title had earned him as high a place in public esteem as did his
friendship with Gladstone; and all his more disinterested activities, all the
hospitals and churches built at his expense, were like so many pebbles dropped
into oblivion in comparison with his one phrase that remained celebrated,
a thousand times repeated, when the matchless ancestor had refused to sell
Bend'or to an American millionaire, saying, "There is not enough money
in the whole of America to buy a horse like that."

How was it that, in an age so rigidly ruled by etiquette, the first duke
managed to persuade the sovereigns he was entertaining to allow a horse
among the guests? A question his grandson was not the only one to ask.
For the day when his grandfather gave a garden party to celebrate Queen
Victoria's Golden Jubilee, the entrance that provoked most comment was
not that of the Prince of Wales nor that of the hereditary Prince of Prussia,
not that of the King of Denmark nor that of the Queen of the Belgians nor
even that of the Queen of Hawaii in her outlandish trappings, nor yet that
of the lovely Madame Albani, the famous soprano. It was that of Ormonde,
horse of the century, Ormonde by Bend'or out of Lily Agnes, perpetuating
through his sire the glorious blood of Doncaster and through his dam that
of Macaroni. Ormonde, whose lineage was more familiar to the little
Grosvenor than his own, and who was authorized by special permission of
the Lord Mayor of London to cross St James's Park and Green Park so that
the Duke of Westminster's special guest might be spared the unpleasant-
ness of city traffic. Curried, polished and curled, prettily curvetting for all
the crowned heads, his forequarters smoothed to a hair and his croup impeccable, displaying with tact and moderation the phenomenal strength of stifle
and hock, Ormonde occupied his place in the center of the lawn with flaw-
less demeanor and nibbled, without urging, the flowers offered him by the

most noble ladies of the land in the beribboned *point d'esprit* gowns that were the rage that autumn of 1877.

Every time Bend'or hearkened back to that formidable ancestor, every time, it was as though he heard a voice from beyond the tomb calling out to him: "What have you done? What are you going to make of our name?" For when Bend'or met Gabrielle the old man was still bearing down, with all the weight of his Victorian virtues, upon his grandson's psyche. And this is not one of the afflictions that fade with the years. In the quarter of a century that had passed since the news of the duke's death had reached him in South Africa – Chester in mourning, all the shops shut, flags at half-mast on the public buildings and the knell tolling in every church, speeches bewailing the loss of the greatest philanthropist England had ever known and simultaneous memorial services in Chester and Westminster Abbey with the royal family in attendance – nothing had changed Bend'or. It was as though, even in dying, the first duke had inflicted upon Bend'or yet another example of the younger man's inadequacy, and for the rest of his life the grandson would reproach himself for not being the equal of the great and good man who had been borne to his final resting place by a detachment from a regiment composed wholly of Westminster retainers since 1797, the Earl of Chester Yeomanry Cavalry. Without Bend'or; for there was that, too. It happened during the Boer War and Bend'or was out there. Bend'or did not see the little note on which the old man had written "no flowers" in his own hand, or the bouquet of immortelles for which his friend the stout old queen had asked that one exception be made. The flowers were placed on his coffin, and there was a card with them: "In token of the respect and esteem of Victoria R.I.," but Bend'or wasn't there. And that preyed upon him too.

In one of those little turns of speech of which she was such a master, Gabrielle Chanel said, on the subject of her secretly downtrodden lover, "To understand what Bend'or was not, you had to know what his grandfather had been."*

But even after we have granted that this grandparent excelled in absolutely everything, had more honors, more success, greater fortune, more horses, and more victories than anyone could imagine – four times winner of the

---

* A biography of the first Duke of Westminster – *Victorian Duke*, by Gervas Huxley (Oxford University Press, London) – was recommended by Chanel to all the writers whom she tried to persuade to write her own memoirs. It was Louise de Vilmorin who told her about the book.

Derby! – we have glimpsed only a tiny portion of his grandson's misfortune.

The worst thing of all was that the old man also had more children than anyone else. Fifteen, by two wives: the first was his cousin; and with the second, thirty-two years his junior and sister of his son-in-law, the first Duke of Westminster, at the age óf fifty-eight, became the brother-in-law of his own daughter . . . Now, by 1924, two marriages, both ending in divorce, had given Bend'or nothing but a couple of daughters and a single male heir who died of appendicitis at the age of four. One of his obsessions was to find a woman who could obliterate both that death and his grief over it.

The woman he kept looking for must have the qualities of both mistress and wife; she must be vivacious enough to dissipate his boredom, sophisticated enough to forgive his infidelities, devoted and fertile enough to supply him with a large number of offspring. He never met her. Did she exist? Those who seemed most appropriate bored him to tears. He fled them. Those he married – on each occasion expressing the sincere wish that he might never divorce again – gave him no children. He eventually was to marry four times.

The Chanel episode was situated between the duke's second and third wives.

His attraction to Gabrielle, his choice of her, his need to impose her upon his world, were the clearest possible indications of the abrupt counterreaction of a man conscious of having been stifled from birth by old-fashioned ideas, of being a stranger in his own age. He was blinded, dazzled to discover a woman who had been liberated by work, and who, because of her unswerving adherence to realities, was so wonderfully in tune with her time.

AFTER LE TRAIN BLEU

On both banks of the Seine the fireworks had died down and the Arts Decoratifs Exhibition was over.

The "official closing ceremony" took place in the hall of the Grand Palais in the presence of the president of the Republic, foreign delegations, and the five colonial commissioners, those highly exotic figures, while the chorus of the Opéra intoned the *Marseillaise*. From the Concorde to the Place de l'Alma, the demolition of the pavilions visited by millions of sightseers, French and foreign, was beginning. The exhibition was devoted mainly to furniture and architecture – there was a church, a cemetery, garden cities, and fountains – and in the big Musée de l'Habitat, which had deprived

Parisians of the Esplanade for six months, a whole new concept of living had emerged. There was even a Palais des Elégances: "The high point of the Exhibition, far from being Paul Poiret's three river-barges, *Amours, Délices*, and *Orgues*, was the pavilion of elegance. There, in an assymetrical architecture by Rateau, behind a huge bay draped by Rodier in white silk with a silver weave, Worth, Callot and Lanvin presented dream gowns beneath a glittering cascade of light."[3] The exhibition had grouped together the gowns of Jean Patou, Chanel, Jeanne Lanvin, and Louise Boulanger, and displayed them along with Poiret's fabrics, with silks and lighting appliances, Lalique crystal, Dunand's lacquerwork, Christofle's gold and silver, ironwork and porcelains, French and foreign; the only unifying condition was that the lines of gowns and forms of objects must be clean, their ornamentation sober, and their relief unexaggerated.

The Arts Déco was an undisputed success. Never was a more imperious keynote more slavishly obeyed.

A new kind of furniture, uncarved and unadorned, was entering the age of industrialization, that is, the age of mass production and mass markets. "The parting of the way between literature and cabinetmaking is definitive," it was said. "No Gallé of the future will attempt to make his wood speak the language of the forest again."[4]

With this decor, women's fashion was perforce to ally itself. It abolished curls, pins, long hair, and nightgowns, the latter being replaced by a garment previously restricted to masculine usage: the pajama. It shrank underwear to invisibility. Lastly, in an attempt to make women even less distinct from those they now wished to see as fellow workers and equals – from men – fashion also did away with breasts and, for the first time ever, ordered every woman's hair to vie with that of Rudolph Valentino in ebony hue and gleam. In other words, brilliantine and the "boyish" cut became essentials.

For Chanel, this meant nothing new. She was that fashion. She had been its initiator nearly five years earlier, she had also been its figurehead. But if the Arts Déco exhibition had brought her no professional revelation, the social significance of the event, in the wider meaning of the term, was enormous: at this great village fair the Parisian woman had shown her true face – and that face was signed Chanel. Without Chanel's having sought or even wanted it, her style had spread through all classes of society.

Thus, alongside gowns executed at great expense and destined for the "luxury trade," more or less clandestine copies were going to become possible, by virtue of the very simplicity of the models, at a fraction of the cost and for far less wealthy women. Where were those dresses coming from? Should their makers be prosecuted? Was it necessary to declare war on all copies? That is what most designers tried to do. With the exception of Chanel. Turn into a policeman? Bring lawsuits? The battle was lost before it began, and she well knew it. Even back in 1925 she reached the conclusion that fashion too was entering the age of mass production, and from that time on would follow the imperatives of commerce more often than its own caprices; one would be making only minor changes from season to season, the way auto-mobile designers alter the lines of their cars.

In 1926 the American edition of *Vogue* predicted that a certain dress, disconcerting in its simplicity, would become a sort of universally adopted uniform. It had neither collar nor cuff, it was made of black crepe de chine, had long, very tight-fitting sleeves, and bloused above the hips, which were closely hugged by the skirt. It was a Chanel dress, a simple sheath. Would large numbers of women consent to wear the same dress? The prediction seemed wildly improbable. So, to persuade its readers that this dress would owe its success to its convenience, and perhaps even to its *impersonal* simplicity, *Vogue* compared it to an automobile. Did one refuse to buy a car because it was identical to another car? On the contrary. The likeness was a guarantee of quality. And applying this principle to fashion in general and to Chanel's black dress in particular, the magazine concluded: "Here is the Ford signed Chanel."

The autumn of 1925 . . . Reverdy was organizing for his departure to Solesmes, and Gabrielle was not happy to see him go. Then, the usual thing occurred: she fell back on her work and her friends, but she also made herself dizzy rushing about in a society that was everything the man who was making her suffer had taught her to abhor.

Her apartment on the rue du Faubourg St Honoré was never empty. More than ever, it became the gathering place for the Ballets Russes and Misia's friends, with the addition of new acquaintances, also from the world of the arts – Colette, Dunoyer de Segonzac, Christian Bérard, Jean Desbordes. Her clientele had also grown appreciably; and Gabrielle began visiting and inviting a few of the women she dressed. North and South Americans, millionaires from Argentina – the Sanchez Elias, the Pedro Corcueras, the Martinez de Hozes, the W. X. Vanderbilts; whatever their background, Chanel's clients welcomed her at their tables and consented to be seen in the most distinguished places in the company of their seamstress.

On occasion, Gabrielle was also seen in the company of her clients' husbands.

In the fashion magazines she got the lion's share of attention. Page after page of it, all for her. "Anyone in Paris who cares about elegance can be seen in Chanel's salons," wrote one source. And, "No collection reflects its creator's ideas better than Chanel's, or is as closely associated with the tastes of the moment." And again, ". . . Subtlety of cut, apparent simplicity: all effort is invisible."[5]

Her presence everywhere was commented upon, in Paris, Monte Carlo, Biarritz, or Deauville.

Autumn 1925 . . . Kees Van Dongen, who had become the most fashionable painter of those years, was preparing an illustrated edition of *La Garçonne*, the raciest novel yet seen.

Autumn 1925 . . . The dollar was at it zenith, and Hemingway, Scott Fitzgerald, Dos Passos, Sinclair Lewis, Thornton Wilder, and Henry Miller were all living in Paris.

Autumn 1925 . . . The Duke of Westminster's divorce from his second wife, Violet Mary Nelson, whom he had married five years previously, was causing an undesirable amount of comment. The decree was pronounced against the duke. There was some distasteful business of adultery, verified *flagrante delicto* at the Hôtel de Paris. All very contrary to the rules of the British establishment, and for a number of years it excluded him from court. But anyway, it was all happening in Monte Carlo that year. And it was there, one evening, that the Duke of Westminster was introduced to Gabrielle Chanel.

Letters carried from London to Paris in an unending stream by His Grace's personal courier; flowers, some from the gardenia house and some from the orchid rooms at Eaton Hall; baskets of fruit freshly picked by the duke's own hand in the hothouse where melons, strawberries, and mandarines ripened in midwinter; salmon from Scotland, no sooner caught than dispatched, in the care of other special couriers – by plane, a great extravagance at the time. By such means was Gabrielle conquered, after a siege conducted in a style not without its disconcerting aspects.

One day, not yet having secured the privilege of sharing her pillow but nevertheless desirous of playing one of his favorite little tricks on Gabrielle, the duke hid a jewel case at the bottom of a crate of vegetables. There was only one stone inside it, but a huge one: an uncut emerald. The butler gasped at the sight of it. Joseph – for it was he who opened the packages – was as delighted with these gifts as if they had been intended for him. His daughter's testimony authenticates that nothing that has been said about this period in Gabrielle's life was invented, and it was truly a carpet of gold that Bend'or spread at her feet.

Yet in spite of it she hesitated. A long time. No doubt about that, either. When asked why, she shrugged. Her answer was there, in that weary gesture and in her way of saying, "I didn't feel like it . . ." It should be understood that even then, she only "felt like" doing her work.

In one sense, she was no longer alone. There was the group of artists around her, and she was prouder of them than of any male conquest. They were better than a good marriage, better than some aristocratic title. And the fact that Joseph still looked upon all painters and musicians as parasites did not prevent Gabrielle from believing that they had become, in part, *her life*. Say good-by to all that? She also said, "I couldn't see what I would do in England . . ." Because she knew how fragile such attachments were. If she tried to bring Bend'or into her society of artists, disintegration would set in at once, her chapel would crumble to dust, her painters fleeing her as others had fled Misia during her marriage to Edwards. Was she going to go through the same thing? With Bend'or tearing her away from her work against her will – away from her one and only certainty; and from her friends – her one and only source of pride? What could she hope for from him? Jewels? But by now she could afford them herself. Not so gorgeous, maybe, and not so many, but what did that matter? What else? As before, with Boy, to become better known to the "Tout-Londres"? There was more weight to that argument, and people did not fail to use it often on Bend'or's behalf.

For the duke had put some inside agents on the job.

One of his lady friends, who possessed that pearly cast of skin and that strange intensity so pleasing to the English, one of those exciting young women of whom there were always a bevy eddying around him, occupied a high rank among Gabrielle's friends. Vera Bate* was her name. But only her professional name.

The lovely Vera . . . No one was more keenly appreciated by London high society, and it was she who, quite without ulterior motives, introduced

---

* Born in London in 1885 as Sarah Gertrude Arkwright, she served as a nurse in France during the First World War. She met her first husband in Paris, an American officer named Fred Bate, married him in 1919 and divorced him in 1927, to remarry in 1929 – an Italian officer who was one of the best horsemen of his day, Alberto Lombardi. Her connection with the English royal family is established beyond doubt, although her birth certificate states that her father was a stonemason. The hypothesis most often encountered is that she was an illegitimate daughter of a descendant of that Duke of Cambridge who, owing to a morganatic marriage, could give no other name to his sons but Fitzgeorge; this explains the close tie between Vera and the Prince of Wales.

Gabrielle and the duke after a party in Monte Carlo. English by birth, American by marriage, an inimitable mixture of boldness and beauty, Vera was in the process of getting her divorce. Her appetite for life put Gabrielle in mind of Antoinette, and her elegance made her think of Adrienne. And her financial problems, of both of them. This explains why she was working for Chanel in 1925, although no one was very clear exactly what it was she did.

A word has still to be invented for this type of occupation which, although indefinable, can be recognized at a glance. Decoy? Vera's job – had she discarded the name Sarah in order to be more in style? – was to give Chanel's business the benefit of her social connections. In addition, she wore clothes so well that that alone was enough to make her friends long to own the dresses they saw on her. Her dresses? People thought they were her own, but in fact Chanel gave them to her. In short, a high-society fashion model, an elegant woman turned out at low cost – Vera was all that and much more. She was also a good adviser, and Gabrielle listened to her. Furthermore, she had such hordes of suitors that Gabrielle, seeing this stream of Archies, Harolds, Winstons, and Duffs at Vera's side, and hearing those exquisite Oxford and Cambridge intonations, finally came to think that Vera alone would suffice to take England by storm. Who needed a duke?

Some witnesses say she repelled Bend'or's first advances pretty sharply. If she had been looking for a way of attaching him to her more firmly, she could have hit upon nothing better. The duke's trips to Paris only became more frequent, and his surprises and little tricks followed at closer intervals. Very late one evening Joseph opened the door to a giant invisible behind an enormous load of flowers. "Put them down there," he told the delivery boy. But just as he was about to hand him a tip, he recognized the Duke of Westminster, come in person to deposit the product of his hothouses.

Not long afterward it was a young man, a stranger, who rang the bell and, knowing that Gabrielle was busy preparing her collection, said he would not dream of disturbing her; but he claimed to have an appointment with Vera Bate.

"She is not in," Joseph informed him. The caller, although his manners were irreproachable, seemed dreadfully embarrassed. He absolutely insisted on waiting in the butler's pantry. Joseph, rather taken aback but thinking that perhaps this was not quite "a proper person," sat him down there and forgot about him. Hours passed. At last, Vera turned up at the door, whereupon Joseph remembered the waiting caller. But he, growing bored in the pantry, had installed himself in the kitchen and was conducting a lively conversation with the cook on the secret of successful profiterolles.

"Mrs Bate has come in. What name shall I say?" Joseph inquired.

"The Prince of Wales," answered the stranger.

Although her friends were mightily diverted by these little everyday occurrences, Gabrielle herself found them only mildly amusing. What lay behind her aloofness? Nothing more than a grudge against anyone who thought he could win her with jewels, flattering connections, and flowers. An old, old song . . . She was being forced to relive the years of her perpetual loathing. The men who kept women . . . Whatever Bend'or did, her reservoir of bitterness overcame him for many a day.

But now the British columnists were saying that the duke had plans for marriage. They were absolutely positive: this time the bride was a Frenchwoman, a world-famed dress designer . . . Thus prodded, Gabrielle decided to unbend. And so one evening on board the *Flying Cloud*, Bend'or took advantage of the departure of most of his guests to raise anchor; and they found themselves off Monte Carlo, she and he, alone. Well . . . "alone" is a figure of speech. The duke had also abducted an orchestra which he had been keeping hidden away.

One last little trick before the delights he was anticipating.

AN ADVANCED COURSE IN OPULENCE

Once again the time for fairy tales had come for Gabrielle. Once again she thought that what was being done would not be undone. Incurable romantic . . . as soon as the first moment of surprise had faded, she lost her head and began dreaming of marriage. She saw each of the houses the duke took her to as a permanent shelter: Mimizan, his "thatched cottage" in the Landes; St Saens, his château in Normandy; his fishing place in Scotland.

She went to England as often as she could. In a twinkling, she became acquainted with her new lover's vast number of possessions. First of all, his two yachts. One in a Mediterranean port, the other in the Channel or Atlantic, both awaiting His Grace's pleasure. The *Flying Cloud* was a four-masted schooner with a crew of forty, entirely outfitted in Queen Anne style – four-poster beds, heavy carved dressers, massive wooden tables, a floating museum. The other, formerly a destroyer, was the 883-ton *Cutty Sark*, built for trade with the Far East by a Major Henry Keswick, the overconfident agent of some China trading company. Unable to pay for her upkeep, he promptly sold her to Bend'or, to the duke's great delight. She was built to brave the fiercest storms, and there was no place on earth where Bend'or felt happier. The moment he boarded her, he began clamoring for heavy weather with the impatience of a child; only then was his bliss complete. His mistresses had to be equally seaworthy: he had cast aside more than one for no more reason than that she was afraid of a heavy sea, or queasy. As a final fillip, the *Cutty Sark* had to pitch and roll wildly, the furniture had to break loose and come bearing down upon the passengers, the terrified ladies had to implore the captain to put into the nearest port. But however fierce the storm, the master's orders were to do nothing of the sort. In the general consternation and alarm, the duke would double-lock himself into his cabin and fall into a deep sleep, not to be seen again until the tempest was over. Gabrielle's fearlessness in the face of the unbridled elements was a major component of her companion's esteem.

In fair weather, Bend'or would give orders to change course under cover of night. Everyone's plans would be all upset. In the morning the bewildered passengers would anxiously question the steward: "What coast is that?"

And, wherever they might happen to be, the order was to reply: "That must be Spain."

Gabrielle was also initiated into the ritual of the special trains – two pullman cars and four baggage cars for trunks and dogs. She was photographed with Bend'or at the Grand National. The columnists commented on her every gesture and Bend'or's girl friends raised their eyebrows at the simplicity of "the celebrated designer's" taste.

In the end, she became acquainted with Eaton Hall too. She wondered at refinements that must have originated in the far-off days of its Victorian grandeur, when members of the royal family used to drop in unannounced and the lord of Eaton Hall, Her Majesty's wealthiest subject, felt compelled to keep his home on a ceremonial footing at all times. In the days when Gabrielle was spending weekends at Eaton Hall – with sixty guests on the premises, among whom Winston Churchill and his wife counted as regulars – a quantity of customs left over from those bygone days were still observed. For the rest of her life Gabrielle retained a dazzled memory of an infinitely soft English lawn, a profusion of flowers, and the masterful skill of the gardeners – along with Scottish tweeds and the waistcoats with black sleeves and striped fronts worn by the Eaton Hall footmen, and the sober garb of the *Cutty Sark* hands in their pea jackets with gilt buttons and their caps pulled down to their eyebrows. This was far and away what she found most irresistible about England.

These elements instantly became the dominant themes of the clothes she was designing.

From 1926 to 1931 the Chanel style was English. Never had her collections shown so many jackets that were "resolutely masculine in cut," as the magazines put it, or so many broad-striped blouses and waistcoats, or so many "sport" coats, or so many suits and outfits "to wear to the races." Gabrielle adopted the English habit of living in sweaters. But she took it further, and with them she also wore jewels such as no lady of English society would have dared to put on except with a ball gown to wear at court. Under her influence, Misia was seen giving luncheons in a black marocain dress under a simple wool cardigan, a combination that did not fail to startle the arbiters of elegance; but their surprise turned to stupefaction when they observed that with this casual outfit Misia was also wearing "her magnificent triple-strand diamond necklace." In 1926, a breeze of opulence caressed the Chanel clientele. But it was a discreet opulence, noticed and then forgotten. Never, until the end of her life, did Gabrielle suppose that luxury could have any other purpose than to set off simplicity.

She was soon more than half won over to the English manner. She could see what she was getting from it. She also quickly felt at home at Eaton Hall. So much so that she became attached to what had originally repelled her most: the architecture of the place, peppered with medieval allusions, the excessiveness of it all. She got used to its gothic flavor, its reminders of the haggard poetry of Hugoesque melodrama. Misia's sarcasm soared, as a result, whenever she went there. She claimed the Westminsters must have a strain of Macbeth-worship in them somewhere, and that whoever erected that forest of dungeons above which one was forever imagining somnambulistic silhouettes about to hurtle into the void had to be a little crazy. But Gabrielle, comparing the haughty setting of the Westminsters with that of the Serts, found more than one point in common. In the end, she loved Eaton Hall for the grace of a certain kind of bad taste. Why? If pressed to explain herself, she would resort to comparisons which were the eternal expression of the wounds of her past: her obsession with cleanliness and neatness, her fear of violating the laws of the natural, in other words her mania for everything that distinguished true society from the world of courtesans and parvenus.

"Eaton Hall," she would say, "could easily have been *disgusting* . . . You see what I mean? If d'Annunzio had lived there, with heaps of dusty tapestries and theater sets and *ridiculous* objects, costume-ball trinketry. What one had to admire, on the contrary, was the cleanliness of that house, its English unaffectedness. It made one forget the ugly bits. A knight in armor stuck into the corner of a staircase, that does look a little overdone – unless it has always been there. Then you see it as something that grew out of the earth, proud and straight, especially when the armor is all shiny and looking ready for action. At Eaton Hall there was one in particular, a sort of hidalgo, whose helmet especially – all it needed was the plume – caught your attention. Shut up inside his heap of scrap metal, he became a kind of friend to me. I thought of him as being young and handsome. I said hello to him every time I went past. I used to say to myself, 'After all, what a clever piece of work that thing is. And how attractive and powerful one must feel inside it.' When I was sure nobody was looking, I used to go up and shake his hand."

What she was just discovering was the *real* world which the kept women of the beginning of the century had tried to achieve, on a smaller scale, with *fakes*. And that was what gave rise to remarks that could be interpreted as a formal indictment. But since she must needs camouflage, she preferred to use an alias – d'Annunzio – rather than make a direct attack upon the soap-opera interiors and fashions of the demimonde. A puny ploy. The ghost of Emilienne d'Alencon haunted the background of the conversation. Hadn't Emilienne also "done" England? "You call yourself the countess of Songeon and I'll introduce you to my cousin Edward." The words in which the King of the Belgians had invited her to follow him. Emilienne, Otéro, Liane . . . all three, in "greaves, thigh-boots, gauntlets, pearl halters, shields made of feathers and baldricks of satin, velvet and precious stones, coats of mail, those chevaliers bristling with tulle,"[6] came back to her memory, and Gabrielle's hatred for every possible form of artificiality was the kind from which there is no escape. So what could she do, except what she did? Exhale her resentment until it conditioned all her judgments. So we must not misinterpret her anglophilia – as unconditional as it was lasting: it derived less from whatever sympathy she may have felt for Bend'or than from her antipathy for those "warriors of love"[7] with whom she so dreaded being identified. Gabrielle was like that, always swathed in a resentment that was the very fabric of her being, leaving her personal genius, her grandeur, her profound disenchantment forever at war with her memories.

Nevertheless, in the days of her English affair the hope she still cherished in her heart, in the face of every wind and tide, remained strong: to marry. To marry, like Marthe Davelli who had given up singing and wedded Constantin Say, "the sugar Say." To marry, like the woman who still called herself Gabrielle Dorziat on stage but who in private life had become the comtesse de Zogheb. To marry Bend'or. Gabrielle exerted all her forces to that end. She followed him. She entered into a sort of whirlwind of amusements, adopting the feckless ways of the aristocrat whose destiny she was now sharing. His delight in constantly changing houses was contagious. She traveled. Wherever he went, he established a sort of divine right to think and act by English standards. His shirts, his hats, his walk, his voice, his jokes, his thoughts, everything made him an Englishman; even his war . . . In his mouth the most trivial anecdote was trademarked English. She listened to him. Of the new, free, turbulent spirit that had reigned over Gabrielle's Paris home during her previous loves – the spirit of Cocteau, Max Jacob, Reverdy – what remained? Nothing. She pretended not to mind, and bent a docile ear to the tale of the Duke of Westminster's Byronic gallop across the African desert. For there had been that, too: Bend'or may have loathed his era, its modern art and airplanes, but he had loved the war.

In 1914 his contribution to the world conflict had been to place his Rolls Royces at the disposal of the British army. He had eight of them. Then, after a brief period on the staff of Sir John French (both Gabrielle's English lovers appear to have been united there – first Boy, then Bend'or), we find the duke in the Lybian desert waging a little private war with the aid of a few friends, the way one might lead a hunting party. Every member of the duke's *cuadrilla* had an armored automobile from which the seats had been removed and with machine guns bolted to the back in place of the trunk. The Rolls Royces were supplemented by touring cars and an impressive array of vans and trucks, representing the contents of the duke's garages, both English and French. The company also had its own doctor, and such members of the Eaton Hall staff as had joined their master: jockeys, coachmen, and footmen were dressed for the occasion in combat fatigues and assigned subsidiary tasks – water fetching, vehicle maintenance, boot polishing, and fuel hunting fell to their lot. Meanwhile, at the triggers of the Hotchkiss machine guns, Bend'or and his friends reserved the noble art of warfare for themselves.

They forged ahead and, more or less by accident, collided with a camp of warriors who, being allies of the Turks and Germans, surrendered in amazement. It was a Senussi camp. The conquerors appropriated all weapons, supplies and ammunition, and in the course of their search came upon several bags full of letters written in English: the letters of British prisoners being held by the Senussi in the middle of the desert. Bend'or reinforced his column with a few camels, loaded his train with booty, and set off behind a guide-hostage in search of his countrymen. He found them ninety miles farther on, dying of thirst. When the prisoners first saw the high Rolls radiators appearing between the dunes, some thought they must be going mad, others were sure it was a mirage.

And from start to finish, the feeling that it was all a great lark.

But one can understand that the duke enjoyed telling tales from his past.

As long as she lived with him, Gabrielle claimed that she found him "perfect in his way." Only after leaving him was she prepared to concede some degree of intellectual inadequacy.

Did Bend'or ever think of marrying her? Let us say that, within a tangle of contradictions, and for as long as passion predominated – until around 1928 – the question remained implicitly open. But for him getting married was less of an issue than producing an heir. Gabrielle soon understood this, and having a child instantly became one of her major obsessions. But she was not getting any younger. Forty-six . . . Her childbearing days were numbered. From surging hope to sinking disappointment she fumed and fretted but would not give up. She scorned her recalcitrant body, she had no more indulgence for it than for any other object – employee, cutter, model, or fractious fabric – that showed unwillingness to serve her. She would have to consult experts? Very well; she turned herself over to the doctors, and to the more or less reputable ministrations of women she thought wiser than she. In her last years, if she felt herself in safe company, she would hint at an operation and "humiliating acrobatics" undertaken on a midwife's advice. But the cause of her misery lay in a single word: sterility. Resentment, rancor, loneliness, failure – everything stemmed from that. But still she succeeded, by linguistic subterfuge or absurd intimation, in throwing the blame on someone else. One time the sterility would be Bend'or's and openly affirmed, another time she would hint at his inability to overcome something like a retroactive virginity in her. But she also said, "I've always had a *child's belly*. Even back in the days of Boy . . ." Then, despite her pathos, it became clear what the trouble was. First Capel, then Bend'or: a twice-told tragedy. One finds it hard to see how she kept up her hopes of marrying Bend'or so long, in the face of her previous experience. But then, every token of love he gave her was proof that she need not yet fear the worst. This heir, after all, was he as indispensable as she had imagined? She told herself, "Who knows? Maybe he'll marry me without that." Because Bend'or was covering her with gifts. She took them as they came – sometimes amazing, sometimes touching, sometimes trivial. They all helped to keep up her illusions.

In 1928 she bought a piece of land, with a magnificent view and an olive grove, at the top of Roquebrune. A purchase fit for a king.* A summer house, a holiday home in close proximity to the leading London social figures and most "swinging" hostesses. A residence on the Riviera, a "place" in France, wouldn't that be an ideal instrument for the seduction of Bend'or? A few miles from La Pausa his old friend Winston Churchill, now out of power, was beginning to write his family's history. He stayed with Maxime Elliot at Golfe-Juan, or with Lord Beaverbrook, founder and owner of the *Daily Express, Sunday Express,* and *Evening Standard,* and Lord Rothermere, owner of the *Daily Mail* and *Evening News,* at Cap d'Ail. And so that La Pausa could actually become the meeting place for all Bend'or's friends, Gabrielle gave the lovely Vera and her husband a little house at the back of the garden: La Colline. Because it was Vera, far more than Gabrielle, who was the bosom friend of all these celebrities – the Churchills and the Princes of Wales.

Bend'or seemed delighted with the arrangement.

So, taking heart, Gabrielle made a survey of the things, apart from her inability to produce an heir, that might stand in the way of their marriage.

Even supposing it became known, her past was not the biggest hurdle. Singing, even singing in music halls, did not put you beyond the pale in English eyes. London was not Paris. But what about the Chanels? She had no more sisters, and no mother. Her peddler father? Dead, most likely, face down in a ditch. No problem. A model aunt most discreetly lived – Adrienne. One could count on her silence. The prospect of imminent marriage was making her more cautious than ever. There remained the brothers. No one but Gabrielle herself knew anything about Alphonse and Lucien. But let some columnist unearth them, or a certain element of the press get hold of them, and the results would be fatal. Yes, her brothers. There was the danger.

Oddly enough the more dangerous of the two, Alphonse, was not the one she worried about. Alphonse had no resources other than Gabrielle, and no occupation. In a pinch, he might be thought of as a small landowner, living on income. He "came up" to Paris several times a year. After every smashed

---

* The sale was made in Chanel's name. The deed of sale for the largest lot was entered in the Nice mortgage office on February 9, 1929 (volume 19, no. 47). All the people who lived with Gabrielle in those years believed that preliminary negotiations had begun three years before that, and whatever else people may have said, the property was bought by Chanel herself, on her own initiative, and was not a gift from the Duke of Westminster.

car, every new gambling debt, or every stormy scene with his wife, who promptly hid the money and put everything else under lock and key, Alphonse would turn to Gabrielle, dropping in one day when there was no one else around, to sit across from her at the table that was never in the same place twice. Alphonse's visits to the Faubourg St Honoré were no ordinary spectacle. To imagine them, we must listen to his daughters. What did they say? "Papa would come back full of stories. Stories about how his sister lived, about her house too, 'like a Hindu palace,' about her servants, fellows in livery and white gloves. Once he told us how, on sitting down at the table, he said to Gabrielle, 'Tell that geezer behind me to f—— off. It bugs me to feel a guy like that standing behind my back.' And Aunt Gabrielle burst out laughing. But the butler made such a face!" Another time their father had confessed a sad truth to his sister: "No more car, Gaby. She's at the bottom of a ravine. Best leave her there. In smithereens . . ." And instead of losing her temper Gabrielle had exclaimed, "I've got just the thing for you! Take that car in front of the door off my hands for me, and the driver with it." And Alphonse was seen returning to Valleraugue in a coupé of unfamiliar make with an enormous great lout in a cap at the wheel.

Here is Gabrielle disarmed by the humor of her long-lost brother; here is the brother – ex-miner, ex-hawker, skirt chaser – boasting and bragging like his dad, here he is seated among the Coromandel screens, dressed in black like the people of the Cévennes and wearing a wide-brimmed hat. And Gabrielle was right: she had nothing to fear from Alphonse. He needed her too badly. And Valleraugue? Who would ever go dig him up in that hole? The Cévennes were at the back of beyond. Gabrielle simply gave him more money, and demanded some improvement in his behavior. Above all, he shouldn't go setting a bad example for his brother. She worked hard enough already and didn't need him to make any more trouble for her. Alphonse promised. He always promised.

Lucien, with his independence, was far more of a problem. She gave him an allowance, true. But that had not stopped him from working. His stall was still set up every market day behind the cathedral at Clermont-Ferrand, and Lucien could be seen at dawn trundling, as of old, his baskets full of shoes. The awful part was that he liked doing it, and earned a good living from it. Selling junk! The future duchess' brother was a common shoe salesman. Just let that become known; let the trusting Lucien fall into the hands of the press, and Clermont-Ferrand would become a gold mine of anecdotes for that gang of riffraff. Paris and London both would be dining out on it for many a day.

The simplest thing to do, obviously, would be to go see the Chanel boys and have a heart-to-heart talk with them. But Gabrielle had neither the time nor the inclination to do that. Return to that province of despair? Not on your life.

Lucien got a letter. Gabrielle wished him to stop working. She now had *enough*. It was only natural that her brothers should reap the benefit. Why did Lucien have to go on touring the markets, when Alphonse was "playing the gentleman"? Wasn't it Lucien's turn now? He'd done and been through enough already. She did not want him to work anymore. Let him look for a fine house and buy it and fix it up, and let it, above all, be a house with a garden. She would send him all the money he needed. But Gabrielle went further than that; giving her desire to retire to Auvergne as her chief motive, she insisted that Lucien should choose a very big house so that, later on, there would be room enough in it for her. Touched by her concern for him, overcome by the thought that this prodigious sister of his was thinking of coming to live with him, Lucien complied. Even though the markets were his whole life, the shouting, the early-morning bustle. Poor Lucien . . . Overriding his wife's objections, he gave up his job, gave up the good faith of his suppliers, even gave up the proposal he had just received: a steady job, with manufacturers known throughout the country. But Gabrielle was talking about coming back . . .

Above Clermont-Ferrand, a piece of land on the side of a hill. It overlooked the whole world. He told his sister about it, and bought it. She made no fuss about the money. Lucien built a house. A sort of small country house, a charming little place in quarry-stone, with a glass-enclosed entryway at the front door, a microscopic front stoop, and stone-framed windows. What would Gabrielle think of it? Lucien trembled. Would she approve, would she like the house? At last her answer came: Lucien had set his sights too low, she would like to see him in an older place. At that, Lucien's common sense took over. The little sister was exaggerating. Was it a château she was wanting? Lucien didn't see himself in some edifice that had more rooms in it than he would know what to do with. Where would he get furniture for it all? And then, it wouldn't look right. What would the local people think of all this money coming so suddenly? He wasn't going to give up his friends, the market traders, the shoe manufacturers, his old customers, just because Gabrielle wanted him to live in a palace. They compromised. The cottage could stay, Gabrielle decided. She repeated that she would come and visit him in it.

She never came.

She had got what she wanted.

Lucien had stopped traipsing around the fairgrounds, her two brothers were henceforth living on their incomes. There were no longer any grounds for raising eyebrows.

But in her last letter she asked Lucien not to see Alphonse anymore, in terms that were highly unflattering to the latter. Lucien knew perfectly well what a hothead Alphonse was. He was better off left where he was, no? Otherwise Lucien might be led astray . . .

And because this was the advice given by so good and generous a sister, Lucien again complied. Part the brothers? Keep them from meeting? This was Gabrielle's last ploy. For if Alphonse learned of her liberality to Lucien, he would immediately have clamored for her to do the same for him.

SO WHITE . . .

No sooner had she got her family into order than the whole exercise became pointless. Bend'or was being unfaithful to her and Gabrielle, in her bitter clearsightedness, saw herself the prisoner of a degrading, artificial liaison, reliving what she had been through before with Capel. Nineteen twenty-nine might have been one of the best years of her life. Work on La Pausa was finally completed, and it was as though building it had helped Gabrielle to soar even higher. The style of the house, Gabrielle's ideas about decoration, were making news. People borrowed from her, copied her. In a related field, No. 5 had become "The Largest-Selling Perfume in the World" and for the time being harmony reigned between her and the company* that produced and sold it. In the fashion world, everything that was to become high style in the thirties – the fabrics: marocain, Roman crepe; the lines – mid-calf skirts, bell-shaped skirts, a degree of fullness, beach pajamas – had been born in the reflections of the mirrors of her famous salon. But where the heart was concerned, the year brought nothing but disillusionment. Gabrielle found the callousness of a companion who did not even try to spare her feelings hard to bear. Officially staying at La Pausa, he spent most of his time at the Casino in Monte Carlo. She turned her scathing tongue on him, but he would not tolerate any form of accusation.

---

* Founded in 1924, the Chanel perfume company marked Gabrielle's association with the owner of the largest perfume factory in France, Pierre Wertheimer. Countless conflicts, violent arguments, and lawsuits of every description divided them for forty years; but the company weathered all the storms, and the war and occupation as well. For details on the story of Chanel's business empire, see Pierre Galante, *Mademoiselle Chanel*, Henry Regnery Co., Chicago.

There were evenings in 1928 and 1929 when fierce quarrels erupted in the silence of the La Pausa olive groves, and there was loud slamming of doors. Almost before it was finished, this dwelling, designed for a life that had been so beautiful in her imagination, had already lost its *raison d'être*.

It was a strange cruise, that of the *Flying Cloud* along the coast of Dalmatia in 1929. There was Misia's caustic and constant intrusion into the privacy of this couple about to part. It is striking to observe how Misia turns up at every crisis in Gabrielle's private life and ultimately takes command. She was on board the yacht, traveling with them. It is true that she had reasons to get away from Paris. José-Maria Sert was inflicting upon her the daily ordeal of his latest passion, a young Georgian woman utterly obsessed with a longing to commit suicide. It was to avoid the demoralizing spectacle of their threesome – "I remember José-Maria Sert slumped in a springless armchair, flanked by his two wives, Misia and Roussy, who were stretched out at his feet," Morand wrote in *Venises*[8] – that Misia had joined them on the cruise. When they anchored at Venice, she set off in search of Diaghilev. Gabrielle went with her. Venice, in her life, always meant an end and a beginning: always a breakdown of love, and always Misia leading to a meeting with Diaghilev.

Misia had been alerted by a telegram from Lifar: Diaghilev was on the Lido, ill and badly cared-for. A condition that had been worrying his friends for the past six months had taken a sudden turn for the worse. His Paris doctor had been categorical: Diaghilev was in the last stages of diabetes. Then, to escape a truth he did not want to face, he had gone for a holiday to Germany, then to Austria where he had been able to disobey doctor's orders with a vengeance. The moment he reached Venice, retribution began. It was like brain fever and typhus together. It was neither one nor the other. But the local physican, a palace Diafoirus who refused to confirm the diagnosis of his French colleague, was proffering the "vaguest speculations."[9] Rheumatism, typhus, influenza, septicemia, he couldn't make up his mind.

Diaghilev saw Misia and Gabrielle on August 17, 1929, in his room at the Hôtel des Bains. He was still in bed but his temperature was down. The last lull. He tried to look better than he felt, he seemed cheerful, he was charming, he was planning trips. Their next meeting must be at Palermo. And the ballet? He didn't feel like talking about it. All of a sudden, a passion for music had replaced his passion for the dance. A unique, exclusive passion.

Misia left convinced that he was lost.

The *Flying Cloud* put to sea again, carrying only two passengers grappling with a dull resentment: Gabrielle, trying for her own sake to make light of her lover's infidelities; and Bend'or, who, although bent on marriage to somebody else, and an heir, recovered energy enough to drag her back every time he felt her trying to break away.

Misia stayed behind in Venice.

That evening at the Hôtel des Bains, Boris Kochno observed a slight improvement. Diaghilev was saying how happy it had made him to see his friends again. He described them, he kept repeating, "They were so young, all in white! They were so white."[10] His joy seemed to be all in that word, in the whiteness that emanated from them, their life.

In the night of August 18–19, Misia received a telephone call and came running to the Lido. Diaghilev was dying.

He did not hear the whispers of those watching at his side. He did not interpret the dry snap of the suitcase closing as the nurse took her leave, remarking that he should just last out the night. He didn't hear it. He knew nothing of what was going on in his room. Or in Venice. To whom did he say, "Forgive me?" The priest, summoned by Misia, had not yet arrived. Outside, lagoon and sea mingled in a single gray blanket. He did not see the slow light growing. He died in the early dawn.

Just as he stopped breathing, those present in the room saw something sparkle at the corner of his eyelid, and one tear roll down. Like the escaping overflow of images, sounds, skies, men, loves, mirages, made-up worlds. A last sign from the dreamer's eyes before inflexible darkness obscured them.

As usual, the Ballets' treasury was empty. Misia used what cash she had on hand. There were immediate expenses to be met, the hotel bill, the nurse, the doctor, there was . . . But then she ran out of money too. She set off to see a jeweler she knew, to pawn her most valuable possession: her three-strand diamond necklace. She had to. Otherwise, how was Diaghilev to have a decent burial?

On the way she ran into Gabrielle, who was just off the ship. A premonition. She had begged Bend'or, and he had agreed to turn the *Flying Cloud* back.

The trip to the jeweler was no longer necessary, the diamonds remained around Misia's throat. Gabrielle took charge of the burial. When was it to be? That same day, at night. Why such a weird time? Because of the hotel customers. They mustn't . . . But a storm broke. And the gondola was unable to come to the Lido for Diaghilev's body. It was put off until very early the following morning. There were the bathers, the customers; they mustn't . . . It was the height of the season.

In the gray hour, three gondolas moved away from the hotel. The coffin was in one: "That floating bed of honor, a Venetian convoy, carried the magician's remains to the funereal isle of San Michele."[11] Four friends followed, in summer dress: Kochno and Lifar, Misia and Gabrielle, all in white. There was no one else at the cemetery. "Despite the paucity of trees in Venice, the storm had littered the path with green branches,"[12] one contemporary wrote. That was not the only peculiarity about the ceremony. If Gabrielle is to be believed, Lifar and Kochno were determined, the moment they stepped out of the gondolas, to go all the way to the tomb on their knees. She brought them to their feet with a stinging, "Stop that nonsense, if you please." According to Morand, "Lifar leaped into the grave." And he concludes, "As Byron wrote to Murray from Venice, on November 25, 1816, 'Love in this part of the world is no sinecure.' "[13]

The Duke of Westminster was not seen at La Pausa at the end of that summer. Gabrielle stayed there with a few artists and the person well-informed journalists were already calling "her dear friend Misia."[14]

In London, the Duke of Westminster was showing signs of ill-humor. Or perhaps jealousy. There was nothing surprising in that. Once back in Paris, Gabrielle quickly resumed her old habits and her old circle of friends. Bend'or, who, although unfaithful, was finding it difficult to tear himself away from her altogether, commented on the situation in an approximative French which his strong English accent rendered most comical: "Coco is crazy! Now she's living with *akiouré* [*curé* = priest]."

His decision was taken, he was going to marry. But without quite wanting to imagine Gabrielle in the depths of despair, he would have liked to see her sorry. Gabrielle, meanwhile, in a Machiavellian gambit, was behaving as though separation meant liberation. She plunged back into action, and the "curé" with whom the Duke of Westminster associated her was none other than Pierre Reverdy.

Thereupon, relations between her and Bend'or assumed a new form. Of course, this didn't happen overnight, or without a struggle. Gabrielle in particular would gladly have forgone the calls which the duke insisted upon paying every time he came through Paris. Having lost the round, she would have preferred a clean break. But in one way Bend'or's congeniality helped her to "save face." She had to protect herself against a hostile world that was waiting for her to fall – ever on the alert for separations and quarrels – that accursed society on which she depended.

What could she do? So Gabrielle imposed a vow of silence upon her vanished dreams, and on her resentment too, and came to terms with them in this artificial friendship which in reality was nothing but wounded pride.

At long last, on April 29, 1930, Adrienne was married in Paris. The demise of her "adored's" father had left him free to marry the woman who had been waiting to bear his name for over twenty years. "Mademoiselle Gabrielle Chanel, dress designer, residing at 29, rue dú Faubourg St Honoré," was witness for the bride.

And the Duke of Westminster's engagement was announced.

He was to wed the Honorable Loelia Mary Ponsonby, daughter of the first Lord Sisonby. And now – one can hardly believe it – the future bridegroom's first thought, with the unintentional cruelty of those whom unlimited wealth envelops in a sort of absolute power, was to introduce his fiancée to Gabrielle. He was even magnanimous enough to inquire whether she thought the young woman a suitable choice.

A REVIVAL THAT FAILED

Smoothing over, patching up, retying – this time it looked as though Gabrielle was suffering from an occupational disease that led her to treat the heart in terms of the sewing room. Reverdy again? There she was, off in the clouds once more. Didn't she know love can't be made over like last year's winter coat?

She probably resorted to a most curious ruse to get him back: an offer of collaboration. In the absence of evidence of a definite connection between her proposal and Reverdy's return to the Faubourg, however, this cannot be claimed with any certainty. When exactly was the offer made? Before the revival, or immediately after it? Was it a pretext or a consequence? We will never know. Of their correspondence only a few of Reverdy's answers have survived, and none bears a date. In any case, the letters[15] are enough to establish that an offer was indubitably made, somewhere in the 1930s when Reverdy was "undertaking to write notes"[16] – the notes that later formed his *Livre de mon bord.*

What did she want? She wanted them to write together. Just short thoughts and notes which she intended to publish in various magazines. But she considered that nothing she wrote would be publishable unless Reverdy revised it for her. In fact, what she really wanted was to supplement a few existing notes referring solely to her work, with more general thoughts on love, grace, and charm. She clearly needed help. Who better than Reverdy to give it to her? After the publication of one volume of notes[17] in 1927, there could be no doubt: all of Reverdy was there, in this almost unbearably concise confrontation with reality.

She must have had some real power over him; otherwise, would he have accepted such a proposal? But he did, without demur. Rising to the bait, he emptied his files – ". . . these are the latest, they were in a writing pad"; sent part of his harvest off to her – ". . . these are only the most trivial jottings. The rest, those I don't even want to see published in my lifetime, are only worth anything if you take them all together"; and when she sent him her manuscripts, used all his tact in "interpreting," never "correcting," her ideas. In addition, every one of his letters contains a brilliant analysis of the techniques of literary creation.

"Of course, dear Coco, what I say about my notes refers to them as a whole and only in relation to myself . . . Moreover, they are the residue of my inner activity and so I don't know when they will stop accumulating . . . I have extracted just a few from the old manuscripts, those that are only one line long. I write them even when I'm drunk. I burn masses of them."

Five years had passed since his break with Paris, and Reverdy was still living at Solesmes. But his initial joy, the peace he had found in living the life of the monks – rising at dawn, mass at seven, a hard morning's work, back to the abbey for high mass, and finally vespers and compline, "and no distractions from God," he had written, "and it will last as long as He pleases in the sun under the gray sky"[18] – it was all gone now. Reverdy found himself confronting a cruel dilemma: he had either to admit that he had lost the Faith and leave Solesmes, which was equivalent to resigning himself – an impossibility ("it meant accepting the man's failure through the failure of his work, and vice versa"[19]) – or to stand fast and stay on.

He chose the latter. As a result, he was writing less and less, and publishing hardly anything – "as his bibliography reminds us, with the titles and dates coming at close intervals between 1915 and 1930, followed suddenly by a long gap between 1930 and 1937."[20] And he frequently abandoned his retreat for increasingly long trips to Paris.

Far from bringing relief, these truancies left him feeling that he had doubly failed. At Solesmes, God may have abandoned him, but he remained chained to the idea of the deity he had forged and everlastingly stricken by the illumination he had experienced six years earlier. In Paris, he was dismayed by the worship of the artificial and the general consent he saw given to all forms of mystification. He soon felt excluded and compelled to flee Paris just as, a few days earlier, he had felt compelled to flee the desert of Solesmes.

In 1931, having abruptly opted for failure, Reverdy decided to carry it to extremes. "He seemed like a man who had broken off relations with something," observed one friend from that period.[21] The sky was empty? So be it. All that remained was to let himself be carried along. Particularly as Gabrielle was doing her utmost to awaken in him a very different kind of faith: faith in his talent and future, faith in pleasure. The longing to *get him back* was intensified in this ambitious woman by her conviction that he was her absolute antithesis. To conquer her opposite: that was a challenge made to order for her.

So Pierre Reverdy was again seen with Gabrielle. Who was more the prisoner? Reverdy of his indecision, or Gabrielle of her poet's manic-depressive states? One day he wanted to live alone, and she urged him to accept a studio that she had gone to great trouble to find and rent for him in Montparnasse. But the mere thought of being settled somewhere gave him cold shudders and he scurried back to Solesmes where he remained cloistered for another few weeks. From there he wrote Gabrielle one of those letters that were a specialty of his, a message that labored to appear soothing but only succeeded in unmasking his utter confusion. He nevertheless contrived to put into the letter, whatever else it might contain, the reassurance Gabrielle was entitled to expect: "As soon as I reach Paris I shall fly to kiss you, as I do here now a thousand times in my mind."[22] Or, "I certainly did not leave Paris with no idea of coming back, but I did not think to return so soon – your call intercepts my plans, but will do no more than delay them. I cannot resist the joy of seeing you . . ."[23]

And indeed, he was seen again.

He installed himself on the terrace of the Dôme, "seemingly quite relaxed, open, cordial, talkative, a shade cynical, sometimes frivolous."[24] His friends of old, those of the heroic days of the Bateau Lavoir and *Nord-Sud*, greeted him ecstatically, the Braques, Max Jacob, the Laurenses, Fernand Léger, the Derains, Brassaï, Cendrars, Cocteau, Tériade. He went to bed late, "seeing lots of people, 'going out,' constantly lunching and dining." Where else could one meet this wolf who had quarreled with his solitude; and to whom was he referring, in his letter to Gabrielle, when he spoke of his "drunkards" and of certain "unjustifiable friendships"? Let us consult the accounts of his contemporaries: "Long days, and nights with numerous drinks." And, from the same source, "He would take me off to one or another of the bars or restaurants he liked, or sometimes to see English or American friends, with whom he spent a lot of time in those days." (And what about Gabrielle!) "I can still see him as he was some evenings, in his ever-spotless double-breasted gray flannel suit, and his imperious shock of hair and glittering eyes, with a glass of Scotch in his hand, talking interminably of everything and nothing." Those were the days when Derain, meeting him one morning near the Closerie des Lilas, a famous restaurant in Montparnasse frequented by the intelligentsia of the 1930s, and assuming that his haggard aspect was a consequence of his monastic life, said, "You've lost weight. Those monks of yours aren't making you fast all the time, I hope?"

To which Reverdy retorted, "It's the fox trot, not the fast."

Because there were nightclubs, too. He and Gabrielle were seen at "Jimmy's and in many another place in which the Montparnasse of those days performed its amazing here-today, gone-tomorrow ballet with the four corners of the earth."

Lastly, there was the allure of a long holiday.

In 1931, Reverdy's visits to La Pausa extended over a large part of the summer. This was when Gabrielle's files were being augmented by new "thoughts" which appeared a few years later over her signature. It would be worth comparing these texts with some of Reverdy's notes, culled from *Gant de crin* and the *Livre de mon bord*. One would note disturbing analogies. What is one to make of their identical choice of subject: the value of chance in creation, the distrust of taste, the abhorrence of the decorative, the distaste for untidiness, the fear of "retouching, which, unless it is miraculous, can ruin everything"?[25] And we should add: a fondness for the quick retort, the stinging summary, together with an undeniable identity in choice of words. But the evidence renders the demonstration pointless. It is enough to quote those of Chanel's thoughts with the most Reverdian ring to convince oneself that he, far more often than she, was their author. Can there be any doubt?

"There comes a moment when one cannot touch a work anymore: when it is at its worst."

"Good taste ruins certain true spiritual values: such as taste itself."

"Disgust is often the rear guard of pleasure, and often its vanguard too."

"One can be driven to deceit by an excess of tact in love."

"If you are born without wings, do nothing to prevent them from growing."

"For a woman, betrayal has only one sense: that of the senses."

"It is the nature of a weak spirit to boast of advantages which chance alone can give."

Informed of Chanel's literary ambitions, the women's magazines hastened to inspect her work. Their disappointment was keen. Fashion was what they wanted. One American magazine sent her its best-qualified representative,[26] with instructions to "get something a little more fashion-design out of her."

"Leave me alone with your gabbling. Adornment is never anything except a reflection of the heart," snapped Gabrielle.

And as the other woman insisted, she added:

"You can take your fashion and ———."

The year before the war, disappointment having given way to resignation, the women's press decided to publish the Chanel-signed thoughts, however "intellectual" they might be. A laudatory introduction prepared the female public for the latest bombshell from the distinguished designer who decidedly "was not like anyone else."

By the end of 1931 the trial reconciliation had failed definitively and the lover's niche in Gabrielle's life was empty again. The patch-up had lasted a year. Reverdy was left to his mental torments, they were his destiny. And Gabrielle, exhausted by this hopeless repetition, gave up for good. Unhappiness is catching, she knew. She turned away from him for fear of contagion, as much as for love of life.

It remains to determine how many outbursts, tempests, fierce arguments, and reconciliations interrupted by further flare-ups preceded the end of this merciless struggle. Hard to tell. But an examination of the few surviving letters shows beyond doubt that many an angry word was exchanged. At what exact moment of their disinfatuation did he send the following epistle: "I should blame myself if I put off answering your little note, which I have just read, for so long as one second. Nothing could have produced a sharper emotion in me. You know well that, whatever happens, and God knows how much already has happened, you cannot contrive to render yourself anything other than infinitely precious to me, forever. To love someone is to know him, in one way, from a viewpoint and to a degree which nothing can affect or destroy. A way of seeing his nature as he neither sees nor knows it himself. In any case, if it were in my power to be unkind it is not to you that I should ever want to express such a feeling. I only believe that it is infinitely wiser, given our personalities, not to see each other anymore; that is, to oppose each other in a moment when violence would sweep everything else away."[27]

One sure thing is that, coming from anyone else, Reverdy's shuttling back and forth between Gabrielle's Paris-the-Futile and the peace of Solesmes might eventually begin to look like the incidents in a rather bad comedy.

But for him it was a calvary, and the incidents only the inevitable stations of his cross. The following letter – containing the word "war" – enables us to determine very exactly the period at which Reverdy returned to his prison for good:

"I have had to make a long journey into myself," he wrote, "a slow and profound retreat. In short, I have thought very hard and, after going over everything and weighing everything up, I have concluded that I must live here again, as before, alone. First of all, because of the state of my nerves and mind, which demands that I treat myself as an invalid – which I am – and which other people need not take into account, nor can I ask them to understand it. Secondly, because it is time for me to change the way of life to which I have uncourageously abandoned myself for *some ten years* now, if I do not want to end by becoming totally disgusted with myself. Now that that existence no longer has the justification of *tender attachments* and *deep emotions*, it has become unendurable. I have too long given free rein to that part of me that asked only to run after pleasure, wholly scorning the rest. I was running after the wind – you lose your breath and are left with nothing but a very painful bitterness. I am too heavy, too serious, too naturally inclined to probe the deepest roots of things, to let myself be carried like a feather at the whim of every breeze without falling back even more heavily than before. The frivolity of others and their agitation, however refreshing they may be, are powerless, then, to soothe the intensity of the bruises.

"I should like to have the faith I had before, and enter the monastery. Although there is too much artificiality in that as well. But there can be no question of it. I shall have to go on being a lay monk, alone, unordained and without faith. That is even more austere and more heroic.

"More modestly, I have to preserve that minimum of balance and self-control which I can only achieve away from the world, in a life of almost ascetic simplicity, by creating for myself a few sane and restful habits. And lately, this war has put me back into perilous financial straits and it is absolutely imperative that I cease my follies if I do not want to lose, along with everything else, the little relative freedom my few remaining pence may be able to preserve. I kiss you. P."[28]

Are we to take him as completely sincere? Or was Reverdy merely outlining, with the help of this letter, the character of the hermit, a role in which he had decided to cast himself in the book on which he was then working?[29] When the subject was broached to Gabrielle, who always forbade herself any reticence where he was concerned, she let slip a smile:

"Whenever he claimed to be very unhappy in his letters," she said, "I knew he had thrown himself into his writing again. That was a way of telling me, 'I am saved.'"

But at the time of his second break with Gabrielle, his self-inflicted misery was too new for him to be wholly steeped in it. And in a conversation with Stanislas Fumet we find the flagellant of 1931 still seeking to deny his lost faith and his perplexity:

"I assure you I am very, very happy," he alleged.

And the moment the words were out of his mouth, he burst into sobs.

That scene took place in 1937, on the rue St André-des-Arts. Six years had passed since he had fled Gabrielle and the temptation of Paris for the second time.

In the summer of 1932 Reverdy did not come to La Pausa. It was Misia who occupied the right wing of the villa, the rooms adjoining Gabrielle's, whose only previous summer occupant had been the Duke of Westminster. Misia, always Misia, present whenever she was needed, enlivening the emptiness, populating the blank spaces in Gabrielle's love life; Misia and the artists who followed her wherever she went, Misia and her piano . . . No more lords. That page had been turned. And no more poets. That summer at Gabrielle's there was music every evening.

Whenever an invitation came, Misia and Gabrielle went together. The columnists announced their presence at Monte Carlo in the company of Misia's old group: Philippe Berthelot, Etienne de Beaumont, etc. The two friends' elegance was much praised. Misia always in Chanel clothes that year, in "a dress of aquamarine georgette and feather boa of the same hue."

In fact, Misia had been around ever since the break with the Duke of Westminster. That is how she happened to be present at a memorable event: Gabrielle's meeting, in Monte Carlo, with Samuel Goldwyn.

Grand Duke Dmitri was the instrument. Chanel's 1920 lover whom she had helped in his time of trouble met her again now at the summit of her glory, and gave her a hand in return; the scion of the Romanovs introduced her to the tsar of Hollywood.

Here Gabrielle's destiny reveals another of those unique moments described in no book – for history immortalizes only the events that stir up vast human masses: plagues, wars, invasions, cities in flames; and pays scant heed to the unforeseeable encounters between individuals. As though history were not also the patient accumulation of images of the time, each containing a modest share of truth, each showing something, sometimes hardly more than a speck of dust, of what those days were like. That, too, is history, after all.

Amidst the storms America was undergoing in the early 1930s, the economic crisis worsening with every passing month and preparing, although no one yet had an inkling of it, for Franklin D. Roosevelt's accession to power; in that precarious moment of American history the son of a Polish emigrant, now a loyal citizen of the continent that had given him freedom to forge a destiny befitting his grandeur, Samuel né-Goldfish, who became Goldwyn at the same time he became pioneer of the American cinema, was engaging in earnest discussions with Gabrielle Chanel, trying to convince her to come to Hollywood.

Might there have been some dark premonition behind his approach? In March 1932, forty million Americans were jobless. You had to have known the full weight of privation, as Samuel Goldwyn had, to know that when you are down to your last pennies and the choice is between a piece of bread and a ticket to the show, you choose the bread. Goldwyn had quickly seen that bringing a higher level of sophistication to his dream factories could help keep him afloat in the dark days ahead. This was not the time for caution and timidity. It was the time to dare, the time to bill the big names and buy prestige. That way, if one could not draw greater hordes of the common people, at least one would be assured the presence of growing numbers of the urban rich. To give women another reason to go to the movies: that was his plan. They would go, "One, to see the pictures and stars; and two, to see the latest in clothes."[30] He had to have Chanel.

The contract guaranteed Chanel a fabulous sum of money: one million dollars. What she had to do in exchange was go to Hollywood twice a year. The famous producer's decision was final: from now on his stars would be dressed by Gabrielle and no one else, on stage and off. This was the big innovation: the object was not just to "dress" films, but also to reform the fashion habits of the great ladies of the screen. How would they react to this ultimatum? In Hollywood there were two schools of thought. That of the fashion editors, who were optimistic: "The stars will accept because it is Chanel"; and that of the columnists, who, knowing the individuals concerned, expressed doubts: "Chanel, nothing but Chanel?" On location and in the studios, maybe. But in everyday life? Didn't the stars have their own temperament and taste, even their bad temper and bad taste?

Goldwyn was firm: he had to have Chanel.

Nevertheless, he was surprised. Seven years before he had bagged the designer Erté for his extravaganzas; the designer had bubbled over with gratitude and enthusiasm and had consented to live in Hollywood for over a year without a murmur. The offer he was making Gabrielle was vastly more handsome. How was it that she seemed so little thrilled by it? To be the person who would clothe the creatures who set the whole world to dreaming and desiring, to clothe them from dawn to dark, was far more tempting than what Erté had been offered. To be given every screen in the world for one's personal publicity . . . to make "Chanel silhouettes" out of the bodies of Mary Pickford and Gloria Swanson: was that all it meant to her? No Frenchwoman had ever been made such an offer; was she finally going to make up her mind and accept? After much hesitation, Chanel gave in; she would go to Hollywood.

But about this glorious journey which would have become anyone else's sole topic of conversation, she never uttered a word. The odd thing about this chatterbox was that she never talked about herself.

Yet there was certainly nothing to hide, nothing that could do anything but magnify and glorify her. So why the silence? By then, it had become second nature to her to keep her mouth shut. To her it seemed dangerous to reveal any episode in her life, major or minor, because they were all links of a single chain, all clues exploitable by someone seeking to dig up what she wanted at all costs to keep buried: her age, her early poverty, her first loves.

Better to say too little than too much. When pressed, forced to yield up a few memories, she would wriggle out with jabs and gibes. Hollywood? "It was the Mont St Michel of tit and tail." Why wasn't her memory of it more vivid? "It was like an evening at the Folies Bergères. Once you've said the girls were beautiful and there were a lot of feathers around, you've said it all." But still . . . "There isn't any still. You know perfectly well that everything 'super' is the same. Supersex, super-productions . . . It had to collapse sooner or later. Television put things back in their proper places. Anyway, I only like crime films." What about the atmosphere in Hollywood? "Infantile . . . It affected Misia more than me. I laughed at it. One day we were entertained by a famous actor who had painted all the trees in his garden blue in our honor. I thought it was nice, but so silly." And the stars? "Them! On that trip I met only one who was worth the bother of going over there." Who was that? "Eric von Stroheim." Why him? "Because with him, at least, there was some justification for the extravagance." What justification? "He was taking a personal revenge. He was a Prussian persecuting Jewish inferiors. Because Hollywood was mostly Jewish. Jews from Central Europe, finding an old familiar nightmare in the person of Stroheim. At least with him there wasn't any pretense! He and his victims reliving an old story

together, and they all knew every twist and turn of it by heart, and underneath it all, they were actually rather fond of it."

Her trip took place in April 1931. Misia went with her. Together they
made a triumphant entry into the film capital, skillfully orchestrated by Sam
Goldwyn. He spared no expense. Despite the depression, Hollywood was
still the maddest place in the world. It was still the capital of excess, of films
with three thousand extras, gigantic studios, the absolute power of the stars.
Every manner of top performer turned up to meet the visitors, and from
Garbo to Stroheim, Marlene to Cukor, Claudette Colbert to Fredric March,
they all considered themselves greatly honored to be able to converse with
the person said to be "the biggest fashion brain ever known."

When she returned to France Gabrielle had not just *seen* Hollywood, as a
tourist would. She had gone there for business, we must remember. And just
as, hardly seven years before, she had learned what a ballet costume was when
she worked for Diaghilev and what a theater costume was when she worked
for Cocteau and Picasso, now she learned about the imperatives of film costuming,
from her work with the best-known technicians of the day. She saw films being
made, met the top experts in scene and fashion design – such as Mitchell
Leisen (DeMille's artistic director, in which capacity he dominated the Hollywood
scene for twelve years, signing the settings for almost all of his films until 1933),
Adrian (discovered and launched by Leisen, who used him for the costumes
of most of his films until 1930), and Cecil B. DeMille. From that time on she
knew them and was known by them. In the minds of her contemporaries she
had achieved a new distinction: she had "done" Hollywood and was "under
contract" there; her creativity had turned her into one of those European
commodities to which Hollywood was looking for assistance. The young
Mademoiselle from Moulins, the would-be singer of Vichy, the bachelor-
apartment seamstress had forged her way to the top. What a long way she had
come! By acquiring an international reputation, the sign of arrival in any field,
she had outdistanced her competition by many lengths. And lastly – and this
may be the most important thing – she had just learned, from the best possible
source, what the word "photogenic" meant; a notion that, consciously or not,
figured in a great many of her subsequent creations.

But that was as far as it went; and after *Tonight or Never*[31] with Gloria
Swanson, the first film costumed by Gabrielle, the stars rebelled. They
would not wear the creations of the same brain in one film after another,
even if that brain was Chanel's.

Gabrielle considered herself released from her second trip, and Goldwyn
was out of pocket. But as far as publicity went, nobody was the loser. All

the daily papers printed long articles on *Tonight or Never*. The *New York Herald Tribune* hailed "Miss Swanson's undeniable talent and the wonderfully natural touch she brings to light comedy." It also observed that this new film seemed to suit the young actress better than her recent creations, which had done her little good. *Variety* was glad to see her giving up the nasty parts which were definitely not right for her. It added, "Here she gives a capital performance." Most critics used terms like "good taste" and "common sense." And *The New Yorker* published a very witty commentary on the *why* of Gabrielle's break with Hollywood, in the form of a tribute: "[The film] gives Gloria a chance to dress up in a lot of expensive clothes . . . The gowns are credited to Chanel, the Paris dressmaker who recently made a much publicized trip to Hollywood, but I understand she left that center of light and learning in a huff. They told her her dresses weren't sensational enough. She made a lady look like a lady. Hollywood wants a lady to look like two ladies." So the good gossips' paradiddle had worked magic, and nobody could be ignorant of the brief alliance between the inventor of Hollywood and the great Chanel.

What was less well known was that in Paris, in the shadow of the Coromandel screens, an influence was already at work without which Gabrielle would never have accepted Sam Goldwyn's invitation.

VIII

Of Divers Dances 1933–1940

"When your feet danced so hard in anger, Paris! when you were pierced by so many knives . . ."

— ARTHUR RIMBAUD, "L'Orgie parisienne"

ENCOUNTER WITH THE DEMON

"My Darling, it is a beautiful day. How to tell it? It would have to be described in music. So much cool, heat, scent, who could describe them . . . A full moon on the sea, the kind that makes you want to say: 'If that's for me, not quite so much, please.' The rest is sea, bathing, flowers, walks alone and you not being here. An explosion of pink lilies: twenty-nine stems on one side, twenty on the other, have all opened at the same time in two rows. Magnificent. Against the open-brick wall, you know, the wall the tool shed leans against? Another explosion of pink lilies mixed with a waterfall of pale blue plumbago and streams of deep blue volubilis. And you're not here!"

Colette, her flowers, her animals, her garden: one letter among the many she wrote to Maurice Goudeket, whom she married in 1935, in the summer of 1933. Motionless, the little Mediterranean port was living through its last years of true celebrity. The connoisseurs shared it among themselves. For the sheer pleasure of communicating a little of her wonderment to the person who loved her, Colette re-created all the charms her south of France still possessed: the lazy sea, the boats with their furled sails, the Treille Muscate, Colette's house at St Tropez, and the flowers storming over it. But her letters were also those of an observer who, in addition to her tenderness, humor, and delight, remained on terms of absolute objectivity with the human race. Unmasking the implacable mechanism of the invasion – St Tropez gradually eroded by "the alert Parisian idiocy" and the reality of individuals caught and held – in short, this was where Colette the letter writer excelled. As here, for example, in this series of candid shots in which she illuminates the actors and actresses of the Tropezian comedy in the days of its stammering opening lines.

Nothing could outline more clearly the disturbing figure suddenly glimpsed at Gabrielle's side.

"Late yesterday afternoon I was in town with Moune and Kessel to pick up the 6:30 post and go to the little shop* to see Jeanne

* Where the cosmetics Colette manufactured were sold.

Marnac,* who was to be having her nails done. As I was buying something at Vachon's two hands covered my eyes, a pleasant body leaned against my back. It was Misia, full of caresses. Effusions, tenderness.

" 'What, you here?'

" 'But of course I'm here!' etc.

"But she had something urgent to toss into my ear:

" 'You know, she's marrying him!'

" 'Who?'

" 'Iribe. Darrrling, Darrrling, what an unbelievable business: Coco in love for the first time in her life!'

"Comments, remarks, etc.

" 'Ah, I can assure you, that man knows his business.'

"I didn't have time to ask what business.

" 'We've been looking for you, we've been to your place, we want to take you to dinner in St Raphael, Cannes . . .'

"I decline, fall into her arms again, leave with Moune, and we go to collect Kessel, who was buying something or other. We take three steps, two arms encircle me, Antoinette Bernstein† and her daughter. Effusions, etc.

" 'We've been looking for you, we're taking you to dinner at Robert de Rothschild's at Valescure . . .' etc.

"She already knew that I was taking over as critic for the *Journal*.[1] Re-effusions, kisses. Moune and I start off again, we take three steps, two reaper's arms embrace me, it was the Vals:‡

---

* Jeanne (stage name Jane) Marnac lived the life Gabrielle Chanel dreamed of so long. Brought up by nuns, she made her debut in 1907 at the Gaîeté Rochechouart. Was lady MC in the revue *Tu l'as l'cri-cri*, when the press sang her praises for a week. Studied singing with Litvine, starred in operettas, then successfully made the transition from singing to "West End" or "Broadway" comedy. Became Mrs Trevor in 1927 by marrying an Honorable British colonel. Given top billing at the Casino de Paris almost as often as Mistinguett; her career led her quite naturally to "take a theater" and become a shrewd lady theater-manager. The contemporary press said of her, "Part fashion model, part rue de la Paix, and part high-class 'dolly,' the whole well-frosted with wit." In Colette's world there were people like Jane Marnac and Spinelly, the very women Gabrielle avoided like the plague, forever fearing that their shared past of music halls and light living would lead to disclosures.

† Wife of the playwright Henri Bernstein. They were Chanel's neighbors in the days of Bel Respiro.

‡ Valentine Faucher-Magnan.

" 'I've just come from your place, I've been looking for you, I'm taking you to dinner at the Escale with . . .' etc. etc.

"I decline – and I mean it literally and increasingly. Moune and I take three steps, two very fine cold hands cover my eyes: it's Coco Chanel. Effusions . . . somewhat less effusive:

" 'I'm taking you to dinner at the Escale . . .' etc. etc.

"I decline further and further, and a few steps later I catch sight of Iribe, blowing me *bezers*.* Then, before I have time to perform the ritual exorcism, he embraces me, tenderly squeezing my hand between his cheek and shoulder:

" 'You're so unkind to me . . . You called me a demon!'

" 'And that's not enough for you!' I tell him.

"But he was overflowing with joy and affection. He is sixty years and twenty summers old. He is thin, wrinkled, and white and laughs all over his brand-new teeth. He coos like a dove, which is an odd thing, moreover, for you will find it written in the old texts that the devil assumes the voice and fragility of the bird of Venus . . ."

Why was Colette in such dread of Iribe that she began making gestures of exorcism at his approach? Clearly Gabrielle's latest "fiancé" inspired her with feelings of gravest mistrust. Was it a sort of animal suspicion of all things adulterated? She couldn't have been Colette without that obscure instinct.

Iribe was the self-conferred pseudonym of Paul Iribarnegaray, assumed when he made his debut as a satirical cartoonist around 1900. Gabrielle's exact contemporary, he was born at Angoulême in 1883, of Basque parents. And although an impermeable glaze of worldliness and some degree of cosmopolitanism had removed most traces of his native soil, he still had an indefinable accent – whence the *bezers* recorded by Colette in allusion to Iribe's speech, and the lisp that thirty years of Paris-worship had not managed to efface.

His beginnings are to some extent reminiscent of those of Cocteau, another man subjugated by the fads of the day and infected to the highest degree with that "red and gold sickness," the love of the theater – one particular type of theater, however, that was the craze of Paris in those days: vaudeville. Iribe had a harder time of it, though, than Cocteau. His father, a writer on *Le Temps*, opposed his vocation. Paul wanted to draw. At sixteen, he was apprenticed to a typesetter in the *Le Temps* print shop. Two years later he

---

*   His pronunciation of *baisers* (kisses).

quit his job and enrolled in an architecture course at the Beaux-Arts. Iribe was only seventeen when *L'Assiette au beurre*, the famous early-twentieth-century satirical weekly, published his first drawings, and only twenty-three in 1906 when he founded his own paper, *Le Témoin*. It lasted for four years. No one could define the event with a sharper line than he, whether the incident he was portraying was serious, trivial, or nonexistent. His was the drawing that gave it life. *Le Témoin* also published the drawings of another beginner, who was Iribe's equal in the field. This person signed himself "Jim." It was inconceivable that the two dandys should not meet. Now "Jim" was none other than Cocteau himself. Together they displayed in their illustrations a slashing keenness that was an intimation of the chilly aesthetic innovations of 1925. One can sense what they gave each other. The elder, Iribe, had a kind of voracity that could easily dazzle "Jim." He was greedy for everything: money, honors, women. While for Iribe, Jim had the appeal of the middle-class boy with a solid background, who "worked as though for pleasure."[2] Cocteau's *style* left Iribe gasping. If only he could have that self-assurance, that ease. What a lousy piece of luck to be stuck with this impossible name that told too much about his origins. Ah, to be able to proclaim, as Cocteau could: "I was born Parisian, I speak Parisian, my accent is Parisian!"

Iribe would have given anything to make people forget that his real name was Iribarnegaray.

Le Témoin, "edited with verve in an entirely new mode," earned Iribe a call from Poiret, the first step toward his ardently coveted Parisification. The anecdote is familiar, the man known as "Poiret le Magnifique" having related it in detail in his memoirs.[3] The portrait of Iribe that prefaces the tale, however, may not have received sufficient attention, although its sole merit is that it adds considerable weight to some of the impressions left by Colette's description. "He was a most unusual young fellow, a Basque, chubby as a capon, with something of both the divinity student and the composing-room foreman about him. In the seventeenth-century he would have been a court priest; he wore gold-rimmed spectacles, a wide-winged detachable collar with a loose sailor-knot tie . . . He spoke very softly, as though there was always some mystery, and placed a sort of crucial emphasis on certain words, articulating every syllable, as when he said: 'That's ad-mi-ra-ble!' "

Thus Iribe's language was modeled after that elite whose poise and composure he so envied.

And here was the illustrious designer asking him to make drawings of the models in his collection. A publicity enterprise of enormous prestige

value, for the album was to be offered as a tribute, to the "great ladies of
the whole world." Iribe asked to see the gowns, and instantly "fell into
raptures," exclaiming, "They're ad-mi-ra-ble! I must set to work im-me-
di-ate-ly." Whereupon he said he would bring one of his friends along to
meet the designer, "a-ma-zing woman," a certain Mme L. who would wear
his gowns "di-vine-ly."

What strikes one now, half a century later, is how little the language of
affectation has changed in spite of two wars and a few revolutions. Does it
mean that this manner of speech is inseparable from a certain life-style, and
is inherited along with one's fortune and aspirations? If one wanted to apply
it to today's snobs, not a single word or intonation would need to be altered.
But the funny thing about Iribe is that this character who so longed to be
urban remained quite unplaceable; the process of Parisification was slow to
bear fruit. As Poiret said, "Iribe happened to need money. I paid him for
his first set of drawings and he vanished. It seemed a long time before he
came back. I had forgotten to ask where he lived. When he brought me his
sketches I was delighted with the way he had understood and interpreted
the models, and asked him to finish off the job in a hurry . . . 'But first of
all,' I said to him, 'give me your address so I can get in touch with you.'
He replied that *he had no permanent address* in Paris but breakfasted every
morning in the home of Mme L. Then, after a second payment on account,
he vanished again. This time I had great trouble retrieving him and extracting
the work from him. I seem to recall that I had to make quite serious threats
. . . At last, he sent me the final drawings and the printers could begin work.
The book is well known, and can be found today in the libraries of artists
and artlovers. Its title was *Les Robes de Paul Poiret racontées par Paul Iribe*."[4]
A copy was sent to every crowned head in Europe, all of whom were pleased
to receive such a distinguished gift, apart from the Queen of England, who
had it returned with a letter from her lady-in-waiting requesting the coutu-
rier to abstain from any further gestures.

An Iribe without a penny, with no fixed address, waiting for advance
payments so he could frequent the better parts of town and be admired and
fed by Mme L.: the description arouses conflicting sentiments. What was
he, in reality – great seducer or gigolo?

It was by cementing his collaboration with Cocteau into a partnership that
Iribe ultimately gained a foothold in Parisian life. Together, in 1914, they
founded *Le Mot*, leaving the realm of journalism proper to launch something
that at the time was relatively new: journalism *de luxe*, with the accent on
illustration. He had turned his two years in the print shop to good account,

and was a first-rate technician: the presentation of *Le Mot* marked an epoch. There was just one little problem – the war. Because of it *Le Mot* was doomed, and publication ceased after one year. But Iribe had seen his light: *luxe*, luxury in every form, was to be his sole preoccupation, despite the fact that when peace came it was far from restoring the golden age, and actually interred it. The Europe of pleasures was dead? Everything was running counter to the Paris of *Le Mot*? Never mind: Iribe, who loved only riches, sought salvation by denying the realities of his age. Which did not prevent him from emerging as one of the foremost creators of new forms and substances in the "roaring twenties," for he achieved the *tour de force* of designing furniture, fabrics, rugs, and jewels without sacrificing by one iota to the spirit of geometrical simplification that haunted his contemporaries. His fabrics, in particular, were irresistible, and great collectors such as Robert de Rothschild and Jacques Doucet commissioned furniture from him. Nor, we would add, did he ever accept the idea that art by and for luxury alone had lost its appeal. As to the fall of Paris, that loss of "moral supremacy in the world"[5] that followed the war, he would never allow it. Iribe hankered after "*la grandeur française*," even in its most frivolous and superficial forms. Aware of the changes going on around him and of the growing difficulty of convincing people that luxury was an asset that must on no account be shared, any form of artisanship became a symbol to him. Clothes, necklaces, hair styles, embroidery, minor or major accessories – anything, so long as it had charm – they were all part of the national prestige, and he was their caustic guardian. From there to regarding elegance as the expression of certain ways of thinking (those of the upper class, of course), as an innate quality (it being implied that those of meaner circumstances could aspire only to *chic*, the access to elegance being forever forbidden them), was only a step. At the time his romance with Gabrielle was beginning, that step had been nimbly taken.

The surprising thing in their relationship is that it looked as though Gabrielle, in choosing Iribe, was seeking to delegate part of her authority to him. Is that what made Misia say she was in love for the first time? One cannot fail to see that in a sense Iribe fulfilled all her aspirations at once. At last, here was a man for whom questions of origin did not count, who avenged her for Boy; a man who was decidedly not burdened down with his family and past, in a word the very opposite of Dmitri and Bend'or; a creator who was sufficiently a part of the world of the arts for her to feel she had things in common with him, yet who had no sign of the curse inherent in all artists and poets – in short, what she needed to forget Reverdy. Gabrielle could throw off the yoke of genius.

Such thoughts may have crossed her mind, but one cannot be entirely certain that she did not also take a malicious pleasure in being courted by someone who, twenty-five years before, had been her old enemy Poiret's choirboy. For not only had Iribe "related" Poiret's gowns in a famous book: he also invented the symbol adorning every item turned out by the avenue d'Antin workrooms. His design, and the rose punctuating those magic words "Paul Poiret à Paris" had made a sensation at the time. One can wager there was some glimmer of professional satisfaction in Gabrielle's latest conquest. And finally – another source of satisfaction – Gabrielle was jealous of all women and could not bear anyone to have more conquests than she; and she could see her affair with Iribe as scoring a neat little point against her rivals, by seducing their seducer.

Because Iribe (would "an agitated love life" be strong enough?) defined himself in terms of his feminine conquests, no aspect of which was left in the dark and every one of which represented another step toward notoriety. He would stop at nothing when he needed money. If one of his lady friends owned a string of particularly fine pearls, Iribe would insist that they looked ostentatious and "nouveau riche" and advise her to remove a few and put onyx beads in their place. By the end of the affair, the whole necklace was onyx.

He began by seducing and almost certainly marrying a delightful actress who gave him her whole heart, her life: Jane Diris, star of vaudeville and silent films.

She came to fame as Marie Bonheur, the lead in the film *L'Equipe*, from a novel by Francis Carco. The film was directed by Maurice Lagrenie and produced by Diris Films. Its opening in 1921 was a major event in Paris, attended by Colette, Gabrielle Dorziat, Polaire, Spinelly, Marguerite Moreno – in other words, Colette's entire team. It was the story of a little working girl who became a music-hall entertainer and an army camp queen and then fell in love with a baddie who went off to Africa and was put in a disciplinary squad . . . of course. Pure Carco and more. The film ended with Marie Bonheur as a high-class kept woman, but more in love than ever with "her guy." Jane Diris portrayed her with "all the necessary fatality," according to the press.[6] Actually, the part fitted her like a glove: she even played it in her private life.

When Iribe found himself in financial straits – which was often – it was as Jeanne Iribe that she submitted to the exigencies of professional photographers. And when *Comoedia* published a portrait of her "elegantly attired in an ermine cape," which was in reality an advertisement for Reveillon the furriers; or showed her at the window of a luxurious coupé borrowed for the occasion and driven by a hired chauffeur ("Madame Jeanne Iribe in her motorcar garnished [sic] with *Triplex* glass"), all of it – the ermine, the haughty mien of the driver, the young woman's beauty, the high dashboard of the coupé, and the costly accessories for which it served as pedestal; the black-lacquered tool chest, the spare tire coated with white and secured like a life-preserver to the flank of some funereal ship – every jot and tittle of that sumptuousness went to enhance Iribe's own publicity.

We tend to forget what a secret complicity there was between the mid-1920s and the color black. Those velvet sofas . . . the cavernous gloom of the first cabarets . . . in interior decoration, gold gradually giving way to silver, and in Iribe's philandering pearls giving way to onyx . . . And the ill-starred Jeanne smiling away at an absent Iribe behind the lowered window of that species of hearse.

If happiness was her goal, marriage with him was a poor way to attain it. Was it because of his obliviousness to his mistresses' sufferings, his fierce determination to please *himself*, that Colette called him a devil? As Jeanne's friend, sensing that she was seriously ill at the first symptoms of the affliction that was to carry her off, Colette notified Francis Carco in these terms: "Jane Diris very ill . . . I feel bitterly useless facing that large handsome body possessed by something active, capricious, and invisible."[7]

When Jane Diris died in 1922 Iribe was busy with other loves: the dollar, and the American belles. One of them, Maybelle Hogan, had spread the nets of her comfortable fortune. He married her in New York in 1919. Upon his arrival in New York, Iribe made a rather shattering statement from which it emerged that there was something "en-chant-ing" about skyscrapers and that he had found "more to learn on the illuminated avenues of Broadway than between the facades of the mansions on the Place Vendôme." A confession followed:

"To be quite honest, the worst enemy of the United States is their terrible taste."

The reporter who harvested these pearls[8] explained that they issued from the foremost foreign cartoonist. At that point, losing his last vestiges of modesty, Iribe deemed that the time was ripe to capitalize upon what he had hitherto sought to hide. Certainly he was famous enough now to boast of his origins. He claimed that all the most powerful nations had, at one time or another in their history, owed their greatness to the people of the Basque country. Beginning with the United States: Wasn't Christopher Columbus a Basque? And Noah? No less than Columbus. In short, this truth was self-evident, and it went back to the Flood.

The reporter conscientiously transmitted every parcel of these novel views, but permitted himself one or two reservations as regards the specialization of this "jack-of-all-arts," remarking that he worked only for the luxury trade. Iribe dismissed the reproach with a wave of the hand:

"Taste always comes from above," said he, "never from below. It is harder to make a lacquered commode than a kitchen table."

Thereupon he moved into an exquisite California cottage with his young wife, made the Hollywood rounds very thoroughly and, like everybody else, dabbled in films. Those were the supreme days of the gilded legend. He met C. B. DeMille. The man who was later to pose as an authority on biblical films was excessive in all things and a priest of gigantism. Iribe's style, his multiple skills – in drawing, architecture, history of costume, furniture – could hardly fail to appeal to DeMille. Even his faults, for they were the same as DeMille's.

He began by commissioning the young Frenchman to research various films, in particular the sets and costumes for *Manslaughter*, which he was directing himself. Leatrice Joy, once a child star, then a has-been, then a Samuel Goldwyn rediscovery, made such a sensation in this film wearing gowns by Iribe that he was instantly promoted to the rank of Artistic Director, which gave him authority over a group of designers and decorators, some of whom had worked for DeMille since 1919. One, the gifted Mitchell Leisen, took a dim view of this ascension. And Iribe, unlike DeMille, did not possess the gift of making himself loathsome without jeopardizing the loyalty of the people working under him.

DeMille was adored. Whereas Iribe . . . His skirmishes with Leisen, the slamming doors, shouts and quarrels, became legendary.

In 1923 he was in sole charge of costumes and sets for *The Ten Commandments*. Leatrice Joy again headed the cast – but there was no Leisen, who would not work under Iribe and refused to have anything to do with the mammoth spectacle.

Iribe's Egypt was an Egypt of the 1920s, lacquered, glittering with gold, dominated by a sphinx more imposing than the real one at Giza and littered with immense temples from which no god, seated, standing, dog- or ram-headed, had been omitted. Innumerable divinities, a whole nation of extras: it all showed an extraordinary wealth of invention.

He took another step up in 1924 when, with DeMille's blessing, he improvised himself into a director for *Changing Husbands*, but the critics spared no one but Leatrice Joy. "Amateurish," proclaimed *The New York Times*, and even found the film absurd in places.

So then C. B. DeMille tried to get Leisen back.

He used every possible argument: he had just left Paramount, now was not the time to let him down, especially as this time he himself, not Iribe, would be doing the directing. And to top it all off, the high point of the film, *The Road to Yesterday*, was a railway crash: a train had to fly apart in a few seconds. Who but Leisen could bring that off?

Leisen took pity on DeMille; but war broke out between him and Iribe and by the time shooting ended, the two men were not speaking.

Yet DeMille began filming *King of Kings* with the same crew: Leisen for costumes and Iribe as Artistic Director. This was not sheer blindness on his part: he wasn't averse to a group that had one or two violent antagonisms in it.

Elsewhere, however, he took lavish precautions: the moral character of his actors had to be totally unblemished and remain so. His Christ had to swear by contract never to be seen with a cigarette in his mouth, to eschew nightclubs, and most important of all, under no circumstances to divorce before the film came out. Only thus could the public safely award some degree of credibility to his performance.

The bubble burst at the foot of Golgotha, when DeMille learned that Iribe had forgotten the storm and made no arrangements at all for the Crucifixion. Did anybody have any idea how Harry Warner was supposed to be fastened to his cross? Were his hands going to bleed, or what? Nobody knew.

DeMille dashed off an instant death sentence: Iribe's. Leisen agreed to take over from him on one condition: that he would never hear the Frenchman's name again.

By the time *King of Kings* was submitted for approval to a board of ecclesiastics consisting of a Roman Catholic priest, a rabbi, a representative of the Orthodox Church and a Buddhist monk, Paul Iribe had left California. He was back in Paris, where Maybelle had given him a shop on the rue du Faubourg St Honoré, on whose front her husband's name gleamed in golden letters against a lacquered background. Iribe returned to his first love, the applied arts.

His furniture, fabrics, rugs, and jewels were now supplemented by interior decorating projects. He would work only for prominent persons; Spinelly, for example, whose entrance hall and drawing room had been "done" by Martine (the interior decorating agency founded in 1912 by Paul Poiret), commissioned Iribe to do her bedroom. Think of it: to be the decorator of the woman familiarly known to Colette and to her large public following as "Spi" – could any customer be more likely to sympathize with his ideas? "His spirit of adventure, his love of daring, combining two or three tones in a clash that first shocked, then delighted the eye, his aristocratic freedom of choice . . . found their ideal accomplice in Spinelly. There, where I looked only as a lover of color and curve, Spinelly was first to recognize the goal of adornment and consumption, the *incontestable necessity of luxury*."[9] She was Iribe's dream client. He presumably did more than decorate in that bedroom, for no sooner was it completed and "tried out" than it earned Iribe another commission – her dining room.

She enjoyed a rare privilege: the first time the ordinary man saw her on stage, whether from the balcony of the Casino in Montmartre or the slips of the European, he claimed the right, in his dreams, to call her "darling"; between him and her there was instant intimacy. And she also flouted convention openly enough for one part of the press to adore her. Her encounter with an Argentinian produced a superb baby born in the Basque country ("Three turns of a tango – oh, such a dangerous dance!" she was to tell the Spanish newspaper which had come to interview her), and the columnists swooped down. In every interview what she called her "hoohme" was minutely described: "A mixture of Hindu temple, Greek palace, Persian corner, and nightclub loggia. After crossing the entrance hall, guarded by a giant Buddha in green bronze, you enter the atrium, which has a gold mosaic floor and a round pool with two telescope fish imported from China swimming in it. Three marble steps lead on to the main drawing room with its crystal ceiling – and there, seated in a lacquered wooden armchair, Spinelly will tell us what it feels like to be a young mother . . ."[10] Nothing was beautiful enough for her. Iribe's bedroom was on the same scale. He designed a brass bed for her, the foot of which was a golden signature. The willow-green walls and low Chinese lacquered tables: it was all indisputably a success. The essential thing, though, was that the enormous bed and the raised platform on which the mattress was placed *à la japonaise* provoked a great deal of comment.

Would Iribe stop there? Certainly not. He became a photographer, experimented with new publicity techniques, combined typography and photography, made excellent photomontages, and came in second in a publicity competition in New York in 1931, out of fifty European photographers representing eight countries. Iribe beat Hoyningen-Huyne by only a length or two, but left everyone else Europe could offer standing at the post. Baron Meyer and Man Ray came off with honorable mentions.

For a while he would make vast sums of money, and buy himself a Voisin with silver headlights and white-upholstered cushions, or a sailboat, *Belle de Mai*, or a house at St Tropez; and the next moment he would be on his uppers, selling off car, then yacht, then house. Then Maybelle went to bat for him, and it was she who began collecting commissions – jewels for Cartier, and more jewels – for Chanel.

She was resigned to his ups and downs, resigned to his escapades and disappearances, resigned to waiting around. All she needed was a telegram: "Cannot come but love you," to remain the dupe of her absent husband. In whose arms was he sleeping? Maybelle supposed it had something to do with the typical behavior of the French male.

Nevertheless, one day, under pressure from her family, who were upset by the extravagance of these expenditures, Maybelle Iribe, in order to preserve her future and that of her two children, resigned herself to leaving her husband, whose financial exigencies seemed as though they might bring the family face to face with ruin.

This happened a few months before that day in July 1933 when Colette called him a demon. Knowing a little more about his life, the reasons why she did so become clearer.

Colette could not forgive Iribe for possessing none of the qualities that were characteristic of Gabrielle – especially this one: "By good fortune, she has retained nothing about her of the contagious effluvium of gold, the indiscreet glow exuded by the weak and overprosperous,"[11] wrote Colette in her masterful portrait of the designer.

Iribe had clearly caught a bad case of the disease, and therein lay the reason for Colette's antipathy. If he had simply set up camp in the center of his wealth and made himself at home in the ephemeral, she would have found him amusing. But he was a slave to it, and thus "a demon."

THE FAUBOURG FINISHED

What was happening? Weird wax figures had been installed on the ground floor of the Pillet-Will house. Unearthed in the back rooms of Parisian shops where they had slept since the opening years of the century, they looked most incongruous and people might well ask what Gabrielle meant to do with them. They were not dress dummies – only busts, the kind one used to see in hairdressers' windows. Without their chignons. Wax busts with lashes on their eyes, fully made-up, short-haired and, although armless, as though alive. Apart from the 1930s eyebrows and short hair and bright red mouths, one would have thought oneself, as far as their expressions were concerned, fifty years back in time. It was all terribly quaint. Such objects could serve no purpose in the mirrored expanses of the rue Cambon, where fashion was still refusing fantasies.

More unadorned and clean-lined than ever, Chanel's frocks were modeled by young ladies with inscrutable faces. The latest idea, padded shoulders, had transformed them the previous season and was still ruling the silhouette. It was almost two years since the most authoritative designers had begun saying that broad shoulders were the mark of the elegant woman: "If you are the right type, do not hesitate to adopt, for informal wear, a silhouette of quite military erectness."[12]

So what was the meaning of these figurines with the gracious smiles and tilted heads, these chins nestling in the hollows of their collarbones? And why set up these serpentlike creatures on antique pedestals? But it was her house, after all, let her do as she pleased in it.

Joseph had received instructions to keep the courtyard doors closed and admit no one through them. Nevertheless, the neighbors' curiosity was aroused when it was known that the chief inspector of police had been to the house and that he and Gabrielle together had inspected every access and installed an alarm system, a complete network of wires and bells connecting the Pillet-Will house with the local police station. They could hardly have failed to learn about it, a guest having accidentally tripped over the alarm system one night, whereupon a whole vanload of policemen invaded the courtyard, to the concierge's intense horror. Lights went on in the upper floors, exasperated faces appeared at the windows. It was most disagreeable: what was that accursed dress designer up to now? One couldn't even sleep nights anymore.

November 7, 1932, was the opening day of an exhibition such as had never been seen in any private residence: nothing but diamonds, and none for sale. They were designed by Chanel. Odd that a woman who was neither diamond merchant nor jeweler should have taken it into her head to modernize this form of adornment, and that it should be to her – a woman who had championed costume jewelry and sold it on an industrial scale – that the International Guild of Diamond Merchants had turned. Odder still that, after declaring on more than one occasion that, apart from pearls, only colored stones were wearable, Gabrielle should consent to use nothing but white diamonds. Chanel, diamonds? We can imagine her colleagues' astonishment. Not one woman, whatever her social rank, was unaware of the fact that artificial pearls were the last word. Even the dance hall hostesses had them, even Simone in *Aurélien*,[13] in the orange and blue lighting of Lulli's . . . "Have I got some pearls, you bet! They're all the thing this season . . . Even the people who've got real ones, real pearls, well, they've all got by-the-yard ones instead now, yes they have!" And the woman who had imposed costume jewelry was now going into genuine? And what was the point of making people pay to enter her house? It is true that the proceeds were going to the *Oeuvre de l'allaitement maternel* of which the princesse de Poix was chairman, and the *Oeuvre d'assistance à la classe moyenne* headed by Maurice Donnay, a member of the Académie Française. But Chanel as a charity dame, Chanel as philanthropist – and what philanthropies! It was ridiculous. The idea had never entered her head before; yet here she was joining the ruling classes' good-deeds club. What had happened to bring about such a change? People were quite right, there was something new in the air.

The diamond-bedecked busts were reflected back and forth infinitely in the mirror-faced screens. The lights were kept very low, making strange reflections ripple over the stones. The innovations were real, and striking: the bracelets were like broad cuffs that could be taken apart, so that a woman could convert one jewel into four whenever she felt like it. Necklaces no longer lay at the base of the neck but spread out over the shoulders in a shower of stars. There were no tiaras to be seen, only slender crescents attached to the hair with invisible clips. No more brooches either; but there were white sunbursts hanging from long chains like pebbles at the end of a rope. And there was one most unusual piece, something like a forehead jewel which everyone greatly admired without dreaming for a second that anyone could wear it. Forming an Egyptian fringe across the forehead – that fringe or "bangs" that was to become the "Chanel fringe" ten years later – it was made not of hair but of diamonds, all of equal size, in a glittering curtain reaching to the eyebrows.

One could comment at length on the symbolic meaning of this jewel, which was at the furthest possible remove from Fashion. What was this chimerical accessory doing there? Did it arise out of some contrary impulse to resuscitate the traditional female "crowning glory" just when everyone else was busy shearing, pasting down, reducing to nothing a "round head, flat and polished as an ebony apple, gleaming . . ."?[14] Was it, in other words, a confession, a sort of remorse for having been the one who had desexed women by taking away their hair? For hair, don't they say, *is woman herself in her essential difference*.[15] It is also possible, of course, that this jewel was only a fetish, a scalp tossed down at the feet of the victor: Iribe, the diamond man.

Whatever its explanation, the new object, presented alone in a glass case over which conspicuously armed guards stood watch, was the talk of the exhibition.

The event attracted a horde of French and foreign jewelers. It was open only to "the trade." It became one of her aims in the jewelry side of her business to enlist the aid of prominent Parisian social figures; thus, through their acquaintances, she was able to see and get ideas from rare pieces which owners usually kept locked away rather than wearing them. "All those aristocrats stuck up their noses at me, but I'll have them at my feet," she once told the woman who manufactured her jewelry.[16] But whatever the rank of the friends or amateurs for whom Gabrielle made exceptions – whether Etienne de Beaumont or Fulco della Verdura, the former a French count and the latter an Italian duke, both of whom designed costume jewelry for Chanel; whether an arbiter of taste like Charles de Noailles or the saleswomen from the dress shop, the faithful Joseph or his twenty-year-old daughter – everyone who saw the exhibition came away with mixed feelings. It was beautiful, no doubt, and fantastic at times, but there was something "wrong" with it, although they couldn't quite put their finger on it. Something Hollywood. And that *overdone* note was Iribe.

Until this point their affair, already over a year old, had caused little comment. It was hardly even suspected. For a thousand reasons – most obvious among them that his wife hadn't a clue – Iribe had been cautious for once. Maurice Goudeket and Colette were virtually the only people who had figured it out, and then only because they could hardly help it, for it was from them that Gabrielle had bought the hideaway where she and Iribe secretly met, "a place for billing and cooing."[17] High up in the village of Montfort-L'Amaury, thickly planted with trees, it was full of nests; Colette had hung them all over the place, and the birds had been quick to take advantage. They came in throngs. La Gerbière was the name of the house Maurice Goudeket was forced to sell, "strangled by the depression," as Colette wrote at the time, "with a rolling pin between the buttocks."[18] Mention was often made in her letters of financial difficulties: "Great God above, things are so tight for Maurice and me." The effects of the depression were beginning to be felt in France; but they didn't seem to bother Gabrielle, who went to Montfort alone one day in the winter of 1931. It was cold. Colette stayed in by the fire while the business between Goudeket and Gabrielle was transacted in a turn around the garden. Had they finished? Colette knew nothing of the motive of the discussion, and when Gabrielle came back to the house she stood aside to let her pass.

"Don't bother," said Gabrielle. "It's for me to let you go first, since this is my house now."

Gabrielle was changing, you could see it in everything. The jewelry show was one instance, when her statements to the press had a most unwonted patriotic ring. To hear her talk, the sole aim of the exhibition was to gain renown for the Parisian jewelers whom she claimed were "the best in the world."[19] She had no desire to enter into competition with the jewelers, oh, certainly not! All she was concerned about were the craftsmen whom "unemployment had made free and cheerless." Why, of course: luxury was on its last legs, unemployment threatened – diamonds were the obvious answer.

She seized every pretext for attributing salutary and redemptive virtues to luxury; clearly, she had adopted Iribe's language.

Their affair became officially recognized at the time of the exhibition. He moved into her house on the Faubourg. This publicly proclaimed presence at her side was filling in the furrow gouged out of her life by so many abortive loves, so many relationships that had had to be kept in the dark.

In 1933, after twenty-three years of silence, the Paris newspaper kiosks displayed a ghost: *Le Témoin*. Paul Iribe was director, editorial writer, and chief illustrator. His drawings had lost none of their bite. There was still the mordant wit, the pitiless use of black laid on in broad flat surfaces; black – generator of power and beauty, eloquent, designed for uninterrupted crescendo. No giving way to the "decorative," few concessions to "elegance," although the graphics of *Le Témoin* made no innovations. And then he spoiled it all, even the strength of his line, by introducing two colors into his drawings, always the same; printed on the white pages, they brought in the inevitable patriotic note: flag-red and flag-blue.

In the copy, the word *France* appeared in every line. The leitmotiv was all-pervading. It was the capital affirmation, the unique slogan, carried to absurdity. To raise subscriptions, a single appeal: "*Le Témoin* speaks French. Subscribe to it." And in every issue a full page, on which a single red–white-and-blue flower was inscribed with the caption: "There is no luxury industry, there are only French industries." An advertisement? Wasted money. Was Gabrielle aware of the fact? She alone financed the publication, and *Le Témoin* was published by a Chanel subsidiary.

In itself, the idea was an attractive one. She would be making Iribe happy and at the same time taking advantage of the talents of an artist who, by successfully combining political events and business acumen, had made head-lines in the history of publicity. Both the woman-in-love and the woman-managing-director stood to gain from the arrangement.

But although a few years before he had broken new ground with his drawings to advertise a brand-name,* *Le Témoin* was a very different matter.

In *Le Témoin* his humor gave way to an ominous chauvinism. Nationalist, opposed to representational government, reactionary – Iribe was known to be all those. Like every other supercharged bourgeois of his day. But why did his articles have to be so bad? His artistic objectives were apparently dictated by those rabble rousers who were preaching a return to the *healthy* life and the flag-waving self-indulgence then in vogue in Fascist Italy and Nazi Germany. Iribe had become the man who denounced the association of art and "cube" – by that he meant all modern art – and aspired to free men from "the machine," that loathsome object which had engendered all the evils of mankind.

"Shall we sacrifice the flower on the altar of the cube and the machine?"

"The reign of the machine means the French way of thinking attacked by the European, that is, the graceful, feminine, and luxurious attacked by the hard, cold, and hygienic."

These quotations give a clear enough idea of his style. We can add a third, "At a time when flags are striving to be monochromatic and opinions unanimous, it is good to love three colors," to measure the extent of his xenophobia. Reading him, one would think France was the eternal victim of some vast international conspiracy. The enemies within, naturally called "Samuel" or "Levy" – you know, the Aliens, Léon Blum and his "Judeo-Masonic Mafia," "Thorez the spy and his red rabble" – were reinforced by the enemies without: the USSR and its barbarian hordes, perfidious Albion, and America, although one couldn't quite make out why. He did denounce Hitler and deplore Germany's takeover of Austria, but he admired order and force too much to challenge the Reich directly.

However admirably illustrated, *Le Témoin* was only a futile reflection of the press of those years, or at least of that so-called patriotic press which

---

* In 1930 Nicolas, the wine firm, had commissioned a brochure from Iribe which was a masterpiece of unintentional drollery. The approach he adopted was blatant chauvinism, in the service of Nicolas wines. Their virtues were extolled only on the last page, after he had demolished every product that might have a claim to compete with them. The only way to do that was to identify rival products with their countries of origin. A murderer in Russian uniform was there to cure the French consumer of any wild notions of vodka drinking. What about Rhenish wines? Iribe's reply was a factory in the Ruhr – purchasing anything from Germany could only hasten the remilitarization of the Rhine. A tot of whiskey? That was promoting British imperialism. An American beverage? That would only encourage the megalomania of the States. All together, now: Drink French!

encouraged veterans and young right-wing movements, Marcel Bucard's Francists, François de la Rocque's Croix de Feu, and the storm troopers of the Cagoule, to break into action. "France for the French!" Stripped of its publicity content and employed for different ends, Iribe's slogan was one of the pretexts for the violent demonstration of February 6.

To be sure, *Le Témoin* had a small readership and its importance should not be exaggerated; it would not be worth bothering about except that in Gabrielle's life it marked the transition from political indifference to a view of the future which, however inconsistent and perpetually exacerbated by innumerable contradictions, was nevertheless modeled upon the opinions of Iribe. And even that would not matter if Iribe had not also committed her to it in his drawings. The Republic? It was Gabrielle. Symbolizing the calvary of France, she was portrayed as a crucified Marianne giving up the ghost in her inevitable Phrygian bonnet; that corpse was her, that fore-doomed victim naked beneath the shovelfuls of earth being hurled upon her by a grave digger who was none other than Daladier (a baker's son born at Carpentras who worked his way through school, fought at Verdun as a private, and finished the war a captain, he was a member of the Radical Party, a follower of Herriot, and became premier in 1933); and that innocent France facing a sneering bench, that too was Gabrielle. Her judges? Roosevelt, Chamberlain, Hitler, Mussolini. Of course! All in it together, all determined to destroy the hapless *grandeur française*, and all to blame for the *désordres* imperiling it.

Politically, Iribe's drawings made no sense. Historically, they remain an image of a certain way of thinking – that of a class which, seeing its privileges threatened, identified its own possible disappearance with that of French supremacy. Displayed on the newsstands, spread out on tables, perfectly recognizable, Gabrielle's was the face on whom it fell to glorify those jeopardized values. Was she proud to be chosen? Was she touched? The latter is the more likely hypothesis. No man before Iribe had so ostentatiously *displayed* her.

So she sought to do for him what she had done for no one else: bring him into her professional life, share that power she had hitherto guarded so jealously. In a word, no longer having anything to hide, she was happy.

When her quarrels with the Société des parfums Chanel were beginning and she was filing lawsuit after lawsuit against her associates on any or no pretext at all, it was Iribe whom she sent to chair a general meeting in her place, even though he had no right to be there. She saw herself as an injured party. Iribe became her confidential agent, her knight in shining armor defending her rights.

That, too, was a novelty.

People noticed she was turning to a man for advice.

The marriage rumors found confirmation in this, and Colette, that same year of 1933, echoed them: ". . . I've just been told that Iribe is marrying Chanel. Aren't you horrified – for her? That man is a most interesting demon" – again.[20]

The riot took place outside Gabrielle's door. February 6 flung forty thousand demonstrators into the Place de la Concorde.* The best view anyone had of them was from the spot where the first victim fell: Corentine Gourlan, thirty-three-year-old cleaning woman at the Crillon. From the balcony of that handsome edifice, in the shelter of the Gabriel colonnade, you could watch the horse guards charging, now cutting off access to the Palais Bourbon, now barring the Faubourg: you could glimpse the sharpshooters crouching up in the trees to cover the demonstrators, and the veterans on the terrace of the Tuileries chucking paving stones down on the police while other veterans set fire to the ministry of the navy; you could see a bus burning at the foot of the Obelisk, and the mounted police flailing wildly away with their sabers at booted young men in berets, and in the distance, coming down the Champs Elysées, you could see gentlemen with clinking chests singing the *Marseillaise* and swinging their walking sticks. They were not ordinary walking sticks, though: razor blades fastened to their tips made them excellent weapons for slashing horses' hocks.

When the shooting became widespread, the tumult spilled over into the Faubourg.

The lachrymose president of France was being protected by those staunch mounted gendarmes. Nevertheless, the gentlemen with the clinking chests reached his residence. They left fifty people seriously injured on the pavement of the Faubourg but they did not manage to break through the barricade. The Elysée held out.

Shortly before midnight, a police officer who had been sent out even though he was not on duty that evening decided to take the initiative. With what remained of the mounted police he attempted to clear the grounds;

---

*   The riot in Paris on February 6, 1934, was the closest France ever got (not very close) to a Fascist takeover. It put Daladier out of office. Right-wing movements, partly financed by Italy and Germany, tried to adopt the process so successful in those countries, but they hadn't done their groundwork carefully enough – or maybe the ordinary Frenchman was just too contrary.

he ordered a charge and he, Colonel Simon, ended the uprising.

By two in the morning the booted youths had given up trying to drive the members of parliament out of their House, and the gentlemen with the sharp-edged walking sticks had lost. Their aims – the Palais Bourbon stormed, a provisional government proclaimed, the president driven out of the Elysée – all up in smoke.

But Paris had seen nothing like that since the days of the Commune.

What bearing did these events have upon Chanel's next decision? In the spring of 1934 she informed her faithful Joseph that she no longer required his services. She would not renew her lease and was leaving the Faubourg. The effects of the depression were still being felt, French production was slowing down, and poverty was on the rise. Would the franc be devalued? She wanted to reduce expenses. Keeping only her personal maid, Gabrielle dismissed the rest of the staff and took her furniture with her to the hotel that was to be her only home in Paris for the rest of her life, the Ritz.

Gabrielle Chanel and Joseph Leclerc parted on bad terms.

He never told what was said during their final interview. He had witnessed the Capel drama, welcomed Grand Duke Dmitri, opened the door to Reverdy, waited on the Duke of Westminster and how many more. He knew what really happened. And people did not fail to ask him, of course. But he never uttered a word.

Every year at collection time Joseph read the papers a little more closely. But he never saw Chanel again, and never wrote to her.

He probably told himself that what had happened to him was inherent in the condition of servant. Gabrielle was going to marry Iribe, she wanted no memories and no witnesses around, she wanted to be freer and lighter. On the eve of a new life, she would need to shed her old staff, that was obvious. Women were always doing it. When they changed husbands they had to change butlers too. When Misia Edwards became Misia Sert hadn't she done the same thing? She had also sent Joseph away.

Joseph Leclerc was careful never to display the least bitterness toward the woman who had so brusquely discarded him after sixteen years of faithful service. He went on serving her, though, all the rest of his life – with his silence.

He died in July 1957. That was after Gabrielle's "comeback." She had been on the rue Cambon again for three years. Joseph Leclerc must have kept pretty close track of events, for at the moment of his death his family heard him murmur, "It's a collection day today . . ."

*

An undeniable wanderlust had driven Gabrielle out of the Faubourg, too. She transferred her attention to La Pausa; henceforth that would be her home. She had parted from the Duke of Westminster before he ever saw the garden finished, or the drawing rooms in their final state. At the Ritz she rented a suite, stood her Coromandel screens around and created a setting as lavish as on the Faubourg; but the best thing about it was that she had never lived there before. There too she got what she wanted, a new life. So when was this wedding to be, that everyone was so sure of?

When he came to stay at La Pausa, Iribe had just obtained his separation from Maybelle. He dominated Gabrielle, and she gladly let him assume the prerogatives of master of the house. She loved her own weakness, so she must truly have been in love.

She had decided to live that summer as one long holiday. To hell with the pessimists, to hell with the winter events, to hell with the spring ones! She wanted them to leave no mark on this stretch of coast, and on the respite she was savoring there. All around the house the olive trees tossed, caressed by sea breezes. Holiday. La Pausa was enough to make one forget all the rest.

In January the Saar voted overwhelmingly in favor of reannexation to Germany, a right no one dreamed of disputing. But on the far side of the Rhine this had touched off an explosion of martial joy, with songs and mass meetings, out-thrust fists and flowers raining down on marching brown shirts. Nothing to be surprised at, after such a victory. It was enough to turn more than one sensible head.* And then, those young men had something about them. In March, Hitler reinstated compulsory military service and announced that Germany was at last about to acquire an army she could be proud of. Lucky Germans! But really, was it possible to flout the clauses of a treaty so flagrantly? What treaty? What clauses? Versailles and its restrictive conditions were going down for the count. There they go again! Any minute now the whole summer would be ruined by people moaning over a crumpled bit of paper. It was sickening, really. One never got a decent, quiet holiday. And then if it wasn't that it was something else. The summer before ... The summer before, way back then, the failure of the disarmament conference had stirred up quite a storm. Roquebrune was virtually a British enclave, and so Gabrielle's titled neighbors, the Riviera English, worked

---

* The Saar was placed under French mandate after the First World War. Its fate was to be settled by referendum in 1935. The results of the vote were as follows: for reannexation to Germany 477,109, for the status quo 46,513, for annexation to France 2,124.

themselves into a terrible state over it. Winston was wild, people said. According to him, they ought to head off the German rearmament before it was too late. He should mind his own business, he was completely out of things. Social upheavals, war . . . were they never going to stop talking about them? And how many words, how much triviality were needed to hide the truth. Gabrielle applied herself to the task. That her beach pajamas were being worn everywhere and copied like a lesson learned by rote; that bell bottoms were out and that to be in style you had to wear them like Gabrielle, no wider or narrower than men's trousers: this was the substance of conversation at La Pausa, this, and dances, and the new season's evening gowns with funny frothy sleeves that were not attached to the bodice, like ruffled tulle bracelets worn above the elbow. One of Gabrielle's notions . . . And what else was she going to dream up for her next collection, to put that newcomer out of action, that Schiaparelli, that species of Italian who was beginning to tread too closely on her heels. It was no longer possible to shrug her off. She existed. She was stealing Chanel's customers. Women consenting to wear clown's hats and riding jackets – it made Gabrielle see red. For the first time in fifteen years she was going to have to take notice of her competition. Those were postholiday problems, however; then she'd have to work overtime, but not until then.

That was the summer of 1935, when Iribe collapsed on the tennis court just as Gabrielle was joining him for a set. He scarcely had time for a last look at her. He fell. A heart attack. He was picked up unconscious. He died in a clinic at Menton without regaining consciousness.

The Riviera in its summer splendor and, as when Boy died, a second body blow.

Gabrielle suffered terribly.

But, again, almost without a murmur.

Misia came running. Like the skilled musician she was, she offered Gabrielle's silence a lucid, critical ear. She knew how to calculate just how much misery that silence revealed and how much it concealed. She heard it aright: as a ghastly scream. How much succor Gabrielle received from the friend who stood steadfast by her side.

Weeks passed.

In the shimmering heat of the Roman August men in black shirts were shouting: "We want our place in the sun . . ." and sweating. If it was sun they wanted, Mussolini was promising them a trip to Africa. His devastating statements to a British press correspondent had instant repercussions among the Riviera English. Uncertainty reigned on all sides. People hoped he was bluffing, and articles in the *Daily Mail* were solemnly discussed.

On August 29, 1935, the voice was heard of a man around whom so many left-wing hopes and so much right-wing hatred had polarized: "Let our officious colleagues and the government for which they speak get this simple truth into their skulls: once war in Ethiopia has begun, no one, however cunning or clever, will be able to measure or moderate its backlash."[21] But *Le Populaire* . . . Did anybody in those circles read *Le Populaire*?

And summer was over.

October dropped a bombshell: the Italian invasion of Ethiopia. It looked like a bad season.

Gabrielle went back to Paris. Now she was alone again – to settle things, make decisions, have new ideas. She made plans. She consented to listen to Cocteau, who was talking about a play he meant to write, *Oedipe Roi*. He wanted Gabrielle to do the costumes. Jean Renoir was working on a film, *La Règle du Jeu*, and he was after her too. "A good film, you know, with stars . . . Paulette Dubost, Mila Parely." He urged her to accept.

So everyone rallied round and tried to cure Gabrielle with work. But for those who really knew her, there was no doubt that she had changed. She had made up her mind that happiness was an illusion. That was the change, and it accounted for everything that was to come.

A MEMORABLE JOY

Ah, it was a singular year that now began, with violence, madness, and April burgeoning to the accompaniment of accordions. A holiday crowd – but not for long. An unpredictable year from beginning to end, even in its most trivial events, even in its way of pushing people to their furthest limits.

There was . . . But let us begin at the beginning. There was fanaticism, which reached unparalleled heights in France. Like a sort of fit. There was February 13, when Blum was dragged from his car by a group of young "patriots," then beaten and kicked. There were the laborers on a building site nearby who saved him in the nick of time and took him to a hospital. That was France in 1936. It was an old man exhorting his readers to rid the country of "this German Jew, this monster of the Democratic Republic" and hoping he would be shot in the back;[22] it was that or worse when you could read, "Blum is neither English nor German nor French: he is Alien. His destiny is to be the Destroyer . . . That is the man whose boot soles are leaving the greasy print of the ghettos from which he emerged upon our native soil."[23]

Along the Rhine the German army made a show of force, and, to sugar-coat the brazen defiance, there were the delicate verbal gymnastics of the chancellery people. "Symbolic occupation," Baron Konstantin von Neurath (the German foreign minister fired in 1937 due to his lack of enthusiasm for the Hitlerian program of aggression) told the French and British ambassadors; and perhaps this man from another age believed what he was saying. There were words that had a new ring to them, ominous words which made no dent on deep-rooted habits. For instance, *Schulung* (meaning "discipline" or "schooling"), shouted into military telephones, meant that the first in a lengthy series of spectacular operations was to be launched. *Schulung! Schulung!* and the Reichswehr moved into the Rhine zone. That was a Saturday, March 7, and the members of the British cabinet were honoring their sacrosanct tradition of the weekend.

Lower-ranking diplomats who knew exactly what was happening informed their lofty superiors, who refused to take any notice. There were dispatches of a French consul in Cologne[24] giving warning that garrisons were growing, airfields expanding and, allegedly for civilian purposes, troops arriving in vast numbers. There was his insistence, which had no effect. On the Quai d'Orsay, site of the French Foreign Ministry, fastidious civil servants, methodical and respectful of chronological order, received his dispatches, read them, filed them, and paid no heed to them.

Ah, a singular year, when even the weather was out of joint! It was raining in France on April 26, 1936, raining hard. Some put their hopes in that water from the sky: it was election day, and the French would stay home. But instead, 85 percent of the voters turned up at the polls and it was victory for the Front Populaire.*

"A bourgeoisie rigid with fear," was the comment of one foreign observer.[25]

In the "posh" parts of town people waited. Some, behind bolted shutters, were expecting working-class riots which never took place. One aggressive society lady went to see Blum, "to spit in his face."[26] Another, less aggressive but just as out of touch, wrote to a friend in Rome: "My dear, dreadful things are happening in Paris. My hairdresser made me wait: 'Princess,' he told me, 'people like me have a few rights too.' That's what it's like."

---

* A left-wing coalition that barred the way to the traditional right-wing parties – and the great surprise of the 1936 elections in France. It was the Front Populaire that enabled Socialists and Communists to obtain a majority in Parliament. See William L. Shirer, *The Collapse of the Third Republic*.

The hostility of the wealthy was universal, but it assumed varying forms: by their ferocity one could identify those whose money was already out of the country; by their panic, those who had let themselves be caught short. Everybody was buying gold. Such was the state of mind, in 1936, of the social class from which the bulk of Gabrielle's clientele was recruited. But she never sat behind closed shutters, not for a single day; the Chanel salesrooms, with doors wide open, were waiting for customers who had locked themselves in.

And the stock market plummeted.

That was only the beginning.

Other changes followed: nationalization of war industries, new regulations for the Bank of France, extended compulsory schooling, etc. Those were the words that brought to power, for the first time in the country's history, a Socialist premier who was also a Jew. And when the tidal wave rose in May, and more and more factories were being "occupied" by the workers, and the country's very life was in danger, came a sentence simple and clear: "Starting a strike is one thing; but you also have to know how to end it."[27] Nothing ambiguous about that. The men went back to work, the economy was back on the rails, and everybody celebrated Bastille Day.

What a celebration! From the Concorde to the Bastille, four hundred thousand people – you might call it a crowd. They fought to buy badges and streamers at the street corners, and the hawkers cried their wares as though it were market day. It was like an impromptu party, where nothing had been planned. And is any party more wonderful than an impromptu one?

Chewing their fingernails, the people who huddled out of the way as the floats rolled past – the little shopkeepers and little investors – turned and asked one another, "Was that all?" They were actually seeing, seeing face to face, those "striking pigs," "traitors," and "agitators," they were looking at them and they couldn't get over their surprise. Hiding for a whole week in terror of being cut down by revolutionaries' bayonets, only to find a crowd of merrymakers wearing badges and armbands like new recruits and waltzing all the girls! While they had been imagining . . . The cutthroats danced on to a merry-go-round tune.

But what about Gabrielle, in that tidal-wave May, Gabrielle among the strikers, alone at the head of her four thousand workers? Her indignation knew no bounds.

Men went on strike, so be it. That was scandalous enough. But, after all, it was their business. In the beginning, she kept her head. The automobile workers – Hotchkiss, Rosenbart, Panhard and Levassor, Hispano-Suiza – the railwaymen, post office workers, steel and mining industries, construction workers, filling stations, taxis, cafés, restaurants, everybody was on strike, but that was all men's business. She thought it would stop there. But what about bread? The bakers were on strike too? Well, bakers were men.

When the tide engulfed the textile industry, she was dumbfounded. Fabrics, materials, jersey, lace – even if men were needed to look after the manufacture of these goods, they were nonetheless articles of feminine consumption. A strike among textile workers affected her directly. She took it as a personal affront. They couldn't do that to her! Could she understand, could she even guess that it was this very notion of authority, the specific way of thinking of the nineteenth-century captains of industry, that was now being challenged? If anyone had told her that the divine right of the boss would be the first real victim of the events and that 1936 would go down in history as the date of its death warrant, would she have believed it? Negotiate, give accounts to workers – what next? These men were out of their minds, she kept saying. She, a woman, firmly resolved to alter nothing in her methods of government.

And indeed, she altered nothing. She only watched more closely than before to see that her workers arrived on time and showed greater zeal than usual.

When she heard that the leaders of the textile industry, acting as true combat captains, had rejected the Matignon agreements* and refused to pay the wage increases, they regained in her eyes all the esteem they had lost. She sent them tokens of encouragement. That's more like it, now they were coming to their senses again . . . A good thing, too, and their example, she was sure, would be widely followed. But almost immediately, the strike spread into the department stores, affecting women workers and plunging Gabrielle into the deepest consternation. Women on strike! Could such a thing be conceived? Saleswomen dancing around their counters, picnicking on the stairs, and all behind the closed doors of those gilded temples of commerce, the Printemps and the Galeries Lafayette; yes, then, truly, this was revolution.

---

* On June 7, 1936, Blum called a meeting in his office in the Hôtel Matignon between representatives of management and delegates of the CGT, France's biggest labor union federation – the first joint meeting of the two sides ever held in France. This led to a series of compacts, concluded the same day, thereafter known as the Matignon agreements.

Twenty years later someone might argue that the blatant poverty of French workers was enough to account for the 1936 strikes and their spontaneous eruption. "What are you babbling about?" She played deaf and dumb.

Those strikes were a way of celebrating a victory: the right to form trade unions, which existed in the United States and in Germany though not in France until 1936. But she would have none of that, either.

"The United States? Oh, leave me alone with your United States! It isn't people like that who will ever teach us anything, and certainly not about elegance. Ah, la, la! You won't go far with ideas like that, my dear, let me tell you. The next thing you know you'll be getting yourself up like those madwomen, those crazy journalists!"

For her everything was costume; and listening to her, one was still hearing the voice of Iribe.

Let anyone touch on the question of wages, and she went up in smoke. "Oh, stop bothering me with your nonsense!"

And the fact that women, by means of strike action, should seek to affirm themselves in a country in which they were shockingly underpaid simply drove her wild. She maintained that in 1936 wages at Chanel were "perfectly proper" and, moreover, that she was the only one of her species to send "the most delicate apprentices" to benefit from the fresh air of Mimizan.

At this point the discussion became a monologue, and it was no longer possible to stop her.

Her face began to flush as she exclaimed, "Because you think all that was about wages? Well, I can tell you the contrary . . . People caught that thing like the plague, like the Spanish flu, like sheep catch the staggers. Even the peasants . . . yes, the peasants. And with them it couldn't be wages, now could it? Because the land, as far as I know, the land doesn't pay you wages! But that didn't stop it from being occupied too, the land, just like the factories, like everything else. Yes, it was! I keep telling you, you don't understand the first thing about it, not the first thing. In the southwest, the peasants went out and occupied the vineyards. You hear me? The vineyards! You're not going to tell me those people weren't sick in the head? I tell you, 1936 was madness. Occupying vineyards! A farce with about as much sense to it as my workers having a sit-down strike on *my* dresses. A sit-down strike. Graceful, wouldn't you say? Attractive, alluring to think of a woman in such a position, striking on her seat. Well there, that's an idea from your United States, the sit-down strike. A fine thing! I mean, what idiots those girls were! And now you want to stick up for them . . . Really! My workers having a sit-down!"

For that was the last straw, the crime of lèse-majesté, that was the unpardonable act: the Chanel staff went on strike too. But once the occurrence had been acknowledged, not another word. Gabrielle barricaded herself inside her resentment that June day, like her workers inside their rooms on the rue Cambon. Pointless to question her. "Leave me alone. And be quiet. You're out of your mind. A madwoman!"

But there are witnesses who remember.

A picket line two doors down from the Ritz is not the sort of thing you forget.

One morning at opening time, a smocked youngster went to paste up a hastily scribbled poster bearing the word "Occupied" on the door. Gabrielle was immediately alerted. Madame Renard, a gentle soul responsible for keeping Mademoiselle's private accounts, a task she performed at the rue Cambon – the arrangement dated from the time of the duke and was a survival of the Faubourg, the wild old days – Madame Renard, not being an employee of the house, found the door closed and barred to her. We can imagine her amazement. She who . . . She whose . . . She fled to the Ritz. Her sole concern was the danger Mademoiselle was in: Paris would soon be in the hands of the rabble, the inflamed workers need only cross the street. Mademoiselle must get out of town at once. She had a ready-made haven, La Pausa; whereas Madame Renard herself requested permission to run home and hide there and not come out again. Not before having carefully filled up the bathtub. And she advised Mademoiselle to do the same. If worse came to worse, there would always be that, at least, the water in the bathtub.

Madame Renard's terror was shared by most Parisian housewives, and in every home that could boast such an object, the bathtub was full.

During the morning, "workroom delegates" requested an audience. This meant that they turned up at the front door of the Ritz, confronted a doorman in gold braid and, throats taut with fear, demanded that "the boss" be informed. All of which would have been inconceivable a fortnight earlier.

Mademoiselle sent word that she did not know what a "workroom delegate" was and would consequently see nobody. How could you see something that didn't exist? Besides, she was in bed. But when she was ready she would go to 31, rue Cambon as she did every day and if anyone had anything to say to her then, she would listen to *her* workers when it pleased *her* to do so.

The doorman's comment: "They might not let you in."

Gabrielle's reply: "We'll see about that."

She dressed with greater care than usual. She decided against her working suit, what she called her "number 2," and selected among her "number 1's" something she considered suitable – sober, a little navy blue model, and a lot of jewelry to go with it. Whereupon, a gasp from the faithful Eugénie: "Mademoiselle isn't going to get out the *real* ones?" And why not? "Mademoiselle knows perfectly well that in these days one can get oneself cut to bits for less . . . Mademoiselle is asking for trouble, isn't she? Mademoiselle is not reasonable." On the contrary. She wanted her pearls. "Mademoiselle isn't going to wear the big rope, at least?" That was precisely what she had in mind, yes.

A tremor ran through the Ritz. Would *they*, or wouldn't *they*, let her in? *They* would not.

She argued at length and haughtily. It was no. And the firmness of that "no" was a humiliation whose marks did not wear off for thirty years, if ever. She was forbidden to enter *her* house. She was *thrown out*; a situation more intolerable for her than for anyone else.

Negotiations between Gabrielle and her employees commenced in an atmosphere of high tension. At first, she turned a deaf ear to even the most modest demands: a weekly salary, paid holidays, limited working hours, employment contracts. Gabrielle's answer to that was to fire three hundred women – who refused to budge. Things dragged on. Gabrielle tried one last maneuver. She offered to give the whole business to her workers, on condition that she would have sole management of it. A poisoned present, which the delegates would have none of. Summer was coming. Gabrielle's advisers told her that if they had not reached agreement by the end of June there would be no hope of presenting an autumn collection. She gave in.

This was undoubtedly the only time in her long career when Gabrielle could not succeed in hiding her consternation. *Her* house was all she had left; and now it too was escaping her. Could any greater injustice be conceived? What did those girls have against her? Did they even exist? Without Gabrielle, without *her* dresses, they did not exist.

In an abstract way, of course, Gabrielle knew that the girls in smocks whom she never looked at, the little girls who sat and sewed all day long, possessed bodies and heads and mouths which didn't always eat their fill but often sang and hummed at their work, and nice little eyes which sometimes showed behind the folds of a dress carried over their arms – beneath the dress stood the apprentice, proud and frail, as though bearing the Holy Sacrament. And she knew they also had longings, the little girls, and all the impatience of their youth; in theory, Gabrielle knew all that. She knew it all the better for having had the same longings and impatience herself. Long ago, she had been just such a girl bending over her needle until her eyes swam. She had also known the arrogance of customers and the anxiety – oh damn, there goes my bias again! – and the recalcitrant flared hem and the sagging "fall." The days when she used to go to the homes of mesdames Bourbon-Busset and the other châtelaines of the region around Vichy who were then her customers – they were only yesterday in her memory. She also had been twenty once, and what an apprenticeship she had had . . . She had nothing to learn from her employees. So with that "no" they flung in her face, it was as though the early Gabrielle, her own youth, had rejected her. Here was its ghost rising out of the ground and threatening her. Nothing, after this, was ever the same or even looked the same in her house. It was not in her nature to react otherwise. The "people"? Don't bore her with questions about the people . . . It was like trying to get her to explain her own family. The people? How could she answer that she *was* the "people," since that was exactly what she was trying to hide? And if she made no greater efforts to picture what was going on in her employees' heads, it was because she had had to drudge like a slave herself in order to get out, as they say, to rise above the people. Get out? Work was the only way. She believed in that, profoundly.

What shocked her so, then, was not so much the strike itself but the fact that her girls had ruined the profession, trampled *her* work underfoot, *her* achievement, everything embodied for her in the conquest of respectability.

How could she have understood? Everything was against it. Beginning, for instance, with the fact that in dress design, work and worker are so joined together that in the end it becomes impossible to distinguish between them. In Chanel's house the confusion was even greater. Because of the mirrors, perhaps, which helped to mingle fitter and dress being fitted, multiplying ad infinitum the double image of dress-plus-fitter, dress-plus-fitter. And the main staircase, too, which – there being no other one – was used by employees as well as customers. At closing time the workrooms emptied onto it in flocks. People watched them passing like flights of sparrows.

But in other houses as well, always and everywhere, the language of fashion design bears witness to this confusion. If the salon calls for "Madame X's fitting," the order is transmitted as "Manon, it's your dress." Which is the same thing as saying, "Manon, you who dare not show the soles of your slippers and who hide beneath your smock a skirt worn more than is good for it, get up from the long table in the attic, emerge from your narrow corridors and descend to the glittering realm where the multimillionairess

Madame X is waiting for the dress she will wear and you will never wear but which is nonetheless *your* dress and will remain so because it has come from your hands, it is your labor, your masterpiece." *Your* dress! There is no need to wear it. Only give it a role to play, and its success will be that of the hands that made it. The president's wife has only to appear on television or anywhere else, and if the little girls in Manon's workroom happen to have cut her coat it is they the guards are saluting, not the great lady.

And how could Gabrielle help it if, despite her fame, her well-documented love affairs, and her fortune, there remained inside her some of the ghosts of the urchin of old? Her love of order and her horror of waste, lessons she never forgot, came from the orphan, the Aubazine convent child. Is anyone alone inside his skin? We are there, and then there is whatever else other people have put there. In the summer of '36 the heritage of Moulins and Vichy and Aunt Julia, as well as that of Iribe, weighed upon Gabrielle. Could she stop herself from thinking? What would Iribe have said about this mess? Ah, no, enough! *My* dresses! Her dresses were being sabotaged, and Gabrielle was overwhelmingly embittered by the fact.

She held it against her workers for many a day, regretting that she could not do the one thing she wanted to do: fire them all, lock, stock and barrel, and lower the curtain. But she couldn't. Schiaparelli was breathing down her neck. If Gabrielle had taken off so much as a week, that other woman, who had less trouble negotiating with her much smaller organization, would leap into the breach the moment her back was turned. Leave the field open to "Schiap" – she couldn't bring herself to do it.

Besides, there was the Expo again. This time, the exhibition exuded a strong aroma of war, with the German pavilion completed and standing like a slap in the face so close to the French and British ones that were still a heap of bricks and rubble; the exhibition, and the Soviet pavilion already finished too; the exhibition, and the delay nobody had been able to catch up – the exhibition opened on May 24 but the brass bands and ribbons to be cut had been ordered for Labor Day (May 1) instead; it was a setback for the Front Populaire, strikes and more strikes and the right wing was sneering, the exhibition and its great fountains playing and its end-of-the-world melancholy, a sunset exhibition with pleasure haunts, parades of models, cooks in chefs' hats, black-aproned wine waiters, restaurants every hundred yards – as if food and glorious wines were all that could be counted on anymore to bring in the customers . . . that was the 1937 Exposition des Arts et Techniques in Paris.

It was being counted on, however, to revive the economy. Gabrielle was constantly being invited to galas, parties, inaugurations. Making an appearance was an obligation. She had to show herself, as Adrienne and little Antoinette had done way back when her first shop opened at Deauville. Where were they now? Sometimes, curiously, she missed them dreadfully. If there had been the three of them, they would have shown that Schiap a thing or too. But from now on she was alone. So she showed herself. On that terrain she was a cinch to win.

For Gabrielle the Expo was an opportunity to build up a court of photographers and journalists. No, she would not let herself be beaten. And indeed, she had never been handsomer than when she arrived one evening during the exhibition on the arm of Christian Bérard. In a dress so weightless that one wondered what on earth it could be made of. What could be used to make that pale foam around her hips, that cloud of flowers. Lightness was another of her secrets. She offered it as a challenge to the other woman, that Italian, as a charm only she knew how to work. No, she would not let herself be beaten and so there she was, self-assured, treading the paths of the exhibition in her organdy veils, wearing a diadem of flowers as Diana her crescent moon, wholly dedicated to the idea of winning. And if it weren't for the contrast between her gay expression and what one would call a smile, if it weren't for the corners of her mouth only half-hiding her confession, down-turned, falling so that it made you want to cry, if it weren't for that, one might have thought her cured. She had never been less "cured."

Nevertheless, she assumed her disguise. She was seen as a "Fair Cruel One" at comte Etienne de Beaumont's spring ball. She was seen that summer at La Pausa climbing trees in flannel slacks, lithe as a cat. The next year, with Misia, Dali, and Auric, she celebrated the renaissance of the Ballets Russes spirit with the matchless Danilova. That was at Monte Carlo, where René Blum, a defector from Colonel de Basil's Ballets Russes, founded a company in 1937 with stars trained in the Russian school; it was supported by the Principality of Monaco and given permission to use the name Ballet de Monte Carlo. Chanel was seen entering the Hôtel de Paris hand in hand with Grand Duke Dmitri Pavlovich. In Paris, again with Misia, she went to the opening of the Athénée, where Jouvet welcomed them in raptures and Stravinsky, her accomplice from Bel Respiro summers, seated himself next to Gabrielle wearing an expression of tender affection. There was a brief revival of the Slavic Period – just for fun, for no reason, for the melancholy of it. But the hat she was wearing was not pretty. And Gabrielle smiled, and went on smiling at her friends and at the photographers, as though she were holding a mask clapped tight against her face with both hands.

But what an abyss! Inspiration had fled. Luck too, maybe. She consulted a fortune teller. The woman advised her to work. That told her nothing she didn't already know. But because she was easily swayed by masculine beauty, when a young and unknown actor, a beginner, asked her to do the costumes for Cocteau's *Oedipe Roi*, she accepted. It is hard to believe she was responsible for them, though, so hideous were those bandages which made the actors look like victims from a casualty list or diapered infants, depending on whether they were tall and pale or pink and pudgy. It took all the beauty of a young god to get away with it, it took Jean Marais. But apart from him – pathetic. Phrygian bonnets you'd have sworn were socks, Lady Abdy wearing a necklace made of a double row of spools of thread; and all so heavy, so outmoded. Neither press nor public refrained from saying so.

On September 21, 1938, the western powers abandoned Czechoslovakia to its fate. At Hradcany Palace in Prague, Beneš woke with a start at two in the morning. The governments of London and Paris were informing him of their treason, and Masaryk's successor could not keep back the sobs. The Czechs were alone. In the peaceful Bubeneč district General Faucher, head of the French military mission, tore up his French passport and enlisted in the Czech army. In London the morning papers published a statement issued the previous midnight: "The division of Czechoslovakia, under pressure from England and France, is equivalent to the total surrender of the western democracies to threats of Nazi force. Such a collapse will bring peace and security to neither England nor France." Signed Churchill. "Well, well! Old Winston again!" as Chanel might have said. She was also saying, "He is like one of those big dolls with weights in their feet. The harder you knock them down the quicker they bob up again." And because she too was capable of surprising somersaults, despite the weight she was dragging around inside her, Gabrielle managed yet another virtuoso stunt. Her long gowns in particular were greatly applauded that season. The dresses of spring 1939: gypsy dresses. But the most popular model came in colors that had nothing to do with gypsies. Is there anything surprising about that? Was it a reminiscence? That was her secret. But the fact was her gypsy dresses were red, white, and blue. Just a few light touches, a bit of blue in the skirt or red in the bodice, like a whispered allusion to the colors dear to Iribe, and to the time, not so long before, when Gabrielle was posing for *Le Témoin*.

Those were the dresses for the last spring when people danced.

A few more weeks of rebuffs, swallowed insults, shouting, hysterical speeches and vociferations, and suddenly one September Sunday it was war. The "phony war," the *drôle de guerre* if you like, but nobody could know that at the time.

In the midst of the confusion and commotion, while millions of Frenchmen were answering the general call-up, Gabrielle made a decision that earned her the strong disapproval of all her colleagues, a sort of unanimous blame which nobody made any pretense of hiding: Chanel announced that Chanel was closing down. Without notice, she laid off her entire personnel. Only the boutique would stay open. That was her way, some said, of getting back at them all, the opportunity she had been waiting for since 1936.

PLAYING DEAD

This was what, in couture circles where exaggeration is part of normal speech, was known as Chanel's treason, her desertion. But was it really? And should she still have considered herself in any way bound to employees who, scarcely three years before . . . To thumb her nose at such an obligation, was that what people called deserting? And besides, why not desert, after all? Everything had deserted her. Now it was her turn to go. And if they wanted to call it deserting, well, let them. She couldn't care less.

She was spurned and reviled. The trade union association tried to stop her. The negotiators were instructed to soften her heart: please would she not close down, they implored her. If she couldn't see her way clear to doing it for the sake of her employees, let her do it for her customers. Wartime customers? She had served them before and wasn't about to again. There was a reason for this: in those days she had had Boy, this time she was on her own; but that was not something she could explain to strangers. All she found to say, with infinite disdain, was "Pooh!" They insisted. She wanted no more of such customers. So negotiations shifted to different ground. Perhaps by flattery . . .

They declared that she had to stay for the prestige of Paris. There would be charity balls and fashion parades, they were going to organize masses of them for the fighting men. And what would a gala be without Chanel? She replied that she had taken part in entertainments of that sort twenty-five years ago in Deauville and they wouldn't catch her doing it again. And that was not all she said; she added, in icy tones, that this time *something* told her they were all going to make precious and total fools of themselves.

"High fashion working for the boys in blue? No, thank you very much." Her distraught supplicants tried to tempt her with work. Orders? Certainly she would get plenty of them, they told her. Air-raid alarm clothes, for instance . . . She'd done them, back in '16. If the ladies wanted more now, let them consult their mothers. "The mamas would remember, for sure! And nobody needed Chanel for that." Then Poiret was held up to her as an example: why shouldn't she do as he had done in the last war, show a little spirit of sacrifice, invent new forms of dress for officers and nurses. They couldn't have chosen a worse tack. "Me!" she exclaimed. "You must be joking! Me! Dress those women! Thanks awfully. Already back in '14 they gave me indigestion. Scandalously incompetent . . . I'm sure they finished off heaps of nice boys who would be alive and happy today without them." Why didn't they just leave her alone. War was men's business. That was all fine for a big fat baby like Poiret, what they were suggesting. That was just his cup of tea; "He's not dead yet, as far as I know?" All right, they could just ring him up and ask him. A megalomaniac like him wouldn't be able to resist offering to reequip the entire French army from head to toe. But as far as she was concerned, nothing could change her mind; she was leaving and she was closing down, come what may. She repeated "come what may"; and also said that nobody could make her work against her will, no, nobody.

What was foremost in Gabrielle's personality at that point came from the distant past: it was Cevenole mulishness. And that *something* that had suddenly warned her: that was peasant magic, the force that drives the farmer's nose up into the air long before the first fat drop falls.

And Gabrielle was sure of it: what was coming now would not be a time for fashion.

One person, however, approved of her decision.

When Gabrielle said, "This is no time for fashion," Reverdy agreed. Their reasons, no doubt, were not the same, but what does that matter. As she felt the hostility rising around her she had that, at least, to console her: Reverdy, in his retreat at Solesmes, thought as she did. He too was saying that the only thing to do in the circumstances was to lie low and keep quiet.

And besides, what happened a year later, when the Germans invaded France and some of them, passing through Solesmes, made their way into Reverdy's little garden, his little priest's garden, and stole his vegetables and then broke into his house; what did he do? He decided it was no longer possible to live there. Where must he go? Where he would not *see* any more Germans, not ever see them again, and to do that he must go where he would no longer see what they had seen. His place of work? His home? He sold it overnight and moved into a barn, where he walled up the windows facing the street. His garden? There was a risk that he might see some of them there. He decided to raise the walls. It was a time for neither seeing nor being seen.

When anyone referred to this episode in Reverdy's life she would comment shortly, "We're alike." And in at least one way it was true.

On Reverdy's first wartime visit to Paris, during the early months of the Occupation, he met Georges Herment and exclaimed, "How's that? The Germans are here and you can still write?"

Chanel's business was shut and Gabrielle was invisible.

Where was she? Where was she hiding? She was at the Hôtel du Pèlerin in a little village in the Basses-Pyrénées. Corbères . . . where her nephew's family had fled.

But Gabrielle carried her impulse to break off even further. There are certain vulnerable moments when anguish takes over from reason and causes unpredictible reactions. Everyone has heard the story of the lioness from the Chad who, the moment she found herself captured, assiduously began to devour her own paws. That was almost what Gabrielle did the year the war began, when she cut her last remaining ties with her family. Destiny ordained that her life was to be a desert, did it, and the men she loved must always be torn from her side? Well, destiny would get its money's worth! She was going to make sure there was nothing missing from that desert. No more lovers. Two sisters dead. There remained Julia's son. He was a well-behaved lad, decent-looking, in very poor health, and she had taken responsibility for him ever since the days of Boy. Him she would not abandon. But her brothers . . . She was about to break with them, and it would be all her own doing.

The only explanation for the brutal letter she wrote Lucien could be a desire to be *nothing* to *anyone*, but with this qualification: here again her origins showed through, for "shutting up shop" also meant ceasing to earn, and even though she was immensely wealthy, this brought the fear of "running short," the ancestral terror as old as the peasantry. Breaking off with her brothers was also, no doubt about it, "an economy."

The letter Lucien received in October 1939 hinted at anything and everything: bankruptcy, total ruin . . .

"I am very sorry to have to bring you such sad news. But now that the business is shut down, here I am nearly reduced to poverty myself . . . You cannot count on me for anything so long as circumstances stay the way they are."* She was cutting off his allowance. Lucien was terribly hard hit by it. Now was not the time to begin feeling sorry he had given up his business and abandoned the fairgrounds and markets and turned down the string of offers just because Gabrielle said so. For a fact, now was not the time. Poor Lucien! He would have done better to trust his wife and go on working, whether Gabrielle liked it or not.

And now here she was on her uppers herself. His savings, that was all Lucien had in the world to live on, his savings . . . instead of which, he wrote and offered them to Gabrielle. It would be his turn to send remittances. What did she think of this? Was she touched? She never saw Lucien again. He died in March 1941 of a heart attack.

But Adrienne was there, near Clermont, family-minded as ever even though she was now a châtelaine, and good-hearted as ever. Hadn't she taken in the unfortunate dancer from the Théâtre de la Monnaie – handsome d'Espous's little friend. He had died. Victim of a kind of widowhood before she ever became a wife, this *irrégulière* had been promoted to the rank of companion by Adrienne, sweet, gentle Adrienne, who was not ashamed of her origins.

Her château became a vacation home for some of her nephews, while others, like Lucien, went there for visits. She presumably intimated to the latter, if only to allay his fears, that Gabrielle might not be so totally ruined as she tried to make out.

In his village of Valleraugue, Alphonse received a similar message. No more cars, no more allowance, no more trips to Paris. Gabrielle was broke. Besides, ever since the end of the Faubourg and her break with the Duke of Westminster, relations between her and Alphonse had become intermittent. This time it was something else again, however. He must cease thinking of Gabrielle as his "last resort." But Alphonse was very different from Lucien. "My Gaby, you're in the drink. Had to happen," he wrote her. She'd been living too high on the hog. Alphonse had few enough resources at his command, but that wasn't going to bother him. He simply went on running his café-tobacco shop, and he too died without seeing his sister again.

Ten or fifteen years later things in Valleraugue were going badly, and Gabrielle was notified. When Yvan, Alphonse's eldest son, died of a bad

---

* The letter is addressed from 160 boulevard Malesherbes, the apartment Balsan had given her for her first hat shop; she had kept it, and it was the only address that ever appeared on the remittances to her brothers.

chest leaving several orphans, she remained mute. And there were marriages and births and happy events, too, continuing long after Gabrielle's comeback. But she went on playing dead.

One day the girls came up to Paris – Alphonse's daughters, Gabrielle and Antoinette, the ones who had taken in Yvan's children. They turned up at 31, rue Cambon on a day when the salons were thronged. They weren't asking for anything, all they wanted was to say hello and maybe take a look . . . Yes, see the dresses . . . Aunt Gabrielle's dresses.

They were informed that their aunt was not in and that you had to have an invitation to look at the dresses. The Chanels from Valleraugue didn't need to be told twice. Out of courtesy, they inquired at what hour and day their aunt might be in Paris, and repeated that they had not come to ask any favors. No one had any idea.

They went back to Valleraugue humiliated and determined never to return.

It may have been their two names joined together, Gabrielle and Antoinette; maybe that was what she couldn't take. But whatever the reason, after October 1939 Gabrielle considered that she had no more family in the Cévennes, and none in Auvergne either. Nothing!

IX

The German Period 1940-1945

"Time and space affect the word 'treason' in various ways."

— YURI TYNYANOV, *The Death of Vazir Muktar*

VON D.

You can take the expression "a handsome man" in a thousand different ways. From the way people speak of him, beauty evidently counted for more in the life of von D. than in that of the ordinary person. Everyone agrees on this point – those who never liked him or grew to dislike him, and those, both male and female, who feared or looked down upon him. And let no one conclude from this that the author shares any particle of their contempt. I would only point out that it exists, while observing that it is most often to be met with among the mistresses von D. had abandoned. Should anything further be said? Only that it would be uncharitable to hold it against him, for that is the very essence of the seducer: rightly or wrongly, somebody is always scorning him.

He was not the "average man"; that, too, nobody denies. Those who knew von D. remember him as a tall, slender, well-proportioned figure. Everyone is in complete agreement on that point – that he was tall, extremely tall. Also superficial. Otherwise what could be the meaning of his nickname, Spatz, which means "sparrow"? Curious, when one thinks of its being applied to a fellow of far from ordinary stature who, at the time of this story, was no longer a youth. Some people would also add frivolous, and the reader would be surprised (and also know how much credit to attach to the criticism) to learn from what prominent German dignitaries it emanates. But as these persons have expressed a desire to remain anonymous, we are compelled to state, simply, that von D. was not only superficial, he was positively frivolous. The two often go together and, in the world of feminine conquests, are not much of a disadvantage. More than one woman wasted her life waiting for him. Some societies, when they have passed their prime and begin to wear out, become more susceptible than others to the singular charms of – shall we say, of sparrows of that species?

Von D.'s family were of the middle aristocracy, no more. Hanoverian gentry. His father had contracted a marriage with an Englishwoman both richer and better-born than himself, which explains why Spatz liked to boast of a British background to which he owed the sort of cosmopolitanism that suited him so well. Nor was he totally devoid of learning. He spoke English and French and wrote fluently in both languages, judging by a few samples of his amorous correspondence in which the writer can be seen switching from English to French or vice versa, as the occasion – that is, his senti-ments of the moment – demands. The expression most commonly employed is *Je t'embrasse comme toujours et pour toujours. Love, ton Spatz.* (I kiss you as always and forever. Love, your Spatz.) Von D. often had occasion to use it, as it happened, for he was much loved. Madly, in fact, and he was never short of conquests.

His baptism by fire had taken place on the Russian front in 1914, in the days when he was a lieutenant in the Königs Ulanen Regiment No. 13. Wilhelm II was the chief of his regiment, a unit of high Hanoverian density in which the senior von D. also served. There was nothing unusual in that: the gentry often made war by family, and in recruiting their officers the regi-ments respected traditions several centuries old and would really have found it rather tiresome to change them. It was taken to be self-evident that real brotherhood-in-arms could develop only among people from similar back-grounds. The same held true for marriage; so that everyone had no alterna-tive but to applaud Spatz's choice, somewhere around his twenty-fifth birthday, of a young lady of acceptable birth and excellent health answering to the name of Maximilienne. It was all very right and proper. Only later did it occur to them how deplorable it was that in addition to her honorable dowry and other rare qualities, the said Maximilienne possessed several drops of Jewish blood. A disadvantage that really could not be overlooked. Spatz divorced in 1935. Not that he wasn't fond of Maximilienne, that would be saying too much. But anyone with a touch of ambition, in short anyone German, found it quite unmanageably awkward in those days to be shackled to a spouse who was even the littlest bit Jewish. And besides, even if some people in his own country criticized Spatz and called it most cowardly of him to divorce, it can also be said that, Jewess or not, the poor Maximilienne . . . Because as far as being unfaithful to her went, Spatz was the man for the job.

The nuisance was that our hero seemed to display less interest in work than in amusing himself. He also had a tendency to spend lavishly, some-times more than he possessed. A significant detail, as you may imagine. For therein lay the seed of the whole trouble. But in his first youth, and in his circle, nobody minded much. Being unoccupied, and even to some degree positively idle, was less frowned upon then than nowadays.

Spatz's first visits to France took place around 1928. A touring von D. . . . often made use of that Train Bleu where, in the mahogany secrecy of the sleeping compartments, between René Prou's marquetry and the accessories by Lalique, he left a trail of fire in numerous ladies' hearts. True, he was a flattering companion and, fine specimen that he was . . . He might easily have passed for one of the passengers on that other *Train Bleu*, the ballet Diaghilev had produced a few years earlier. For Spatz, with his hair just as slicked down but blond and his eyes not velvet-dark but water-pale, was the German version of "Beau Gosse"; and, like the Don Juan of the seaside resorts so beautifully impersonated by Anton Dolin, he was also a fine athlete.

October 1933 saw the return to Paris of a civil-servant von D. He took an apartment on the Champ de Mars and a job that would allow him plenty of leisure time. Maximilienne had not yet been repudiated. Spatz described himself as an embassy attaché, which nobody doubted. In people's eyes a disciplined body, an imposing presence, a well-born wife, a job as attaché, an office in an embassy – they all went together to form a diplomat. And as von D. said nothing to the contrary, people in the best society gave him the warmest possible welcome. One might be tempted to observe that the year in which the Nazis seized power in Germany, the year of the burning of the Reichstag, when the *Horst Wessel* song was more or less replacing *Deutschland über alles*, might not have been an ideal moment to fling wide one's doors to every German in sight. But more broad-minded types may deem otherwise, and argue without anyone's being able to say them nay that one cannot be expected to think of everything. And Spatz danced divinely. People positively fought over him.

This did not alter the fact that there were other people, in other circles, who concerned themselves less with what made him so irresistible than with the reason he gave for being in France. Almost as soon as he arrived, Spatz attracted the attention of the French counterespionage services. Which would tend to indicate that he was either dangerously careless or remarkably clumsy, both of which, in a business like his, were highly portentous.

Just how well-informed were the French as to the nature of Spatz's activities in Paris? That we shall never know. Certain archives in the Federal Republic, on the other hand, provide sufficient indications as to the source, if not the scope, of his mission. *Hans Gunther von D. born in Hanover on December 15, 1896, was under the orders of the Reich Ministry of Propaganda, using a post as press attaché as cover. His activities in Paris were authorized by a private service contract for one year, effective October 17, 1933.* Hitler's first lieutenant, the orchestrator of the extravaganzas of the Third Reich, the specialist in mass intoxication and banner-bristling parades – that was Spatz's employer, that was the sinister little man who needed less than ten months to set up the entire Nazi propaganda machine. Spatz was working for Dr Goebbels.

Recalled to Germany when his contract expired, Spatz went but returned to France almost immediately. There is no evidence that his contract was renewed. Everything would seem to indicate, on the contrary, that it was not. After 1934 von D. was finished with propaganda. He had opted for a form of activity regarded as shameful by Latin peoples although it enjoys some repute in Anglo-Saxon lands, even in the highest society – a form of activity known in London as intelligence and in Paris as espionage.

From that date, clouds of darkness gather over von D.'s head; he is to be found in none of the files where so many eminent specialists trained in all the latest research techniques might have expected to come across him – and we know with what icy passion the Germans carry out this sort of research. So many professors and so many doctors of contemporary history, anxious to help and to omit no word of this story that relates to their country, have been compelled to conclude that the remainder of von D.'s career is, in their own words, "silence, shame (on the part of the historian) and mystery."[1] There is no slightest mention in the military archives of his service in the army, so that one could be led to believe he was never either lieutenant or uhlan under the late Kaiser's command; the political files contain no syllable of his activities in occupied France, whereas he should by rights have star billing there, for there is no doubt that from 1937 on, in addition to divers civilian and assorted clandestine appointments von D. was, in Paris, what Prince Max-Egon von Hohenlohe Langenburg[2] was in Madrid and Baron Turkheim in London – in other words a loyal vassal of national socialism; and finally, the ex-members of the Abwehr,* who form a most closely knit little unit and publish an astonishing bulletin, *Die Nachhut* (or *Informationsorgan für Angehörige der ehemaligen militärischen Abwehr*), in which both their greatest exploits and most trivial endeavors are reported – this honorable society swears by all that is holy that never was anyone named von D. on its membership lists, and we have no reason to doubt its word: all this offers absolute proof what a first-rate spy our man

---

* German army information service. An entirely military organization which was involved in open conflict with the state secret police (better known as the Gestapo), on more than one occasion.

became. For the fact that he left no trace of his activities in either German writings or German memories is not sufficient cause to deduce that the investigations of the French counterespionage services were unfounded. If von D., as some claim, was effectively acting under the orders of a certain Colonel Waag (whose name is shrouded in so much uncertainty and is, in short, so . . . vague that any spy must be proud to claim it), and if he was ordered out of the country the minute the war ended – and the ban has never been lifted – it is presumably because he did not confine his activities, during his years in France, to fluttering about like a sparrow and pecking here and there in women's hearts.

Anyone acquainted with the army of spies, informers, double and triple agents, and more or less sworn strong-arm men who made up the Reichssicherheithauptamt* and aware of the ruthless internecine struggles dividing it at every level from 1942 on, also knows that no one except von D. himself could tell to which particular gear in the elephantine machine he was attached.

At 7 P.M. on August 26, 1939, the French ambassador to Berlin made his final attempt to persuade Hitler to abandon the idea of taking Danzig by force. And it is a fact that the representative of France did succeed in wringing unwonted scruples from Hitler. "Ah, the women and children . . . I have often thought of them!" he murmured;[3] which consorted oddly with the storms and rages with which the Führer had previously favored his audience. But was it a hesitation? Hitler recovered himself almost at once.

Joachim von Ribbentrop, on the other hand, showed the same "face of stone"[4] throughout the interview.

Five days later the Führer's scruples, if any, had dissolved into one of those historical snapshots that talented ambassadors know so well how to reduce to a few pithy lines. "I may have touched Hitler. But I did not make him change his mind,"[5] M. Coulondre wired home. And so it was: his conversation with Hitler was the last diplomatic contact between France and Germany.

On August 31, *Directive No. 1 for the Conduct of the War* was issued. The date of the attack was set for September 1, 1939, the time 4:45 A.M., and the whole document, marked "Top Secret," was signed Adolf Hitler.

---

* Founded in 1939 by a decree by Himmler, the RSHA (Reich Central Security Office) united not only the Gestapo and SD or security services, but the criminal police and all Nazi information services abroad as well.

And the man with the face of stone directed von D. to leave Paris.

He went to inform his mistress accordingly. With regard to the identity of the woman who then occupied his spare time, we shall confine ourselves to a mildly camouflaged form of her first name: Elena, for this imprudent creature of fine and ancient lineage – a beautiful woman, moreover, and at the time of writing this book in the pink of health and life – perhaps as the result of cherishing an overoptimistic view of love, got herself into so much trouble on his account that we should not forgive ourselves for causing her any more by inscribing her true name in this story.

When bidding her farewell, von D. claimed that he could not bear the thought of being involved in bloodshed. He, a pacifist? Surprising, perhaps, but how can we doubt him? He would have no part of this war, he repeated. The woman in whom he was confiding was ignorant of what was the most open of secrets to the intelligence services, and she offered to help him. He wanted to get to Switzerland and stay there. Could she send him to any safe friends who would offer him hospitality? She could and did, and von D. left France for a country with which relations remained as before.

So here he was, on neutral territory, with an address and a post office box into which envelopes from France dropped without difficulty. A facility his loving lady used and abused. Which need not have led to anything, if von D. had not been under close surveillance. But before his correspondent had sent and received a dozen missives she found herself under arrest and charged with collaborating with the enemy. The incident became public and created a great uproar in the accused's circle, her love affair now being exposed. The military muscled in. For the reading and interpreting of other people's letters, there was no one like them. But as for understanding them – that was a very different matter. People flocked to her side, testified to her innocence and good faith, labored to prove that whatever might appear obscure in their correspondence was merely discretion and reserve, that what looked like double meanings were simply stylistic refinements, but all to no avail. For her accusers, every word of love had a hidden meaning; even the words crossed out and the spelling mistakes which the couple let slip by in the heat of the moment were patent proof of treason.

This woman's anguish has no place in our present story; let it suffice to say that she risked her life for love of a liar. Eight months later he was back in France a conqueror, at the end of a speedily won war and notwithstanding the vigilance of France's correspondence censors.

What is highly pertinent to a description of von D.'s character, however, is his reaction upon learning that Elena was still in prison in the unoccupied zone. He presented himself at the château where his victim's mother was living. She was not acquainted with her daughter's lover, had no intention of knowing him, and had kept herself totally aloof from a situation that had caused her nothing but shame and sorrow. Her caller seemed perfectly amiable although ever so slightly arrogant. Suddenly she realized who he was. He then gave her to understand that he would be able to obtain her daughter's release if . . . well, if a lady of her rank would agree to place herself at his disposal, so that he could use this as an argument to his superiors, could assure them that she would not refuse to receive them or arrange meetings which might interest them, well, then, in short, on those terms, her daughter would be released much sooner. She replied that even at the cost of her daughter's freedom, and should her daughter lose her life in the process, it was completely out of the question; and that, seeing nothing further to be said, she also saw no reason to detain him.

Without wishing to condemn an action that may not have been wholly von D.'s own idea but was perhaps carried out under orders from above, we can still conclude that the air around this particular spy, as the marquise de Sévigny would have put it, well, "the air was a bit thick."

As everybody knew, the "unoccupied zone" was a mirage, and when it vanished Elena was free. Spatz, by that time, no longer was. He had met Gabrielle.

At the time of her romance with von D. Gabrielle was fifty-six years old. That was thirteen more than he, which, however overpowering her charm, left her holding precious few trumps in her lovely hand. But why speak of age? No one can arbitrate love, and Gabrielle was ageless since, whatever people may say, he loved her.

Let us try to imagine this singular adventure in the Paris of those days.

Gabrielle had not lasted long at Corbères. After a few short weeks there and a brief sojourn at Vichy, she returned to Paris at the end of August 1940. Playing refugee was not her style, and besides Julia's son had been taken prisoner. For once the lad's poor health might help him. She wanted to see if she could do anything to get him released.

Anyone else finding the Germans ensconced in the Ritz would have gone elsewhere. Gabrielle did nothing of the sort and insisted that the manager hear her out. He had "put her out," had he? Well, she would change her room but not her address. The handsome apartment with the windows overlooking the Place Vendôme, the vast room in which she had re-created the decor of the Faubourg in the days of her affair with Iribe, had been cleared within hours of the hotel's requisition. Where could she go? Moving to another part of town meant moving farther away from her shop, losing sight of her daily bread, and she couldn't bring herself to do that. Anyone else would have considered himself in line for mortification from both hotel manager and Germans and, in a word, not wanted. But such considerations were simply not relevant to Gabrielle. Her strength lay in heading straight for what *served her*. And she was attached to so little. No roof or walls, no scheme of decoration had ever seemed permanent to her, and she couldn't have cared less if someone "touched her things," that fabulous bugbear of the bourgeoisie. The danger began when they reached her cash, the purse hidden in the mattress. That was the only threat – that she would be left high and dry. But apart from that? So her things had been moved, so what? Now those Coromandel screens could fill their proper function. Hadn't they been made to be folded and unfolded indefinitely? She would unfold them a few doors down from the Ritz, just over her shop, and there she would furnish her drawing room to suit herself, as an Arab furnishes his tent. A reaction dictated by her childhood and the years she had spent on the move. As for what the Ritz was offering, one scrappy little room on the rue Cambon side: she had known worse and asked for no more. It was all that was necessary to keep warm at night.

Besides, she had no choice.

To anyone who advised her to live elsewhere, and to Misia in particular, who was amazed that she could be satisfied with such shabby surroundings, she retorted: "What's the use of changing? Sooner or later all the hotels will be occupied. Then what? I may as well stay here. My room is too small? That will make it cheaper." Her eternal eye for economizing and that ancient virtue of simplicity she had no trouble recovering. Her words are proof enough. A friend she had seen in Vichy had asked why she was in such a hurry to get back to Paris, and she had said it was because of the price of gasoline: "Wait? Until the return trip costs a fortune? I wouldn't dream of it. At the rate things are going now, it's going to cost as much as perfume." As Chanel No. 5! Her one unit of measurement, her gold standard. Yet she was rich. But with her, no precaution was silly and no profit negligible, and however rich she might be she took everything that came her way, like those peasant women who will throw nothing away in times of defeat or invasion but hoard it all, saving the bread and old bones from one month to the next. Gabrielle definitely belonged to that breed and was, we may as well confess it, a miser.

*

Spatz and Gabrielle . . . how and when did they meet, and how did they become acquainted? Are we to believe her when she said they had been friends "for years"? Perhaps that meant they had met before the war. But then, what would knowing tell us? Whether it was in this place or that, or last year or the year before, or in this or that person's house, will that make us better able to understand the secret landscape of this love, its special lighting, its tenderness and violence, its truths or lies? And what difference does it make whether she knew him before the defeat, or only saw him for the first time on the day she went to ask him to have Julia's son repatriated? For those were the circumstances of their meeting, or reunion, and that is how it all began between them.

Henceforth von D. was sufficiently devoid of ambition to be forgotten by his superiors, but also sufficiently adroit for his presence in Paris to be accepted without question. A delicate game, a subtle maneuver whose object was simply to remain in France. That was his only aim, and his only apprehension was to find himself honored with some special mission that would compel him to plunge into the hornet's nest of Berlin with all the risks that implied, the worst being that some court clique would lay hands on him and he would be helpless to prevent it. That was what von D. feared more than anything else in the world, that was what he wanted to avoid. Even if his closest associates were to tax him with a lack of zealousness, which they hastened to do. Even if this was the first thing for which Gabrielle reproached him – although not at once. For in the beginning what Gabrielle liked best was the discretion of von D., always in civilian dress and with the English language rising readily to his tongue.

The desire to live in hiding with their happiness, and a physical harmony so often proclaimed by von D. that no one, not even the most jealous of his former mistresses, could challenge it, explain the fact that there was now a sort of hiatus in her life. Spatz and Gabrielle were invisible because they were happy, and it lasted for nearly three years, happy in a world in which mountains of misfortune were rising around them, happy while Misia was slowly going blind and pretending not to – "she has to guess where the doorknobs in my house are," wrote Colette.[6] "Her noble coquetry, how much more moving to us than any complaint . . ." – happy while Grand Duke Dmitri Pavlovich, the companion of Bel Respiro days and that summer of sun on the bay at Arcachon, was dying of tuberculosis at Davos in 1942, happy while the martyrdom of Max Jacob was beginning at St Benoit-sur-Loire; those two were happy. What else can we say – happy. Are we to blame them?

The love of his woman brought out the Oriental in him; he never went out anymore, nobody ever saw him anywhere, either in the "de luxe" restaurants* where, in exchange for a contribution to the Secours National, you could eat whatever you liked, or at Carrère's, the "in" nightclub of the moment; never in any bar, whether the Belier d'Argent or the Veau d'Or – bars near the Villette slaughterhouse; taking no part either in the prodigious jocularity in which "the extremely useful lightheartedness of the national character"[7] was displaying itself, or in the great sorrow and depression of a debased people; never anywhere.

And so they lived, above a shop through which passed throngs of uniformed buyers. Whenever stocks of Chanel No. 5 ran out, these strange tourists simply picked up the display bottles marked with the intertwined double C. It was something, anyway . . . something to take back home. A souvenir of the Occupation, an "article from Paris" as they say.

THE BLACK PERFUME OF ADVENTURE

What is one to make of a life that leaves no room for the unexpected? It wouldn't satisfy Gabrielle. Whereas von D., who was not an imaginative man, basked in bliss at her side, in an atmosphere in which everything was somehow vaguely enveloping.

It is more than likely that the initiative for change would have come from Gabrielle. She always had to be *doing something*. To challenge fate? That was her delight.

For a time her legal entanglements with the Chanel perfume company kept her occupied. *Her* perfumes . . . It was fifteen years since she had given the Wertheimer brothers the right to manufacture and sell them, but she had never been able to bring herself to sign a permanent contract. Very noted lawyers advanced irrefutable proof of her associates' loyalty and talked and talked and talked, but the moment she was alone her doubts came surging back. Come, now, it was plain as day! Her invention had been purloined. She had been swindled. It was an *idée fixe*.

When the Occupation regulations offered her a chance to dissolve the partnership, the opportunity seemed too good to miss. Could she get back her perfume from the Wertheimers? One of the occupying forces' regulations stated that companies whose management had been forced to leave the country would find themselves under new, imposed management. That was

---

* The Tour d'Argent, Lapeyrouse, Maxim's, Drouant, and Carton.

her chance. A trick to try – a dirty one. Now it was her turn to play, she, the exploited, the swindled, and the Wertheimer clan would see what she was made of. She was Aryan, they weren't. She was in France, they were in the United States. Emigrants . . . Jews. In the eyes of the occupying power, in short, she alone existed.

She wanted to impose a manager of her choosing. In a fight against the representatives of a Jewish company, a woman who would stop at nothing and could count on German support? In that France, she couldn't possibly lose, it would seem. But oddly enough, she did. There were shrewd players on the opposing team, too. She thought she was the only one with a particular kind of support, did she? What an innocent. Didn't she know there were Frenchmen in Paris prepared to act to protect Jewish holdings, and that in Paris as elsewhere some Germans were disposed to let themselves be bought? With that mixture all you had to do was be quick and not make mistakes.

First of all, the opposition needed an Aryan.

They needed one to whom they could sell the company for a pittance. They found him, in the person of an industrialist specializing in airplane construction: Amiot.

Next, they needed a German.

They would ask him to certify the validity of the transaction, to endorse a massive shuffle of false transfers of predated documents, a complete set-up which would have to be made to look plausible, unassailable. A German? Just a question of money. They found him too, but he was expensive. Thus the Chanel company would be able to prove that it no longer belonged to the Wertheimers. And there was nothing to be said, the trick had worked.

But that wasn't all. A representative of the new owner had to be para-chuted onto the board of directors – a man able to beat any candidate Gabrielle might put up.

To add insult to injury, they sought out this person in a circle Gabrielle knew only too well. So she found herself losing to her eternal adversaries, but this time under the ironic gaze of a man who had been put there to undo her, a socialite from that particular society she could never think of without a surge of resentment. He had been in the Moulins set. She was confronted by a witness to her own past: the chairman imposed upon her was the brother of Adrienne's "adored." What could she say to that, except that she had lost? Which did not mean she was going to give up, not by a long shot.

On his return to France, however – let us mention it and then say no more – Pierre Wertheimer, resuming control of his company, seems to have felt that generosity was his only possible revenge. But we need not over-sanctify him. Where does generosity end and cynicism begin, in business matters? Pierre Wertheimer could have accused and attacked, he was in a strong position. But he was most careful not to. With Gabrielle alive and flourishing, what would a Chanel company be without her? But with Gabrielle reviled and dishonored, what would a Chanel company be *with* her? That, presumably, was his line of reasoning.

In any event, relations resumed and their battles raged on more fiercely than ever. But rather that, a thousand times rather, than nothing. Because for people of their type such seasonable hostilities, contradictory affirma-tions, lawyers constantly maneuvering to get their knives into one another's backs, were the very substance of their lives. They were like a luxury, a special treat.

They played the nastiest conceivable tricks on each other. Booby traps, ambushes, feints and double dealings, every form of machination – the list of hooks they baited for each other would be a long time completing. New perfumes surreptitiously dropped onto the market by Gabrielle and instantly ordered withdrawn by Wertheimer . . . Samples smuggled into the United States, where Wertheimer immediately had them confiscated by the customs officials . . . A threat from her to launch an improved Chanel No. 5 good enough to sink the old one, whose success was the foundation of his fortune . . . Machiavelianism of this order, as conducted by the opposing parties, left the participants themselves gaping. Wertheimer was the more amazed of the two: after so many years, there was his Gabrielle again, that tigress, Gabrielle, his dearest enemy, still in the ring and on her feet – nobody else would have dared to challenge him so. Really, determination like that deserved the top lawyers.

Even more than the appeal of profit, there was unconfessed admiration in the tie that bound M. Wertheimer to Gabrielle. There was also regret, that between them there had never been anything but conflicting interest. Never any question of anything else. But how dearly he would have liked to receive what she was not giving: encouragement, an expression of satis-faction. No matter what new coup he brought off, there was never a word from her. Not even the day a horse from the Wertheimer stables won the Derby at Epsom. One word, just one word, would have made him so happy! The truth of the matter was that he loved her. Or almost . . . For no one reminded him so acutely of his past as Gabrielle. Nobody. Pierre Wertheimer, you see, had been one of those *entreteneurs* (like Balsan) of a type that no longer existed, whence Gabrielle's attraction for him. How could he have regarded her as anything but an *irrégulière?*

At last the day came when, certain promises having been given, Gabrielle accepted the principle of a cease-fire. That was in 1947. In the enemy camp a few more sleights-of-hand were tried, but more or less just for the sake of the thing, or from force of habit. In the end Pierre Wertheimer capitulated, consenting, in addition to her other returns, to pay Gabrielle a 2 percent royalty on the gross sales of her perfumes all over the world.* At that point, she settled for peace.

She was sixty-five years old.

It really was time to lay down her arms.

But her old foe was a few years younger than she – a thing she judged intolerable – so when the contracts were being drawn up Gabrielle managed to falsify her birth certificate.

She had become a woman with a colossal income. That more than justified taking ten years off her age.

But let us return to the Occupation, and to the stage of the dispute in which Gabrielle was watching her opponents organize their network of allies and seeing appear in their ranks one of those fine-looking fellows from the Moulins days she so devoutly longed never to meet again.

Defeat is infuriating; it weighs you down intolerably. Can anyone conceive of Gabrielle letting someone else have the last word? No sooner did the perfume reappropriation campaign prove impracticable than she was overcome by another obsession. What was it this time – ambition? Presumptuousness? Unless there is another term that would be more appropriate: love of conquest, will to dominate, pure daring, the need to dazzle. Take your choice. Her friends, the Germans, saw it as pure and distinterested self-sacrifice. Some went so far as to affirm that she had "a drop of the blood of Joan of Arc in her veins"![8] Well, Joan or not, Gabrielle's next mad scheme led her into far more compromising and dangerous waters than her previous one: the official or semiofficial realm of war intelligence.

Since January 24, 1943, and the Casablanca Conference, the terms were certain. Roosevelt and Churchill had announced their decisions, unconditional surrender would be exacted from Germany, and there would be no peace on any other terms. What emotion those words inspired! There was the satisfaction of those working in the underground in occupied territories,

* About $1,000,000 a year.

carrying on the struggle and seeing no future or honor in any other solution; and there was the cruel disenchantment of the others: for voices were heard – why deny it – regretful voices saying that the bloodletting had gone on long enough. They were heard in Pétain's France and even in England – although there, it is true, they found few listeners. There were politicians in Lord Runciman's party, but what could you expect of them? And aristocrats, too, who hoped for negotiation, for an end to the bombings – the Duke of Westminster among them, whose arguments made his old chum Winston see red. And there were those who would have liked to spare Germany – a view undoubtedly shared by the Duke of Windsor, a sort of exile in his far-off isles, although he denied it when questioned in later years.[9]

Thus more than one of Gabrielle's English friends, more than one of the fair Vera's admirers, those callers to whom Joseph used to open wide the Faubourg doors, were now on the side of the would-be peacemakers whom Churchill's announcement had brought down to earth with a thud.

And what about the Germans?

In Germany too there were pacifists, of a very different kind, some of whom – those plotting against the regime, officers of the Wehrmacht and members of the Abwehr – were heroically daring and selfless. We know what became of them . . . Sir Winston's demands did not make their task any easier, yet the announcement seems to have encouraged them, in fact, rather than dampening their ardor. First, persevere, put down the regime; afterward, they could negotiate and perhaps on better terms: that was their only objective.

Finally, there were the calculators.

They were legion, those whose hopes were dashed by the British prime minister. Their sole aim was to destroy the Red Army, and they wanted a separate peace only because it would enable them to continue the war against the Soviet Union, with or without England. But although their ends were different, sometimes radically opposed, all the partisans of a negotiated peace had one thing in common: a constant desire to communicate with the English authorities; and they left no stone, however minute, unturned, in their efforts to do so.

Except in this context, which gives a true picture of the period, the undertaking on which Gabrielle was now about to launch would look like the act of someone living in a fantasy, or of a megalomaniac. But when it is placed in the doubt-ridden atmosphere of those years, the episode appears as the almost inevitable consummation of a destiny such as hers – that of a woman with no status, a woman born of rootlessness and resentment, who had been able to tear herself loose from her original condition only by her own hazardous initiative. In short, this was just one more throw of the dice. And in this crazy scheme, what was she after but a means of affirming herself by "winning"? Can you ever cure a gambler?

What an extraordinary fate hers was ... to find herself in a conquered country, bound to its conquerors and yet on intimate terms with the person on whom the outcome of the war would largely depend. What tricks life had played on her! Churchill ... To think that one brief encounter might be enough to convince the ruthless old man that by continuing his death game he would only bring about the death of Europe, *his* Europe, the good old Europe of privilege and tradition. This war must be stopped, Gabrielle told herself. Stopped at any cost.

Could she succeed where others had failed? Could she persuade Churchill? Would he even listen to her? She determined to stake everything. Wouldn't Churchill find it *natural* for her to come and visit him, as in the old days of the holidays at La Pausa when the Duke of Westminster used to take her along and drop in on him unannounced?

She was dreaming, of course, but there's no reason why anyone should be surprised. Had she ever lived in any world that was not imaginary? Her entire life was one long dream suddenly erupting into bursts of action. True, this particular dream was also slightly mad. But once again, why should we be surprised? All her schemes, from the very beginning, had been fundamentally impossible. And had succeeded *in spite of* it. She was used to it. So she went on.

The strangest part is not that she ever believed in this dream, but that she got other people to share it, to believe in it as strongly as she herself. True, they were German. And in that summer of '43 the Red Army was at their door. But is that reason enough? The ingenuousness of some people ... Germany.

It was about six months after the Germans occupied Paris that von D. introduced one of his boyhood friends to Gabrielle. As was to be expected, efforts to have Julia's son returned to France had met with no success. Such an unreliable fellow, that Spatz. But his instincts had been right when he turned the matter over to someone more capable. The boyhood friend occupied a position of responsibility, he was an officer, a man who worked and had experience. Indeed, knowing him, one can see how Gabrielle came to trust him. Rittmeister (Cavalry Captain) Momm was one of those

Germans whom the events of those days made it hard to believe could still exist.

And when Momm said, on his first visit to Gabrielle, that his family had been "textilian" for five generations, father to son, he could not have hit upon a happier opening. And so charming, that made-up word "textilian," with the guttural intonation that is the essence of German speech. Gabrielle repeated it, "Textilian! You don't say . . ." After which, he informed her that he had been born and raised in Belgium, where his father managed a dye factory. Their suppliers were the Manchester cotton manufacturers. Really; imagine that! And in 1914 his family had gone back to Germany; what else could they do? Of course, of course, always the war. And it was back in '15 that he had met von D. Where? In the 13th, of course, the 13th Uhlans. What a small world! In addition, he announced that the most redoubtable competition showjumper, the celebrated Momm who won God-knew-how-many World Cups in 1935–36, that star of stars, was a cousin of his. Your cousin! Whoever would have imagined it! Gabrielle had admired, applauded him. She was most impressed. Horsemanship was one of the subjects on which she knew she was unbeatable, and then, horsemen can always find a common ground, can't they? And lastly, and this was the main thing, Rittmeister's job in Paris was to supervise the French textile industry under German administration. It was clear what that meant.

He looked into the matter of Julia's son, decided that it was absolutely imperative to reopen a little textile mill near St Quentin, and testified that Gabrielle was its proprietor. This being the case, the German authorities should see fit to release a prisoner who was so obviously the ideal person to assume management of it. The child whose upbringing Boy Capel had taken in hand, Gabrielle's nephew, returned to his homeland at last. The Rittmeister had done wonders, and she continued to show him signs of friendship. Who could have done less? In her situation . . .

When her obsession about meeting Churchill had reached fever pitch, it was to the Rittmeister that she turned. The fact that she chose him instead of von D. indicates that the latter already had fallen short of the mark. The Rittmeister was mildly surprised. Curious female, who made no secret of the fact that she gave her heart to one man and her trust to another. What had gone wrong between her and Spatz? But once he had gotten over his surprise, Rittmeister Momm found, all things considered, that what she had told him was safer in his hands than in any others. (After the war Theodor Momm returned to his former career. He traveled widely and, notwithstanding his advanced age, held positions in the textile manufacturing field in Chad and the Cameroons.)

Her plan was to persuade Churchill to agree to the idea of Anglo-German talks, held in strictest secrecy. She began by shaking her listener rather badly, giving him to understand that the Germans "didn't know how to tackle the English" – they simply made one mistake after another; because in order to get along with them you had to know the British well and know them for a long time, and, fortunately, that was her case. She laid before the Rittmeister the line of reasoning she thought most likely to overcome the prime minister's reluctance – and, carried away by her subject, acted out the conversation they would have. Pacing up and down in her narrow drawing room on the rue Cambon, on the crest of her enthusiasm, she addressed herself to the German officer as though he were Churchill in person. She scolded him: "You foretold blood and tears and your prediction has already been fulfilled. But that won't give you a name in history, Winston." And in a voice that brooked no contradiction she added, "Now you must spare human lives and end the war. By holding out a hand to peace you will show your strength. That is your mission." Suddenly the German, plunged into a semistupor by this incredible performance, heard Churchill's answer. It was enough to make you wonder . . . Was he dreaming? How could anyone refuse this woman . . . He saw the prime minister of the United Kingdom solemnly mouthing his cigar and nodding. He listened to him acquiescing in such strange words:

"You're right, Coco," he was saying, "you're right."

"The force of a unique personality," as Theodor Momm was to acknowledge when, in a faltering voice, he tried to relive that memorable moment thirty years later. "What then began, in secrecy, could be the subject for a fascinating story," he added. But he confessed that he had hesitated . . . "Oh, yes! Hesitated damned long!"

To be Gabrielle's go-between involved more than one risk. What assurance could she give him? None. Less than none. And what would people think in Berlin? Would she be given permission to leave France? Permission for a return trip, signed by the MBF,* that's what she was asking for. Because she would have to go to Spain. She was personally acquainted with Sir Samuel Hoare, and it was actually there in Madrid, through contact with the English ambassador, that the success or failure of her mission would be decided. But what if she didn't come back?

---

* Militärbefehlshaber in Frankreich (Military Command in France).

Rittmeister Momm set out for Berlin, not very sure whose bell to ring. First, as a matter of precaution, he tried the ministry of foreign affairs. Alerting the diplomatic services would forestall danger. There, Baron Steengracht von Moyland, a secretary of state, agreed to see him. He was a highly distinguished but inexperienced civil servant who had just taken up his duties. And he was more than preoccupied by the recent alarming turn of events. Moreover, the foreign affairs department was not conspicuous for its brilliancy in those days. There, as elsewhere, the Nazi takeover had wreaked havoc, and its officials had become mere passive order endorsers, but this did not worry their minister overmuch. The extremely mediocre Joachim von Ribbentrop "wanted no thinking officers in anything having to do with him" and the Rittmeister's man was no exception. "His noble and empty physiognomy was a warrant of respectable and infrequent cerebration."[10] But we must admit that there were reasons for reticence just then. The higher echelons of Berlin were living through a reign of terror; and the "drawing room folk" aroused the sharpest suspicions. The Gestapo was laying traps. "The affair of Frau Solf's tea party"* was hardly two months old, and prominent diplomats were threatened with execution. It is not difficult to imagine the motives for Baron Steengracht's prudence. What was this Parisian dress designer up to, wanting to rush off to Madrid? All she seemed able to count on there were her lofty connections, and who knew where they could lead. No confidence. He politely ushered his courteous caller out, intimating that no further action would be taken on such a scheme. The plan, he added, was of the sort "not to be pursued."

A poor start. The man who had taken on the mission of defending Gabrielle's project had little choice. Army intelligence? Out of the question; one would have to be an innocent or a fool not to know that Hitler blamed the Abwehr for every conspiracy. Admiral Canaris' days were numbered and his organization threatened,† and his was certainly not the door for a wise man to knock at.

---

*   Frau Solf, widow of a German ambassador, kept a salon where people spoke their minds. On September 10, 1943, an agent of the Gestapo was among those present and on February 12, 1944, everyone who had been "to tea at Frau Solf's" was arrested, sentenced, and executed except Frau Solf herself and her daughter, who were deported to Ravensbruck and found there alive in 1945.

†   The department was effectively abolished two months later, but Admiral Canaris himself was only demoted and given a subsidiary position. He had six months left to live, before Schellenberg in person came to arrest him.

There remained the services of Himmler, the only person whom the Führer trusted. The Reichsführer of the SS reigned over a universe of mystery and darkness. One wasn't exactly eager to venture into his labyrinth. Nevertheless, it was to the Reich Central Security Office that Rittmeister Momm finally turned, reluctantly and as a last resort. "A world in which nothing was too fantastic to be impossible, where any action without ulterior motives, any forthright and unconcealed gesture was regarded as an aberration, where no one was judged by his appearance but rather by what that appearance was likely to be concealing."[11]

The fate of anyone penetrating that maze hung on all manner of imponderables. Toward whom or what would he be sent? The first contact was decisive, for if the caller's information was of any interest at all he would never get a chance to discuss it with anyone else, it became the sole property of the first person who listened to him. Far better, one hardly need say, to arouse the interest of AMT VI, which was responsible for the supervision of foreign intelligence, than of AMT IV, whose field was counterespionage in Germany and the occupied countries, and which was nothing more or less than the Gestapo. In addition, the divisions of the Central Office were rigorously compartmentalized; no one working in it had the slightest idea what the man at the next desk might be up to.

When he realized whom he had to deal with, Theodor Momm could only rejoice: the chief of AMT VI in person had agreed to see him; and so it was to the youngest of the leaders of the SS – one would be tempted to call him their charmer – that he explained the object of his mission.

Despite his youth, his Hollywood good looks, and his polished speech, Walter Schellenberg was neither a beginner nor an amateur. True, he had entered the SS more or less by chance, he wouldn't deny that. A lad who had grown up in the occupied Saar and known hardship at first hand, with a piano-manufacturing father and seven brothers and sisters, all older, then a return to Germany where the family's livelihood vanished in the economic crisis, followed by a university career at Bonn where the scar-faced student he had become proved exceptionally gifted – that was in the spring of 1933, he was twenty years old and virtually penniless. And then, suddenly, a judge he was studying under assured him that his chances of success would be much improved if he joined the Nazi Party; what else could he do? It was not particularly tempting. He didn't really fancy himself in a brown shirt among brewery brawlers. But the uniform of the SS was an altogether more stylish affair . . . and so his choice was determined by a question of costume.

He came up the ladder the usual way. Having started at the bottom, he had to prove himself. His first exploit was to make a surprise raid on the Nuremberg prison where two SS men were serving ten-year sentences for having hammered a Jew to death – because in 1934 there were still a few towns not in Nazi hands, and Nuremberg was one of them. Schellenberg managed to unlock the cell door of the prisoner who had simply lent the other one the hammer, released him, and was warmly congratulated by his superiors.

But other proofs were required, in more abstract areas. Did he know how to speak in public? As a law student, he was asked to give a series of lectures on antireligious themes. He had been brought up a Catholic; oh, well, never mind. He was so skillful at indoctrinating and, really, so talented. One could easily imagine the lawyer he might have become. Two discreet observers placed in the audience to listen immediately seized upon this rare specimen and transferred him to a "top secret" branch of activity. Thus, without leaving the SS, Schellenberg became a spy.

He was an educated lad; they gave him only "classy" jobs.

His first mission abroad was to attend the Sorbonne, where there was a particularly worrysome professor. Four weeks were needed to complete a delicate investigation, which he did successfully. But before passing final judgment on his case, it was thought advisable to send him farther afield. He was ordered to photograph every aspect of the port of Dakar. Mission again successful. Whereupon he was set a new task. Was he a man of the world? This was another of the less dominant qualities of the early recruits. So Schellenberg found himself responsible for setting up a house of joy in Berlin for the use of senior civil servants, higher officers, ministers, and foreign guests. Nothing was lacking: polished service, exquisitely tasteful decor, highly qualified female staff. No one could doubt that floors, walls, ceilings, and even beds were stuffed with microphones like a turkey with chestnuts. In recruiting his personnel, Schellenberg had creamed off the best the European capitals had to offer. First class goods only. The enterprise being successful, offers of service came in so thick and fast that he hardly knew where to turn. Extremely youthful volunteers, from the best families, came forward in regiments to serve their fatherland "in that way." It is true that in addition to a better-than-average salary the "Salon Kitty" offered a top-quality wine cellar and the best food in Berlin.

Whereupon his superiors decided there was no need to prolong his probation, and Schellenberg's lightning rise began. He was present at all the great moments of Nazism, all Hitler's triumphant entrances – Vienna, Prague – ever watchful

over the Führer's safety. And on all occasions he showed the same spirit of
initiative, pocketing any secret documents that came his way – as happened
in the Hradschin Palace; defusing bombs set to threaten Hitler along his
victory parades – as in Vienna; burning the three million rubles the USSR
paid in exchange for documents that were to lead to the death of Marshal
Tukachevsky. He was in on all the big deals. In Prague, when the SS were
surrounding the church of St Charles Borromeo after Heydrich's assassination, who was conducting the inquiry? Schellenberg. He was never one to
hold back: a spy of scope and daring. Whenever a job wanted genius in addition to deftness, they turned to him. Laying a telephone cable across the
Maginot Line, securing the "understanding" of persons in high places at
Schneider or Creusot, establishing the list of lords, ladies, authors, scholars,
Boy Scouts and their leaders who were to be interned the moment England
was invaded – such were the missions entrusted to Schellenberg. He had one
specialty: abductions. The most spectacular had been that of two British intelligence agents snatched up in a hail of bullets on Dutch territory; the biggest
failure that of the Duke and Duchess of Windsor, when they stopped in
Lisbon. But could he have expected some old friend of the duke's to make a
special trip out from England just to insist that Their Graces set off at once
for those Bahamas they seemed to have so little desire to visit? One of the
rare fiascos of Schellenberg's career. He was soon forgiven, though, and at
the time Rittmeister Momm came to see him, young Obergruppenführer
Schellenberg – by virtue of the fact that he was now assuming, in addition to
the running of AMT VI, the weighty responsibilities of which Admiral Canaris
had just been divested – was the chief of all Germany's foreign spies.

And he was just thirty-three years old.

Contrary to all expectations, Schellenberg found Theodor Momm's proposal
highly interesting. Although his closest associates were far from suspecting
it, Schellenberg himself was actively engaged in making contacts in the
western camp and was one of those who still hoped for a separate peace –
the Reich's last chance to go on fighting in the East.

But one would be wrong to suppose that Schellenberg was acting without
Himmler's knowledge. On the contrary, he enjoyed, if not his approval, at
least his benevolent neutrality. For one day, taking the Reichsführer of the
SS by surprise, Schellenberg had won him over to his own pacifist point of
view.

"Reichsführer," he had asked abruptly, "tell me in which secret drawer
you keep *your* alternate solution for ending the war."

Himmler looked at him in amazement. To have an alternate solution implied that one had it *without Hitler's knowledge*. Negotiate with the Allies and not let him know? Betray the Führer? "Have you taken leave of your senses?" he exclaimed. Nobody had ever dared use such language in his presence before. Schellenberg was undeterred. Surely, the consequences of such negotiations must be clear? If they succeeded, the Allies would not negotiate with Hitler and he, Himmler, master policeman of the Third Reich, would alone be able to take Germany's destiny in hand. He, successor to Hitler! Tempted but unwilling to admit it, Himmler simply allowed Schellenberg an unusually free rein. That happened in the year following the Stalingrad disaster, or in other words at the time of Rittmeister Momm's visit to Berlin.

Gabrielle's confidant was accordingly assured that the Paris services of the Reich Central Security Office would be authorized to issue him the necessary travel orders. The operation must be carried out in total secrecy. Gabrielle would travel incognito. A code was adopted. Her trip could only be designated *Modellhut*. And so, "Operation Hat" was born.

Schellenberg took no notice of his visitor's qualms regarding the absence of guarantees, or proofs of the friendships about which Gabrielle boasted. This was sufficient evidence that he had nothing and no one to fear. "Madrid was the best organized and most highly developed stronghold of German espionage." Schellenberg had often been there and, having a commando unit of the best-trained strong-arm men at his disposal, felt as secure there as in Berlin. His services were on the best of terms with the Spanish police, occupied an entire wing of the German embassy, had no fewer than a hundred agents, quantities of transmitters, a weather-forecasting station – and the entire organization remained in working order until 1945.[12] Also, there was no one among his *V-Männer* more active than Prince Hohenlohe, who was a close friend of his and actually lived in Madrid. As a high-class privateer and noble servant of the National Socialist state, Schellenberg had entrusted him with more than one top-secret mission. In January 1943 it was Max Egon von Hohenlohe who made contact with "Mister Bull," the pseudonym of Allen Dulles, who was directing the American OSS in Switzerland. This being the case, what was there to fear from Gabrielle? If she got out of line, could she escape Schellenberg's men? Whence his decisiveness. However skeptical he may have been about the outcome of Operation *Modellhut*, it was better to risk failure now than live to regret his pusillanimity another day.

*

A cruel disappointment lay in store for Rittmeister Momm when he returned to Paris. He expected Gabrielle to set off at once, but she informed him that it was impossible for her to start without a traveling companion. His "Joan of Arc" had suddenly lost her nerve. Gabrielle said she had never traveled alone in her life, and would furnish no other explanation. Surely he could understand, couldn't he? She had to have someone. The major expected her to name von D., but it was Vera Bate whose presence she required, and in requiring it she created an impossible situation. Vera Bate! An Englishwoman married to an Italian! Had Gabrielle lost her mind? How did she imagine he could go back to Berlin with such a request? How would Schellenberg react to this mad notion? And who did she take him for? Didn't she realize that he was guaranteeing the seriousness of her mission? She would make him look like a fool before it ever began. Her amateurishness would get him into trouble. This was no time for fainting females.

But no argument could sway Gabrielle: she would go to Madrid with Vera or she would not go at all. Could she tell the truth? Admit that without Vera her mission had not the remotest chance of success? Only Vera was close enough to Churchill, and dear enough to him, for his pleasure at seeing her again to overcome the obstacles to the interview. And then there were Vera's connections with the English royal family which, skillfully handled . . . To admit this would be to lose all her prestige in Theodor Momm's eyes, to hand over the leading role to Vera, and there could be no question of that. In the event of success, Gabrielle wanted it all for herself.

So in November 1943, resigned and as though somehow in thrall, the Rittmeister went back to Berlin. If Gabrielle had told him what she had already tried: von D.'s venture and their vain attempts at intimidation; if he had been able to guess what she was hiding, would he have gone?

But Theodor Momm requested his second interview with Schellenberg in complete ignorance of what had already been perpetrated in Rome in an attempt to secure Vera's collaboration.

WHY THE ROSES?

Two weeks earlier, in a secluded district of Rome, a German officer laden with roses . . . a very tall officer and an enormous bouquet . . . red roses. This was not the sort of visitor one would expect on October 29, 1943, and so his arrival at 31, via Barnaba Oriani did not go unnoticed. The officer knocked at the door of Colonel Lombardi's home. A surprise all the more unwelcome as the colonel had left Rome on October 11 and was hiding out in the Frascati hills, where he was not alone. More than one colleague had done the same.

The Eternal City was occupied and more than two-thirds of Italy remained under German control. So when Vera, the lovely Vera, found herself face to face with a German officer, her first thought was that he had come for her husband. But why the roses?

The roses were from Gabrielle.

The sole mission of the caller (some say he was von D. but there is no proof of this) was to deliver into the proper hands a letter from Paris dated October 17, on the Chanel letterhead. Gabrielle gave no explanation for her long silence – it was almost four years since Vera had heard from her. But very suddenly she was remembering her old friend: "Now, my dear, I am sad not to know what has become of you," she wrote. She said she could not bear the thought that Vera had been reduced to painting screens to earn a living. And so she begged her to come and join her at once, giving as a pretext that she wanted to reopen the fashion house. "I'm going back to work," the letter said, "and I want you to come and help me. Do exactly as the bearer of this message tells you. Come as soon as possible, don't forget I'm waiting for you in joy and impatience." The closing expression was in English: "All my love."[13]

How could Vera have guessed at the true motives behind this invitation? She took it at face value, without dreaming for a moment of accepting. The "bearer" insisted. She gave him no hope. It was no, definitely and absolutely.

Exactly what happened when the roses turned out to have no effect? Did von D.'s minions carry out his orders, or did they exceed them? Was Vera a victim of the stupid zealousness of some subordinate, or had von D. decided upon strong-arm tactics from the start?

Early in the morning of November 11, 1943, she was arrested and taken to prison; and there, in the women's prison of Rome, known as the Mantellate, Bastard of England though she was and dear friend of Sir Winston, she was left among the prostitutes and common criminals to meditate upon the cost of refusing certain types of invitation, even when the inviter "says it with flowers."

Arrest Vera? That was a faux pas. One can imagine the noise it made in many a circle. Von D. had piled error upon error and Gabrielle must have been kicking herself for entrusting such an important mission to him. She immediately ceased to have any use for his services and it was at that point, without informing Spatz, that she turned to Theodor Momm.

The Rittmeister had more shocks in store. Back in Berlin for a second talk about Operation *Modellhut*, he was not surprised to see Schellenberg express acute impatience at the news he brought. Operation *Modellhut* was going sour on him, becoming almost unworthy of a man of his stature. The Obergruppenführer's concept of espionage made it unthinkable that he should dabble in second-class matters. His contacts were all at top level. He was in direct touch with General Masson, the chief of Swiss intelligence, and with the British consul general in Zurich, and *he*, at least – and he could prove it, moreover – was permanently in liaison with Churchill, who had even authorized the consul to pursue his "investigations" with the German intelligence services. Schellenberg had had personal assurance of this; so why was he wasting his time on *Modellhut?* And why had this Rittmeister come all the way from Paris to tell him that the operation could not get under way unless the principal were accompanied by a traveling companion? It was absurd, grotesque. Schellenberg had far more serious matters on his mind.

This was the time of Cicero.* The secret services were all on edge, attempts on the Führer's life were becoming increasingly frequent, and the infighting had reached a level of violence well beyond anyone's wildest dreams – Himmler against Canaris, Kaltenbrunner against Schellenberg – aggravated by the clumsiness and fatuousness of Ribbentrop; in short, with the threat of disaster looming ever larger, madness was slowly taking over. For that was exactly what it was, a form of collective insanity. One day Hitler solemnly considered deporting the pope to Avignon, and Himmler spent the whole day persuading him to change his mind. A short while later it was Ribbentrop, summoning Schellenberg and informing him of weighty decisions – he was going to ask for an audience with Stalin and shoot him point-blank in the course of it. Would Schellenberg agree to accompany him on this suicide mission? So, *Modellhut*, after all – was it as farfetched as it sounded?

Walter Schellenberg asked the name of this traveling companion. Rittmeister Momm, knowing nothing of Spatz's doings in Rome or of Vera's fate, told him, along with her address and certain other particulars. The Obergruppenführer ordered an investigation and his services in Rome produced the information almost immediately. It came like a bolt from the blue: the woman had been in prison for a fortnight. On whose orders, yelled Schellenberg. Agents not working for AMT VI. That was not good enough; and Schellenberg repeated that he wanted to know who was responsible and within the hour. Then those who were responsible, Gestapo agents who were

* Cicero was the mysterious spy working for Germany in Istanbul who showed Hitler Allied D-Day plans. He has been the subject of many books and films.

made extremely nervous by these queries from such high quarters, confessed that Vera had been imprisoned on their orders and added that they had most pertinent reasons for their action. They alluded to some act of espionage. Vera Bate an English spy! Rittmeister Momm, stupefied by this revelation, observed in his report, "It was surprising to see Schellenberg swallow the pill, which was especially bitter to him."

Was it really all that unpalatable? And if it had been, why need he swallow it?

Vera in prison for espionage was an excellent thing from Schellenberg's point of view. At last, Operation *Modellhut* was beginning to shape up. That taint of amateurishness had been removed. And besides, Vera, a relative of the Windsors – albeit bar sinister – was a prize catch. An enemy agent, dragged out of prison and skillfully employed, can almost always be turned into a sort of hostage.

From then on, Operation *Modellhut* was launched with a vengeance.

The agents chosen to retrieve Vera from prison on November 29 were handpicked by Schellenberg himself. He got in touch with the SS chief in Rome and ordered him to supervise her release in person. Vera must be treated with all the consideration befitting a woman of the best society. Everything was done to eradicate the loathsome impression undoubtedly left by the memory of her arrest and the conditions of her imprisonment.

The colonel of the SS acquitted himself of his task and repeated that Vera must return to Paris where, he said without further explanation, her friend Gabrielle Chanel was anxious to see her at the earliest possible moment. He drew attention to the very special treatment she would receive and the arrangements that had been made to render her removal as painless as possible. Rather than taking her home, where no preparations had been made to receive her, they had reserved a suite of rooms for her in the best hotel in Rome. Princess Windischgraetz, who lived there, had been notified of her imminent arrival. The two ladies were dear friends. They would be in adjoining rooms. The next day Vera would be taken to the via Barnaba Oriani to pack whatever personal effects she might require, then two officers would drive her to Milan and, to allay any apprehensions Vera might have concerning the object of their trip, one of her friends, an old, prewar friend, had agreed to accompany her. This friend, who had been living in Rome for many years without anyone's being able to figure out how he had avoided the draft, was a German aristocrat, a great connoisseur of the arts, a person of refinement, and an extremely fastidious dresser who assumed sly expressions of complicity when informing you of some masterwork which an acquaintance of his was trying to sell off, poor dear . . . Something of an antique dealer, in short, but not without charm, and a man who wouldn't hurt a fly: Prince Bismarck, or rather Eddie, as he was known to the ladies of Rome and his youthful boyfriends. Because this Eddie who was to be traveling with Vera was an absolute pet of the palazzo set.

As further proof of his solicitude, the SS chief warned Vera that she mustn't be surprised to see Prince Bismarck in an SS uniform; a mere formality, you understand, but otherwise he would not have been allowed to come with her. Orders were strict on that point and vehicles carrying civilians were stopped without question. So . . . the prince had been very understanding.

Now, nothing in all this speech altered Vera's intentions.

Convinced that the invitation was a cover for some threat, she gave Gabrielle's second emissary exactly the same answer she had given the first. It was no. She repeated that she would not leave Rome on any pretext or for any destination whatever.

The colonel referred back to Berlin.

Schellenberg sent word that one was terribly sorry to offend, but it was either Paris or an immediate return to prison.

Vera took the night to think it over. What was the meaning of all this superproduction? All this fuss, just to help Gabrielle reopen her fashion house? It was not credible, and Vera couldn't make up her mind to go. Where were they taking her? Paris was exile. And when would she see Berto, her husband, again? If this departure, as she believed, was merely a disguised deportation, wouldn't it be better to go back to prison? In the Mantellate the conditions of hygiene and the promiscuity were atrocious but at least it was Rome. And the Allies were in Salerno and the liberation might come any day. If the English entered Rome her brother George Fitzgeorge, an intelligence officer, would soon hear of her plight. And her husband – whom she dared mention to no one – her husband, too, was not far away; he had found a hiding place at the Aldobrandinis'. In other words, on papal land; and Berto, for sure, the moment Rome was liberated, would be able to get her out. Whereas in Germany, in Germany . . .

What counsel did that last night in Rome bring to her? The next morning Vera had changed her mind. She accepted. She would go to work in France. But since they were trying to make this forced departure look like a picnic, she would insist upon taking Taege with her. And too bad if they didn't like it. In her husband's absence, who else could look after him? Poor Taege. He would live in Paris with her. He would keep her company.

Long-legged, the size of a young bull calf, Taege belonged to a venerable breed of dog unknown outside Italy. A mastiff of Calabrian origin who, with his harsh short coat and his easily revealed canines, was highly intimidating. The SS's reaction to the news that the lady intended to take this monstrous brute with her was rather cool, but they didn't dare disturb Schellenberg again. Would he allow the lady to travel with her dog or not? Hadn't she been politely requested to make herself as inconspicuous as possible? Whereas she was actually doing just as she pleased. And now . . . On the roads of Italy a party of SS with an Englishwoman and a dog: such a thing had never been seen. She was taking liberties; who did she think she was? Despite all their little attentions, she had refused to wear the military coat in which Prince Bismarck had suggested she wrap herself, and she seized every opportunity to needle them.

But however taken aback the members of her escort may have been, their dismay was nothing to that of Theodor Momm when he met Vera in Milan. So here was this traveling companion, and with her came a dog . . . Might as well have been a horse. What was he supposed to do with this Taege? At close quarters, the brute was terrifying. And he took up so much space! How could he persuade Vera to leave him behind, what line should he take? At this point it occurred to him that Gabrielle had some rather peculiar friends.

It was night, time to rest. Overnight accommodation had been arranged in the home of a great Milanese lord whose residence was like a royal palace. Arcore – the handsomest castle of the region. Everyone did his utmost to cheer her up. In vain. The host worked like a trojan. Tried to be amusing. But, for God's sake, what was she so afraid of? If this trip had been made into such a grand affair, she couldn't possibly imagine she was being abducted? It might be an unpleasant interlude, yes, and he could understand her anxiety, but still, she really had no cause to complain. Her escort was worthy of her. In the car, Prince Bismarck and two superb young men; in Rome the company of Princess Windischgraetz; in Milan that of Count Borromeo; what more did she want? She answered that she was not happy to leave Rome. She said Rome because she couldn't say Berto; if she did, they'd go making trouble for him too.

The next morning at dawn, exasperation flared up anew. Vera found herself deposited on a flying field where the plane awaiting her was so tiny that there was only room in it for herself, the pilot, and the Rittmeister. Once more she expressed, with vehemence, her views of the disgusting behavior of people who took people places against their will. The worst of it was that

Taege was being separated from her and she was powerless to stop it. Then Prince Bismarck, looking miserable in his borrowed uniform and wholly undelighted at the prospect of transporting the beast – he clearly would have far preferred the sole company of the two young drivers whom he could have engaged in artistic conversation, with allusions to Roman antiquities – Eddie, a true prince, solemnly swore to look after Taege until the end of the war.

And the plane took off for a tumultuous flight during which, despite all the Rittmeister's good intentions, Vera never once opened her mouth. About as hospitable as a prison gate. You'd have thought talking hurt her jaw. The worst was when they were flying over Ulm. Heavy ice formed on the wings and the pilot had to make a forced landing. Paris was too far, he couldn't make it. It occurred to Vera that this was a ruse. Where were they going? To Munich. The logical deduction was that they had lied to her. She imagined herself dead. At this point Momm nearly killed himself, trying to reassure her. The moment the wheels touched ground he found a car. Now where were they going? He was driving her to the railway station. A gloomy ride through the city beside a woman more resentful than ever. The sight of the train and the fact that they both got into a car marked Paris did nothing to reassure her. When they were seated, Vera, who refused to speak any language but English, also refused her companion's polite invitation to accompany him to the dining car. She was so very sure they meant her harm. Whatever the Rittmeister tried, Vera's attitude, unaltered, rebuffed him.

At last the words "Gare du Nord."

There they finally found themselves in agreement on one point: they were in France. But Vera did not really relax until she got to the Ritz. Gabrielle was waiting for her. Then came the only pleasant surprise of the entire trip: it was not in Paris they were going to start sewing again, but in Madrid. Gabrielle's plan was to resurrect Chanel in Spain.

THE SPANISH IMBROGLIO, OR A WEEK IN CASTILLE

Gabrielle kept her friend in ignorance of her true intentions to the end. She talked nothing but fashion. As a result, freed from the doubts that had assailed her throughout her long trip, Vera felt a fresh surge of affection for this Gabrielle with whom she was at long last reunited. They were sisters in work, after all, sisters in adversity. Their alliance, of long date, had stood the strain of time. In her wandering years at the end of the First World War when Vera, a stranger in Paris, her marriage on the rocks and pretty thoroughly discouraged, had been looking for work, where had she found it but with Chanel? People of heart don't forget such things. Now it was Vera's turn to help Gabrielle out. If she felt such an irresistible need to have Vera with her it must be because she didn't feel up to the job herself, and the "reopening" must be compulsory, Vera felt sure of it. But now, a few days after her ordeal, Gabrielle was annoucing their departure for Spain. It became plain to Vera that the adversary had not got the upper hand of Gabrielle after all, that this new development was a pretext to get them out of a tight spot, and that they were going together to a country where the Germans weren't.

So Vera managed it so that she seemed to be rid of every trace of her resentment, even forgetting what she had endured in Rome. But what an extraordinary sight they made, these two women, neither enemies nor allies, playing a faked match and both playing blind. For if Gabrielle was not telling Vera that what impelled her to go to Spain was her certainty that the English ambassador there would see her, Vera was not telling Gabrielle that as soon as she reached Madrid no power on earth would stop her from going to call on that very same ambassador. She had a plan: to join the English in the part of Italy where the Allies were now firmly entrenched. And then? Well, she would try to get in touch with Berto. Once there, Vera would get her husband back for good. A simple message: "Am in Salerno." And he was imagining her in Paris! Salerno! He would certainly wonder what on earth had taken her there. But he would come galloping up in an instant, she was positive, together with Taege, of course. Vera could see them, him on a horse streaking across the slopes, and the other with lolling tongue, following belly to the ground. The dream taking form inside her head, of breakaway horsemen threading their way through military convoys with their hounds, was like one of those English hunting scenes, the kind she painted on screens.

Their stay in Paris was short, the atmosphere amicable, and there were almost no problems, except that Vera often had the impression that all contact with the outside world was forbidden her. Gabrielle never ran out of arguments. Misia? Well, Misia wasn't well, she was out of town; and besides, the telephone being a risky business, it was better not to try anything. Without openly declaring herself, she made sure Vera saw no one but her.[14]

There was a real danger, of course, that someone might express surprise at not having heard before about the fashion house's reopening, or, even worse, about a trip to Spain. For in the days of that long ordeal people were hardly interested in tourism, and trips to Madrid were scarce as bread.

Living in Madrid meant staying, once again, at the Ritz. The elegant coterie encamped there listened delightedly as the page boy trumpeted out the names of the most authentic aristocracy. Here, in conditions of prewar ease, were perpetual arrivals and departures of gentlemen who, although German, for the most part wore civilian dress, spoke Spanish, drove heavy American cars, and lived in dread of the defeat of their fatherland. They watched their adversaries' numbers steadily swelling: other gentlemen – equally well-born, also in civilian clothes, driving the same make of car, and also speaking Spanish – who had been put there to watch them. They were English or American. There was something farcical in this face-to-face confrontation, with each side contriving to keep the balance of power exactly equal. When a new agent made his appearance in the English camp, the Germans immediately received permission from the Spanish government to add an additional spy to their roster. However, General Franco's notions of neutrality being highly individual, only the secret services of the Third Reich received unconditional support from the Spanish police.

We know next to nothing of the trip from Paris to Madrid, except that Vera and Gabrielle were traveling on German safe-conducts; and there is no proof that von D. went with them – he says so, but his intimate friends deny it. Their stay in the Spanish capital, on the other hand, did not pass unobserved.

Immediately upon arrival, they set to work.

We see Gabrielle pretending to have some errand to run, scurrying off to the English embassy. And we see Vera, providentially freed by that alleged errand, unwittingly setting off in the same direction. She is deeply moved; the sounding doorbell and the English employee it instantly summons are shrouded in intense emotion: at last, friendly territory.

A short time later the inevitable occurred: the two women found themselves face to face on their way out the door.

Both stood transfixed, frightened, almost trembling, trying to think of something to say.

It seems to have been Gabrielle who first recovered her aplomb. She is alleged to have said, "Well, this is a fine thing! Are we going to stand here forever staring at each other like a couple of cats?"

And they left the embassy.

Their only recourse now was to show their hands.

Gabrielle told Vera what had brought her to Spain. She withheld nothing. Schellenberg's existence and his involvement in the entire business were minutely described. Now Gabrielle had just seen Sir Samuel Hoare, and her message to Winston Churchill would be passed on, or so she said. Many people believe the Duke of Westminster supported her scheme from the beginning. And although there remains no trace of this encounter in the British archives, both the audience with the ambassador and his acceptance of a message whose contents could easily be verified are conceivable.

But because secrecy was the only thing Gabrielle really trusted, she had taken an unforgivable risk, one that would make her mission forever suspect in the eyes of the British delegation in Spain. Even without this, it might have been so, but her omission was the deciding factor. For with the idea of keeping Vera in reserve as a trump card to play should Churchill seem hesitant to see her, Gabrielle had not even mentioned her presence in Madrid to the ambassador. How was she supposed to know that the other woman was talking to an intelligence officer at the very same moment? And Vera had left nothing out. She told it all, everything – Rome, the dreadful ordeal of the prison, the conditions in which she had left Italy, her stay in Paris, the German safe-conducts . . . The question immediately arose why the two women contradicted each other. One said all, the other almost nothing. One claimed that Churchill would be glad to see her, the other wanted permission to join the army in Italy. So how did it happen that they were traveling together with safe-conducts issued on the same day by the same authorities?

Their case looked highly fishy.

However, not everything in the enigma was negative. One of the women had made herself famous, the other had the highest possible connections. Without hazarding so much as a half-step forward, the British agents decided they could not simply ignore the affair. They asked London for instructions. But the trouble with Gabrielle's scheme was that it was one tiny drop in a huge bucket of far more serious ones. London did not see any need for haste; but in Madrid the ladies were showing signs of impatience. So the ambassador decided to set up a sort of permanent liaison with them, judging, whatever else might be true, that they deserved his attention. The person chosen to perform the liaison was a young man who, although English, never gave any other name but Ramon. Gabrielle never discovered what was behind the pseudonym that so irresistibly summoned up the days of brilliantine and the tango, however totally it was contradicted by the fair good looks of the person bearing it.

The following days were decisive. Ramon showed more signs of trusting Vera than Gabrielle, a distinction instantly perceived by the latter. Her antennae now told her that Ramon was not going to put himself out on behalf of her mission.

And it seemed to her that Vera was also failing to exert her full potential to that end.

Ramon, indeed, had something to do with this.

He clearly implied that it would be greatly to Vera's advantage not to appear in the company of Chanel. According to him, the only thing to do, if she wanted to return to her country on the terms she desired, was to leave the Ritz and stay elsewhere. With what money? she wondered. Help must be found. Vera met more and more people, anywhere and anyhow. Gabrielle saw that she was no longer even consulted about the right people to see or not to see – a detail that might at first hand appear trivial but was actually significant.

One time, Vera invited the Marchese di San Felice, an Italian diplomat who had refused to join forces with Mussolini's "Fascist Republican Government" and who lost his post as a result. He and his wife, victims of a social cold shoulder as general as it was ignoble, had been living as though imprisoned in the scorn of those who, a few weeks before, had been all smiles.

Their appearance in the Ritz lounges inevitably provoked various reactions. Gabrielle thought Vera was playing her for a fool, abusing her hospitality. To prove that she was not taken in, and using an insulting tone of voice just to annoy her, she held out her cup to Vera during the sacrosanct tea hour and smirked, "English prisoners are always given free tea."

Which could be translated, "Don't forget you're in my hands." Strange words, and they cut Vera deeply. She, a prisoner? Just you wait and see. The incident, small as it was, confirmed her determination to end an association that no longer had anything positive to offer. She gave herself two days and not a minute more. Events, overtaking her, were to hasten her decision.

Suddenly the news spread through Madrid that Churchill was unwell. In London, Attlee told the House of Commons on December 16, 1943. A hastily drafted health bulletin was issued. Before they even knew he was ill, the English learned that "the Prime Minister had a quiet night. A certain improvement in his general condition was observed."

Ramon, besieged by questions, confessed that Sir Winston had caught "a bad cold" on his return from Teheran. That was the official version and no one knew anything more, except that the consequences of the "bad cold" were a prescribed period of rest. No one could tell in advance how long it would last. Sir Winston's meetings, despite the urgency and enormity of his task, had all been canceled. This gave Gabrielle clear notice that she would have to abandon any idea of obtaining an audience with the Prime Minister, who, under doctor's orders, was seeing neither his own cabinet nor the Allied commanders.

Both Gabrielle and Vera trusted their informers.

Would she have succeeded in communicating with Sir Winston if he had been well? Nothing is less sure. But now she was convinced that he was seriously ill. Old Winston . . . "He's really and truly ill," she told Vera in an anxious voice. "Maybe even going to die . . ."

"At the end of his tether," noted his personal physician on December 10, 1943. "He is certainly heading straight for collapse."[15] And the next day, "As the Prime Minister was moving slowly towards the plane I observed that his face had turned a shade of grey that I didn't like at all." Churchill was on his way to meet General Eisenhower, who was waiting for him in Tunisia. "When he finally reached this house he literally fell into the first armchair," the doctor continued; and later, "He did nothing at all today, he seems not even to have strength enough to read the usual telegrams. I am very worried." Capsized . . . Suddenly there in Carthage, a bad night, a threat of pneumonia. And fear gripping his friends and a specialist coming from London and the question nobody dared ask: "Is Churchill going to die?"

At last, the old sailor who had so long navigated the raging swells of war, stopped in his tracks, laid out by bad luck, suddenly recovered that strength to hope that was the source of his vitality. As soon as he could travel, the Prime Minister went to convalesce in that unique poem of summits, sand, sky, and palm trees called Marrakech.

Gabrielle had waited in Madrid. In vain. No more illusions: she would not see Sir Winston and Operation *Modellhut* had failed.

She told Vera that she was going back to Paris.

Was she to count on her friend?

Vera said no, she was staying on in Spain. Gabrielle assumed that she would change her mind, having no money, and turn up at the railway station the next day. But Vera left the hotel that evening and Gabrielle heard no more of her. Where was she? To have made that whole long trip just to lose her. A bitter pill! For Gabrielle the entire incident had become nonsensical.

Vera stayed first with the Marchese di San Felice; then the mysterious

amon, possibly Brian Wallace, an honorary secretary to the embassy, became
er host. She went back to earning her living by painting equestrian scenes
n cocktail tables and screens. The suspicions she had aroused proved tena-
ious, however. After several months, news came from London that she
ould not be allowed to return to Italy until Rome had been liberated. The
.llies entered the city in July 1944, yet Vera had to wait until January 1945
ɔ go home. The Spanish imbroglio transcended all the bounds of imagi-
ation, however – it was the exiled queen of Spain who, wishing to assist
his "left-handed" relative of hers, undertook to transmit from Switzerland
ɔ Italy the letters Vera wrote her husband from Madrid.

Back in Paris, Rittmeister Momm was becoming intolerably anxious
bout Gabrielle's absence, and he was extremely relieved to see her back.
'era had let him down? So what! It was in the cards. One of the two had
eturned, and that was enough; by that time, nobody hoped for more.

Gabrielle possessed that strange power of preserving her faith in unfore-
eeable futures. Who could say what was inside her?

Despite the fresh reverses that the armies of the Third Reich were suffering
n every front at once, despite everything that was reported – towns being
ulverized all over Germany, the fate of women and children weighing heavily
ɔn the fighting men's morale, and thousands of homeless wandering the
treets specterlike day and night, unable to find the least trace of a shelter
- Gabrielle, at that time and in that world which was falling apart whole
ities at a time, was coolly settling accounts.

First of all, with Vera – that woman-in-love whom she must convict and
.entence. Her first act was to write her, and what a tone she took: Cursed
ɔe all husbands! It was happening all over again, just as in the days of
Adrienne and Deauville. And under every phrase one could feel the surge
ɔf exasperation of the eternally disappointed woman confronting the Other,
.he false friend who confessed that all she was waiting for was the moment
when she could rush madly away to rejoin the man she loved.

So in the last days of 1943, Vera received a letter from Gabrielle,
ɔrought by no one knows whom: four hurried pages written in pencil in
a firm hand, never mind the mistakes, and with no words crossed out. In
appearance somewhat haughty, her writing was still redolent of the lessons
she had learned at the turn of the century from the canonesses of Moulins.
It was one of those proud, curving hands designed to prove how very
much one really was "a lady." A lady with a sharp voice and a stern tone
ɔf command:

Dear Vera,

In spite of the frontiers everything travels quickly! I know of your betrayals! You will gain nothing from them, except to have hurt me deeply.

I did everything in my power to render your stay less painful. Patience, money, etc. But I could not become rabid on the Italian subject, or, on the German subject, hear or say low things which I leave to the retarded. To scorn your enemy [she writes *ennemie* in the feminine, which is ambiguous: was Germany the enemy, or Vera? Both are feminine in French] is to debase yourself.

My English friends cannot blame me, at any rate, or find the least thing wrong in what I have done.

That is enough for me.

I have seen M.* I said nothing that could make trouble for you. If you want to go back to Rome, forty-eight hours after you reach Paris you'll be there with your real friends!!

Your indifference on the subject of my business in Spain makes it unnecessary for me to talk about it! But I have good news and hope for success.

I have a most pleasant memory of your friend "Ramon" although his help in business matters seems negligible.

I will also tell you that I did not leave Spain under orders – I have given a lot of them in my life and not taken any yet. But my visa was up. S.† was afraid I might have problems.

I hope with my whole heart that you find your happiness again.

But I am surprised to see that the years have not taught you to be more trusting and less ungrateful.

Times as cruel and sad as these should be able to work that sort of miracle.

The letter was signed "Coco."

There will never be an opinion of Chanel expressed without a "but." Knowing her, would we suppose that she could feel obliged to go to Berlin and report on her failed mission? Surely not. But that is what she did.

Which of her friends, which of her employees or customers, seeing her working on one of her creations with the maniacal concentration, the fussy

---

*   Gabrielle employed only the initial, and gave neither his name nor that of Schellenberg in full.

†   Clearly stands for Schellenberg.

nd sometimes infuriating pernicketiness she brought to her work – Gabrielle neasuring the freedom of movement of a sleeve, gauging the length of a kirt, vigorously denouncing this or that fault which she then proceeded to ssail with great snips of the scissors; which of them could have imagined he same Gabrielle ten or more years before, confronting insecurity in every ossible form: traveling across the Europe of that day and the German towns - she had to sit out a long air-raid alert the night she spent in Berlin – and vholly possessed by the idea of justifying Schellenberg's confidence in her? Was it for him, for that unknown man, the German, that she sought to ppear as an incarnation of feminine valor? Was it because she was sixty ears old that year, was it the fear of having passed the age of love, that nade her so greedy for reassurance? What was she so afraid of that made er risk so much? And as for pretending she didn't realize the possible consequences – that would be to call her stupid, and who could be made o believe that?

Something very sad took Gabrielle to Berlin, a clutching hand from the depths of the interminable disappointment into which she felt herself sinking. What light can you turn to when that kind of chill grips you? What about Spatz? Wasn't he enough? Oh, please leave me alone with your Spatz and what importance did he give it. Between the comfort she enjoyed in a Paris of war and want, between her cloistered life and the madness of her ultimate attempt to exist *other than* in the pages of fashion magazines, there is room only for Gabrielle's secret truth, made of melancholy and a dark despair.

So in the closing days of 1943 there she was in Berlin, with Schellenberg, in her moment of greatest glory. Did he see her in the office-fortress he was then occupying as head of all the German secret agents – the office he describes proudly, one is tempted to say joyfully, plainly showing that he found his role exceptionally pleasant? "There were microphones everywhere, in the walls, under my desk, in every lamp, so that every conversation, every smallest sound could be recorded . . . My desk was like a miniature *blockhaus*. Two automatic weapons were built into it, which could fill the entire room with repeating fire at a moment's notice. If in danger I had only to press a button and two machine guns began firing simultaneously. Another button set off the alarm signal ordering the guards to surround the building immediately and block every exit." How much time did Schellenberg give to his famous caller? And if it is true that "France is *par excellence* the country of the dangerous forty-year-old,"[16] then did our sixty-year-old do better, did she raise the record? Did she succeed in captivating the fair young host of that black palace? And what did she think of this man who, as part of his job and without one twitch of a face muscle, had watched the menace growing one by one, followed by the worst conceivable cruelties, and finally by the greatest shame the western world has ever known? Attractive, this beast of prey? There would be no point in denying it. Admirably courteous, loftily reserved. Above the discreetly scarred chin was a mouth with fleshy lips that knew neither insult nor sneer and seemed made only for laughter and love. The faultless nose showed, as it should, no slightest trace of deviation: a conqueror's nose, as though expressly manufactured to illustrate the purebred Aryan pedigree. And then the eye – by its immobility, the eye alone terrified, and one gasps to think of the horrors that eye witnessed.

Did Schellenberg, when Gabrielle saw him, exhibit one or another of the special attributes of his job of which he was so proud? Hollywood* could have asked no more of one of its actors. You listened to him speaking casually of that hollow tooth he screwed into his jaw whenever he went on mission – to be used in case of capture. "It contained a dose of poison large enough to kill me in less than thirty seconds."† But for added safety he also wore a unique ring adorned with a cabochon stone of finest blue. Beneath the gem lay a capsule containing a sizable dose of cyanide.

Will anyone tell us which of the two, Gabrielle or this servant of Nazi Germany, listened to the other more intently? All we know is that what happened in that office was neither a routine meeting nor an incident that can be left unmentioned in her long story; for on the day of reckoning, when the twilight of the false prophets was at hand, Gabrielle was the woman to whom Schellenberg appealed, and Schellenberg was the man she helped in a moment in history when nobody else would have dared.

Whoever would be a clear-sighted witness scrutinizing the successive stages of this woman's life, torn between respect and irrepressible aversion, between desire to absolve and rejection: such a witness can but keep silent and think in pain of the unfathomable tragedy that was being enacted in

---

* "Hollywood could not have asked for more," says Alan Bullock in his preface to the memoirs of Walter Schellenberg. And he adds, referring to the two passages quoted here, "But the point which is only too easy to miss is that Schellenberg was not exaggerating when he wrote this."

† It is known that Himmler had recourse to such a capsule, hidden in a cavity in his gums, which he used to commit suicide on May 23, 1945. Just as an officer of the British intelligence went to inspect the prisoner's mouth, "Himmler bit on his vial and was dead in twelve minutes, despite frantic efforts to keep him alive . . ." (Quoted from William L. Shirer, *The Rise and Fall of the Third Reich*, Simon and Schuster, New York, p. 1141.)

men's hearts then. A tragedy all had to watch, a tragedy that went beyond even the overt warfare and the conflicts opposing men and nations, a destiny of suffering born simply from war, yes, from war and from blood.

In comparison with what women who collaborated openly had to endure, or with what was inflicted upon those whom a German romance designated as the victims of popular revenge, Gabrielle's hell was brief.

About two weeks after General de Gaulle was cheered down the Champs Elysées in a melting-pot of people of every class, arousing the indignation of nostalgics of the German order and many others, Gabrielle Chanel was arrested.

A holy rage would engulf her every time she had to recall the day when two young men had dared to enter the Ritz at eight o'clock in the morning. They went straight to her room and there, quite casually, they asked her to come with them, by order of the Committee. What Committee, if you please? The Clean-Up Committee.*

One could understand, listening to the rare witnesses to the scene as they described her allowing herself to be seen by the hotel staff in such low company, wild with panic but mastering her terror and walking out of the hotel between two youths wearing *sports shirts* and the most hideous sandals imaginable, two thugs with revolvers stuck in their belts, two brutes, in a word, two fomenters of revolution, why she was so vicious on the subject of *fifis* and *résistants* after that.

The worst thing of all was that they had said "tu" to the doorman.

A few hours later she was back, and could tell her friends, to whom the intruders' gross behavior was so insulting, that she had been arrested by mistake and that one must be careful never to trust such people. So that's what it was, their "people's army"! France had fallen into the hands of madmen, they were all sick in the head. Anyway, she was leaving the country. But could she go? Then she must have been cleared of all suspicion. Those who heard her could not help wondering. Who had saved her? To whom or what did she owe her impunity?

For the Clean-Up Committee to hold her such a short time, Gabrielle must have possessed (and kept up her sleeve for the day that could not fail to come) the high ace that would trump her judges. Because after the Liberation there was no getting away with evasions or fobbing off the

---

* In French, *épuration*, purge or purification. The organization that settled accounts with collaborators after the Liberation.

inquisitors with fairy tales. Only protection from very high places could restore to Gabrielle the freedom which others less guilty than she had lost.

So she must have been saved by an order that could not be disobeyed.

Whose order? No trace of it, nothing remains that will enable us to answer this question with the slightest degree of certainty.

A very short time later, while other soldiers, GIs this time, were crowding into the Chanel shop after those bottles of No. 5 whose qualities the Germans had been savoring only a few months before, Gabrielle, free to travel and apparently unhindered, speedily left for Switzerland; and less than two years later, the ease with which she obtained permission to go to the United States, where she stayed for a short time, is no less unaccountable.[17] Applications for visas to the States were very severely scrutinized during the five years following the war. But while others were interrogated at length and forced to wait and to prove their innocence, crossing the frontiers into America created no more problems for Gabrielle in 1947 than had her previous precipitous departure for Switzerland. The need to tell things the way they are compels us to observe that even then, in that brand-new peace, justice was not the same for everybody.

CONCERNING TRUTH GLIMPSED AMONG THE CORNFIELDS OF CONVERSATION

The truth is difficult, sometimes maddening. Nothing is ever where you go to look for it. People who are said to know and universally regarded as knowing, yield, in the moment when their memories serve them at last, nothing but anecdotes for which one has no use. The enigma is left as entire as before, and the thing sought continues to refuse to be found. The truth is seldom a fleck of foam on the surface of a conversation; more often it is a black hole into which one is pitched as at the back of a cave – scratchings are there to which, at first glance, one attaches hardly more significance than to a slip of the pen, some accident of writing or recital, some parenthesis which an often tedious interlocutress opens after one has already ceased to listen.

Sometimes one puts all one's hopes in the work of historians, analysts, and chroniclers; one pores over, sorts, and classifies, takes apart invisible gears and for one mad instant expects to see rising from the dust of ancient files the thing that is slipping through one's fingers. And indeed, very rich in truth are certain archives, which become heartrendingly barren once one is convinced that they will not yield the thing one hoped to find in them.

And how true it is that "rich" does not mean the same for everyone, and what a good thing that some can shout, "What treasures!" while others think, "How insignificant!"

But what was it Mme Denis, the gardener's widow, was saying, in the little sitting room on the rue Alphonse de Neuville at Garches to which she has retired? What was it she said that suddenly stripped all the insignificance away?

In appearance, the only value of her testimony was its amazing futility, which seemed to correspond fairly well with the atmosphere of Bel Respiro, that black-shuttered house where Gabrielle once lived. But then suddenly, without having in the least situated the rooms in the house or given the objects their "feel" or the garden its thousand moods, here was this witness from the twenties telling things that seemed more sensed than known, things one didn't very much want to hear because, if you think about it, indiscretion is often a burden and one comes to resent the person who proffers it. In the theater things are very different, and entanglements can be moving there which, when revealed late at night in the shadow of the thickets ... But for that, one needs *The Marriage*, one needs Mozart, and not every storyteller is as good as the abbé Da Ponte, just as Henri Bernstein was no Cherubino and besides, one can't quite make out how the widow of the former gardener at Bel Respiro would have gone about singing "*Ratto, ratto, il birbone è fugito*,"* she being English and not having the right voice anyway.

So what she was implying – namely, that Gabrielle and Henri Bernstein, whose gardens were adjoining, used to meet every evening on a hidden path which the narrator's gardener husband promptly baptized "lovers' lane" – was a prime example of the type of anecdote about which, if you'll pardon the expression, one couldn't give less of a damn. For one thing, cataloguing the loves of Henri Bernstein would be as arduous an undertaking as compiling an annotated bibliography of the telephone directory; and for another, one can't see why those particular two, if they took it into their heads to be lovers, should refuse themselves the comfort of some furnished accommodation or other; and for a third and most important, never did Gabrielle speak ill of Bernstein – which would tend to indicate that she had never been his mistress. For all her short-term lovers were the objects of her deadly hatred – those men she had yielded to long ago to forget, to exorcise the memory of Boy, in the days when she gave her body its freedom the way other people dive into the Seine.

---

* "Quickly, quickly, the knave has fled!" from Mozart's *Marriage of Figaro*.

But now, how should one put it, somehow in the gardener's widow's tale the lighting changed so abruptly that one would have thought a fuse had blown or the lighting technician had made a mistake. Because there were no more black shutters in the woman's story, and hardly any Gabrielle. And Stravinsky, where had Stravinsky gone? And why had the piano suddenly fallen silent? We truly heard the melodies of Pergolesi played on that piano, though; and *Le Sacre*, for goodness' sake, what about *Le Sacre?* Not a sound now, and what on earth was the woman saying? She was saying, "Years and years went by." Suddenly some tragedy had stilled the little tune of melancholy and libertinage she had been singing here. What was it about? The arrival of army officers. At Garches? Yes, at Garches. Nothing surprising in that. The Germans were quartered there for four years, this time it was the English. What a mix-up! The owners of the luxury cottages and handsome villas hardly had time to realize what was happening when one requisition followed another. All of a sudden Garches became pure English-speaking.

As is the rule with every army in the world, the best rooms, those with the bay windows and the walls hung with bouquets of flowers on chintz or silk, had been allocated to the higher ranks, while the subalterns . . . Ah, well, billeting officers, English or German, it's all the same thing. So the cooks and chauffeurs, secretaries and telephone operators made do with what was left over. There was no shortage of bungalows about the place, and little villas with gardens. The rooms where Gabrielle's Raouls used to sleep, and Grand Duke Dmitri's Piotrs, and the maîtres d'hôtel and their wives, the Josephs and Maries, now nursed the slumbers of the staff of the British command. They made out very nicely, thank you; but they did cause a considerable commotion in the district. Would the streets of Garches ever recover the refinements of the first years of the century? It had been a long, long time since anyone had met one of those sports roadsters or convertible cabriolets, those Isotta Fraschinis or Delaunay-Bellevilles in the rues Edouard Detaille or Alphonse de Neuville, and the young man who had found a roof not far from Gabrielle's former gardener's widow, high command chauffeur or not, drove a jeep like everybody else.

A soldier far too busy to be much interested in the past history of the pretty suburb he was quartered in, but happy even so to find an English neighbor he could talk to.

And so it was that one day he heard her tell some vague tale about a fashion designer, some famous woman who had lived for years in the last house as you went down on the left, you know, the one with the black shutters and the big cedar . . . And the soldier had inquired – out of politeness, perhaps, because really he hardly cared – why the woman was so famous and what her name was. Come again? He asked her to repeat the name twice, because it rang a bell somewhere.

He had heard the name the previous night, first in the mouth of his captain and then in that of the colonel. And they had talked about it in the mess hall that day, there was a great fuss and fury about it. The name had remained engraved in his ear: *Cha-nel, Cha-nel.* An officer had been ordered to look everywhere for her, that very Chanel, why, it was really too bad she didn't live on the rue Alphonse de Neuville anymore, then it would have been easy to find her. The rub: impossible to lay hands on her. At her business address people acted as though she had disappeared for good. At the hotel across the way, same story. In the end, they had run her to the ground in a hotel on the outskirts of Paris and it was high time too because from the way the radio chaps were talking London was getting very antsy over the thing. London, was it? asked the gardener's widow. The young man confirmed that it was in London that people were worried about Chanel and that although he couldn't swear to it (but like that, you know, just a guess and on account of the general bustle) it must have been one of the *Old Man*'s secretaries who had telephoned, yes, madam, one of the secretaries of the Old Man in person!

It must be added that the old woman at Garches had not followed her young compatriot's explanations too closely because she confessed to not knowing who this person was that he kept calling the "Old Man." Who was he? The young man exclaimed that he had never heard such a funny question in his life. And burst out roaring with laughter because the Old Man, good Lord, woman, who else could it be but Churchill?

And so it is that, contrary to all expectations, through a sort of indiscretion, or by accident if you prefer, a gleam of truth flickered in the night of words, on the question of who might have saved Gabrielle after the Liberation. But one wouldn't want to insist upon it, for it would really be quite absurd to take any of this as gospel.

First Epilogue 1945-1952

"Such is peace-loving France, and she will exterminate all who come to trouble her seamstresses, philosophers, and kitchens."

— JEAN GIRAUDOUX, *Siegfried et le limousin*

BEING OUTSIDE

Switzerland may not really be what one could call exile, especially as they speak French in Lausanne. But that's what it was in those days, and nobody thought of it as anything else.

Staying in palaces at Ouchy or Geneva, shuttling from one ski resort to another, dragging from one hotel to the next – Gabrielle lived there as an *émigrée*; and the brief periods she spent in France, the freedom she enjoyed to go to La Pausa for a few weeks every summer, made no difference.

Danger had driven her out. She behaved like the peasant who knows what it means to "hole up." She abandoned country and work, and her whole past was far, far behind. Would anyone claim that that's not exile? That state of permanent uprootedness and, even worse, of inactivity? Then, if we add what the Switzerland of those years had to offer in the way of misery and confusion, the swarm of refugees who had been treated so well as long as they held the whip – high-ranking Nazi officials, Fascists, Pétainists – but were now pronounced outlaws in their native lands and subjected to endless administrative heckling, and lucky at that if they weren't asked to clear out, because Helvetian hospitality does leave one or two things to be desired; and would anyone claim that the agonizing encounters with this guilty mass of men and women who were criminal in the eyes of the rest of Europe was not exile?

To tell the truth, when Gabrielle headed for shelter she also headed for von D. And that may well have been the main thing – who knows? Perhaps she really decided to live in Switzerland largely so that she could live with him. For her lover had left France; he had crossed frontiers and changed countries as easily as he changed his shirt, and had set about it early enough to be in no danger. One can't help finding it odd, and yet in reality there was no possibility of things happening any other way. Gabrielle's money was in Switzerland, where the profits on foreign sales of perfume had been quietly accumulating throughout the war; and can one imagine Spatz anywhere but where the money was?

They were constantly seen together, Gabrielle and he, and people often assumed they were married. He still cut a fine figure, whereas she . . . Curious how much older she seemed then, at sixty-four or so, than she did ten years later. Maybe it was the inactivity that was gnawing away at her; and then there were signs now and then that things weren't going so well between them. Some claim he beat her, others that she beat him, others that they beat each other. And one knows how violent he could be. To a friend he intimated that her one and only desire was to force him to marry her. You see what sort of "gentleman" he was. But that doesn't alter the fact that they were virtually each other's prisoners. He was held by her money, she by his silence. What a fortune he might have made if he had decided to talk . . .

Nevertheless, just as she had followed those "ghastly thugs" from the Clean-Up Committee with her head held high, so now, despite the general confusion and a romance that was anything but idyllic, Gabrielle kept walking, bloody but unbowed.

For a time, it is true, there was the battle that began in 1945 between Pierre Wertheimer and the Chanel perfume company and herself to keep her occupied. Her victory, in 1947, left her tragically idle. She was rich, worth millions, but where was the joy in all that? And also, the inevitable threats hanging over her were now intensified by a dreadful series of deaths and mourning.

From the moment of the final collapse and unconditional surrender of the German armies,* it was plain as day: Schellenberg did not intend to let himself be forgotten as easily as all that. Gabrielle, therefore, must continue to live in perpetual fear that Operation *Modellhut* might become public.

As the dénouement drew near, the Obergruppenführer of AMT VI was engaged in a sort of last-minute negotiation with Count Bernadotte in Sweden, where news of the capitulation reached him. Did he realize his good fortune? While his chief, Himmler (whom he had left five days before), was committing suicide in Germany, Schellenberg was hastily accepting Count Bernadotte's protection and, on the latter's advice, taking advantage of the brief respite his luck had accorded him to draw up a memorandum in which he recapitulated all his efforts and attempts to wrest a negotiated peace from the Allies.

His extradition order came in June 1945, and Schellenberg went to sit in the dock with the other accused, Hitler's twenty-one former close associates who were now war criminals facing the military tribunal at Nuremberg.[1] But he was left to rot in prison and could not even find out when his trial

---

* On May 7, 1945, in a school building in Reims. The war had lasted five years and eight months.

would begin. Three years went by thus, during which it is unlikely Gabrielle ever knew a moment's peace.

In 1947, as though misfortune were determined Chanel should never catch her breath, José–Maria Sert died. He had taken her by the hand long ago, dragged her out of the night and led her like a child, in Venice. In art, he was a mere remnant. The Duke of Westminster had inherited his gargantuan palaces, whereas Sert had gone on endlessly dreaming them onto the ceilings he decorated and the great theater curtains where he fashioned his sumptuous fantasies, a whole world of disheveled mirages opening onto infinite vistas. A sort of monster, with rather irritating, overly pretty good looks; but who says one can't love monsters? He had divorced Misia, and then remarried her. Gabrielle knew his disappearance would leave her friend broken, and foresaw that nothing now could stop her from abandoning herself to the lethal intoxication of opium.

But that was not the end. Vera went next.

Really, Gabrielle was wondering, was that all there was going to be in 1947? In Rome, in Paris, her life was being torn to shreds. Vera, the beautiful Vera of 1925, back from Madrid at last, Roman once again, and then dead. Even supposing that her first thought when she heard the news was "One less witness!" we have no reason to suppose she escaped the ghoulish summons of the thing no one can prevent: memory, like a dream circling on a conveyor belt, memory alone, like the unmade-up face of the person one no longer loves.

On February 12, 1947, amidst thunderous applause, the "New Look" was born in Paris. A new woman emerged in a dress that went down to her ankles, and a new star appeared in the fashion firmament: Christian Dior. Behind the newcomer – the beginner who dared to sell models to the United States that could not be copied industrially because they required such artistry to cut and such yards and yards of material to make and because of the detail, the opulence of accessories – stood the industrialist financing him: a highly intelligent man, a "textilian" as Rittmeister Momm would have called him, Marcel Boussac. He supplied this beginner in whom no one else believed with a capital of 700 million (old francs – somewhere in the neighborhood of $58,800,000 at that time), and that was only a start.

The American press had to admit that it had been a long time since anything quite so pretty had been seen.

The American dream of holding the western world in thrall by inundating Europe with dresses "made in USA," expressed on more than one occasion with a cynicism lacking the most elementary civility, now became an impossibility. By upsetting every prediction, going against everything reasonable, plumping firmly for the opposite of what one would expect from a conquered country exhausted by years of privation, Christian Dior made Paris a capital of elegance again, and gave back to France the leadership it had lost in both clothing and textile industries.

The American riposte was not long in coming. If one were to tell what was in the air even then, if one were to tell the shameless pillage of ideas or, even worse, the illicit traffic in barely disguised models practiced in every form, if one were to tell . . . But this is not the place, and all that is simply a way of showing how Chanel's sun was being eclipsed. For as the fashion industry was transformed and the international fame of Christian Dior continued to grow, people increasingly forgot what the reign of Gabrielle Chanel had been. What could she do about it? Fashion, hitherto led by women (Jeanne Lanvin, Schiaparelli, and Madeleine Vionnet, among others), suddenly fell into the hands of men such as Balenciaga, Piguet, Fath, and Rochas. It was an inescapable end, and Gabrielle clearly saw something like an implacable "off-season" growing up around her.

But at the same time, perhaps out of sheer habit, she was becoming convinced that the source of the new king's prestige and appeal lay in nothing more than another backward glance, and that the *élégantes* dressed by Dior would, sooner or later, feel an overpowering urge to fling away their waist pinchers, wired bras, heavy interlined skirts, ribbons, and laces. So why get involved in a fight that was not and could not be hers? Her role was certainly not to give women back the corsets she had taken off them more than thirty years before; it was to dress them to live in their time.

She was burning to say so, again and again. But even if she had tried, the position she was in would have stopped her. Better keep quiet.

That silence, that absence, that being outside of her profession which began in 1939, was to continue for almost another ten years.

There is nothing more exhausting in everyday life than the threat of ghosts. Will-come-again-won't-come-again? In Gabrielle's existence the delay of the Schellenberg trial began to assume that role. She assuredly hoped for his acquittal out of sympathy for him, but she hoped for it also and primarily because of the repercussions it would have on her own life. If Schellenberg were cleared at Nuremberg, how could Gabrielle be guilty?

Of the twenty-one accused at the Nuremberg trials, seven of the war criminals got off with prison sentences* and the rest were condemned to death. Apart from Goering, who had managed to get hold of a poison capsule, Frank, Frick, Jodl, Keitel, Kaltenbrunner, Rosenberg, Streicher, Seyss-Inquart and Sauckel had gone to the scaffold by the time Schellenberg was summoned before the judges. His trial lasted fifteen months. The verdict came in April 1949, when Schellenberg saw himself sentenced to "the lightest penalty this Court has inflicted"[2] – six years in prison.

After that date he was permitted to receive letters and parcels from his friends. The first to appear was Theodor Momm, who sent Schellenberg a copy of *Le Siècle prend figure* by Alfred Fabre Luce, along with Count Bernadotte's book on the vicissitudes of the cease-fire, and one imagines with what interest the prisoner perused the latter. Without Bernadotte's advice and protection, how would Schellenberg have escaped alive? But Momm's parcel clearly contained something else, to which he was even more sensitive.

On April 11, 1950, Momm received a letter of thanks from the Nuremberg infirmary, posted by Sister Hilde Puchta, one of the prison nurses. Here is what it said: "Dear Sir, I thank you with all my heart for your Christmas wishes and especially for passing on those of *Modellhut*. Please convey my special thanks to her. Tell her also, in suitable terms, how very much I should have enjoyed taking part in that little reunion!" Gabrielle's good wishes were evidently what had touched him most. The allusion to a sort of memorial reunion of the chief actors in Operation *Modellhut* had aggravated his customary gloom. The worst of it was that he was terribly ill. "I had an operation here on April 7, 1949. In November extreme unction was administered several times and they wired my wife to come. Now I'm a little better again. Depending on how things go, they're thinking of operating again. Let's hope I make it through!"

And then the loneliness. What is longer to live and shorter to tell? To be alone . . . Gabrielle's life began to be entirely built around the word. But had her loneliness ever ceased? How would living in the same city as von D. alleviate it? Their association was a dubious *modus vivendi* at the best of times. It had to be ended.

Beginning in 1950, she was seen less in Switzerland and more often in France, especially at La Pausa. 1950 . . . Judging by dates alone, this was one of the cruelest years of her life, the year Misia died. Gabrielle had imagined everything except that. Misia had been her one and only true ear, the only woman

---

* Life, for Hess, Raeder, and Funk; twenty years for Speer and Schirach; fifteen for Neurath; and ten for Admiral Dönitz.

she ever cared for. She had broken every tie in her life, rejected everything, lied unceasingly, except to Misia. If she had spent her life covering up her tracks – no letters, no photos, no souvenirs – it was because Misia was her memory, and with Misia everything became real again. Without her, Gabrielle found herself cut off from her past, severed, and as though a total puzzle to herself.

No other death left her with this sense of being cast adrift.

Hurrying back to Paris, she did for Misia what she had never done before for any man or woman and never did again. She went into the room where Misia had died and there, humbly, she went through the motions of her trade: she dressed, adorned, embellished. That was her business, wasn't it? She owed her living to that, and that alone. She dressed Misia, combed her hair, put on her jewels, trying to efface the last image which was not quite what Misia would have chosen. Gabrielle smoothed the turned-down sheet for a long time, making the mechanical gesture that came from long years spent teasing away the faults of a piece of material with that knowing hand that nothing ever resisted. She wasn't frightened. None of these gestures frightened her. Straightening the edging of the pillow, plumping up the bolster, making the bedspread hang gracefully – they were the gestures of her trade. The only awful thing was that she was doing for Misia dead what had so often been done for Misia alive. The awful thing was that she was no longer dressing Misia, she was disguising death.

When everything had been inspected down to the smallest detail, and she saw that there was nothing more she could do to bring back any fragment of the past, of the violent and beautiful woman Misia had been, then Gabrielle sat by the side of her friend's bed, as at the edge of night.

In June 1951 Schellenberg was released. Discreetly dressed, courteous as always, but thinner and looking more like a young lawyer without a practice than the engaging "Benjamin" of the SS, Schellenberg took refuge in Switzerland under an assumed name and, as soon as he got there, sent word to Gabrielle. He was penniless; she helped him. It was imprudent, but it would have been still more imprudent to do nothing: Schellenberg had decided to publish his memoirs. His first act upon arrival had been to get in touch with various literary agents who might find him a publisher.

At the time, private diaries were all the rage, and posthumous confessions, and correspondence – any little word left by Hitler's companions or the witnesses of his downfall. Dead, alive, in prison, or on the run, it hardly mattered so long as their testimony existed. There were plenty of buyers in the market, and they all came to see Schellenberg. He talked to them, making no mystery of anything and no effort to hide either his true identity or Gabrielle's friendship for him. He welcomed everyone interested in his project, possibly making more promises than he could keep and even hinting, to the most eager of the agents, that he was prepared to relinquish part of his royalties.

But before he had time to sign a contract the Swiss police requested that he leave the country without further ado. A bad blow. Schellenberg took it better than one might expect. For him even more than for Chanel, being outside had assumed the proportions of an obsession. Out of everything, was he? If they were making him leave, it was because he existed, no? Because they were afraid of him. Then in Italy . . . He found shelter in a house at Pallenza on the shore of Lake Maggiore, all his expenses paid by Gabrielle.[3] There Schellenberg experienced the greatest indignity for a spy, that of no longer being spied upon. He, chief of German intelligence; he, the young and handsome Schellenberg who joined the SS because he fancied the uniform, was no longer of interest to anyone, not even the local police. He sank into apathy. His health deteriorated. He requested a visa for Madrid; its being granted without the slightest difficulty took all the joy out of going for him. And yet how voluptuously he had imagined the thousand and one complications that might have arisen and prevented his going there to make up with his old enemy Otto Skorzeny.* The most ordinary, everyday reconciliation. Everyone, apparently, refused to treat Schellenberg as anything other than a peaceful tourist. What a comedown.

Meanwhile, in Switzerland, Gabrielle was having some unpleasant moments because of him. The literary agent Schellenberg had seemed to prefer turned out to be a cheap crook. It did not take him long to find the link between Schellenberg and Gabrielle Chanel, and he used his discovery to practice "shameless blackmail" and to demand, in return for his silence, "a large sum of money."[4] The sum was paid. Always people to pay off, always silences to buy, and, forever

---

* An Austrian, one of the most enterprising of the gangsters employed by Hitler. It was he who landed on the summit of the Gran Sasso and managed to free Mussolini; he who restored order out of the general chaos in Berlin, leading his armed gangs during the night of July 20, 1944, a few hours after the attempt upon Hitler's life; he who kidnapped the Regent of Hungary in October 1944; and he who, in December of the same year, having assumed command of his special brigade of young Germans who spoke English and wore American uniforms, succeeded with unbelievable boldness in sowing mortal confusion behind the American lines in the Bastogne sector. Acquitted by the Americans, he emigrated first to Spain, where he was cordially received in 1947; and then, like most of the top Nazis who emerged from the ruins unscathed, he settled in South America and lived in prosperity.

and always, evidence to destroy. Would she have to go on defusing bombs until she died? How long could she endure this nerve-racking torture?

On March 31, 1952, Schellenberg died, in a clinic in Turin. He was forty-two years old. With him disappeared the chief witness to Operation *Modellhut*. What did that mean to Gabrielle? At last, the curtain was falling on the most compromising episode of her life. Vera was dead, Schellenberg too. She knew she would have nothing to fear from Vera's husband, Berto Lombardi, who knew everything but would never stoop to the slightest indiscretion. That left Theodor Momm. She obviously knew what to expect of him, too. A man as silent as the tomb. He would sooner die than expose himself to the most innocent question. Gabrielle could congratulate herself upon the fact on more than one occasion.

In 1952 he even discouraged Mrs Schellenberg, of whom he was very fond, from writing to Gabrielle: "With regard to your question concerning Mademoiselle Ch., I believe she has gone to the United States for some time. Things being as they are, I would not advise you to correspond with Mademoiselle Ch." Could a woman who had just lost her husband be more plainly told that she was out of order? Years later, the courageous woman, still battling, was engaged in lengthy litigation with the various Swiss sharks who claimed to be sole owners of her husband's copyright. She had left the shores of Lake Maggiore and gone back to Dusseldorf with her children, and she vainly sought a statement from Gabrielle. Why did Gabrielle not answer? Mrs Schellenberg could not understand this inimical silence. "I understand only too well why she should not have replied," Theodor Momm wrote to her. "In the present state of affairs, one must not hold a grudge against that generous and helpful woman. She knows how much more exposed she is than anyone else, and does not want to bring up the events or turbulence either of the wartime or of the immediate postwar period again."[5] He always found excuses for Gabrielle. He was there, ready to interpose his full height between Gabrielle and whatever might be threatening her.

But despite his loyalty he was unable to account for something that happened, unknown to him, on December 12, 1952, hardly nine months after the Obergruppenführer's death. Passing through Dusseldorf, von D. went to the Schellenberg home, ostensibly to collect for Gabrielle two objects* that Mrs Schellenberg wanted to give her; and he asked for a death certificate, not from the widow's hand – that would not have been enough – but

---

* It has been impossible to learn anything more about these objects. Wouldn't they be more likely to be documents?

an official document. What game was Spatz playing now? And what did he want with it? More blackmail in the air. Maybe some sharper was continuing to persecute Gabrielle, and they had to have the certificate, she and Spatz, in order to silence the people who were still trying to make money out of Operation *Modellhut*, once and for all.

But this is just a hypothesis.

The only thing wrong with it is that it is resolutely unfounded and premature. For there comes a moment when the atmosphere of trickery and complicity in this unending nightmare makes one long to cry out, "Enough!"

Second Epilogue 1953-1971

"Sewing, in the last analysis, means re-creating a world without seams . . ."

— ROLAND BARTHES, *Sade II*

DUE HOMAGE

Here is Gabrielle, at seventy, back in Paris. The remaining years of her life are a second beginning.

No more support of any kind.

From the "elsewhere" that England used to be came news, in 1953, of the death of the Duke of Westminster, the companion of both laughter and tantrums with whom she had lived a few beautiful years in the rain and wind of Scotland, and in the sun too, and the azure of cruises with the sea to send back reflections of carefree faces. How could she not be affected, when it was impossible to doubt that Bend'or, along with Churchill, had helped to save her. But why try to define a feeling that was closer to fear than to any real regret. The man was gone who, without ever making it obvious, had never ceased to wish her well.

Also in 1953, she sold La Pausa. What was the point of a house intended for holidays she no longer felt like taking? Eight years of exile and fifteen of inactivity had quelled all desire for them forever.* And she was carrying so many secrets around inside her, and needed so much strength to convince herself that none of the things she kept pent up in silence would ever come to light. Soon it would be seven years that she had been lurking, ready to slay any shadow that might try to rise out of the darkness of the past, seven years she had been trying to make herself believe that human memories are short and that what one has never admitted never really existed. It was done, yes; but at what cost in wretchedness and fatigue. So now she had but one desire: to cast off useless ballast, houses that had no purpose, gardens she would not enter again, rooms echoing with lost loves. Go away, sell it all, keep nothing but one hotel room and a place to work in, and live for that.

For that's what she had in mind, that and that alone. She wanted to reopen the only house in which she still felt like living, her fashion house. Open it wide, start the workrooms going again, fill them up with employees. Here is Gabrielle Chanel, at seventy, back where she started.

---

* By a curious irony, Winston Churchill then began spending long periods at La Pausa, which had been bought by Emery Reeves, his literary agent.

The woman who, ten years later, had found *through* her work and *in* her work a new vitality and almost a power of seduction, returned from these involuntary holidays marked, one might almost say rusted. What had worn her out most was the constant daily effort of dissimulation. She had also lost all trace of whimsy or frivolity. All that was left was the rigor. Only later, once the triumph of the great comeback was assured, only then did she go back to playing with her gold necklaces, the whiff of chiffon around her neck, a flower stuck in her lapel. But in the months before her resurrection – Robert Doisneau's photograph is there for proof if proof were needed – she was dim and tarnished, and faced the reporters' curiosity brittle, in a woolen skirt and a little black working jacket so unassuming that one would have thought it made in Switzerland. Gabrielle Chanel, this woman who was pretending to resurrect fashion, seemed somehow, in 1953, irredeemably provincial. She was almost outmoded.

The reason was that in matters of dress, the opulence of some and the romanticism of others had become accepted. It was all extremely attractive, moreover; why deny it? To pretend that nobody in Paris knew how to dress women as long as Gabrielle was not around would be to rob her of her victory. Who will believe that Balenciaga, Dior, Givenchy, Fath, Lanvin, and so many more were nonentities? Their fame was at its apex, and to imagine that anyone, at the age of seventy-odd, was going to bring about any transformations in a field they had so brilliantly captured was highly irrational.

The astonishing thing is how perceptive Gabrielle was, choosing just the right moment to prove that fashion as Paris saw it was no longer made for the women who wore it. Because however beautiful it might be, what the Parisians were being offered could only be seen as outside time and space, and every creation contained some allusion to the styles of the past. In fact, all the innovations were reminiscences. So in order to succeed it was necessary *not* to try to compete with the imaginations of the current gods but, without neglecting virtuosity or good workmanship, to strive above all to provide a new purity for everyday life.

The magic of Gabrielle's success is completely summed up in the following passage: "Clothes, abstracted from the flux of the present and considered in themselves, as a form, in their monstrous life on the human body, are weird sheaths, strange vegetations perfectly compatible with the nose jewel and the lip ring. But how fascinating they become when one looks at them in terms of the qualities they lend their possessor. A phenomenon takes place then which is just as remarkable as when a maze of lines traced in ink on a sheet of paper come together to form the significance of some great word. In a well-cut garment, we see proof of this ability to interpret the invisible every day."[1]

Gabrielle was going to fight the "strange vegetations," brilliantly, with garments made remarkable by their pure, *invisible* structure.

THE INDOMITABLE

What was the atmosphere like *chez* Chanel, that afternoon of February 5, 1954? Like a supreme court a few seconds before the verdict. The journalists of England and the United States were seated in the front row next to the French fashion editors, and the combined forces of these ladies on their little gilt chairs formed something in the nature of a supreme court bench. Their anticipation was somehow unsavory, expressing half-hidden eagerness, frank nastiness, or a sort of sneering superficiality. One couldn't quite make out what it was about them that seemed so out of place. Perhaps, after all, it was only the mess they made. At their feet spread the contents of unfastened handbags that looked like beggars' packs. Coats and fat spiral notebooks littered the floor. Cigarettes cocked, pencils poised, the press sat ready to pass judgment.

But where was the accused?

Many women who had come just "to see her" sought Gabrielle in vain. She remained invisible, sitting hidden in her favorite place between the mirrors at the top of the staircase.

Few young people in the crowd. Chanel's clients were all getting on. And the rich beauties of the day were dressed by Dior, or by copies of Dior, and had never heard of Chanel.

Choosing the fifth, her lucky number, as opening day had no effect on the verdict: capital punishment. "The French press was revoltingly vulgar, stupid, and nasty. There were gibes at her age, self-satisfied assurances that fifteen years of silence had taught her nothing. The models paraded through an icy stillness. At the end there were even a few crude remarks uttered in loud voices."[2]

The Paris dailies' headlines and stories on the event tell the whole tale. "Melancholy retrospective," said *Aurore*. "Ghosts of the 1930s gowns" was *Combat*'s view, and the headline even worse – "Chez Chanel à Fouilly-les-Oies," which could be translated, "Out in the sticks with Chanel."

We should add that the French press was not alone in heaping abuse upon her. The London papers showed equal ferocity. "A fiasco" was the

Daily Mail headline. And if anything really hurt Gabrielle it was, beyond all doubt, this sudden contempt on the part of her English friends. For the rest she couldn't care two hoots, and in any event her opinion of the French press was extremely low.

Her behavior during the hours that followed this resounding flop, after all the hard knocks in Gabrielle's long life, was certainly something that commands our respect. The little girl in black, the child of Aubazine, the pupil of the sisters of the Sacred Heart of Mary, the eternal orphan – Gabrielle had been through it all before. Why did people want so fiercely to see her go under? She listened to her friends paying her compliments that sounded more like condolences; listened to them and wanted terribly to laugh. Did they imagine she was taken in? They told her she had won. What semblance of truth was there in all that?

She listened with the implacable cold clear peasant sense that nothing had ever cured her of. Can you persuade a farmer his crop is good when it isn't? And what about the sons of the Ponteils tavernkeeper? If you had told them that the chestnuts weren't really in such bad shape, would they have believed it?

During that night of February 5–6 she confessed to one of her former fitters who had come back for the reopening that in her years of inactivity she had "lost her touch." She conceded it. Between craftsmen you can't pretend. Well then? All she wanted was to get back to work. And you could search her face, her gestures, and her words in vain for any trace of discouragement.

The next morning, facts had to be faced: the appointment book was empty and the place deserted. Gabrielle informed her employees that the opportunity was too good to miss: instead of preparing the collection in the cramped space at the top of the building, she would do her fitting in the main salons. "At least, let's be comfortable. That will be one good thing." The collection? What collection? They'd just had one, thank you. But with stubborn brow, jerking at her scissors on their ribbon, Gabrielle talked of nothing else: "The next collection."

The atmosphere, however, was far from euphoric, and "Chanel stock" had taken a nose dive.

At the perfume company much soul-searching ensued. Was it reasonable to go on financing the efforts of a woman who visibly could no longer "catch on"? A repetition of her failure would be the worst possible publicity for their perfume. The news from the rue Cambon only confirmed their doubts. Gabrielle, her face set, was living in an atmosphere of false confidence. It was as though she was trying to drug herself with words. She carried out her fittings kneeling on the floor in a sort of fury.

Pierre Wertheimer thought he had better go see for himself what was happening to his bellicose associate. What was up with his valiant, his *irrégulière*, his mule-headed Gabrielle? There was no more rivalry between them, no more fits of temper; their quarrels were ended.

He found Gabrielle hard at work, disappointment and anxiety etched in her eyes. Weariness as well, in a new way of walking with lowered head, unlike her old style. She confessed, "I can't go on." And a pang went through her old admirer's heart. How he would have liked to help her . . . Of course, she had betrayed him many a time, and unjustly suspected him many another. But he admired her, and never more than then. What an easy life she might have had if . . . Wasn't he still there? Why did she want this revenge so badly? But then, what could he do about it? And who could stand up to such a woman . . .

So when Gabrielle muttered, as he was slowly walking her back home, "You know, I want to go on . . . Go on, and win," ah, what was the use of telling her that her board of directors didn't believe in her; because he had made up his mind to urge her on.

"You're right," he told her. "You're right to go on."

The next day he informed one of his colleagues that, despite everything people kept telling him, he had decided to trust Gabrielle: "I know she's right."

It took her a year to regain her omnipotence; her first official recognition came from the United States. Contrary to all expectations, her initial creations, those of the reopening – the little dresses judged so insignificant that buyers had been kicking themselves ever since for placing too much confidence in the name and ordering sight unseen – well, those much-maligned little dresses were selling better than anyone expected. Inexplicable choice, mysterious manifestation of the female "flair."

Quickly alerted, the New York garment industry – all the Seventh Avenue experts – woke up. What was going on? Six months later, at that "next collection," they perceived that America yearned for nothing so much as to rediscover the woman whom a public of connoisseurs was already familiarly addressing as "Coco."

The American press did the rest.

At the third Chanel collection, *Life*, then the most widely read magazine in the States, admitted that the famous designer had made a slightly premature comeback but added, "She is already influencing everything. At seventy-one, Gabrielle Chanel is creating more than a fashion: a revolution." And every edition of *Life* gave four pages to the "Chanel look."

When asked for the secrets of her triumph, she offered very simple recipes. A garment has its own logic; all she had done was respect it. The extravagances and pretensions of "those gentlemen" – by whom she meant the male designers, whom she clearly conceived of as a rather degenerate breed – were all contrary to logic, and it was one of the strong points of American women that they had not let themselves be "led around by their noses."

With vicious verve Gabrielle demolished any garment that seemed to her to represent an obsolete aesthetic. If one of her competitors used whalebone she would annihilate him: "Was the fellow mad?" What were his customers supposed to do when they had to *bend over*? "And that other fellow with his 'Velásquez style'! Do you fancy those women in brocade who look just like old armchairs when they sit down?" No, decidedly, men were not the right people to dress women. She nevertheless gave them a decisive role to play: in the public. They had to be pleased, that was the main thing. Her personal success, the triumph of the "Chanel look," could have no other justification. She owed it entirely, she said, to masculine approval, and especially to that of the man-in-the-street. They were the acolytes of her canonization.

Everything had been hard, and dangerous, and she had overworked herself, true enough. But now it was done: for the second time she had changed women's dress and imposed a style upon the ordinary people – her style, which consisted in being incorruptibly sober and pure.

"I care more about the city street than the drawing room," she would say. She also said:

"I like fashion to go down into the street, but I can't accept that it should originate there."

Which may have been forgetting a little hastily what she owed to her own first sources of inspiration. But it would have been in poor taste to remind her. To be sure, she had found the letters in her private alphabet in the clothes of work and everyday use, in school uniforms and the shirts worn by sailors, grooms, and jockeys. But that had been so many years ago. And it had undeniably been necessary, in transforming men's clothes into women's, to reinvent them all from A to Z.

BUT WHAT FLIES CLEAR . . .

For seventeen years more she was to reign alone, respected by time and still beautiful. Work ennobled her, smoothing away the very wrinkles of her exile. Vulgarity was one of her bugbears, and she refused to qualify as "progress" the changes that were constantly threatening her fragile universe of perfection.

To the very end she stood there "embattled and erect as a captain on the bridge of a sinking ship."[3]

No one could say anymore where her strength came from. You could even wonder whether it was more than a reflection of herself, a sort of ghost one left behind, long past midnight, still hard at work, now half-fainting, now exasperated, obsessed with the sound of scissors, peering with all her eyes at the creation about to take form.

She remained deaf to protests, deaf to anything that was not that new form slowly becoming more distinct as she modeled it, with so sure a hand that it seemed she *could not* make a mistake.

A few people believed she was infallible. Her fingers gripped the cloth like pliers, her fists thudded down like hammers, she hollowed out, she kneaded. The flaw *had to* yield, the rebellion of the fabric *had to* be quelled. Then, finding, as she said, "the use of her feet" again, abandoning her "prostrate laundress"[4] position for the gesture of a painter at his easel, she would stand back to get a better view of her work, muttering raveled phrases in a low voice. "There, that's got her . . . Come on now, not too bad . . ." She clearly took fewer pains with her speech than with her job. Patch words together? What for? Words? In her old age they were at best a stopgap for her loneliness. She did not talk: the words burst from her lips, and then only at night. A wild stream of words . . . a delirium. She used words the way you take revenge, scorning and abusing anyone who listened. Words? They were only good for damning, for excluding. Her words suited her life: cruel and unjust. But what matter; it was not with words that she held her place at the top of the heap. It was with that unflagging labor and her inexhaustible patience.

She was dramatically alone. Many people surrounded her and took advantage of her, and she knew it. But she liked that better than the loneliness, the dreadful loneliness. "There are," she would say, "those who come and listen to me thinking they can get a story out of what I say. There are those who are bored listening to me but they eat better here than they would at home. And most of all, there are those who want to ask me for something. They stick the tightest. Money. Always money."

Now and then a faint far-off echo reached this closed-in kingdom where she ruled. Her past. Sometimes a single word would bring it back. But so briefly. Past a certain age, remembering is wasting one's strength for nothing; and taking the measure of time gone by is like wanting to watch oneself die.

Occasionally, however, she would turn back in her tracks, but cheerlessly, and always with a certain harshness.

There was one word, though, when served up to her memory, one name that never lost its power: Reverdy. The last word not to stick in her throat.

It wasn't that the attraction she felt for him had stood the test of time better than any other. At bottom, it was no more than gratitude. For now she had only one way of loving or hating: depending on whether she had been absolved or condemned. Her behavior during the Occupation . . . Spatz . . . That was her damnation, her hell. Whatever she said was either a plea from the defendant or an indictment, either revolt or a desperate attempt to justify herself.

And Reverdy had forgiven her.

It seems hardly credible, when we know how violently, during the war, he proclaimed his hatred of the Germans, his loathing of collaboration and everything connected with it: Vichy, the admirals in power, the government of Laval. It is nonetheless true that the poet who greeted the Liberation by abandoning himself to demented joy, the upright and severe artist for whom the mildest qualification was sacrilege, this Reverdy who had broken off relations with his dearest friends on the most meager of pretexts, did not break off with Gabrielle. Why?

Perhaps the explanation lies in the answer he gave one day to a journalist who was interviewing him:

"Who is your favorite saint?"

"St Peter."

"Why?"

"Because he betrayed."

In his eyes, Gabrielle had betrayed.

He never saw her anymore, or so seldom that it came to the same thing. But from time to time, measuring better than anyone else the weight of the words "remorse," "distress," "solitude," and aware of the irresistible power of tenderness, he telephoned. In a book he gave her, he wrote a poem. In 1949 she received a copy of *Main d'oeuvre*[5] with this dedication:

Voilà, Coco très chère	There, Coco most dear
Ce que de ma main	Is the best I have made
J'ai fait du meilleur	Of myself
De moi-même.	With my hand.
Bien ou mal fait	Ill- or well-made
Je vous le donne	I give it to you

Avec mon coeur	With my heart
Avec ma main	With my hand
Avant d'aller voir	Before going to see
Au plus sombre chemin	On the darkest path
Si l'on condamne ou	Whether they damn
Si l'on pardonne	Or forgive
Et vous savez que je vous aime.	And you know I love you.

In 1951 she also received *Pierre Reverdy*[6] in the "Poètes d'aujourd'hui" edition, with another poem and another dedication, the last:

Le temps qui passe	Of passing time
Le temps qu'il fait	Rain and sun time
Le temps qui fuit	Fleeting time
De mon obscure vie j'ai perdu	In my dark life I have lost
La trace.	All trace
La voilà retrouvée	Here it is found again
Plus sombre que la nuit	Blacker than night.
Mais ce qui vole	But what flies
Clair c'est ce que de tout mon coeur	Clear is that with all my heart
Je vous embrasse	I embrace you
Et qu'importe tout ce qui suit.	And does it matter what comes after.

"He sent that to me without any warning," she said, "a little as though he had slipped a letter under the door." And she was so grateful to him for doing it.

Pierre Reverdy died at Solesmes on June 17, 1960. He had given stern injunctions to his wife and the fathers in the abbey: "Notify no one, don't give in to anecdote." By the time news of his death reached Paris he was already buried. His wife and two monks had gone with him to the cemetery.

Gabrielle learned about it in the same way as his last friends – Braque, Picasso, and Teriade: from the newspapers.

When someone spoke to her about him, she would say that of all the silences, Reverdy's was hardest to bear. And she would add, "Besides, he isn't dead. Poets . . . poets, you know, they're not like us: they don't die at all."

DEATH ONE SUNDAY

She held out. She held out for seventeen years, going from workroom to bedroom. One street to cross, that was all. She held out, with an outing or two every week and a few days' rest during the year, preferably in Switzerland.

Her work had grown into her hands and fingers and head so deeply that her nights had become travesties of her days.

She had appalling bouts of sleepwalking.

She would be found standing in her room fast asleep and sometimes naked. And, naked, she would talk. What was the meaning of this conversation with the invisible?

Scissors in hand, she would get ready a dress, blindly, for some woman who didn't exist. Or, dismantled with inexplicable precision, her nightgown would lie in a heap of scraps littering the bed. Sometimes it was a pair of pajamas . . . She no longer knew how to perform any gestures except those of taking apart and putting together again, unstitching and restitching, and she was all three Fates in one. One night Clotho the spinner, and the next Atropos, who measured; sometimes she would abandon herself to a kind of fury, searching for something missing, feeling about in the dark. But what was it? What was she looking for? Her death, maybe. On those nights she was the third, Lachesis, who made the final cut.

One day at dawn she was seen hurrying down the narrow hotel corridor, her expression wild and lost, all in white, impeccably neat but in her nightclothes. Where was she running? Visibly, she was dreaming. Monsieur Ritz, who was passing by, managed to guide her back to her door without awakening her. A story he was not fond of repeating. He never knew whether this reminiscence helped or harmed the memory of a woman he had enormously admired. After that, her maid waited until she had dropped off and then locked her into her room.

Sometimes her nightmare assumed a very different form. Someone was ordering her: "Wash yourself, Gabrielle." The obsession . . . She fell prey to an ancient fixation, the dream of cleanliness and whiteness. To be clean . . . to be clean . . . But the water's touch woke her with a start and she would find herself in the bathroom with a wad of soaking linen in her hand. She would go straight back to bed. Say nothing. It mustn't be known.

Once back at work, there was no way anyone could tell . . . If she had related the story of her night the people would have listened, incredulous. To them, she seemed so coherent, so much in command of herself.

She held out. And every season her house turned out the same number of models. She was eighty years old the year the blood of an assassinated President left a scarlet trail across a pink skirt that came from her workroom. But nothing could amaze her now. That same day the new President of the United States hastily took oath standing beside the same suit worn by the same young woman with the beautiful lost expression. What did Gabrielle have to say about it? "Yes, Jackie Kennedy was wearing a Chanel suit in Dallas." And what else? Nothing. Nothing else. She was at an age when emotions are also a waste of strength. And misfortune had existed since the world began, and she had to hold out.

She held out. She had eighty-one, –two, –three, –four years in her hands and in her eyes and she still held out. Her success was prodigious. In her way, she was making history, dressing the women in the street, the movie stars and queens.

At eighty-eight, it had to come. But on the only day it was possible: on Sunday. Because the rest of the week she was working and to die at work in the infinite reflection of her mirrors would have looked theatrical. Bad theater. As Reverdy said, avoid anecdote.

She could not have been more discreet.

Coming back from her walk that January Sunday, in her bedroom at the Ritz, she did not intend to disturb anybody. She lay down fully dressed on her brass bedstead decorated with four big gilt balls. A single bed. A bed to sleep alone in or to die like a Chanel . . . Again, it would have been difficult for things to be otherwise. Her maid Céline, to whom she confessed that she felt atrociously tired, could not get her to take off anything but her shoes. She would undress later, after dinner. All right.

Céline – whom she called Jeanne because she was one of those absolute masters who change their servants' names if their real names don't please them – Jeanne, then, left her to rest without going out of the room. Gabrielle always got her strength back on Sunday evenings, and on Monday she got up and went to work.

On her unpainted pine bedside table there were two objects: a cheap little religious image, a gold-painted St Anthony of Padua standing on a sort of altar base, which was a souvenir of her first trip to Venice with Misia. To get better . . . health in Venice. And an icon that never left her side. A present from Stravinsky, in 1925, after his long stay at Bel Respiro. The bedroom walls were hospital white. Gabrielle used to say that she loved that room for its simplicity: "A real room for sleeping in." Nothing on the walls, not one painting, not one drawing. "Ah, no! None of that here. This is a bedroom, not a drawing room." In the next room stood a very ordinary little screen which she called "My travels." On it she pinned the postcards her friends sent her. There were more of them lining the mirror of her dressing table under a strong light bulb. "Ah, no! No fuss! It's not a mirror for showing off. It's a mirror that throws a true image right back in your face."

Such was the decor of the room on Sunday, January 10, 1971, when Gabrielle was lying on her bed and a motionless figure sat in the room watching her from a distance. Alone, then, alone with a woman to help her entertain her last caller. She was going to die alone.

Suddenly Gabrielle cried out. "I can't breathe . . . Jeanne!" Céline-Jeanne went to her. Gabrielle had seized a syringe she always kept within reach. But she no longer had the strength . . . And the vial wouldn't break. She had time to say, "Ah, they're killing me . . . They'll have killed me." *(Elles me tuent . . . Elles m'auront tuée.)*" But who? Who were these monstrous female "theys" who were killing her? Were they dresses, women? All together, *they* became the criminals. Her employees? Weren't *they* killing her too?

Vainly, Gabrielle tried to beat off the final insurrection. What did *they* want now? She had to take those shadows apart. She had to unsew them. But *she* no longer had strength to do it.

"So that's how you die," she said.

Céline-Jeanne was there. She closed her eyes.

Panarea, 1972–Marseille, 1974

NOTES

A FALSE START 1903–1905

1. We owe this information to the precious testimony of Carlo Colcombet. In 1911, while he was serving in the 14th Dragoons at St Etienne, he often went to Moulins with his captain, who had been garrisoned there five years before. This captain, a habitué of La Rotonde, was always talking about a girl named Coco, who was unforgettable. They both met her at the races at Vichy with Adrienne, with whom she was staying. Colcombet had a career in textiles, and remained a loyal friend to Gabrielle all his life.
2. Description in a letter by Maupassant, quoted by Paul Morand in his *Vie de Maupassant*, Flammarion, Paris.
3. "People never washed," we read in the memoirs of the comtesse Jean de Pange, *Comment j'ai vu 1900*, Grasset, Paris.

THE KEEPERS AND THE KEPT 1906–1914

1. Sale of the estate of Prince and Princess Murat, May 29, 1902. Archives nationales.
2. Report of a commissioner of police of the Eure to the minister of the interior, informing him that he had chastized them. Archives nationales.
3. Marcel Proust, *Within a Budding Grove.*
4. Letter from Colette to André Sagho, director of *La Vie Parisienne*, St Tropez, 1908. Archives nationales.
5. Elisabeth de Gramont, *Clair de lune et taxis-autos*, Grasset, Paris.
6. Leon Bailby, letter to Guillaume Apollinaire, March 5, 1914. Paris, Guillaume Apollinaire Archives, private collection.

THE FOUNDATIONS OF AN EMPIRE 1914–1919

1. Elisabeth de Gramont, *Mémoires*, Grasset, Paris.
2. Unpublished letter from Paul Morand to the author.
3. M. Contini and Yvonne Deslandres, *5,000 ans d'élégance*, Hachette, Paris.

4. François Boucher, *Histoire du costume en Occident*, Flammarion, Paris.

5. Marcel Proust, *Swann's Way*, Part III.

6. Philippe Erlanger, *Clemenceau*, Grasset, Paris.

7. Charles de Chambrun, *Lettres à Marie*, Plon, Paris.

8. *Times Literary Supplement*, May 10, 1917.

9. Paul Morand, *Journal d'un attaché d'ambassade*, Gallimard, Paris.

10. Maurice Paleologue, *La Russie des tsars pendant la guerre*, Plon, Paris.

11. Ibid.

12. Ibid.

13. Speech, November 10, 1917.

14. Unpublished letter from Paul Morand to the author.

15. Diana Cooper, *The Rainbow Comes and Goes*.

16. Evelyn Waugh, *The Life of the Right Reverend Ronald Knox*, Chapman and Hall, London.

17. "Some have been preserved, in particular one evening gown adorned with peacock feathers which the Flemings wanted to lend Katharine Hepburn when she came to Toronto to play in *Coco*, but the feathers were all frayed!" Letter dated February 9, 1972, from Mme Campana to the author. Mme Campana, now Ambassadress of France, was then (1972) Consul General in Toronto.

THE SLAVIC PERIOD 1920–1925

1. Roland Barthes, *Système de la mode*, Editions du Seuil, Paris. The following quote is from the same book.

2. *Misia par Misia*, Gallimard, Paris.

3. Paul Morand, *Venises*, Gallimard, Paris.

4. Article by Cocteau in *Paris-Midi*, 1933.

5. Published in the *Grand Journal* for 1896. Quoted in 1973 in the catalogue produced by the Musée des Arts Décoratifs for the *Équivoques* exhibition.

6. Cocteau article, op. cit.

7. Paul Morand, *Venises*, op. cit.

8. Charles de Chambrun, *Lettres à Marie*, Plon, Paris.

9. Ibid.

10. Boris Kochno, *Diaghilev and the Ballets Russes*, Harper and Row, New York, p. 89.

11. *La Treizième Heure*, volume IV of the memoirs of Elisabeth de Gramont.

12. Charles de Chambrun, *Lettres à Marie*, op. cit.

13. Figure published in *Time* magazine on January 25, 1971.

14. Louis Aragon, *Henri Matisse*, vol. I, chapter "Apologie du Luxe."

15. Roland Barthes, *Système de la mode*, op. cit.

16. Maurice Paléologue, *La Russie des tsars pendant la guerre*, Plon, Paris.

17. Pierre Reverdy, *Le Livre de mon bord*, Mercure de France, Paris.

18. André Masson, "Remémoration," *Mercure de France*, no. 1181. Also in this article

we read: "I have known and know other southerners of that same family: Artaud, Char, Montale."

19. Georges Pompidou, *Anthologie de la poésie française*, Hachette, Paris.

20. Pierre Reverdy, *Cravates de chanvre*, published by Nord-Sud. Chanel's copy was number 9, bound by G. Schroeder.

21. *Tendres Stocks*, a novella by Paul Morand. Preface by Marcel Proust. Gallimard, Paris.

22. André Warnod, *Ceux de la Butte*, Julliard, Paris.

23. Fernande Olivier, *Picasso et ses amis*, Stock, Paris.

24. In *Le Livre de mon bord*, op. cit.

25. Ibid.

26. Ibid.

27. *Les Lettres françaises*, June 29, 1960.

28. From *En vrac*.

29. From *Le Livre de mon bord*, op. cit. Most of the quotations in this passage, including this one, were ticked in the margins or underlined in Gabrielle Chanel's hand in her well-read copies of the works of Reverdy.

30. *Le Livre de mon bord*, op. cit.

31. Paul Morand, *Nouvelle revue française*, 1923.

32. Letter from Reverdy to Jean Rousselot, March 1951. *Entretiens*, Subervie, no. 20.

33. Michel Leiris, "Reverdy, poète quotidien," *Mercure de France*, no. 1181.

34. *Récit de ma conversion*. Quoted in the appendix to *Max Jacob*, by Pierre Andreu, Wesmael-Charlier, Paris. "Conversions célèbres" series.

35. Reverdy, *En vrac*.

36. From a manuscript in Chanel's library.

37. *Le Livre de mon bord*, op. cit.

38. Ibid.

39. Louis Aragon, in *Sic*, no. 29, May 1916.

40. André Malraux, "Des origines de la poésie cubiste," January 1920; reprinted in *Mercure de France*, no. 1181.

41. Pablo Neruda, "Je ne dirai jamais," *Mercure de France*, no. 1181.

42. Pierre Brisson, *Le Théâtre des années folles*, Editions du Milieu du Monde, Paris.

43. Interview in the *Gazette des Arts*, February 10, 1923.

44. Program notes by Jean Cocteau.

45. Antonin Artaud, *The Theatre and Its Double*, Grove Press, New York.

46. Igor Markevich, *Diaghilev et la musique française*, Guilde Internationale du Disque, Paris.

47. Jean Cocteau, 1922 preface to *Les Mariés de la Tour Eiffel*, Gallimard, Paris.

48. Sergei Diaghilev, *Lettre à sa belle-mère*.

49. Darius Milhaud, *Notes sans musique*, Julliard, Paris.

50. Boris Kochno, *Diaghilev and the Ballets Russes*, op. cit., p. 216.

51. Jean Cocteau, preface to the 1922 edition of *Les Mariés de la Tour Eiffel*, op. cit.

52. Letter from Diaghilev to Boris Kochno, quoted in the latter's book *Diaghilev and the Ballets Russes*, op. cit., pp. 216–17.

53. Letter from Cocteau to Diaghilev.

54. Jean Cocteau, *Revue de Paris*, June 15, 1924.

55. Music: Francis Poulenc; Curtain, sets, and costumes: Marie Laurencin; Choreography: Nijinska; First performed by Diaghilev's Ballets Russes on January 6, 1924, at Monte Carlo.

56. Words and music: Stravinsky; Sets and costumes: Larionov; Choreography: Nijinska; First performed on May 18, 1922, at the Paris Opéra.

57. Music and words: Stravinsky; Settings and costumes: Goncharova; Choreography: Nijinska; First performed by Diaghilev's Ballets Russes on June 13, 1923, in Paris.

58. Francis Poulenc, quoted in *Serge de Diaghilev à Monte Carlo*, Guilde Internationale du Disque, Paris.

59. Letter to Boris Kochno, *Diaghilev and the Ballets Russes*, op. cit., p. 206.

60. Boris Kochno, op. cit., p. 219.

61. Quoted in Pierre Galante, *Mademoiselle Chanel*, Henry Regnery Co., Chicago, p. 101.

62. Colette, *Prisons et paradis*, Hachette, Paris.

63. *Revue de Paris*, June 15, 1924.

64. Boris de Schloezer, *La Nouvelle Revue Française*, July 1, 1924.

65. In the French edition of *Vogue*, 1947.

66. Pierre Reverdy, *En vrac*.

A VICTORIAN ILLUSION AND ITS AFTERMATH 1925–1933

1. Pierre Reverdy, *En vrac*.

2. Sir Winston Churchill, "Tribute to Duke of Westminster," *Manchester Guardian*, July 22, 1953.

3. Hélène Demoriane, in *Connaissance des Arts*, no. 266.

4. Henri Clouzot, *L'Illustration*, no. 4307.

5. French edition of *Vogue*.

6. Jean Cocteau, *Portraits-souvenirs*, Grasset, Paris.

7. Jean Cocteau, preface to the catalogue of the exhibition of Paul Poiret's paintings at the Galerie Charpentier in 1944.

8. Paul Morand, *Venises*, Gallimard, Paris.

9. Boris Kochno, *Diaghilev and the Ballets Russes*, Harper and Row, New York, p. 278.

10. Ibid.

11. Paul Morand, *Venises*, op. cit.

12. Michel Larionov, *Diaghilev et les Ballets Russes*, Bibliothèque des Arts, Paris.

13. Paul Morand, *Venises*, op. cit.

14. Bettina Ballard.

15. Collection of M. Hervé Mille.

6. "À la rencontre de Pierre Reverdy," Maeght Foundation catalogue, p. 186.

7. Pierre Reverdy, *Gant de crin*, in the Roseau d'or series, Plon, Paris.

8. Letter to Stanislas Fumet, *Mercure de France*, no. 1181.

9. Jean-Paul Sartre, *L'Idiot de la famille*, Volume III (1972), Gallimard, Paris.

10. René Bertelé, "Un poète en vacances," *Mercure de France*, no. 1181.

11. Ibid.

22. Unpublished letters, Hervé Mille collection.

23. Ibid.

24. From René Bertelé, op. cit., as is other quoted material in this and the following two paragraphs.

25. Pierre Reverdy, *Gant de crin*, op. cit.

26. Marie-Louise Bousquet, Paris representative of *Harper's Bazaar*.

27. Unpublished letter, Hervé Mille collection.

28. Ibid.

29. "I stand on the threshold of oblivion like a night passenger," he says in *Livre de mon bord*.

30. Interview with Sam Goldwyn, signed by Laura Mount, in the *Collier's* of April 1931, quoted by Pierre Galante in *Mademoiselle Chanel*, Henry Regnery Co., Chicago.

31. Directed by Mervin LeRoy. A light comedy in which Swanson, playing a great soprano, was widely praised by critics. Premiered in December 1931.

OF DIVERS DANCES 1933–1940

1. Like Reverdy, Colette – who painstakingly recorded the day of the week and hour of the day of every letter she wrote – neglected to put any dates on any of them, so that the chronological classification of her correspondence is a singularly arduous task. However, this sentence referring to her collaboration on the *Journal* – her first drama criticism was published in it in October 1933 – enabled Maurice Goudeket to determine when Colette was writing to him on this occasion, i.e., the summer of the same year. And Colette's writer's precision made it possible to go even farther: this particular letter was written between the first and the thirteenth of July, which is when the lilies blossomed and the moon was full that year. The letter is unpublished, as is the whole of Colette's correspondence with Maurice Goudeket.

2. Colette, in Georges Sion's book, *Cocteau ou l'illustre inconnu*, Editions Dynamo, Liège.

3. Paul Poiret, *En habillant l'époque*, Grasset, Paris.

4. Published in 1908.

5. Paul Morand, *Venises*, Gallimard, Paris.

6. Review by J. L. Croze in *Films de France*, 1921.

7. Colette, *Lettres à ses pairs*, Flammarion, Paris.

8. Cornelius Vanderbilt, Jr., *The New York Times*, January 25, 1920.

9. Colette, *Prisons et paradis*, Hachette, Paris.

10. "Spinelly Maman," article, signed L. G., in *Le Parisien*.

11. Colette, *Prisons et paradis*, op. cit.

12. *Vogue*, October 1931.

13. Louis Aragon, *Aurélien*, Nouvelle Revue Française, Paris.

14. Colette, *Prisons et paradis*, op. cit.

15. Roland Barthes, *Erté*, Franco Maria Ricci.

16. Related by Mme Gripoix, of Maison Gripoix in Paris, in Pierre Galante' *Mademoiselle Chanel*, Henry Regnery Co., Chicago.

17. Letter to the author from Maurice Goudeket.

18. Letters to Marguerite Moreno, written in August 1930 and September 1931.

19. Interview with Albert Flamant, in *L'Illustration*, no. 4680, November 12, 1932.

20. Colette, *Lettres à Marguerite Moreno*, Flammarion, Paris.

21. *Le Populaire*, August 29, 1935. "We reject the idea of war as inevitable," by Léon Blum.

22. Charles Maurras, in *Action Française*, April 9, 1935.

23. Portrait of Blum by Lieutenant-Colonel Renaud, in *Solidarité Française*, the publication of an ultra right-wing movement financed by François Coty the owner of *Figaro*. Since 1922 *Solidarité Française* had had its booted, blue-shirted storm troopers. Their motto, like *Le Témoin*'s, was "France for the French."

24. Jean Dobler, as reported by William L. Shirer in *The Collapse of the Third Republic* Simon and Schuster, New York.

25. Ibid.

26. Pertinax, *Les Fossoyeurs*, vol. III, Editions du Sagittaire, Paris, 1946, pp. 74–75.

27. Maurice Thorez, in a speech at the Jean Jaurès secondary school on June 11 1935.

THE GERMAN PERIOD 1940–1945

1. Unpublished letter from Prof. Dr Eberhardt Jäckel of the University of Stuttgart whose *La France dans l'Europe d'Hitler* (Fayard) and *Hitler idéologue* (Calmann-Lévy) are regarded as authoritative.

2. He was instructed to "guide" Lord Runciman through the Sudetans and "inform" him of the imminence of the German putsch.

3. Robert Coulondre, *De Staline à Hitler, Souvenirs de deux ambassades*, Hachette, Paris.

4. Ibid.

5. *Le Livre jaune français, Documents diplomatiques*, 1938–39, Ministry of Foreign Affairs.

6. Colette, *Journal intermittent*, August 15, 1941. *Oeuvres complètes*, vol. XIV, of 15 vols., Flammarion, Paris.

7. Michelet, *Histoire de la révolution*, Bibliothèque de la Pléiade, Gallimard, Paris, 1952.

8. Letter from Theodor Momm to the author.

9. In a statement made on August 1, 1957, made public by his lawyers.

10. Descriptions borrowed from Stendhal's *The Red and the Black*.

11. Alan Bullock in his Preface to the memoirs of Walter Schellenberg, *The Labyrinth*, Harper and Bros., New York.

12. Walter Schellenberg, *The Labyrinth*, op. cit.

13. Letter from Gabrielle Chanel, in the author's collection.

14. Her only meeting arranged without Gabrielle's knowledge provoked a scene. The lifelong friend – Sabine Charles-Roux – with whom Vera did manage to get in touch nearly collapsed in amazement when Gabrielle turned up and addressed Vera like an avenging fury, harshly requesting her "not to do it again."

15. Lord Moran, *Winston Churchill: The Struggle for Survival, 1940–1965*. Constable, London.

16. Colette, *Prisons et paradis*.

17. "The purge was incomplete (the wealthiest and most cunning escaped and resurfaced when the storm was over); it was too often emotional, unlawful, and unworthy of a democracy that wanted to be hard and pure." Gaston Defferre, Preface to *La Libération de Marseille* by Pierre Guiral, Hachette, Paris.

FIRST EPILOGUE 1945–1952

1. "I went down to Nuremberg to see them . . . Attired in rather shabby clothes, slumped in their seats fidgeting nervously, they no longer resembled the arrogant leaders of old." William L. Shirer, *The Rise and Fall of the Third Reich*, Simon and Schuster, New York, pp. 1141–42.

2. Alan Bullock, Preface to Walter Schellenberg, *The Labyrinth*, Harper and Bros., New York.

3. "Madame Chanel offered us financial assistance in our difficult situation and it was thanks to her that we were able to spend a few more months together." Letter dated March 8, 1958, from Irene Schellenberg to Theodor Momm.

4. Letter from Irene Schellenberg to Theodor Momm, March 8, 1958.

5. Letter from Theodor Momm to Mrs Schellenberg, March 13, 1958.

SECOND EPILOGUE 1953–1971

1. From Robert Musil's *The Man Without Qualities*.

2. "Un flair sans pitié," by Michel Déon, in *Les Nouvelles Littéraires*, January 21, 1971. The writer, very young at the time, happened to be sitting next to Gabrielle

Chanel during the memorable reopening. He also wrote, "At times she seemed made of iron . . ."

3. Françoise Giroud in *L'Express*, January 18, 1971.

4. Colette, in *Prisons et paradis*, Hachette, Paris.

5. Poems 1913–1949, published by Mercure de France, Paris.

6. By Jean Rousselot and Michel Manoll; published by Pierre Seghers, Paris.

INDEX